Democratic Elitism

Democratic Elitism

The Founding Myth
of American
Political Science

NATASHA PIANO

Harvard University Press
Cambridge, Massachusetts · London, England · 2025

Copyright © 2025 by the President and Fellows of Harvard College

All rights reserved

Printed in the United States of America

First printing

Library of Congress Cataloging-in-Publication Data

Names: Piano, Natasha, author.
Title: Democratic elitism : the founding myth of American political
science / Natasha Piano.
Description: Cambridge, Massachusetts ; London, England : Harvard
University Press, 2025. | Includes bibliographical references and
index.
Identifiers: LCCN 2024022312 (print) | LCCN 2024022313 (ebook) |
ISBN 9780674295377 (cloth) | ISBN 9780674298989 (pdf) |
ISBN 9780674298996 (epub)
Subjects: LCSH: Pareto, Vilfredo, 1848–1923—Influence. | Mosca,
Gaetano, 1858–1941—Influence. | Michels, Robert, 1876–1936—
Influence. | Democracy—Philosophy—History—19th century. |
Democracy—Philosophy—History—20th century. | Elite (Social
sciences)—Italy—History—20th century. | Elite (Social
sciences)—United States—History—20th century.
Classification: LCC JC421 .P515 2025 (print) | LCC JC421 (ebook) |
DDC 321.809—dc23 / eng / 20240822
LC record available at https://lccn.loc.gov/2024022312
LC ebook record available at https://lccn.loc.gov/2024022313

Dedicated to my mother Lalla—in love, in gratitude, but above all in friendship

Contents

Preface   ix

Introduction: The Lies We Tell Ourselves
An Intellectual History of Political Science   1

1 An Angry Warning
Pareto and Elite Circulation   18

2 Sober Cynicism
Mosca and the Ruling Class   50

3 The Edge of Fatalism
Michels and the Iron Law of Oligarchy   83

4 Sardonic Irony
Schumpeter and the Alternate Theory   114

5 Hopeful Panic
The American Reception   144

Conclusion: A New Realism
Democracy as Good Government   178

NOTES   193

ACKNOWLEDGMENTS   229

INDEX   233

Preface

Over the last twenty years the twin menaces of populism and demagoguery have plagued liberal democracies worldwide. Increasing economic inequality and marked plutocratic capture of political institutions have given rise to what many today call populism. The phenomenon is characterized by general citizen disillusionment with elections that result in plutocracy and legislative decisions that consistently reflect the interests of elite minorities over those of voting majorities. In short, populists complain that elections do not generate leaders who are representative of or even accountable to popular interests. The perceived lack of representativity and accountability has prompted demagogues to call into question the legitimacy of liberal democracies. These demagogic leaders often express the familiar refrain that their victories constitute "the voice of the people" or electoral mandates to do away with liberal norms and practices.

At the same time, both mainstream political science and contemporary political discourse continue to define democracy primarily by the presence of free and fair elections. For at least fifty years, political scientists of all stripes have criticized this operative "minimal" definition as insufficient, but no clear alternative has emerged to differentiate democratic regime types from authoritarian alternatives. This definition of democracy has come to be seen as especially unconvincing in an age of populist uprisings where demagogues have consistently won competitive elections and proceeded to systematically dismantle liberal democratic procedures in the process.

Some have argued that this "disfiguration of democracy" highlights our need for more representative, competitive elections—the foundation of democracy—to combat the infiltrations of technocracy into popular government.[1] Others have called for more direct, deliberative citizen participation in the spirit of

x PREFACE

Athenian politics refurbished for the internet age.[2] Still others demand plebeian constitutional measures that introduce new political institutions based on socioeconomic divisions to both minimize plutocratic capture of office and bolster ordinary citizen extra-electoral participation.[3] Yet the sheer quantity of proposed remedies raises a recurring question in the history of Western political thought: Are these plutocratic and demagogic threats simply bugs of current systems or inherent features of democracy itself?[4]

Is it possible that these twin threats are unintended consequences of defining democracy in terms of competitive elections? What if defining democracy as competitive elections actually breeds citizen disillusionment with liberal norms and procedures, thereby inviting demagogic usurpation?

The Italian School of Elitism—Vilfredo Pareto, Gaetano Mosca, and Robert Michels—voiced this very suspicion. They worried that defining democracy through representative practices creates unrealistically democratic expectations of what elections, on their own, can achieve, resulting in their delegitimization. And yet these authors are a rather surprising resource for concerns about plutocratic capture, populist uprising, and demagogic usurpation. The conventional wisdom understands them as conservative, antidemocratic figures who championed the equation of democracy with representative practices in order to restrain popular participation in modern mass politics. It is generally taken for granted that Pareto, Mosca, and Michels are responsible for the hundred-year-old tradition called democratic elitism, or elite democratic theory, which identifies democracy as electoral alternation of office.

This book contends that those who interpret Pareto, Mosca, and Michels as "elite theorists" fundamentally distort their political thought and completely ignore their main objective: to contain plutocracy in the age of modern mass politics, partially by disassociating elections from democracy. Somehow Pareto's, Mosca's, and Michels's cynical views of elite domination and its perversion of the democratic process have become—in the hands of Carl Friedrich, Charles Merriam, James Burnham, Raymond Aron, C. Wright Mills, Seymour Martin Lipset, Robert Dahl, Peter Bachrach, Carole Pateman, Adam Przeworski, and others—celebrations of electoral competition and representative government. I aim to convince readers that we ought to think of Pareto, Mosca, and Michels, not as elite theorists of democracy, but instead as democratic theorists of elitism.

My alternative narrative questions whether we should continue to identify modern democracy as synonymous with free and fair elections. Reviving the Italian School's original contributions unearths a theory of democracy that might help us disassociate these two concepts in our political vocabulary. The point of this endeavor is not to eliminate elections from democratic theory. Rather, I maintain, deflating the democratic expectations of electoral politics can help restore the legitimacy of elections and actually revive their proper role in modern popular government.

Today, when the future of contemporary democracies appears murky, the definition of democracy as free and fair elections no longer maintains the clarity that it once promised. Retracing the genealogy of democratic elitism might not only purge us of old bad habits; it might also lead us to a fresh conception of modern democracy following the Italian tradition of *buon governo*—democracy as part and parcel of good government.

Illic enim orta, illuc redit   —Petrarch

Introduction:
The Lies We Tell Ourselves

An Intellectual History of Political Science

To explode a myth is accordingly not to deny the facts but
to reallocate them.   —GILBERT RYLE, *The Concept of Mind*

Many readers will be familiar with *Pinocchio* (1940), the animated fantasy film of a puppet's attempts to become a real boy. After many tribulations, Pinocchio learns the virtues of honesty and moral rectitude through the guidance of his conscience, a cricket named Jiminy who narrates the tale. Across the globe, the Walt Disney production is known as a children's masterpiece and optimistic ode to the virtues of individual morality. It also, perhaps unsurprisingly, wildly distorts its literary source material, Carlo Collodi's celebrated *Pinocchio* (1881–1882). Collodi's novel is the quintessential *storia risorgimentale*— an allegory for the birth of the Italian nation.[1] Just ten years after formal unification, *Pinocchio* offered a prophetic warning to the adolescent *l'Italia*, which still had many growing pains to face and whose outcome was far from certain. In the original fable, the allegorical representation of the nation (Pinocchio), the Northern elite (Master Antonio), and the Southern masses (Geppetto) was readily apparent to an Italian audience.

The story begins in Tuscany, the part of the peninsula that is neither Turin nor the Kingdom of the Two Sicilies but that will furnish Italy with a unified language. There a carpenter named Master Antonio finds a block of wood that he plans to carve into a table leg. Frightened when the log cries out, he gives it

2   DEMOCRATIC ELITISM

to his wretchedly poor Southern neighbor Geppetto, nicknamed Polendina (Polenta) because his blonde wig recalled the yellow gruel of the cornfields. Rather than farming, Geppetto dreams of earning his living as a puppeteer and thus carves the log into a boy he named Pinocchio. It is as if from the very beginning the piece of wood yearned to be its own independent object with no interest in serving as an instrument to prop up something else. While the wood's cries panicked the master carpenter, Geppetto was willing to put the work into giving it life, just as the North's southern neighbor was ultimately more willing to put in the grueling preparatory work of revolution and unification throughout the nineteenth century.[2]

Before he is even built, Pinocchio has a mischievous nature. No sooner is Geppetto done carving Pinocchio's feet than the puppet kicks him. Once the puppet has been finished and Geppetto teaches him to walk, Pinocchio runs away into the town. He is caught by a police officer, who assumes Pinocchio has been mistreated by Geppetto, whom he imprisons, just as the South will be inappropriately blamed for its purported political depravity. Left alone, Pinocchio heads back home. After a series of trials that exhaust him, Pinocchio lies down on a stove; when he wakes, his feet have burned off. Fortunately, Geppetto is released from prison and makes Pinocchio a new pair of feet. In gratitude, Pinocchio promises to attend school, and Geppetto sells his only coat to buy him a schoolbook, only for Pinocchio to start ditching classes once he has started to make a modicum of progress. How quickly Pinocchio neglected Geppetto's earlier sacrifice, a sacrifice Geppetto had made in the hope that Pinocchio would acquire the education that Geppetto himself never received.

A long series of disasters ensue as Pinocchio indulges in deceitful behavior and gluttonous excess, most famously with his best friend, Lucignolo, or Candlewick. In the end, after a face-to-face reckoning with Geppetto inside a whale, Pinocchio and Geppetto escape together and Pinocchio gets a job as a farmhand. After Pinocchio has put in months of hard work supporting the ailing Geppetto, the Fairy with (Savoy) Turquois Hair makes good on her earlier promise and turns Pinocchio into a real boy, gifting him a new suit, boots, and a bag that contains forty gold coins. Pinocchio begins to prosper as he works to improve his circumstances. Even Geppetto miraculously regains his health.

Pinocchio's mischievous adventures represent the ways that Italian identity was formed through newly developed attachments, voluntary and otherwise, to the nascent nation.[3] Yet in the face of these trials, disasters in his identity formation ensue as Pinocchio continues to lie about his circumstances and capabilities in order to indulge in excesses that certainly do not correspond to his stage in life. In effect, the fable does not consist merely in a moralistic reprimand of Pinocchio's disobedience.[4] The problem is more that Pinocchio pretends to be something he is not: a wealthy adult spending his money on pastries, drugs, and the theater instead of attending school, which is more appropriate to the season of his life. Ultimately, excess and deceit are what turn both Pinocchio and Lucignolo into asses.

The most destructive lies are the ones Pinocchio tells himself. Early on, more than anything else, he is unwilling to hear that he is not yet a real boy. In the opening chapter the Talking Cricket pedantically reprimands Pinocchio: "You are a puppet and what's worse is that you have a head of wood!" This later becomes the refrain of the tale. In frustration, Pinocchio throws a mallet at the cricket, accidentally killing him. Throughout the narrative the Cricket periodically reappears as a ghost furiously reproaching Pinocchio to reform his ways and return home to attend school. Far from serving as his conscience, Pinocchio's talking critic was killed immediately, and many external interventions are required for Pinocchio to begin following the path toward reform.

This book tells the story of the Italian School of Elitism and its role in the Risorgimento and in the development of political science across the Atlantic. We should think of the members of the Italian School as being like the Talking Cricket—furious, pedantic critics who continually lambasted the wannabe Italian republic's corrupt ways. In the republic's youth, the talking critics reprimand the plutocratic corruption of a young nation that simply could not afford this kind of excess on multiple registers. On a smaller scale, the new Italy was not ready for fiat currency, nor could it afford the political effects of exploiting the South through economic practices associated with free-market liberalism. More broadly, the infant nation was in no position to impose a parliamentary system on a peninsula that had no experience with liberal political institutions in a context of severe regional economic inequality and with no shared language, leadership, or political tradition. Universal suffrage was used to hide Northern domination of the South, which was further impoverished through corrupt forms of electoralism that created and subsequently empowered the mafia. Most of all, Italy had no business boasting that this new shell of a parliamentary government was a democracy. It was an offense to Geppetto, who had sacrificed everything for the birth of the nation, and Collodi reminds the reader that the nation could never survive without a healthy South.[5]

What happens when a nation lies to itself about its circumstances and essence? Can a republic really grow and evolve while pretending be something that it is not? What happens when an electoral government tells itself it is a democracy? Perhaps the nation prefers a strictly liberal order and would rather not engage in the kind of participation and institutional elite contestation that democracy requires. What, then, is the value of calling such practices democratic?

As we shall see, in identifying the Italians as protofascist authoritarians, we, like Pinocchio, accidentally killed off the talking critics Pareto, Mosca, and Michels from the beginning. Political scientists optimistically ignored their message about the plutocratic and demagogic dangers of conflating elections and democracy—most likely because we did not want to hear it because it interfered with the lie we had begun to tell ourselves: that elections could serve as an imperfect but helpful proxy for democracy, or that free and fair elections offered the most elegant definition of democracy available. At one point in the midcentury, American political science even entertained the Pollyanna idea that a lack of participation in elections was a sign of political approval and health of the democracy itself.

Of course, this is not to say that democratic theorists have blindly conflated elections and democracy. Over the last thirty years, democratic theory has been particularly attuned to how democracy and elections came to be intertwined through a set of historical contingencies that developed after the revolutions of the eighteenth century. Many political scientists have forcefully articulated different historical formations in democratic theory that detailed the contingent braiding of democracy, elections, and representation into a singular phenomenon. Nevertheless, these accounts all seem to suggest that it is too late to go back to a time when elections and democracy were easily separable. After all, the popular imagination understands modern democracy as free and fair elections—and even if that identification is based on a series of historical contingencies, it has seemed as though, at least at this point, it would be futile to distinguish the two.

Parallel to the distance between Collodi's initial ominous warning and the midcentury Disneyfication of *Pinocchio* that has permeated all corners of the world, this book shows how political science was born out of a violent misappropriation of Italian elite theory and how this distortion developed into the idea of democratic elitism, more broadly understood as the popular definition of democracy as free and fair elections. Recounting this secret history of political science might help us better understand whether the lie we have been telling ourselves about democracy still holds water in the twenty-first century, and what, if anything, we may want to do about it.

INTRODUCTION 5

On Democratic Elitism and Elite Theories of Democracy

The second half of the twentieth century witnessed an explosion of synonyms for democratic elitism—an abundance that attests to the salience of the category. Minimalist, empirical, economic, proceduralist, Schumpeterian, pluralist, neo-pluralist, equilibrium, realist, and even "contemporary" theories all came to denote a model of democracy that champions elections as an institutional mechanism; a model of democracy that simultaneously allows for popular participation while actively containing it. Democratic theorists spent the twentieth century debating whether this model provides an accurate description of our current political practice and / or a desirable normative ideal.[6] What is more, the prevalence of this model encouraged thinkers to identify themselves within the confines of a convenient binary: either as advocates of the elite model or as opponents favoring a more participatory alternative.[7]

In fact, the historical genesis of democratic elitism currently remains undisputed: democratic elitism purportedly originated with the so-called Italian School of Elitism, comprised of Vilfredo Pareto (1848–1923), Gaetano Mosca (1858–1941), and Robert Michels (1876–1936), who drew upon experiences with failed mass party regimes like Italian parliamentarism and the Weimar Republic, and whose thought then was refined by Joseph Schumpeter (1883–1950) in response to the twentieth-century rise of fascism and communism.[8] Yet despite the uncontested identification of democratic elitism as a twentieth-century construct, democratic theory has invoked the elite ideal far beyond these temporal confines. Today many thinkers retrospectively apply our modern understanding of democratic elitism to the history of Western political thought. Whether critical or supportive, some circles of scholarship make sense of the theory by constructing a genealogy of its institutions, logic, and rationale that spans back to ancient Rome, through the Italian republican city-states and the French and American Revolutions.[9] Even though Bernard Manin's *The Principles of Representative Government*, for example, explicitly asks how two concepts as antithetical as democracy and elections became coupled, the work ultimately connects Cicero, Francesco Guicciardini, James Harrington, Emmanuel Sieyès, and Publius into a narrative that suggests a fusion between democracy and elitism long before its twentieth-century iteration.[10] This genealogy has fostered the impression that democratic elitism comes with a two-thousand-year history, and that we ought to structure arguments about what democracy means by investigating such moments in the tradition through the lens of elite versus mass participation.

6   DEMOCRATIC ELITISM

Even when the elite theory of democracy is not explicitly at issue, democratic theorists easily become divided between two camps: one is more visibly "elitist," while the other proclaims itself to be non-elitist because of its self-professed commitment to a participatory ideal.[11] The latter contingent centers its energies on demonstrating the elitism inherent in the former's political vision while still accommodating it as a conception of democracy.

Are aggressive attempts to expose elitism in various forms of contemporary democratic theory productive for those interested in encouraging participatory norms of a forward-looking democratic progressivism? To be clear, I find genealogical inquiries that assess the sources and lineages of elite theories of democracy valuable, but I would like to investigate elite theory derivatives differently. Instead of mining the texts of canonical figures for the elitist antecedents of democratic elitism, I focus on whether these purported elitist and antidemocratic figures in the history of political thought are as elitist as we take them to be.

This study thus reexamines where, exactly, the twentieth-century conception of democratic elitism came from, why elite theories of democracy became so central to American political science, and how the construction of democratic elitism as a formal category *sui generis* facilitated the current hegemonic understanding of democracy as free and fair elections.

Conventional wisdom holds that democratic elitism is a direct offshoot of the Italian School of Elitism begun by Pareto, Mosca, and Michels. My point of departure is to ask whether these forefathers of the tradition are accurately portrayed in later formulations. I contend that the subsequent iterations mark rather startling departures from the original formulation, both substantively and methodologically. Specifically, I ask how the Italian School's concern about plutocratic tendencies inherent in liberal institutions completely disappeared in this current of intellectual history, and how these theorists perversely came to be seen as unqualified defenders of representative systems instead of what they actually were: democratically motivated critics of the conflation of democracy with electoral government.

I reveal in the course of the narrative that these dramatic departures do indeed exist, and in the rest of my analysis I take up the question of how American political science preserved the focus on the study of elites but ignored the Italian theorists' obsession with the relationship between liberal institutions and plutocratic sociopolitical arrangements. Relatedly, I ask why Pareto, Mosca, and Michels are mistakenly thought to advance "scientific" methodology, and what this says about the relationship between their work and the postwar explosion of positivism and behavioralism in American political science.

Most importantly, this book asks what these distortions say about the state of American political science. Why did twentieth-century American political thought so forcefully articulate the elite theory of democracy and construct a rather suspect genealogy? What purpose did it serve in developing contemporary democratic theory? And are we now still constrained, politically and theoretically, by the myth of a school of thought rather than the reality?

The Italian School: Democratic Theorists of Elitism

For the last century, then, the Italian School of Elitism has been regarded as the foundation of elite theory. Pareto, Mosca, and Michels are remembered as champions of elite power who were distrustful of increased mass political participation in industrialized society. As a result, these authors, it is maintained, endorsed representative institutions because such procedures allow for popular participation while actively constraining its most deleterious effects.

My genealogy reverses this narrative of the Italian School's contribution to democratic thought. Pareto, Mosca, and Michels, I maintain, investigated elite power in order to constrain plutocratic infiltration of representative government. More specifically, they were methodologically driven to combat plutocracy by exposing the myth that electoral outcomes express popular sovereignty, and therefore facilitate democracy. Presuming that pessimistic exposure of plutocracy would revitalize animus against it, they sought to curtail the growth of plutocracy and neutralize its most objectionable excesses in representative systems. Each of their expositions analyzes different features of representative politics to reveal how electoral procedures enhance elite domination of the majority; such procedures, for the Italian School, neither secure majoritarian interest nor pose an adequate constraint on leaders' authority. These authors take up the following three issues:

Pareto highlights the connection between governing and nongoverning elites to show that parliamentary elections render politicians beholden to financial and military leaders by virtue of economic interests (Chapter 1).

Mosca details the ways minorities use the organization of representative institutions to increase their access to wealth and consequently consolidate their power under the color of a legitimizing "democratic" façade (Chapter 2).

Michels investigates political party structure to conclude that parties require a necessarily plutocratic organization to advance their platforms, a feature that precludes egalitarian distribution of resources and power (Chapter 3).

8   DEMOCRATIC ELITISM

Rather than harboring disdain for mass political incompetence, Pareto, Mosca, and Michels harbored a distrustful orientation toward elites and a "realistic" or pessimistic posture toward the democratic possibilities of liberal (representative or parliamentary) government. They expressed this attitude not to encourage resignation, but to spur action to fight these tendencies. Of course, pessimism is not foreign to the history of political thought, but unlike, say, the Frankfurt School of critical theory, the Italian School is almost never considered in such a light.[12] To the contrary, they are considered the most conservative, anti-egalitarian coterie of fin de siècle political scientists—more clever, cynical heirs to the continental counter-revolutionary thinkers Louis de Bonald, Joseph de Maistre, and Juan Donoso Cortés.

To be sure, none of these figures would have ever called himself a democrat because they identified democracy exclusively with Athenian-style assemblies, lot, and sortition. At the time of their writing, liberalism had not yet gained ideological dominance over the Western consciousness; democracy still indicated a system of government antithetical to electorally based institutional models. These authors most certainly did not think within the peculiar binary of liberal institutionalism versus Athenian "participatory" governance that preoccupied contemporary democratic theory and therefore never would have imagined that their critiques of liberalism would be interpreted as "elitist" attempts to stifle any form of popular government, electorally based or otherwise.

Contextualizing the environment in which the Italians wrote corrects this misunderstanding of what motivated their pessimistic orientation toward liberalism. Moreover, it helps unearth their political contribution to democratic theory, a theory of *buon governo* (good government) that defends electoral practices only alongside democratic institutions that aggressively regulate the plutocratic corruption of representative institutions and more regularly allow for popular contestation and judgment of elite performance outside of the electoral moment. This theory of *buon governo* champions a popular, pluralist, and anti-plutocratic platform, which can be summarized by the following three precepts:

1) Democracy requires continual contestation of elite power and vigilance against plutocratic encroachment, which can easily go undetected under liberal-representative arrangements.
2) Democratic action must focus on continual redress of material inequality. For Pareto and Mosca this meant addressing economic *regional* disparity between North and South; for Michels it meant

imposing mechanisms that would equalize access to education and
"economic status."

3) Democratic theory must consider elites, their motivations, and their
modes of operation just as much as it promotes mass movements,
a horizon-broadening that in no way undermines its popular or
egalitarian character.

This conception contrasts with the other currents of democratic thought
because it is attentive to the majority / minority divide and alive to the necessarily contestational element of democratic politics but nonetheless specifically
directed at an elite audience. Pareto, Mosca, and Michels are intent to show
their peers within the ruling class that democratic institutions and accountability are stabilizing forces on a polity; instead of inviting tumultuous mob
rule, such procedures are actually the only forces that keep such violence at bay.

The Italian School's view of democracy thus does not confine itself to specific institutional conditions that must be fulfilled in order to identify a state
as democratic. Most obviously, Pareto's, Mosca's, and Michels's works reject the
static criterion of free and fair elections that postwar political scientists from
Dahl to Przeworski would invoke as the necessary condition for designating
a regime democratic. Neither does their thought bear any resemblance to a
Rawlsian conception of justice, which demands a priori identification of the
principles that would underpin a "well-ordered" society and the institutional
means to satisfy such principles.[13] The Italians insist that such principles can
seem to be advanced by the very institutions that pervert them, and therefore
they reject any a priori conceptualizations or "ideal theory" in their formulations. Far from being interested in the Habermasian "siege model" or Sheldon
Wolin's "fugitive" ideal of democracy, which are fixated on popular movements,
Pareto, Mosca, and Michels were not advocating fleeting, insurrectionist, defensive positions of mass organization in moments of crisis.[14] Their conception
of democracy speaks to elites about the necessity of continually reconstituting
democratic procedures before such moments of breakdown, and their pessimism aims to prompt a preemptive, aggressive posture—an offensive / defensive strategy, as it were—rather than a purely defensive one.

In this sense, the Italian orientation toward democracy does not simply rest
on the presence of constant "movement," nor does it regard contestation of elite
power as an end in itself to promote "agonistic pluralism" of the political
sphere.[15] From the Italian perspective, pessimism must be seen as an instrument. It is, in fact, supposed to *do* something: When married to a combative
orientation, Pareto, Mosca, and Michels intimate, pessimism can help enact

change for the better. As such, contestation serves as the means to implement procedures that advance economic equality, often by demonstrating the interest elites have in adopting such measures.

In the Italian case, contestation of plutocracy is part and parcel of advancing the elite project of the Risorgimento—the Italian unification process and its aftermath. Long before the wave of nineteenth-century nationalism that swept through Europe, the Italian political classes and intelligentsia had envisioned the assimilation of the peninsula's city-states into a consolidated sovereign entity, at least since Niccolò Machiavelli's exhortation in the concluding chapter of *The Prince*, if not earlier in Francesco Petrarch's clarion call "In difesa dell'Italia [Contra eum qui maledixit Italie]" (In defense of Italy).[16] But even with the formal beginnings of unification finally underway, the Italian authors warned their peers that l'*Italia* would never survive as a nation-state—*even under conditions of universal suffrage*—without regional economic redress. For Pareto and Mosca in particular, circulation of elites or competition among them, fostered through liberal institutions, is simply not enough to qualify a regime as democratic, whether in its modern formulation or otherwise. Both of their life projects were devoted to the permanence of Italian unification. As such, they tirelessly fought against the conflation of elections and democracy because they thought that, through plutocratic domination, this equation made modern popular government in Italy impossible. They believed that the nexus of representation and democracy sullied the benefits of representative forms of popular government because it increased democratic expectations of elections and facilitated plutocratic outcomes. When electoral institutions fail to provide the democratic results that they promise, the enterprise's entire legitimacy is called into question.

Michels, as discussed in Chapter 3, presents a more ambiguous understanding of the conflation of elections and democracy. Most commentators argue that if any of these three thinkers could be conceived of as a democratic theorist, it would be the non-Italian of the group, the German-born Michels. In the conventional understanding, the German émigré to Italy applies Pareto's and Mosca's thought to a conception of modern democracy defined by competition among elites, thus rendering his infamous "iron law of oligarchy," or the inevitability of oligarchy, not nearly as inflexible—and in fact far more democratic—than one might think. According to the existing literature, Michels used Mosca's and Pareto's elitism to produce what in actuality was merely a "bronze law" of oligarchy from which we could convincingly develop a new view of democracy based on liberal elections.[17]

Through the first three chapters I challenge this view that Michels democratized Pareto's and Mosca's thought through his emphasis on elite competition. If anything, Michels—who was far less sensitive to the problems and the promise of the Risorgimento—initiated the corruption of Italian democratic theory: Michels's more German-inspired political thought opened the door to efforts validating the conflation of elections and modern democracy, an idea that has now become so pervasive that it seems too formidable a force to resist.

Chapter 4 reveals how the Austrian Schumpeter deployed the German-born Michels's thought and radicalized the conflation of elections and democracy. The chapter offers an alternative reading of Schumpeter's seminal *Capitalism, Socialism and Democracy*, in which I demonstrate how Schumpeter's sardonic dare to identify democracy as competitive elections simultaneously inherited and transformed the major precepts of elite theory, but not for the reasons that would later be claimed by postwar political science. His alternative to representative democracy, the "alternate theory of competitive leadership," proposed identifying democracy simply as an electoral method. As such, it utilized the approaches of his Italian predecessors to invert their most sacred lesson: If we define it this way, he dared, democracy can just as easily be understood as its opposite.

Chapter 5 investigates the reception of the Italian School and Schumpeter's thought in the development of American political science as a discipline. I assess how American political scientists such as C. Wright Mills, Robert Dahl, Peter Bachrach, Carole Pateman, and Adam Przeworski took Schumpeter up on his dare to redefine democracy as competitive elections through a misunderstanding of Pareto, Mosca, and Michels, thereby transforming both the original contributions of the Italian School and the thrust of *Capitalism, Socialism and Democracy* as a whole.

My revisionist genealogy hopes to recover an Italian political precept that may serve us in our own moment: as the Italians argued, equating elections and democracy is not a mere matter of semantics; rather, it occludes plutocratic and demagogic threats that reside within representative systems, ultimately destroying the distinct contributions that both representation and democracy potentially offer popular government.

Pessimism Constrains Plutocracy

How did this wild perversion of the Italian School happen? If it turns out that Italians were not antidemocratic "elitists" after all, then how did they earn this reputation that has dogged political science for the last century? And if their critique of plutocracy was indeed so explicit, how was it so easily ignored by American political science?

The Italian affiliated intellectuals are not remembered as critics of plutocracy for a variety of interconnected political, historical, and theoretical reasons. The story of the Italian School of Elitism is a classic game of telephone in which the final American utterance is nothing like the original Italian one: the Italian elite theorists Mosca and Pareto found their natural progeny in Mittel-European figures Michels and Schumpeter, who ferried elite theory to the US academy, where it was assimilated, transformed, and distorted by Lipset, Dahl, et al. In this case, the layers of redescription generated a category of democratic elitism that justified the equation of elections and democracy, thereby ironically occluding the Italians' warnings about the dangers of conflating them.

Most obviously, the Cold War and its effects on social science formation in the postwar period played a significant role in the vilification of the Italian theorists as conservative proto-authoritarians. The postwar ideological desire of American political scientists to construct a foreign, more extreme understanding of "elite circulation," "the ruling-class theory," or "the iron law of oligarchy"—one conveniently linked to fascism—partially motivated them to falsify Italian theories so as to position their own theories as being less elitist and therefore more palatable to an American "democratic" public in the midst of a "Cold War" struggle with a more totalitarian enemy. This foil allowed thinkers like Seymour Martin Lipset and Robert Dahl to articulate a theory of democracy that not only made more permissible the plutocracy that the Italian thinkers feared but also eliminated the intellectual concern over plutocratic tendencies in liberal democracy.

This ideological motivation coalesced with the problems posed by historical and contextual translation. Twentieth-century American political scientists faced a very different set of political concerns than those Pareto, Mosca, and Michels confronted, and therefore interpreted these forefathers of the tradition from another perspective. Thomas Piketty, in *Capital in the Twenty-First Century*, demonstrated that the post–World War II generation in Western Europe and North America experienced an unprecedented and highly abnormal level of material equality.[18] Consequently, he argues, although plutocracy had previously appeared to social scientists and historians as a transhistorical phenomenon, the second half of the century was able to legitimately marginalize this issue and instead focus on what political and intellectual elites found to be a more pressing concern: containing totalitarianism and authoritarianism, which at the time many believed originated in the failure of excessively participatory government structures. Theorists as different as Charles Merriam and James Burnham, on the one hand, and Seymour Martin Lipset and Robert Dahl, on the other, thus looked to the Italian

School with different eyes and a new set of problems to resolve. As such, American scholars read Pareto, Mosca, and Michels with more optimism about plutocratic containment than had been possible for the Italian School, and therefore underscored other elements in their texts at the expense of ignoring their most explicit anxieties.

Postwar socioeconomic conditions exacerbated the extent to which Americans could not recognize the context of nineteenth-century Risorgimento politics—a rampantly plutocratic environment wildly different from the uncharacteristically equal political-economic landscape of the postwar period.[19] Importantly, these Italian authors did not dedicate their lives to fighting plutocracy as an end in and of itself. Instead, they were committed to realizing the Italian unified state as a lasting project and insisted that combatting the Risorgimento's parliamentary plutocracy was crucial for generating a salutary modern popular government in Italy.[20] Postwar American readers could not appreciate the extreme plutocratic fragility that threatened the very existence of the Italian state at the turn of the nineteenth century, and consequently misread the Italians' concerns as a full-scale denunciation of liberalism tout court.

Recognizing the way in which plutocracy drops out of the equation is key to understanding the history of American political science, its behavioral turn, and its peculiar "realistic" or "empirical" approach to the study of politics. The disappearance of the concern about plutocracy induced American authors to misunderstand the "scientific" character of the Italians' orientation toward the role of elites. Despite the exclusively empirical register in which we now understand ideas like "elite circulation," "the ruling class," or the "iron law of oligarchy," the Italians treated politics historically and normatively: they were trying to understand how and why representative institutions developed in a disappointing way through a Vichian approach to science, a position that rejected the simplistic Cartesian emphasis on causal reasoning and empirical observation and eschewed moralism in political discourse.[21] Drawing from their acceptance of the inevitability of elite domination, postwar American political scientists set out to establish scientific laws for the development of institutions—laws so absolute that they permitted no effective mitigation of elite influence. Works like Dahl's *Who Governs?* were offered as models for how political rule develops everywhere, despite his book having been based on a study of New Haven city politics. This model became paradigmatic in the interest-group approach to the Western study of elites, which held that interest group competition was a standard that even the Soviet Union was thought to share with the United States. Ironically, the committed anti-historicist Leo Strauss was

14   DEMOCRATIC ELITISM

the only major resource for midcentury political scientists seeking to critique "value free" positivist scientism. Had Pareto and Mosca been properly recovered, then we might have avoided the worst excesses of behavioralism, antiinstitutionalism, and myopic obsession with elections.[22]

Some might wonder whether the Italians' warnings of the connection between elections and plutocracy are particular to the social and political conditions of post-Risorgimento Italy or whether they hold more broadly. But in the Italian understanding, the particularities of the Risorgimento's plutocratic parliamentarism did not conflict with recognizing the more generalizable connections between electoral institutions and plutocratic corruption. The Italian nation-state was a particularly egregious example of how unfettered electoral processes generate plutocratic outcomes and unrepresentative government. While the Italian School theorists diagnosed plutocracy as endemic to electoral institutions, their normative projects investigated a wide variety of comparative (geographical and economic) contexts in order to identify which social, economic, and institutional variables have historically controlled for plutocratic capture of electoral government.

In other words, the Italian case distilled the inherent connection between elections and plutocracy that can ultimately lead to the corruption of those very same representative institutions. Pareto, Mosca, and Michels understood their approach as "scientific" because they posited the intrinsic relationship as a generalizable law, but this did not mean that they saw the post-Risorgimento period as perfectly emblematic of how elections operate in all historical circumstances. They stressed the variable success of representative governments across the Continent to emphasize that this law need not be fatalistically interpreted. Ironically, the Italians would have classified Dahl's *Who Governs?* as quintessentially "anti-scientific" precisely because it uses anecdotal evidence of city politics in Connecticut as a proxy for how politics works universally.

Finally, the misinterpretation of the Italian school thinkers also stemmed from a misreading of the pessimistic tradition to which they belonged and the accompanying literary sensibility they expressed. Pessimism is a philosophical approach that emphasizes human limitations in order to provoke self-conscious confrontation with fundamental obstacles to human flourishing.[23] Educated in the late nineteenth century—a time when pessimism reached its apex within European discourse—Pareto, Mosca, and Michels, and in some respects Schumpeter, are better situated within the tradition of pessimism than within the tradition of elitism with which they are currently affiliated. Much like famed pessimists such as Nietzsche, Weber, and Ortega y Gasset, the authors discussed here offered pessimistic accounts of democracy and posited grim warnings about the future of European liberalism that were mistaken for celebrations of oligarchic domination.

Of course, authors who subscribe to pessimism are not all the same, and one does not need to be aware of this philosophical discourse to appreciate the pessimism of a particular figure. In order to assess the value of various kinds of pessimism and other affective postures, I propose a mode of reading that focuses on what I call literary "sensibility" or "disposition" within a particular historical-intellectual context. Here, I refer to a rhetorical tone and nuance clearly detectable within a text—a tone available to any readership, accessible beyond the esoteric level intended only for an elect audience. Dispositional readings can alert us to such sensibilities so that one may find in texts something critical that otherwise seems dispassionate or prescriptive, as was the case with the Italians and Schumpeter; or conversely, something that seems ambivalent but should be considered resigned or sanguine, as was the case with Lipset and Dahl.

This book traces the shift in the literary dispositions that undergird what we now call "elite theories of democracy." The chapters identify the rhetorical sensibility expressed in each moment, contrasting Italian variants of pessimism and Schumpeter's sardonic irony with American postwar optimism. By isolating these dispositional expressions, I demonstrate how these different literary moods served as imperatives for various—and contrasting—political ends. I claim, somewhat counterintuitively, that the pessimism and irony expressed respectively by the Italian School and Schumpeter left open possibilities for democracy seldom recognized within the "elitist" model, and that, conversely, the Americans infused optimism into this understanding of representative government with perniciously complacent consequences for subsequent democratic theory. Specifically, Lipset's and Dahl's hopeful ambivalence expressed in their "nouveau elitism" induced American political science to live content with narrow empirical orientations to democracy, with constricted liberal institutional choices, and with plutocratic tendencies. While Schumpeter's work undoubtedly provoked the perverted American reception of the Italian School, attention to the irony through which he conducts his socioeconomic analysis and conveys his political prescriptions ought to change the way we perceive the elite "tradition."

In what follows I complicate what we understand as "elite" democratic theory, and question whether this school has been mislabeled all along.[24] I refer to the Italians as the "forefathers" of this tradition in deference to the common understanding of these thinkers, and not to designate them as genuinely elitist in any normative way. On the contrary, I aim to convince readers that we ought to think of them, not as elite theorists of democracy, but instead as democratic theorists of elitism. In a discipline where "elitist," "minimalist," and "Schumpeterian" are used interchangeably and pervasively, it is time we recover how these terms came into existence before we pass judgments over their normative import. A genealogical recovery of the Italian School of Elitism not only disrupts the habit of debating the empirical validity or normative desirability of contemporary elite models. Such a recovery may also newly equip proponents of greater democratic participation, as well as others who fear the increasingly pernicious impact of plutocracy upon democracies worldwide or those who have become suspicious of the conflation of democracy and elections but struggle to find viable alternatives.

Democratic Elitism as a Trope

Given the argument articulated above, one might suppose that this book aims to banish any discussion of democratic elitism from contemporary political thought. If the elite theory of democracy is in some respects a myth, why continue relying on it when analyzing current democratic practices?

Here I find a parallel with Renaissance studies instructive. Canonical Renaissance figures employ a famous trope whereby they insert speeches into their texts, and they impute authorship to the speaker or they attribute corroboration of its content to some other personage. This trope often comes accompanied by a forceful insistence that such a speech did indeed occur, more or less verbatim, at a rather specific historical juncture. Petrarch, Bruni, Machiavelli, Guicciardini, and, as a matter of fact, most Italian Renaissance figures often include such speeches and "transcriptions" as rhetorical devices in their political thought.

Contemporary interpreters were not only familiar with the trope, but they knew, at the very least, to proceed with caution when they came upon its use. Most readers are inclined to completely reject the notion that the speech (in fact or via transcription) actually took place, and instead look to its broader function in the work, or consider how to make sense of its substantive claims in light of the knowledge that the speech most likely never occurred (at least not in remotely such a form). Following the etymology of "trope," which originally connoted a "turning away from," the use of the trope in Renaissance scholarship is an invitation to pivot and change direction precisely because the veracity of the claim is in question.

Each of my chapters advances the suggestion that democratic elitism is a trope that contemporary political theory relies upon in order to make its own diverse claims about what democracy means today. The problem with this usage is not the reliance on the trope itself, but that we do not acknowledge, either implicitly or explicitly, democratic elitism as such a foil. Instead, we think of democratic elitism as some kind of ontological foundation of twentieth-century democratic theory as opposed to a trope, which beckons us to pivot and play with other conceptions of democracy because the legitimacy of democratic elitism is doubtful. The Renaissance trope operates on the assumption that the contents of such speeches are false for the purposes of the authors composing them, but we take the invocations of the "elitist theorists" by Lipset, Dahl, Bachrach, Pateman, et al. at face value.

This book seeks to make democratic theory more aware of democratic elitism's function as a rhetorical device in contemporary political thought. While it argues that democratic elitism is indeed a myth that twentieth-century American political science constructed, it also aims to convince readers that we ought to look at such a straw man as an invitation to pivot and explore new avenues of democratic justification, and perhaps furnish a new political vocabulary for democracy that primarily relies, not on the celebration or disparagement of competitive elections, but instead on the democratic foundations required for *buon governo*, or good government. In this sense, the lie constructed in the twentieth century can still be fruitful.

CHAPTER I

An Angry Warning

Pareto and Elite Circulation

> Votaries of extreme laissez-faire may cull plenty of passages from
> [Pareto's] writings in support of their views. Yet there was nothing
> he despised so thoroughly as the "pluto-democracy" or "plutocratic
> demagogy" of liberalism.
>
> —JOSEPH SCHUMPETER, *Ten Great Economists*

As Talcott Parsons once observed, Vilfredo Pareto was most certainly a
"'knocker' not a 'booster.'"[1] No study of Pareto fails to mention the particularly aggressive, desperately critical tone that has come to define his oeuvre. This
"unpleasant," "utter cynicism" often helps interpreters explain the wildly varying
political positions that Pareto purportedly maintained throughout his life.[2]

On this register, studies of Paretian politics invariably fall into two camps.[3]
The first underscores the early Pareto: the engineer and industrial railway
president, journalist, and political activist who embodied the fanaticism of a
"Manchester" liberal—a severe laissez-faire type, typical of the nineteenth
century, who excoriated government intervention of all types.[4] The second
camp instead focuses on the more mature Pareto: the disillusioned and aris-
tocratically fastidious scholar who, after emigrating to Switzerland in the
1890s, wrote the "protofascist" academic tomes that gave concrete expression
to the authoritarianism that would engulf Europe soon after his death.[5]
For both those who valorize the politically active journalist of the liberal
period and those who disparage the older, embittered protofascist, 1899 presents an abrupt turning point in Pareto's orientation, but one that ultimately

makes sense given his alleged dread of "mass society."[6] At different points in Pareto's life, it is consistently argued, Pareto's pessimism reflects a supreme distrust of increased mass political participation in industrialized societies, channeled through his early disdain of socialism and his later "vilification and hatred of democracy."[7]

In other words, the last century has painted Pareto as having been always deeply distrustful of the effects of mass participation. Consequently, the aim of containing these tendencies in the economic and political spheres emerges as the motivation for his shifting politics.[8] As a young man he took a "libertarian" orientation against socialism, and in his later years he expressed conservative, "counterrevolutionary," or even proto-authoritarian antipathy toward democracy.[9] Charles Merriam's critique of the "founders of elitism," Mosca and Pareto, devoted special attention to the "seemingly undespotic liberal" Pareto who, in Merriam's estimation, "proved hostile to the very possibility of democratic self-government."[10]

This long-standing paradigm obscures not only Pareto's central preoccupations but also the nature and function of his pessimism. Far from worrying about the pernicious effects of increased mass participation, Pareto anxiously feared elite corruption and its pernicious effects on a polity—and specifically, on the new, fragile Italian state. Throughout his life, in both his journalistic and his academic endeavors, Pareto sought to combat corruption by exposing the myths used to legitimate a decaying plutocratic ruling class.[11] In his own historical moment, this meant debunking the reigning myth that popular sovereignty can be expressed through parliamentary representation. Most crucially, Pareto aimed to reveal the plutocratic stranglehold of political life that electoral institutions engender, and he unfailingly warned of the dangers that could result from this kind of corruption.

As opposed to understanding Pareto in terms of the fervent classical liberalism of the Anglo-American tradition or the counterrevolutionary fervor that swept over continental Europe in response to the uprisings of 1848, this chapter analyzes his political thought within the context of the Risorgimento. Studying Pareto with an eye to the distinctly Italian, "skeptical" orientation toward liberalism in the midst of state unification unearths entirely different preoccupations than the ones typically emphasized.[12] More than anything else, Pareto warned against both the exploitation that structurally accompanies electoral forms of government and the risks of intensified economic inequality, because he saw how these two factors generate a governing class that can easily evade accountability to popular sentiments and desires. Not only does such a reconsideration invalidate the classification of Pareto as a laissez-faire liberal or

20   DEMOCRATIC ELITISM

protofascist authoritarian, but it also accentuates the anti-elitist (rather than the anti-popular) continuity in his pre- and post-1899 political concerns.

Instead of interpreting his pessimism as an expression of disdain for illusory faith in the progressive prospects of mass political participation, I contend that Pareto's deployment of pessimism seeks to combat the plutocratic risks associated with electoral government by ruthlessly exposing them. While many would later read his aggressive cynicism as suspicion of popular government of any kind, Pareto's angry, rebuking tone functions as potentially productive, in that it militates against equating democracy with elections.

In his appraisal of the Italian economist, Joseph Schumpeter insists that Pareto's scientific contributions must be understood biographically, for "the whole man and all the forces that conditioned him entered so unmistakably that it is more necessary than it usually is . . . to convey the idea of that man and of those forces."[13] This chapter thus begins with a biographically anchored investigation of Pareto's early writings to reveal his core concerns with economic inequality and elite corruption under electoral schemes. Given this context, I then argue that the theory of equilibrium and elite circulation highlights the perils of liberalism by focusing on the relationship between competitive minority elites in a given society, or polyarchy, and refusing to acquiesce to the inevitability of elite rule. By way of conclusion, I take up Pareto's purportedly most "protofascist" text, *The Transformation of Democracy* (*Trasformazione della democrazia*), which studies how electoralism hampers democracy and prophesies the authoritarianism that looms after the imminent collapse of parliamentarism.

The Fiery Revolutionary: 1848–1899

From his earliest days, Pareto exhibited passion for the public policies that would make Italian unification a success. Until he was fifty, he fought tirelessly against the Italian ruling class by illuminating the dynamic between elite sects in the nascent parliamentary state, and the many ways electoral corruption facilitated the ability of these minorities to despoil the polity despite their best intentions. Unlike British or continental contemporaries such as John Stuart Mill or the Marquis de Condorcet, Pareto understood parliamentarism as a regime based, not on openness and discussion, but instead on the primacy of the electoral mechanism.[14] This is not to say that Pareto opposed universal suffrage or the mere existence of elections in a polity. Rather, he held that the intrinsic features of elections that lend themselves to corruption must be combatted through democratic mechanisms. Equating elections and democracy, in his view, facilitated corruption by allowing for an unconvincing, legitimating veneer of equality, ultimately destroying faith in elections writ large.

Pareto was born in 1848 in Paris, the son of the Genoese Marchese Raffaele Pareto, an uncompromising Mazzini supporter who was exiled to Paris as a result of his revolutionary fervor. Despite his father's title, the family was not wealthy, and Pareto grew up in middle-class conditions. Pareto achieved financial independence only after he became heir to his uncle's sizable fortune in 1898, an inheritance that permitted him to live comfortably as an academic. At age ten, Pareto returned to Italy and began studies that resulted in an engineering doctorate in 1869. Thereafter he embarked upon a career in industrial management, rising to the rank of managing director of the Italian Ironworks Company (Società delle Ferriere Italiane). After struggling to navigate the "deal-cutting" with government departments that was necessary to raise the capital needed to modernize at competitive prices, Pareto resigned his post in 1884.[15]

This is not to say that Pareto became politically inclined only after his career in industrial management. As early as 1870, the year before the formal completion of Italian unification, Pareto lectured on political economy, regularly wrote editorials on the policies of the day, and in 1881 ran an (unsuccessful) bid for office on a highly "anti-elitist" platform.[16] After resigning from the Ironworks Society, he published a plethora of "antiestablishment" articles and organized radical democratic meetings, for which the Italian police marked Pareto as a wanted man.[17] He supported the popular insurrections of 1894 and 1898. In 1898–1899, he sheltered Italian socialist refugees after the government opened fire on peaceful protests in Sicily and he continued to encourage a coalition of republican, socialist, and democratic activists against government corruption.[18]

One might think that seeing his dream of the Risorgimento come to fruition, under the structure of a parliamentary regime no less, would have been a cause for optimism. Yet Pareto saw no reason to celebrate the triumph of liberalism in Italy. He identified nothing but incompetence and corruption in the new Mecca and fought mercilessly against each administration and *trasformismo*, or the rapid absorption of contesting forces into the governing majority through sacrifices of policy positions through corrupt or suspect electoral "compromises."[19] Outside of Italy, Pareto gained a reputation as an ultra-laissez-faire liberal, partially because of the ferocity with which he repudiated government intervention as nothing more than the craven workings of politicians' machinations against the public interest.[20]

22　DEMOCRATIC ELITISM

Analysis of his early thought, however, reveals that Pareto's orientation should not be classified as liberalism of the English variety—the "Manchester" type or otherwise.[21] Pareto railed against government, not because he was against government activity per se, but because he was against unrestrained governments of parliamentary rule—the same parliamentary governments that English liberals held so dear. In comparison to its English or French counterparts, he maintained, the Italian establishment was a sordid caricature of the worst vices of electoral politics.

For Pareto, Italy's difficulties were the product of collusion among politicians, speculators, and military leaders who, despite misaligned interests, managed to steer the government toward their own pecuniary advantage. Under electoral governments, he says, "the subtle ways in which the politicians manage to purloin the wealth of the nation and to divide it up among their friends" are so complex and opaque that they can easily go undetected.[22] His relentless exposés of these maneuverings, or *combinazioni*, can be loosely organized within his critique of the Italian economic crisis, financial scandals, and military expansion.

Pareto belaboredly argued that the economic crisis resulted entirely from a party system that encouraged and rewarded collusion. The country's dire financial straits could be explained by three factors. First, no matter which party came into power, each cabinet promised to increase armament expenditure without tax hikes in order to appease the military.[23] Initially Pareto held out hope that eventually some administration would have the courage to take a "firm grip on those untouchable institutions that are the ministry of war and the admiralty," but it quickly became clear to him that reform was elusive. Antonio Starabba di Rudinì's accommodating attitude toward the military was just as bad as Francesco Crispi's, and Giovanni Giolitti's blithe spending in this regard was "even worse."[24]

Second, each government seemed beholden to a class of financial operators and speculators. In 1892, commenting on rumors concerning the possible sale of the railways, Pareto proclaimed the sale price of 600–700 million lire to be "ridiculously low" given its 1,200-million-lire capital value, or the 60 million lire per year that the state was earning from the sector.[25] In effect, politicians were giving away one of Italy's major going concerns for pennies to the already well-to-do. Despite Prime Minister Giovanni Giolitti's proclamations that privatization would enrich public coffers, Pareto countered that this simply could not be the case at such a low valuation. Perhaps every enterprise has a price, he concedes, but the only effective way to balance the budget would be to reduce public spending, "starting with military expenditure."[26]

Finally, Pareto contends that the crisis could be traced back to protectionism: new tariffs had exacerbated the trade deficit (increasing the value of imports and decreasing that of exports) because they had unexpectedly increased production costs.[27] Yet his campaign against tariffs was not resolutely anti-protectionist: Pareto's diatribe was specifically directed against Italian duties, imposed primarily on agriculture (specifically on grain), which disproportionately disadvantaged the Southern region. For him, the solution was not to make it more expensive for the Mezzogiorno (Southern Italy) to export its agricultural products.[28] No one on the global market would buy Southern goods at those prices, and the region would become even more impoverished: emigration would rise, bank deposits would fall, and unification would be threatened by aggravating the already precarious economic disparity between the North and the South.[29]

Pareto's anti-protectionist crusade thus unsettles the typical assumptions of classical liberals. Anti-customs policies in Italy were not affiliated with the liberal, moderate, or nationalist parties, but instead were championed by socialists. In fact, the young "liberal" Pareto vocally advanced the proposal of socialist Gregorio Agnini to abolish the duty on grain.[30] But irrespective of the political labels that anti-protectionist policies assumed in Italy, Pareto was never an anti-protectionist tout court. In certain stages of development, he argues, government subventions and protective tariffs are positively conducive to industrial growth because they afford time for the necessary capital accumulation that enables national industry to compete in world markets. While tariffs entail a significant transfer of wealth, he accepts that such transfers can be beneficial in the long run, depending on the circumstances of the tariff in question and its beneficiaries.[31] In this circumstance, tariffs on agriculture benefit only the North: such duties would exacerbate the disparity between the Northern "haves" and the Southern "have-nots," and justifiably render *meridionali* (Southerners) more suspicious that unification had just transferred the exploitative power of the Bourbon monarchs to the capitalistically sympathetic House of Savoy.

Protectionism was not the only issue that differentiated Pareto's position from the free-trade platform of traditional economic liberalism. In the sphere of monetary policy, he vehemently opposed fiat currency and free issuance of banknotes. "For all intents and purposes," the issuing of paper money unbacked by coinage, he insists, constitutes "a tax" on the working population because increasing "the spread vis-à-vis gold" decreased the value of the lira, thereby reducing the purchasing power of those earning "fixed salaries."[32] The "important thing," Pareto writes, "is that notes should be convertible into coinage."[33]

Although he knew quite well that free-trading economists of the time hoped "to see freedom of issuance," non-obligation to accept banknotes for coinage was also "compatible with *a regime characterized by a monopoly of issuance*." And such a Northern monopoly would exacerbate the rampant inequality between *settentrionali* (Northerners) and *meridionali* (Southerners).[34]

Put simply, in order to improve this regional economic disparity and the country's general economic situation, the best policy would (1) reduce the issue of notes so as to eliminate the premium on gold and (2) require that all banks carry enough coinage to back paper money. While in theory enacting this policy would not be difficult, Pareto recognized that it would require that "politicians . . . stop drawing on the deposits of the issuing banks for their own needs"—an event that seemed unlikely in light of their previous record.[35]

Pareto's monetary policy effectively accused politicians of drawing on public reserves at the expense of the working class. But his analysis of the question vis-à-vis issuing banks also cast light on the collusion *between* political elites and economic elites. The Banca Romana's financial scandals were some of the many sensational examples of such maneuverings, or *combinazioni*. In short, this period is marked by financial elites' bribing politicians to allow them to continue benefiting from bond issues.[36] Pareto began monitoring the issue in 1891, when he first observed that, at the prompting of the Banca Nazionale (one of the six issuing banks), the government had created a land credit union, the Istituto di Credito Fondiario. Immediately he noted a series of suspicious real estate loans on the Istituto's balance sheet.[37]

Two years before the Banca Romana scandal erupted, Pareto clamored about the canary in the coal mine. The land credit union, he wrote, creates a nexus between banking elites and real-estate tycoons, along with the politicians who cave to their demands in exchange for kickbacks. The union will never achieve anything in the interests of the nation because the whole aim of the venture, he asserted, was "to come to the aid of compromised building companies and to clear the portfolios of the banks that had propped them up thus far."[38]

This episode demonstrated for Pareto that even the Rudini-Luzzatti administration with its "vague intentions of honesty and integrity . . . will submit to any type of coordinated pressure" exerted by economic elites seeking to financially engineer organs of profit.[39] And indeed, the Istituto di Credito Fondiario was quickly rescued by the Bank of Italy. This is not simply the typical complaint of the convergence of political parties into a cohesive elite class: here Pareto laments that no matter which party holds power, differences in competence, intentions, or platform cannot stop elected representatives, supposedly accountable only to the people, from catering to leaders of the finance and banking sectors. The worst part, for Pareto, was that the show trials cleared politicians of responsibility and allowed the company administrators to circumvent their terms of imprisonment.[40] Even without the formal election of economic elites to office, Pareto intimated, the consolidation of a plutocracy in Italy was near.

Over the course of the 1890s, Pareto fought against fiat currency based on the corruption that electoral institutions engender. In his view, when issuing banks were not required to redeem paper notes with sound money for average citizens, the banks could mobilize capital and deposits in unprofitable transactions working solely to the advantage of the government and private financial institutions. The banks had allocated the savings entrusted to them, he says, "among various entrepreneurs . . . [not] according to [their] productivity in a fair manner . . . [but] according to the kickbacks the entrepreneurs were able or prepared to *pay the politicians*, which is not at all the same thing."[41] The legal tender regime had thus helped enact a system of legalized bribery masquerading as responsive government: banks had been relieved of the obligation to redeem their notes with sound money, and legislative controls were ineffective because both political and economic elites stood to profit from fiat currency.[42] The only way to ensure that banks would redeem their notes was to give citizens the right to "take legal action against them, exactly as for a trader or a banker who does not redeem a bill of exchange at the due date."[43] Perhaps other nations could reap the benefits that fiat currency allows in facilitating capital accumulation, but Italy could not bear the risk, given such egregious displays of parliamentary corruption.

The problem was not simply corruption. To Pareto's mind, the electoral system created a ruling or governing class that transcended political leadership to include military and economic elites, but that could not hold the latter two groups accountable. Pareto's pacifist writings against the First World War best reveal how the plutocratic "connection" among political, military, and economic sects makes it impossible for elections to hold this broader ruling class accountable to the majority of the people.

In the summer of 1892, Pareto began to attack the Triple Alliance as "a catastrophe worse than any in historic memory."[44] "What benefit can come for the Italian people from the government's support for Germany in regard to the possession of Alsace-Lorraine?" he asks in one letter.[45] This alliance was capable of "obliging Italy to take part in a war that is none of its business and that could cost much more than just vast sums of money, because [if] we win we will gain but little reward, while [if] defeated we will be destroyed."[46] There must be

26 DEMOCRATIC ELITISM

another reason, he muses, that the Italian establishment was eager to destroy "the whole of Europe so that Germany can keep control of Alsace-Lorraine against the wishes of its inhabitants." Delusions of national grandeur could not even explain this policy of "plain stupidity."[47] There must be more to it.

Pareto encouraged his readers to think about who might economically benefit from war. Certain capitalist interests in the North, he intimates, would obviously like to have a paying customer for armament production.[48] But a military-industrial complex could not be the whole reason, either. In 1893 Pareto suggested that ruling-class corruption was behind both the war effort *and* the new protectionist policies. The government, he said, facilitated a trade, granting tariffs to economic elites seeking to increase the prices of their products in exchange for their support of armament expenditures.[49] Parliament had acted as a clearinghouse to satisfy economic and military interests, presumably only to line the pockets of the members of parliament.

Clearly politicians were responding to the demands of economic and military elites, Pareto said, and not enacting policy in the people's interest. He thus proposed one way—hardly classically liberal but "infallible"—to render Italy "more pacifist than Switzerland": finance the proposed military expenditure "through additional taxes on landholdings," because the culpable elites in this circumstance were more likely to own property.[50] Pareto demonstrates that instead the military budget had been financed through a system of indirect taxation with covert loopholes for the ruling class, which burdened the popular classes without benefiting them at all.[51] There is a reason, he wrote, that the nation, as a collectivity, was never asked to choose among possible strategies for balancing the budget—namely, through debt, reduction of military expenditure, or tax increases.[52] Direct consultation of the people, our supposed "elite theorist" intimated, would have resulted in a more just and efficacious outcome.

Pareto began to clamor for democratic action. Only "true" democratic regimes, and not the shams known as "parliamentary democracy," could forestall the threat of war because parliamentarians were enabling interested parties to control policy.[53] In 1895, speaking of the Italian defeat at Amba Alagi, he encouraged Italians to use the Ethiopians as a model: "instead of going to fight the Africans . . . the Italians should fight their internal enemies"—the politicians who were working for other elites. He noted that the working class was acutely aware that the "millions . . . wasted fruitlessly in Africa would be better spent in Sardinia, in the Roman countryside, where there are lands to be reclaimed and roads to be built everywhere."[54] Because "the art of governing consists in plundering citizens' property, rather than safeguarding it, and the goal is for all the politicians to receive their share," the only way for Italians to "defend their land and their liberty," he proclaimed, is to collectively fight against the political class in an anti-war campaign.[55]

No matter the policy in question at this stage in his career, Pareto sought to expose the corruption of a ruling class that transcends the political sphere. In the modern state, the ruling class's nodes of patronage and influence cluster around economic interest. While Pareto often called the governing class "the bourgeoisie," the derogatory label referred not to the middle classes but instead to the "rich and well-to-do" ruling minorities who were not a part of the pre-1860 nobility.[56] To be sure, these new, querulous elite sects were constantly competing with one another, but there was still sufficient cohesion among them to warrant calling them a "class" because they live by political and economic mutual back-scratching.

In his early years Pareto hurled vitriolic attacks at Italian politicians who were "not only dishonest but also incompetent, ignorant, dithering and lacking in determination" such that "everything they try ends up going wrong."[57] But at this time his view of *structural* electoral corruption in parliamentary governments was already forming. *La classe governante* consisted not only of politicians, but of a consortium of sects who live through this sort of back-scratching without explicit design or intention. At the most general level, the governing class was increasingly splitting "into two distinct groups"—those who were in explicit pursuit of power and those, in much larger numbers, who had "nothing in mind but making money."[58] Although this second category relinquished formal political power to those who procured capital for them, he asserted, the political "industry" was becoming "more lucrative" for all parties concerned.[59]

Even when confining his discussion to *la classe politica*, Pareto never saw competitive elections as reflecting anything about the people's choice of leadership. In his eyes, politicians were united in a feudal fraternity, with the parliamentarians at the top, followed by the influential electors economically incentivized to campaign for them. The parliamentarians and secondary-level officials worked by exchanging offices in return for votes.[60] As a result, the candidates who were elected were those with the best ministerial contacts, and not those who received anything that could be interpreted as a popular mandate. Electoral outcomes, he states, bear no "inference as to the political views that prevail around the country."[61] Worse still, this did not mean that an administration with enough secondary-level ministerial power would remain there for long periods, because these sub-deputies would at a whim switch their allegiance to another politician who promised greater handouts.[62]

28   DEMOCRATIC ELITISM

Part of the issue lies in the particularities of Italian parliamentarism. Pareto contended that no matter what they might claim about their "parliamentary democracies," other European states did not concentrate as much power in their legislatures. In contrast, the Risorgimento had imposed a Bismarckian system of authority on an English parliamentary monarchy that was centralizing the state *à la française:* "Nothing good was to be expected from such a monstrous assemblage," given that "a well-established tenet of political science is that one of the worst forms of government is a parliamentary dictatorship that has control of centralized powers."[63] By over-empowering electoral institutions, Italian unification brought out the ugliest side of representative regimes. Extension of suffrage, however important, would not contain these deleterious effects in Italy.

Nevertheless, after having expounded at length on Italian electoral corruption, Pareto also asserted that all representative systems exhibit these features. The lack of genuine political parties and universal corruption were "the consequences of more general causes," some typical of all Latin countries, some particular to Italy, and some common to "almost all civilized states."[64] At the University of Lausanne, Pareto would take on this larger project of analyzing "almost all civilized states" and theorize the same plutocratic problems within representative politics more systematically.

Professing Equilibrium: 1893–1916

Between 1893 and 1916, as the successor to Léon Walras's chair of neoclassical economics at the University of Lausanne, Pareto published the academic volumes in which he developed his famed theories of equilibrium, which scholars have alleged contain the germs of his protofascist thought or, at the very least, attest to his elitist hatred of democracy, because they treat society as cleft between a passive mass and an active elite. Many suggest that these texts, with their insistence on the inevitability of elite rule, demonstrate Pareto's disbelief in salutary mass agency.[65] Rather than insist on the primacy of the mass / elite binary, I argue that the most salient aspect of Paretian equilibrium, and more specifically his theory of elite circulation, is its focus on elite heterogeneity and various problematic *combinazioni*—the "combinations" or maneuverings it produces in a given society.

Before turning to his political thought, it is helpful to acknowledge why so many readers see the works from this period as constituting Pareto's pessimistic resignation over elite domination. Most obviously, Pareto was the first to employ the term "elite" in a prominent fashion, and his French appellation, *élite*, enjoyed more success with continental and Anglo-American audiences than did Mosca's counterpart phrases *la classe politica* and *la classe dirigente*.[66] Moreover, Pareto, unlike Mosca, did not have the opportunity to distance himself from fascism, because he died in 1923; consequently, Pareto is often remembered as the more protofascist thinker of the pair. And generally speaking, Pareto's misanthropic demeanor and aggressive rhetoric were easily misunderstood as exhibiting antidemocratic proclivities.[67]

More fundamentally, Pareto's economic studies demonstrate a consistent interest in economic inequality, and the elite / mass paradigm forms the guiding element of his equilibrium models. For example, the law of vital few, which showed that 80 percent of the land in Italy was owned by 20 percent of the population, seemed to suggest that nothing could change this inherent division between masses and elites.[68] As Joseph Femia explains, "in his determination to 'unmask' the hypocritical elitism and tawdry self-seeking elites of liberal 'democracy,' he [Pareto] was a match for any left-wing firebrand," but the problem lay in the finality of his economic laws.[69] Of course, Pareto's economic work can be broadly characterized by the elite / mass partition, but myopic focus on these categories occludes the way his critique of liberalism, as we will see, actually complicated them.

On the surface, his conception of social equilibrium did not appear encouraging, either. In contrast to authors who likened the social body to an organism, Pareto proposes a model of equilibrium, or a dynamic balance among interdependent parts constantly moving toward a stable state, as a heuristic for understanding a polity.[70] According to this model, the form of society depends on the nature of the minority that dominates the rest of the populace, and regime change occurs when one set of elites replaces another decaying group in search of equilibrium—a theory he calls elite alternation or elite circulation.[71] By focusing on elite "heterogeneity," or the composition and fluctuations in membership of the dominant minority, Pareto sought to dispel the Marxist fairy tale that there was unity in a singular, monolithic ruling class, one that would be overcome by the dictatorship of the proletariat.[72] In response to his repudiation of Marx, later commentators, as we shall see, interpreted this emphasis on equilibrium between different classes of elites as denoting either fatal resignation or celebration of elite rule.[73]

The aim of this sociological theory, however, was not to encourage quietist acceptance of domination but instead to contest it by unveiling the distinct dangers elites pose and the fragility of a decaying governing class. In the *Trattato di sociologia generale* (literally "Treatise on General Sociology," published in

30   DEMOCRATIC ELITISM

English in 1935 as *The Mind and Society*) (1916), Pareto deploys elite circulation vis-à-vis the equilibrium model as a way to contrast two forms of polity that are particularly relevant given the corrupt practices of present ruling minorities. Each archetype corresponds to a distinct type of *classe dirigente* (ruling class) and their contrasting means of governance.

The first type of ruling class, which Pareto does not formally name but censoriously refers to as "Byzantine," constitutes an autocratic state in which power is explicitly vested in a hierarchical, centralized structure.[74] These governments operate directly on the governed through the use of physical force and explicit coercion. This ruling class is replete with what Pareto earlier in the work calls "Class II residues," or the "persistence of aggregates."[75] These residues, or instincts and abilities, incline the state toward violence and direct reinforcement of authority through clearly "organized" bureaucracies.[76] For the sake of simplicity, Pareto beckons his reader to use Machiavelli's labels and think of the elites who rely upon these attributes as "lions." In this form of government, a rigidly defined, cohesive, and clearly identifiable ruling class dominates. The sub-leadership directly responds to the elite minority, and all agency flows from the top of the pyramidal structure. The Greek tyrannies, Sparta, China, medieval feudalism, the Reformation, and the ancien régime are all classified under this typology.[77]

The second type of government is a decentralized clientelist state. This regime disseminates power latently through various and even competing channels—channels operated indirectly through artifice and cunning. The power of this group emanates from a fluid consortium of patrons who dominate through "Class I residues," or the "instinct of combinations."[78] The shrewd ability to combine (*combinare*) allows for those in power to constantly create new coalitions of dependents through manipulation and intrigue, and these coalitions are always actuated by economic interest. In keeping with Machiavellian categories, Pareto calls this ruling group the "foxes."[79]

Pareto does not bestow a formal title on this secondary typology, but its "plutocratic" form corresponds with the government of Athens, Republican Rome, medieval municipal structure, Venice, Italian parliamentarism, and all forms of modern electoralism.[80] Employing the vocabulary of twentieth-century political science, Samuel Finer defines this form of administration as a "polyarchy" because a plurality of minority elite groups compete for power.[81] Giovanni Sartori agrees on the polyarchic, pluralist nature of Pareto's second type because the ruling class consists of many "leading minorities."[82] Three elements of this typology are of particular note, as they showcase the continuity with Pareto's diagnosis of the Italian parliamentary system.

First, while the ruling minority should be considered a consortium of competing sects, they develop cohesion through economic incentivization, rendering monetary compensation a primary component of this regime. This form can flourish so long as it generates more wealth than it reallocates through patronage.[83] The Roman Republic and modern liberal, representative governments are the best examples of this system because electing a legislature necessarily requires the formation of "cliques, intrigue, and gangs" beyond the political class, Pareto says, and economic rewards are the only incentive strong enough to draw such disparate parties together.[84] Plutocratic power thus is a necessary feature of this state.[85]

Second, the cohesion generated through economic back-scratching does not come about by a specific plot or conspiracy. Pareto denies that the governing class is a "concrete unity" or a "person."[86] Its principal characteristic, he asserts, is "the order, or system, not the conscious will of individuals who may, indeed, in many cases, be carried by the system to points they never would have gone to by deliberate choice.... The road ... followed ... is the resultant of an infinity of minor actions."[87] Even the most earnest opponents of the plutocratic state act as its unintentional purveyors. Taking the United States as an example, both Woodrow Wilson and William Jennings Bryan, he maintains, "went into power as professed and probably sincere opponents of trust and financiers, but actually they worked in their favor in maintaining anarchy in Mexico with a view to securing a President there who would be subservient to American finance."[88] Put differently, because all actors are highly motivated by pecuniary interest, they act in concert without any need for shared intention or preconceived design.

And lastly, although a variety of distinct sects form a broad-based ruling group without an explicit mutual objective, they are made all the more cohesive as a result of the "inner government"—a political cabinet—which facilitates the concerted action of the competing minorities.[89] Elected assemblies function as a go-between for the various nodes of power and influence.[90] Importantly, according to Pareto, this political form does not impinge upon minority domination by allowing for competition between a plurality of distinctive minorities; rather, it facilitates such domination by acting as a legitimating façade that veils the inordinate power that the other, competing elite minorities hold over the formal political entity.

Although he harbors contempt for the Byzantine state, Pareto spends little time developing the typology because it does not correspond to the current, dominant form of polity. In his own time, the second genus of electoral or "democratic" rule prevails, but at a moment when it begins to show signs of decay. Though he includes so-called "democratic" states in this category, he distinguishes between democracy and—what everyone calls "democracy"—representative government. "The best government now in existence, and also better than countless others that have so far been observable in history," he clarifies, "is the government of Switzerland, especially in the form it takes in the small cantons—forms of direct democracy."[91] This democracy, he continues, "has nothing but the name in common with the governments, also *called* democratic, of other countries such as France or the United States."[92]

One might wonder why Pareto does not more forcefully distinguish between representative rule and democracy as he understands it. If he defines democracy as the devolved government and participatory politics of the Swiss cantons, why include "democracies," always in quotation marks, in the second category at all?

A major component of Pareto's argument emphasizes the problems with contemporary representative regimes that tout themselves as democratic. He constantly distinguishes between democracy as a form of government and democracy "as a religious creed."[93] "Who is this new god called Universal Suffrage?" he writes. The "Worshippers of Universal Suffrage," the elites who champion this creed, "are not led by their god." Instead "it is they who lead him," that is—who use this myth—and "often by the nose, determining the forms in which he must manifest himself."[94] Pareto goes to strenuous lengths to elucidate why electoral government cannot be faithfully understood as synonymous with a popular democratic one. The informal constellation of power in these electorally based regimes bypasses the official circuits of representation, posing systematic disadvantages to the majority of the people.[95] This virtually disqualifies liberal representative government as a necessarily popular form in the democratic register.

Incidentally, Pareto was an advocate of universal suffrage. He railed against both those who opposed the extension of suffrage on the grounds of literacy (by proposing that the North should fund compulsory education in the South) and those who, by manipulating the electoral constituencies, ensure that the number of members of parliament is not proportional to the number of electors who vote for them.[96] Against those opposed to proportional representation, Pareto pointed out that if the principle of nonrepresentation of minorities were to be accepted, elites themselves would be banished as they were a small minority, being the educated part of the nation.[97] Nevertheless, he found that universal suffrage, while necessary, could never address the dangers that electoralism presented in the context of a unified Italy. Worse still, when universal suffrage is conflated with democracy, the result is lethal to both forms of institutions.

This issue is not merely an example of benign hypocrisy in modern political discourse. The "fiction of 'popular representation,'" or the myth that elections generate democratic accountability through representative delegation, Pareto argues, bears pernicious, concrete consequences for the health of the polity.[98] He makes sure to include so-called electoral "democracies" of his day, the ones that supposedly construct adequate avenues of popular participation and accountability, in order to underscore that the conceit of democratic representation actually creates disillusionment with the system, thereby encouraging its delegitimization.

Given the stark failures of electoral outcomes to reflect popular interests, Pareto contends that the conflation of elections and democracy does not mollify the people by inducing them to believe that elections produce accountability of leadership to the majority. Parliamentary "democracy," he suggests, only generates democratic expectations that electoral institutions will always undermine. This gap between the expectations and the political reality of representative politics makes space for a cunning "democratic plutocrat," "a wealthy financier who becomes a demagogue for the sake of political influence rather than from any real conviction," and who exploits the inadequacy of elections, consequently ushering in a new stage of authoritarian rule.[99] In other epochs, this demagogic plutocrat came in the form of a Crassus, a Caesar, or even a Napoleon III, but Pareto fears that a contemporary manifestation will be far worse than the ones previously experienced, given the many recombinations possible within a capitalistic and liberal regime.[100]

To recapitulate, the elite circulation model contends that regime change occurs when one ruling class replaces another group whose power has begun to decay. Pareto highlights the ways that pluralist or polyarchic, electorally based systems create channels of plutocratic domination through the economic cohesion of highly diverse, competing minorities. In such systems' manifestation as "parliamentary democracies," the expectations for this class of leadership contrast sharply with the leaders' actual behavior, precipitating the disintegration of their authority and presenting a plutocratic demagogue with the opportunity to initiate a regime alteration toward autocracy.

Pareto never hides his frustration with his own typologies. He admits that his binary of the two regimes is inadequate because many governments do not fit in either category, as the clientelist practices of feudalism demonstrate.[101] Additionally, he identifies far more "residues" than the relevant two described

34   DEMOCRATIC ELITISM

above (there are six in his schema); therefore, infinite combinations of these human tendencies will never generate a "perfect repetition of political structures in history."[102] Nevertheless, for the purposes of understanding social change from the perspective of equilibrium, these impoverished categories help capture his main aim: to identify a perceptible "undulation" or "alternation" between the Byzantine, "centripetal" accumulation of power and the "centrifugal" dispersion of power in the polyarchic form.[103] In the most abstract sense, the history of civilization ping-pongs between these extremities, and equilibrium analysis seeks to understand the reasons for such vacillation and to isolate moments of transition. To put it somewhat differently, history does not repeat itself, but it rhymes.

For some, this "undulating curve" between the pair of elite types may seem excessively narrow and undifferentiated.[104] Yet it would also be a mistake to classify his theory of social change as a constant, abrupt transition between the two poles of centripetal and centrifugal domination. Pareto stresses that all ruling classes are eventually replaced, but one variable can mitigate violent transitions and the worst excesses of each form of government. In order to inhibit the stark oscillations between these two types of power, a ruling class must continually check itself by remaining open to contestation from below. Elite circulation within a ruling class determines the moments of transition between government alternation because it keeps the minority more responsive to the majority. How each *classe governante* maintains an open "aristocracy" (always in quotation marks) and fights the pitfalls of its own corruption depends on the society in question. Those occupying elite positions are not necessarily the most qualified or the genuine *aristoi*, and therefore the fourth volume of the *Trattato* devotes hundreds of pages to analyzing the countless permutations that this "openness" or "closedness" can take.[105] Most obviously, Pareto claims, democratic contestation from below, followed by institutional inclusion, allows for a natural flow of equilibrium. In fact, when classes in a nation are suddenly allowed to "mingle," or

> when class-circulation that has been sluggish suddenly acquires an intensity at all considerable, almost always observable is an appreciable increase in intellectual, economic, and political prosperity in the country in question. And that is why periods of transition from oligarchic to more or less democratic regimes are often periods of prosperity.[106]

Examples of such democratic contestation, institutional inclusion, and consequent prosperity include "Athens in the time of Pericles, Republican Rome after the victories of the plebs, France after the Revolution of '89. But one could go on."[107] Elite groups that remain genuinely open to lower-class influx through majoritarian contestation are the best off, as they will most assuredly enjoy periods of "boom."[108]

Along with democratic contestation from below, Pareto claims that co-optation of competent lower-class members into the ruling class and policing of corruption among elites can be just as important to the maintenance of equilibrium. In fact, Venice and Sparta began with open ruling classes, and even though neither was ever really accessible to the lower elements, throughout most of their histories the governments compensated for their narrowness through constant "egress," or expelling their most corrupt members.[109] Once Sparta became a fully closed system, he writes, the revolt of Agis was on the horizon.[110] Counterintuitively, Pareto uses the examples of Venice and Sparta to stress that the constant influx of new members from lower classes and the constant expulsion of corrupt elites helps maintain social equilibrium by preventing radical oscillations.

At some points Pareto makes the critical purchase of elite circulation and the equilibrium heuristic explicit: "Our democracies in France, Italy, England, and the United States are tending more and more to become demagogic plutocracies," and he predicts that they "may be following that road on the way to one of those radical transformations that have been witnessed in the past."[111] But in his mammoth study of nearly all civilizations, the argument about plutocratic corruption in his own purported "democratic" moment can get lost. Perhaps for this reason, many have highlighted the rambling tangents on plutocracy and obscure tirades on the specificities of Italian parliamentarism as evidence of his disorganized writing style.[112] But in these very tirades and tangents lies the heart of his message: the liberal plutocratic ruling class of his own day has decayed to such an extent that it is on the verge of combustion. If social equilibrium is to be maintained—that is, if the plutocratic ruling classes do not somehow find a way to restrain their own corruption by becoming more open to membership from the lower strata and disciplining their most corrupt members—the current reign of "parliamentary democracies" will give way to a violent form of autocratic rule.[113] Far from constituting an about-face in his anti-elitist orientation, the focus on elite heterogeneity in equilibrium displays his continued effort to fight the plutocratic tendencies of liberal regimes by warning of future authoritarianism.

I have focused on Pareto's analysis in the *Trattato* because it constitutes the culmination of his political theory from his years in the academy. But well before its publication, in four different works—the review of his Paris course

36 DEMOCRATIC ELITISM

(1896–1897), "Sunto di alcuni capitoli di un nuovo trattato di economia pura" (Summary of certain chapters of my new treatise on pure economics) (1900), *Les systèmes socialistes* (1902), and *Manuale d'economia politica* (1906)—Pareto analyzed elite heterogeneity and circulation to advance a rebuke to his readers.[114] Throughout these works he cautions that pluralism within the ruling class does not necessarily make a system more stable or democratic. Furthermore, the seeming global success of "parliamentary democracy," he contends, should not fool anyone into thinking that its "pluto-demagogic" features will inhibit its coming demise. When viewed in this light, even the most "scientific" explications of the dynamics of equilibrium acquire a political valence. As Pareto describes in the opening pages of *Les systèmes socialistes*, the height of a movement indicates an impending swing in achieving equilibrium:

> When a movement is about to change direction, the reversal will not usually start with a decrease in intensity, which would facilitate predication; on the contrary, the movement will attain its maximum intensity precisely at the moment prior to the change of general direction.[115]

Even if Pareto's political message does indeed become lost in the million-word, disordered magnum opus, in his last work he indicates exactly how he wants equilibrium theory to be interpreted vis-à-vis the governments of his own day.

A Furious Invective: 1919–1921

To be sure, Pareto's pessimism has its most hostile expression in *Trasformazione della democrazia* (*The Transformation of Democracy*) (1921). But rather than representing the pinnacle of his "fascist" thought, this harsh rhetoric insists on the separation of elections and democracy in order to forestall the latter's violent collapse. His angry pessimism offers simultaneously a severe denunciation of current ruling elites and his most distilled warning of the authoritarianism that contemporary plutocratic corruption breeds.

The book's title indicates the chief motivation of this short political treatise: How do representative institutions transform democracy into a demagogic plutocracy? From the outset, Pareto admits that he harbors significant reservations about using the word "democracy" because of the general confusion it provokes over, on the one hand, democracy understood as a specific regime type and, on the other, the many arrangements that might make up "popular government." Henry Sumner Maine, he remarks, may think that he resolves the confusion posed by the comprehensive idea of democracy by replacing it with "popular government," yet both terms inadequately capture the "indeterminate" nature of this "fugitive" concept, which does not specify precise institutional requirements.[116]

The difficulty is further compounded by the narrow scope of Pareto's argument. His text, he reminds the reader, studies the "transformation," or "social movement," of popular government into a structure that has nothing to do with democracy itself. Pareto yearns to understand how a seemingly legitimate democratic form so often mutates into its very opposite. While the *Trattato* demonstrates that all bodies politic undergo alteration, democracy presents an especially acute illustration of a polity that constantly threatens to undermine itself. Deconstructing the nature of this particular type of political change, he says, better elucidates "the economic, political, and social consequences" of the "current phenomenon."[117] From these introductory remarks, Pareto makes it clear that he does not think that democracy properly conceived as the direct, mass participation of the Swiss cantons, for instance, poses a problem per se. Rather, his mission consists in uncovering how representative institutions can transform popular governance into an undemocratic regime.

Because he has "already been accused" of making certain "dangerous" normative judgments that he rejects, Pareto begins by qualifying his project. Many, he complains, have interpreted his previous works as condoning or celebrating the consequences he identifies. But if he chooses to detail precisely how the current bourgeois ruling class "runs to its ruin," this does not mean that he encourages them toward that end, nor does it mean that he "advocates particular reforms of customs, prejudices, laws, or behavior to preclude such a destiny." That idea would suggest that he can offer some "prescription for curing the sickness from which the bourgeoisie suffers." On the contrary, he declares that he is "completely ignorant of the remedy." One should think of him, he says, as a "doctor who knows exactly how to diagnose the patient with tuberculosis but has no idea how to cure him."[118]

Pareto even admits that a remedy would be far more valuable than what his treatise contributes: merely a close investigation of "the type of political transformation we are witnessing" (*la trasformazione alla quale assistiamo*) and a prediction of some of the resulting consequences. In order to understand the current type of social movement, he applies the equilibrium analysis employed in the *Trattato* to investigate why contemporary representative governments so often threaten to become demagogic plutocracies.[119]

38 DEMOCRATIC ELITISM

To make a long story short, Pareto says, in every society there exist two contrasting forces: the centripetal force, which concentrates power in a central authority, and the centrifugal force, which pushes toward diversification. These two energies vacillate in search of equilibrium in an infinitely "undulating curve."[120] The diametrically opposed poles attract individuals with different aptitudes for acquiring power: the centripetal force draws those who incline toward direct expression of aggression and the centrifugal attracts those with a predilection for indirect manipulation.[121]

One of these groups gains control over the state only because the "weaker," more numerous parts of the population seek protection from being dominated by the other of these two forces.[122] Pareto argued that at the time when he was writing, the weaker classes were dominated by a *classe governante* that exhibited centrifugal, diversifying instincts; nevertheless, their sovereignty was clearly "crumbling" (*sgretolamento della sovranità*) due to the "discord sown by their excessive greed (*eccessiva cupidigia*) and their commitment to a war that formally summoned a demagogic plutocracy." These circumstances threatened to "force the weak to prefer a centripetal, centralized government which will concentrate sovereignty in itself" (*volgono a favorire questo secondo periodo, un governo centrale persistente . . . torna a concentrare in sé la sovranità*) in opposition to the foxes who currently despoiled them.[123]

Given *la classe dirigente*'s ostentatious corruption, who can blame them? For too long, Pareto says, the legitimating justification of their power has proven to be a myth—a "derivation"—that no one could conceivably accept, least of all those who need protection from abuses of power.[124] "The theory that our Parliaments reflect the nation through representation," he repeats in this last essay, "is simply a fiction." "Our parliaments only represent the sovereign group that [currently] rules through their vulpine arts," a fact that, Pareto said, was obvious to everyone except for the delusional *classe governante* itself. Pareto furiously scolds the ruling group for deluding itself into thinking it would actually benefit from its "insane and suicidal politics" of deceit and corruption perpetuated throughout the war. For some reason, he says, they believe that they retain popular support because they recite the canticle of representation, making chimerical promises without any intention of keeping them.[125] No ruling group, he implies, can get away with this type of leadership for long.

Here again, Pareto accentuates problems associated with the myth that representation facilitates popular sovereignty, and consequently, democracy. He claims that the plutocratic dimension of parliamentary politics eradicates representation's seemingly democratic pretensions. Invoking "the maxim that represents the origin of our parliamentary governments"—no taxation without representation—he writes: "It used to be maintained that taxes must be approved by those who pay them. Today, whether we acknowledge it implicitly or explicitly, the opposite holds: those who evade their tributes approve and impose them on the rest."[126] The "weaker," urban "working classes" (*operai*) may have no means available to fight the current Svengali's evasion, he continues, but they are certainly not blind to it. We cannot be surprised that the *operai* would invite demagogic leaders to gain footing, he suggests, whether that invitation takes the form of suspicious trade union tyrants pretending to champion the cause of the proletariat or a more potent and visible figure who will eventually overtake the entire polity.[127]

At first, representative governments foster plutocracy due to the failures of electoral accountability. As the plutocrats grow in number, Pareto recounts, their corrupt *combinazioni* proliferate, and their power gives way to demagogic energies that become increasingly appealing to oppressed classes. This process constitutes "the plutocratic cycle" of electoral governments.[128] While the shrewd foxes champion representation in order to legitimate their power, the collapse of their sovereignty in so-called contemporary "democratic" states in fact unravels through the exposure of the myth of representation as blatant hypocrisy. This means that the equation of elections and democracy is actually harmful for the resilience of elections, as the ever more apparent incompatibility of elections and democracy proves to be a powerful delegitimizing force.

Through the mythical conflation of representation and democracy, parliamentary government thus effectively functions as plutocracy's "handmaiden," and Pareto denounces these regimes as "the effective instrument" of "demagogic plutocracy" because electoral institutions, or their manifest democratic insufficiency, can encourage demagogues to take control of the state.[129] Crucially, though, demagogic plutocracy should not be considered a genus of the Byzantine, centripetal form of organization. It functions as an intermediary stage between the two government types.[130] For Pareto, a demagogic plutocracy is a system in which representative institutions allow plutocrats—that is, "rich speculators" (industrialists, merchants, financial operators, and so on)—to con the "democracy of workers" into joining a "partial alliance" with them against landowners and farmers (or rentiers), "thereby pulling the wool over [the workers'] eyes." With a demagogue at its helm, this liminal state sanctions the ruling class to continue replacing real economic production with risky speculation and "fiscal tricks." Of course, the demagogue claims to be fighting for the downtrodden proletariat, but "in reality he defends those who know how to pillage them."[131] Remember, he insists, that the demagogue himself is one of the plutocrats.

40   DEMOCRATIC ELITISM

Pareto's substantive claims clearly remain consistent between the *Trattato* and *Trasformazione*, but the latter book's aggressive condemnation of ruling elites intensifies a few aspects of his previous thought—an intensification which, we will see, was later met with serious disapprobation by critics. First, as just mentioned, Pareto's social classification defies the simple elite / mass paradigm that his legacy attributes to him; it instead identifies more nuanced categories to describe the ways that parliamentary systems afford speculators the "upper hand over the state and of exploiting other social classes."[132] His laborious distinctions between speculators and rentiers in *Trasformazione* recall his discussion on the subject in the *Trattato*, in which he complains that the Marxist division between capitalists and proletariat is not sufficiently differentiated because it does not adequately capture the picture of domination as currently experienced by majorities.[133] In both works he states that without singling out the "speculating" sect of the capitalist set, Marxist categories occlude the threatening elements of the ruling group that allies itself with the urban proletariat against rural farmers (rentiers), even though the urban proletariat and rural farmers have more shared interests, and, generally speaking, speculators and workers (*lavoratori*) *never* share any common interests.[134] In *Trasformazione* he further accentuates the division between urban and rural workers and between financial operators and capitalists who engage in less speculative economic activity. Far from reinforcing the ruler-versus-ruled binary that preoccupies the canon of Western political science, Pareto emphasizes the importance of detailing elite differentiation in order to identify the specific threats posed to the polity by each part of the ruling class.

Second, for Pareto this attention to elite heterogeneity illustrates that parliamentarism is inherently unstable and undemocratic because it systematically engenders plutocracy. In keeping with all of his works, he insists in *Trasformazione* that the "recombinatory" quality of electoral regimes structurally breeds plutocracy in modern and ancient popular governments alike: "There is nothing in the present state of affairs to prevent the plutocrats from continuing to make fat profits, just as the general prosperity of the Roman plutocracy was in no way jeopardized by the corn doles."[135] Capitalism's acute tendency to promote recombination, he maintains, simply makes contemporary matters far worse.[136]

In *Trasformazione*, Pareto demonizes plutocracy, anthropomorphizing it to such an extreme that it becomes the greatest nemesis of political life per se. Plutocracy's instrumentalization of parliamentary government is the most insidious problem we face, he writes, because it creates room for the "devious measures that speculators use to dupe the masses" (*per scopo principale di trarre in inganno le moltitudini*). It is striking, given retrospective charges of elitism, that his analysis does not impute to the masses an inherent cognitive incapacity for participating in politics; instead he stresses the protracted, deliberate efforts of speculators to "gull" the lower classes *and* everyone else outside of the speculating class into supporting their own self-interested ends—a vulnerable group that includes the "investors and savers" who are presumably elites themselves.[137] For Pareto, the speculators that reign through modern representative governments are the perpetrators of injustice; he warns that if parliamentary institutions remain unreformed, there will be no remedy for the impending political tragedy.[138]

The tragic, yet imminent, "triumph" of demagogic plutocracy becomes far more pronounced in this conclusion of the treatise. "Plutocracy is weakening, and demagogy is growing stronger," Pareto cautions, because "a downturn in the cycle is on its way."[139] Representative institutions have encouraged demagogues to enter the public sphere, he repeats, which is the reason electoral governments so often allow for the transformation of a popular government into a regime diametrically opposed to it. In this respect, Pareto should be read as issuing, not a call for resignation, but instead an exhortation for all representative regimes that do not restrain plutocratic power to quickly do so.

Trasformazione makes the case against the plutocratic features inherent in all representative systems, but Pareto never stops privileging the Italian case. In the appendix, he returns full circle to the attacks on the Giolitti administration that preoccupied him in his early years and declares that his predictions have been vindicated. The "legal conspiracy among plutocrats" has become undeniable.[140] He accuses the plutocratic ruling class of attempting to lower the exchange rate and cause a currency devaluation in order to hide the schemes that made them billions during the war. The evidence, he writes, "reveals that a number of stockbrokers are at fault," as can be seen by their panicked sale of nine million lire in state bonds in the span of a mere two days. Although the usual "judicial inquiries will continue," he says, the investigations conducted in Turin and Milan already indicate that they will have "the life expectancy of soap bubbles."[141]

At this point, Giolitti's denunciations of the perpetrators of injustice strike everyone, including Pareto, as a cruel joke. Calls for "democratic" accountability will not do because the political representatives allowed those who stood to profit from the war to control policy. New impositions of sumptuary laws cannot hide the fact that "demagogic plutocracy in Italy and elsewhere was only able to support the war by [ruling class] deceit." The duplicity began when those who supported the war—those who stood to materially prosper from it—were able to steer the government into deceiving the Italians into believing

42   DEMOCRATIC ELITISM

that the war would be "short, inexpensive, and require no tax levies on them." Had those "profiteering sharks" and even those "honest producers" not been able to exercise so much influence over the government, he claims, "the war would have never lasted," and things would have been different.[142]

"Now there is some pretense of prosecuting some of those sharks," Pareto acknowledges, lamenting that "no one questioned their actions during the war." In microcosm, this belated attempt to preach "democratic" values illustrates how electoralism creates a plutocracy that inhibits popular government. Giolitti, Pareto says, will now make "impossible" promises to the people of "increased prosperity of the masses" in order to win votes, but he will engineer this façade of affluence by allowing the same plutocrats to stimulate production through "innumerable fiscal tricks and whimsical measures designed to manipulate the economy." These lies, he declares, "belong to the same class of falsehood and deception politicians used to manipulate public opinion during the war and continue to use now that peace is here." The plutocratic electoral cycle thus endures, but at a certain point, he warns, the majority will refuse to support a hypocritical system that only intervenes on behalf of "the downtrodden" and ends the "evil deeds it previously favored" when it can do nothing else. He then worries that it might already be "too late."[143]

"When the state stops being for everyone—that is to say, when it stops being a *res publica*," Pareto writes, "it inclines each day toward a part of the populace."[144] Elections, he reiterates time and again, privilege the speculating part of the population, thereby obstructing the democracy that parliamentarism claims to have enacted. Most obviously, Pareto aimed to dismantle plutocracy by identifying the destructive effects of electoral corruption on the *res publica*. But just as importantly, he underscores the threats inherent in the mythical or "fictitious" conflation of democracy and electoral government. In so doing, he shows his elite readers how current elite behavior poses a threat to the class's own dominance. He may insist that he has no remedy to offer the ruling class of his day, but his heated reprimand functions as a warning, as it were, of the current ruling classes' political suicide pact. If anything, his angry condemnation should only encourage them to reform.[145]

The Posthumous Pareto in Italy, the Continent and Beyond: 1923–1950

After reading Pareto's livid tirade against modern liberal, representative governments, one might be tempted to think that Pareto rejects electoral institutions altogether, and by implication, condones the force and violence characteristic of the Byzantine state. Even those who acknowledge that Pareto was "the prophet, not the apostle, of Fascism" tend to think that his political thought encourages proto-authoritarian conclusions because he speaks so disparagingly of Italian electoral institutions.[146] This assumption, combined with his diatribe against corruption between financial and political elites, has prompted scholars to believe that "if Pareto's theory had not existed, Fascism would have had to invent it."[147]

If one starts from the view that a critique of elections necessarily constitutes a counterrevolutionary attack on democracy, then Pareto will of course sound like a protofascist who hates popular participation. Even though he expressed anger toward the plutocratic ruling class of his day and the ways representative institutions were used to the plutocrats' advantage, Pareto never gives us any reason to think that elections, in and of themselves, are the main difficulty facing modern governments. In his eyes, the problem surfaces when elections are privileged and inaccurately treated as the democratic institution par excellence. When this conflation occurs, it becomes difficult to restrain the structural plutocratic tendencies of electoral procedures. Under the halo of democracy, the intellectual justification for such a critique appears to vanish.

Pareto's political thought teaches us that the mere presence of competitive and fair elections will not create a democratic government. Elections, he insists, often obscure the ways in which unaccountable sects of competing elites can sway the legislature to act against the public interest. His contribution alerts readers to the risks of papering over different types of elites in a given society. Ignoring the plutocratic dimension of representation, he demonstrates, will only facilitate corruption of the system and undermine its credibility, thereby transforming a democracy into an autocracy.

Relatedly, approaching Pareto's political thought from the perspective of Anglo-American liberalism—which often treats democracy and representative government as inextricably linked—also prompts one to ignore his warning regarding plutocracy. It encourages the belief that he aimed to condemn only political elites, and not a broader ruling class that escaped the channels of majoritarian accountability that representative mechanisms are often presumed to provide. This results in the fallacious assumption that he abhorred government intervention as a rule, or that he became so disillusioned with his initial commitment to liberalism that he bitterly reacted against it in an excessively antidemocratic fashion.

Understandably, both continental and Anglo-American scholars seek to understand Pareto's thought within their own political contexts and assimilate him into their own respective traditions. But Pareto was primarily concerned with Italian political life during a time when, Schumpeter writes, "the frosts had not yet fallen upon a theoretical structure glorified by uncritical liberalism."[148] From the perspective of an Italian elite steeped in the plutocratic horrors of the Risorgimento, an angry critique of liberalism, electoral institutions, or representative government and its plutocratic dimensions does not necessarily constitute an attack on a popular form of government. In fact, only from our own peculiar contemporary standpoint does a critique of electoral government so often seem to read as a denunciation of mass participation or of democracy broadly conceived. This explains why Pareto's life and works, at least when considered from the Italian vantage point, do not display a series of performative contradictions or a grand disillusionment with liberal democracy.

The Italian orientation toward politics is characterized by incessant exposure of corruption as a means of combatting its most deleterious effects. In a cultural milieu that identifies political activism with constant critique of plutocratic elites, Pareto's "fiery pen" strikes the reader as neither antidemocratic nor classically liberal in the English sense.[149] In this regard, his reception among his Italian contemporaries may be illuminating. Vittorio Racca recounts in his retelling of "Bloody '98," the socialist popular insurrection of 1898, that at the time Pareto was considered the obvious champion of the people, and activists and protestors instantly knew where to turn when the government violently arrested peaceful protestors who simply demanded bread:

> Why did everyone retreat to Pareto's home in Lausanne at a moment's notice? Because he was considered the fiercest, most courageous defender of the people's rights, of the people despoiled and oppressed *by the myopia and greed of the rich classes.* He was the greatest flagellator of those classes and their anti-liberal policies that destroyed the well-being of the people in the new Italy. These people had the right to see another type of politics after their [the people's] revolution had run their [initial] enemies out of Italy through national unification.[150]

Racca's account is emblematic of how Pareto was seen by intellectuals and activists during his lifetime. Pareto was certainly a member of the elite, but to his contemporaries he was the quintessential antiestablishment "traitor" whose activism and hotheaded tone defied traditional political and behavioral conventions.[151] It is worth noting that after he unsuccessfully sought a university chair in his own country, Pareto was eventually obliged to accept the offer of a professorship next door in French Switzerland.[152]

While Pareto enjoyed a posthumous international reputation, a constellation of contingences led to an immediate distortion of his legacy at home and abroad. These distortions in Italy and elsewhere on the Continent set the groundwork for the later American distortion that would take place in the postwar period. As a young student, Benito Mussolini may have attended some of Pareto's lectures at the University of Lausanne, and later he revered the economist as an intellectual inspiration.[153] Moreover, Pareto initially expressed sympathy for the fascist movement, an attitude taken by many intellectuals of the period. Yet as mentioned above, because he died in 1923, Pareto did not have the opportunity to denounce fascism, which most other Italian academics would do in short order, and he became a convenient scapegoat for similarly implicated scholars who had initially supported Mussolini's ascendance. For instance, Benedetto Croce (Mosca's intimate political ally) had an interest in being remembered as the main anti-fascist intellectual voice in Mussolini Italy, and in 1925 he decried Paretian politics and its proto-authoritarian roots.[154] In a word, whether justified or not (for who could conclusively know how Pareto would have responded to Mussolini after 1923, and apostasy on his deathbed may have made no difference anyway), Pareto's early political identification with fascism occluded his lifelong anti-plutocratic positions, and therefore the thrust of his main theoretical arguments were misunderstood as necessarily authoritarian.

This temptation to condemn Pareto was compounded by a rancorous academic squabble in Italy—the "question of priority," or the debate about which of the two Italians, Mosca or Pareto, first came to the precepts of elite theory. Beginning in 1902 Mosca accused Pareto of plagiarism, and he continued to do so after Pareto's death in 1923.[155] Mostly after Pareto's death, these acrimonious allegations occasioned commentaries from illustrious contemporaries, all of which, with few exceptions, were decidedly in Mosca's defense. To take the most illustrative episode, in 1935 the Paretian economist Alfonso de Pietri-Tonelli suggested that Pareto's work on elitism should have been given proper consideration in Luigi Einaudi's summary article "Parlamenti e classe politica," published in *Corriere della Sera* in 1923.[156] In response, Einaudi—Mosca's intimate friend and colleague at the faculty of the University of Turin (and, after World War II, the second president of the Italian Republic)—replied in reprimand:

> The dates do not lie. Mosca came in 1883 and 1896, Pareto in 1900, 1902, 1906 and 1916 . . . No need to rehash the issue of [Pareto's] plagiarism . . . but as Pareto's fame continues to grow, and after having persuaded that

46   DEMOCRATIC ELITISM

exclusive circle of English academics, Pareto is now conquering the North Americans. The Theory of Elitism is now classified under Pareto's name. This is an injustice.[157]

Yet until 1923 Einaudi had relied upon his elder Ligurian mentor for intellectual and professional support on more than friendly terms. Even though Einaudi was tied to the school of thought of Giovani Vailati (Pareto's sworn intellectual rival in mathematics), Pareto enthusiastically campaigned for Einaudi's appointment to the Political Economy Chair at the University of Geneva, and strongly encouraged Einaudi not to give up his candidacy to Emanuele Sella.[158] From 1900 to 1923, Einaudi consistently sent his work to Pareto and asked for commentary, which Pareto would generously offer even on points of disagreement.[159] As Alberto Giordano details, Einaudi's thought was profoundly shaped by Pareto's specific orientation toward elite theory—especially the concept of equilibrium from an economic perspective.[160] Einaudi's private correspondence reveals that he considered Pareto a founder of elite theory; however, after Pareto's passing, Einaudi's loyalty to his close friend and confidant Mosca triumphed.[161]

Einaudi was not alone, after Pareto's death, in arguing that Mosca had precedence in establishing elite theory. Incidentally, many of the commentators in this debate were either Pareto's admitted adversaries or Mosca's close intimates. Rodolfo de Mattei, Mosca's fellow Sicilian colleague at the University of Rome, and Antonio de Viti de Marco, Pareto's longtime nemesis, were particularly intent on proving Pareto's purported plagiarism.[162] Pareto's taunting of Giovanni Papini, Cesare Lombroso, and Achille Loria were not forgotten by Turin intellectuals when the question of precedence resurfaced in the interwar era.[163] Even Arthur Livingston, Mosca and Pareto's English translator, expressed concern over upsetting Mosca about this thorny issue.[164]

This intellectual and political landscape is not hard to imagine. While Pareto was alive, his elite peers defensively responded to his scathing criticism of their plutocratic excesses in the Giolittian era. If this did not motivate enough animus against him, ironically, both Pareto's death and his international success made it all the easier for Italian intellectuals to defend Mosca and protect the Italianness of elite theories by supporting Mosca's precedence. After all, in sharp contrast to Pareto, who had been a constant thorn in the establishment's side, for nearly fifty years Mosca was the "model of decorum" as a professor, a member of the Chamber of Deputies, and a senator.[165] In a moment where Mosca's presence loomed large in the intellectual and political culture, the academic community was more than happy to distance themselves from the "rabble rouser" Pareto.[166] Let the French—or, for that matter, the English and Americans—have him, thought the Italian intelligentsia.[167] Not only was it professionally and politically advantageous to abandon Pareto in the interwar period, but intellectuals hoped that this distancing could further disassociate fascist and even antidemocratic theory from Italian political thought as a whole.

Our historical vantage point reveals that "the question of priority" helped transform the reception of Pareto's and Mosca's intellectual contributions, enabling *both*, as we shall see in Chapter 2, to be identified as antidemocratic, protofascist thinkers.[168] Focusing on precedence obfuscated the fact that their ideas were paradigmatic of the Zeitgeist—of the plutocratic conditions of the Risorgimento—and, more broadly, revealed the distinctive methodological features of the Italian strain of the pessimistic tradition. Once the Italians began to treat Pareto as a fascist—or at the very least, as antidemocratic—exception outside mainstream Italian political theory, it was easy for continental and Anglo-American scholars to do the same.

On the Continent, Karl Popper and Raymond Aron bear special responsibility for disseminating this view. Popper famously called Pareto "the theoretician of totalitarianism," but as Renato Cirillo later demonstrated, there was no evidence in Popper's work that Popper had even read Pareto before reiterating this common but unsubstantiated prejudice in anti-fascist circles.[169] In the 1930s Aron also identified Pareto's thought as a fascist theoretical weapon developed to combat leftist and Marxist reform.[170] Toward the end of his life, Aron equivocated on the extent of Pareto's fascism, yet, as Stuart Campbell put it, even in his final word on the subject Aron claimed that Pareto's ideas "had been used but not necessarily misused by the fascists"—suggesting that proto-authoritarian ideas had always pervaded Pareto's work.[171]

Nevertheless, the interwar damage to Pareto's legacy had already been done. At the same time, on the other side of the pond, Pareto's increasing fame in economics and sociology further fueled his role as the fascist, proto-authoritarian punching bag for political science. Amid these swirling accusations, Talcott Parsons and Lawrence Henderson, founding members of Harvard's Pareto circle, were committed to reviving Pareto's classical liberal credentials even from their polar opposite political vantage points.[172] Some of these commentators avoided the fascist question entirely; others rejected the label as "sheer poppycock."[173] And while the Pareto circle insisted that Paretian economics ran entirely contrary to all fascist precepts, it never ruled out the possibility that Pareto was a disillusioned liberal who eventually succumbed to proto-authoritarian temptations.

48   DEMOCRATIC ELITISM

In response to such defenses of his economics, two incredibly influential American political scientists reaffirmed the "antidemocratic" nature of Pareto's thought based on its premise of a division between elites and masses. At Harvard, Carl Friedrich complained that because Pareto clearly "believed in an elite, [he] did not believe in the common man; that much is obvious."[174] Similarly, at the University of Chicago, Charles Merriam insisted that the separation between elites and non-elites necessarily revealed an anxiety about the masses that lay at the heart of the new despotism, constraining modern possibilities for democracy.[175] Oddly, Merriam admits that Pareto's animus was actually directed against plutocracy and that Pareto supported the participatory politics of the Swiss cantons. However, in his next breath, Merriam commits the fatal mistake about which Pareto explicitly warned his readers: Merriam misunderstands Pareto's critique of "this new god called Universal Suffrage" as a critique of the "workings of democracy," thereby equating democratic government with suffrage and elections. What is more, although Merriam reserves his harshest words for Pareto, his identification of Mosca as Pareto's intellectual forerunner equally implicated the two Italians as heralds of the "new despotism."[176] The question of who first formulated elite theory—Mosca or Pareto—thus was a lightning rod that decidedly converted the historical memory of the Risorgimento in political science discourse from an anti-plutocratic spirit to an antidemocratic one.

H. Stuart Hughes's magnum opus *Consciousness and Society* was uncharacteristically sensitive to the anti-plutocratic spirit as well as the distinctively "skeptical" tradition of Italian social thought that Pareto, in Hughes's estimation, represented. Nevertheless, Hughes ultimately identified Pareto as an "antidemocratic" figure because of Pareto's "excessive scorn" for the humanitarian aspects of democracy. Despite the fact that Pareto railed against the perils of such a dangerously moralistic, utopian orientation toward liberal "democracy" from an internal critique of liberalism's plutocratic character, this attitude, according to Hughes, rendered Pareto's thought more prone to a "quasi-fascist" view.[177] Pareto's "mocking irony" proved too aggressive for even the most generous and perceptive American commentators.

Pareto epitomized the anti-plutocratic mood of the 1890s. And yet, as Hughes would also later write, 1921 marked the "caesura" of the age—a caesura that slowly gave way to amnesia about the decades that had come before.[178] By midcentury it was inconceivable to think of Pareto as he had been described by many of his Italian contemporaries fifty years prior: as a man who sought to "out-Marx Marx" in his ruthless critique of the plutocratic exploitation, and who, even more courageously, sacrificed his money, life, and reputation defending those who were abused by the exploitation of the degenerate Italian governing classes.[179] And as Pareto warned time and again, when the governing class becomes "degenerate," it "crashes to ruin and often sweeps the whole of a nation along with it."[180]

CHAPTER 2

Sober Cynicism

Mosca and the Ruling Class

Everything must change for everything to remain the same.
— GIUSEPPE TOMASI DI LAMPEDUSA, *The Leopard*

Throughout his life Pareto vehemently insisted that his anti-elitist posture did not make him a socialist. A self-professed contrarian invested in ideology critique, he refused to bow down to any "ism" whatsoever. But the main reason he was not a socialist, he said, was that he could not see "a way to increase state control without increasing the damage produced by politicians."[1] And yet despite his infamous critiques of socialist economic theory in *Les systèmes socialistes* and his refusal to identify with the movement, Pareto was thoroughly enmeshed in socialist discourse.[2] Vittorio Racca recounts that while Pareto's critiques of Italian socialism "had been devastating and far-reaching," at the time they "had been taken as a sign of his fairness of mind."[3]

As we saw in Chapter 1, not only did Pareto champion Italian socialist policies, but he also encouraged a coalition of republicans and socialists against the liberal government and gave popular protestors and socialist intellectuals asylum in his home. At the time of the 1892 popular uprising, Pareto informed his American audience that socialism in Italy was far more complicated than its prevailing exponent in the United States. Socialist thought might prove disastrous from an economic perspective but positive in light of its contribution to political theory and parliamentary reform.[4] He also greatly bolstered socialist doctrine when he became the patron saint of "new welfare economics": Pareto was the first to demonstrate that a collectivist state can improve the level of welfare in a way that is practically unattainable under perfect competition—a hardly laissez-faire position that proves that his economic theory did not conform to ideological dogmas. He often sparred with his friends Antonio Labriola and Filippo Turati in Marxist debates, and during his life he was considered a crucial part of this intellectual community, especially given his open hostility toward the fascist "lunatics" epitomized by Giovanni Gentile.[5]

Far more than Pareto, Gaetano Mosca is remembered in light of his antagonistic relationship to socialism.[6] According to most studies, in contrast to Pareto's respect for Marx, Mosca's detached demeanor could not hide the fact that Mosca "abhorred" Marxist doctrine and dedicated his life to combatting its tenets, even if in his tone he "approached the notion of class conflict gingerly."[7] He sought to undermine socialism, it is argued, by developing a study of politics that was based on a "new science" characteristic of the positivist theories of his time.[8] Despite Mosca's tone of "urbane skepticism" being pierced with "ebullient Mediterranean good humor," his political thought is often described as "conservative" nineteenth-century "positivist theory with vengeance" against socialist hegemony in political discourse.[9]

This chapter reconsiders Mosca against the backdrop of his relationship to socialist philosophy. Instead of aiming at undermining the Marxist conception of class struggle in order to encourage resignation to elite rule, Mosca's critique of socialism, and his famous ruling-class theory, were motivated by an entirely different goal: namely, Mosca's desire to expose the prevalence of elite rule in electoral governments in order to stem the growth of plutocracy amid *regional* economic inequality. Mosca harbored a pessimistic disposition toward both socialist and liberal forms of electoral politics, but this orientation was not driven by an essentially elitist, anti-popular orientation. Rather, he was principally concerned with the way that, under a democratic veneer, the plutocratic parliamentary institutions established in the Risorgimento would propagate even more problematic structures of minority domination than those that existed before Italian unification.

Specifically, Mosca worried about regional economic inequality and pondered the redistributive measures required to generate legitimacy and commitment to the new Italy in the South. It is important to appreciate that—given the lack of shared historical identification, the Catholic Church's opposition to the unified state, and the Piedmontese military occupation of the South that lasted into the 1880s—Southern Italians (*meridionali*) viewed Northerners (*settentrionali*) as a foreign enemy. From Naples to Palermo, Southerners found themselves swindled into a state apparatus that unjustly subjected them to the rule of a Northern elite even though it was Southern revolutionary efforts—first with the Neapolitan-led Carbonari movements of the early nineteenth century and then formally with the Expedition of the Thousand—that allowed for unification in the first place. This feeling was compounded in Sardinia, which had always considered the Piedmontese House of Savoy as their oppressors. Southerners felt so betrayed by unification under Savoy that the rise of local resistance (the so-called *brigantaggio*) at one point required the presence of some 140,000 Piedmontese troops to maintain control of the former Kingdom of the Two Sicilies.[10]

Considering this acknowledged obstacle, Mosca claimed that Northern plutocratic exploitation of the South through Northern industrialist alliance with feudal Southern landed elites (*baroni*), combined with the unconvincing conflation of elections and democracy, would undermine the fragile Italian state.[11] The patently false claim that Southerners were now (economically or politically) better off because they participated in elections that solidified Northern domination, he argues, did not fool anyone into thinking that they enjoyed the benefits of a democracy. In fact, this set of economic arrangements, combined with the pretense of electoral democracy, would only alienate the poor South and render alternative local structures of authority like the mafia more attractive. Much like fellow *meridionalista* Antonio Gramsci, Mosca warns that without drastic regional economic redress that counteracts Northern plutocratic control of the peninsula, the equation of elections and democracy will encourage Southern loss of faith in representative institutions and in unification altogether.

In the following discussion I read Mosca's thought within the context of *la questione meridionale* (the Southern Question) and the politics of the Risorgimento, and identify some of his major political preoccupations and methodological attitudes that have been forgotten, ignored, or inaccurately interpreted as exhibiting necessarily antidemocratic proclivities. In order to unearth Mosca's consistent focus on the plutocratic character of parliamentary government, I compare his two main works, *Teorica dei governi e governo parlamentare* (*Theory of Governments and Parliamentary Government*) (1886) and *Elementi di scienza politica* (literally, "Elements of political science"; published in English in 1939 as *The Ruling Class*) (1896, 1923), contextualizing their methodology, evolution, and reception in early twentieth-century Italy with particular reference to Gramsci's application of Mosca's ruling-class theory. To borrow Nadia Urbinati's formulation, I will be examining exactly how Gramsci's project "picked up where" Mosca left off, in turn suggesting that Gramsci might be productively considered a member of the Italian School of Elitism and, as we shall soon discover in Chapter 3, perhaps an even more fitting successor than Robert Michels.[12] Once Mosca's paradigmatic concern with electoral plutocracy vis-à-vis regional economic inequality comes into view, it becomes easier to understand the ruling-class theory for what it really is: a heuristic device that facilitates a defensive posture against the constant encroachment of elite power—a posture that, in his own time, Mosca thought could guard against the plutocratic propensities of electoral regimes, but also could be useful in combatting corruption and oligarchic domination writ large.

The Young Mosca: Teorica dei governi e governo parlamentare

In Mosca's demeanor we find a quintessential strain of Southern Italian pessimism—concern that revolutions are façades intended to restore dominating power to an existing elite or bestow it upon a new one. *Meridionale* (Southern) political thought maintains a distinct place in the Italian philosophical tradition that predates the Risorgimento, yet in the late nineteenth century the main political expression of the tradition was a virulent skepticism toward the emancipatory promises of parliamentarism for the South. Already by 1876, just five years after the formal completion of unification, Francesco De Sanctis's *Un viaggio elettorale* (An electoral journey) tried to combat the optimistic delusions of those who championed liberalism in Italy, detailing the corrupt realities of the Southern ballot box and its problematic ties to Northern capitalist exploitation.[13] Southern skepticism was initiated by the suspect events of the history of Italian unification, only to be later enflamed by the egregious plutocratic electoral corruption paradigmatic in Giollitian-era *trasformismo.* Building on Vincenzo Cuoco's "passive revolution," Gramsci will characterize the *meridionale* anxiety of the time as worry over a "'revolution' without a 'revolution,'" or a "revolution-restoration."[14]

Mosca's political thought fits perfectly into this *meridionale* skepticism toward the view that electoral government could be a real, lasting revolution that changes the structure of Italian civil society.[15] Taken holistically, his thought centers upon dismantling what he considered dangerously optimistic political paradigms that would only lead to violent insurrection without any resolution or substantive change—or worse still, a purported revolution that actually propagates the more insidious, depersonalized capitalistic exploitation of the South by Northern captains of industry.[16] Mosca articulates suspicion

54   DEMOCRATIC ELITISM

toward optimistic, nineteenth-century conceptions of progress, whether of the positivist or a Marxist variety; his distrust is particularly motivated by the way these paradigms discount the prevalence of plutocracy in modern parliamentary government. As the precursor to *Elementi di scienza politica*, Mosca's first book *Teorica dei governi e governo parlamentare* (Theory of governments and parliamentary government) (1884) exhibits in microcosm the main ideas that will be later developed in his magnum opus: (1) an insistence upon a historical approach to political science, (2) a concern with the parliamentary-plutocratic nexus evident in liberal governments, and (3) an explanation of the political function of his pessimistic orientation.

Appreciating Mosca's account of positivism puts his cynical appraisal of Marxism into proper perspective and additionally accentuates the contrast between his historical methodology and the "empirical," proto-behavioralist reputation he will later acquire.[17] Mosca indeed complained that the study of politics desperately lagged behind the natural sciences.[18] In the opening pages of the *Teorica*, he calls for a "new science" to be developed so that the study of human affairs can be analyzed more "systematically."[19] This call for scientific systematicity has led many to believe that he shared the typical nineteenth-century positivist craving to create a category of "social sciences" analogous to the natural sciences. After all, what could a "new science" possibly refer to if not the continental positivist philosophy characteristic of the German and French traditions prevalent at the time?

Nevertheless, Mosca saw his complaint as being decidedly anti-positivist in the traditional understanding of the term, because the study of "physics, chemistry, geology, botany, etc." and the study of "human affairs," he says, are incommensurable. To uncover generalizable laws in the physical sciences, observation of present phenomena can suffice; but to find generalizable laws in the "social sciences" requires a vast historical record, which is difficult to attain and nearly impossible to master. Moreover, he contends, whereas the natural sciences allow for experiments that can be purposively constructed and executed within a discrete time span, political experiments cannot be conducted along the same temporal criteria or according to the same inductive reasoning.[20]

Given this incommensurability, studying politics requires a global historical approach more akin to the intersection between historicism and what today we call philosophy of history. In his "social science" of the future, Mosca in no way seeks to imitate the scientific method characteristic of the natural sciences. Instead he calls for a "systematic" historical investigation of human affairs in the style of Giambattista Vico's "new science"—a methodology antithetical to

Auguste Comte's or Charles Darwin's teleological paradigms of evolution.[21] In *A Short History of Political Philosophy*, Mosca elaborates Vico's new science and discusses Risorgimento patriots (Vincenzo Cuoco, Gian Domenico Romagnosi, Vincenzo Gioberti, Cesare Balbo, and Giuseppe Mazzini) who attempted to translate Vico's "fantastic presentment of the science he proposed" into a more accessible scientific formula amenable to contemporary audiences with positivist inclinations.[22] By invoking Vico, Mosca argues that optimistic, Cartesian insistence on observable phenomena and verification cannot provide the foundation for social science research because it evades the often imperceptible but recurring ideas and structures that underpin civil life and / or civilizations.[23]

Mosca concedes that it may seem tedious to demand a global historical comparison between the governments of "ancient Greece, ancient Rome, the Middle Ages, and the imperial orders of China, Japan, and India" in order to uncover the particularities of contemporary parliamentary government.[24] But he defends this comprehensive approach as essential for any "real and true social science" because no one in the present can recognize the "absurdities" of their own epoch without the temporal distance provided by rigorous historical comparison.[25]

After *Teorica*'s exhaustive study of each of these civilizations, Mosca discloses what he thinks constitutes the greatest absurdity of modern liberal polities: the problem contained in "the social question."[26] He devises a decidedly anti-Aristotelian "political law" that divides society between rulers and ruled (as opposed to division between rule by the one, few, and many) in order to call attention to the plutocratic challenge facing parliamentary government.[27] Unlike Pareto, Mosca does not explicitly identify this issue as plutocracy, but he defines the social question as the problems contained within a regime type characterized by "economic inequality, or the suffering of the poor caused by the excessive luxury and arrogance of the rich." Mosca notes that this question had attracted "thinkers of all ages," but that the concern remains dormant in the political self-understanding of his own day.[28]

In Mosca's view, the heart of the matter lies in the enormous inequalities in political control that arise from the wealth disparities inherent in parliamentary government.[29] He rejects the two prevailing and, to his mind, overly optimistic dispositions toward this issue. First, Mosca parsimoniously dismisses the Marxist fairy tale that economic inequalities could be entirely abolished in a communist future.[30] In his panoramic historical study of political societies, Mosca finds that elite domination is *always* a problem. Socialists who predict a classless society mistakenly, with unfounded optimism, anticipate a society in which there will be no elites; they think that the answer to elite domination is

56 DEMOCRATIC ELITISM

simply to *eliminate* elites. But for Mosca, the problem of elite domination is intractable: it is a numerical problem. In every society, small cadres of the powerful will form and aspire to dominate large majorities of the powerless. Socialism breeds complacency with domination, because under certain conditions it will surrender its vigilance against elite domination, enabling a new elite to arise. This sort of utopian Marxist confidence, he writes, has already caused great destruction (with the Revolutions of 1848 and their subsequent restorations) without any indication that such an order could ever be stabilized.[31]

More pressingly, Mosca claims, the preposterously sanguine liberal contention that economic inequality is the natural consequence of free competition has generated equal, if not greater, oppression.[32] Liberals maintain that government neutrality ensures free competition; Mosca counters that so-called government neutrality between economic classes really constitutes a defense of the rich and a guarantee that wealth accrues in their hands:

> While soldiers' bayonets maintain order and secure peace, they actually prevent the poor from using their numerical advantage and protect the wealth of the rich, such that the rich are left free to combat the poor with their vastly superior economic means. In these circumstances, the poor, as the weaker group, necessarily succumb. The government intervenes with all of its means, overwhelming the people's numerical strength. Subsequently, the government needn't do anything to keep the force of money from prevailing.[33]

Mosca here anticipates a criticism that becomes rather familiar later in the twentieth century: that liberal regimes and the negative liberty they presuppose do not engender fair or free competition because government neutrality protects the status quo, thereby stacking the cards against the poor in favor of the rich. "This kind of so-called liberty is quite advantageous in the economic sector as well," he continues, "where it extends an open invitation to the economically strong to oppress the weak." Mosca consequently implores his reader to "admit" that the liberal state offers a "well-funded insurance policy" for the rich against the poor, and not a commitment to the ideals of equality before the law or justice. "I will leave it up to those with a heart and a conscience to determine whether this constitutes the alleged 'liberty' that defenders of modern-day popular government wish to uphold," he sarcastically declares.[34]

But there is far more to his critique of negative liberty than a moral plea for justice or political equality. Mosca claims that exposing this impoverished conception of freedom underscores the structural plutocracy endemic in representative government and, consequently, directs us toward the problems that arise when democracy and elections are equated. Modern electoral systems, he writes, must stop declaring that they "guide," "tutor," "protect," or even "represent" the masses. The blatant hypocrisy should encourage us to "renounce" such representative claims as the reigning "raison d'être" of the parliamentary form, he says, because nothing constructive vis-à-vis political stability or the improvement of general welfare comes from such idealistic delusions.[35]

Mosca further complains that defenders of liberalism express Panglossian faith that universal suffrage or other mechanisms for increasing popular participation in elections will resolve the empty democratic promises of representative institutions.[36] *On their own*, he insists, these instruments cannot be effective without massive economic redistribution—especially given the conditions of abject poverty, illiteracy, and vestiges of Bourbon feudal corruption in the Mezzogiorno (Southern Italy). The character of representation, he argues, always propagates plutocracy because it effectively bars the working classes from being elected to the legislature, so that it is impossible for the assembly to genuinely reflect the common people's concerns even when the entire population is enfranchised.

In other words, despite being the most seemingly democratic of practices, elections are inherently instruments of inequality because they unofficially bar lower-class access into the governing body. This informal prohibition manifests itself in more or less obvious ways. Most noticeably, "technical expertise and a high level of cultural attainment" are increasingly required in the modern globalized world, a trend that Mosca says naturally skews the body of representatives toward wealthy sectors of the population. Because of this propensity toward specialization, parliament tends to be filled with technocrats alienated from the masses who are unable to perceive the broader scope of the difficulties facing the majority of people.[37]

Far more importantly, Mosca declares, the notion that elections provide the opportunity for the masses to elect someone who will represent their interests is a fantasy. The people cannot elect one of their own "to represent the country," he says, simply because of the enormous wealth required to run as an electoral candidate. On this point, he considers the recent proposal for salaried offices offensive because it inappropriately slights the general population's epistemic capacities for judgment and pretends to promote lower-class representation in the government. The poor are not effectively prohibited from candidacy owing to the assumption that they would have difficulty "maintaining and deploying capital once they are in office," a task that, he quips, "does not require all that much frugality or competence" despite what lawmakers may want us to believe. The working classes do not fill the halls of the legislature, he states, "because they do not have enough capital to run for office in the first place." Instead of ensuring that incumbents have access to even more funds, an effective proposal would offer an "indemnity to poor candidates in order to overcome campaign expenses, allowing them to develop the affluence and influence initially required to be elected."[38] Here, he proffers a type of political affirmative action for the poor, a policy that certainly defies his later reputation as being elitist or anti-popular.

According to Mosca, "active and energetic" government intervention that redistributes the grosser discrepancies between rich and poor offers a practicable solution to the plutocratic tendencies of electoral outcomes. But, as he claims, the domination of the government by the wealthy obstructs proper redistribution, because the wealthy "will never damage their own interests in order to improve the condition of the poor." Although this parliamentary-plutocratic connection constitutes a "grave" structural drawback of modern representative governments, he vows that proactive redistribution has historically proven to alleviate the issue. If only there were a way to get the current ruling class to agree.[39]

Mosca spends the rest of his time trying to persuade elite readers to adopt drastic preemptive redistributive measures, which he suggests are actually the most moderate approach to the problem of plutocracy. The Mezzogiorno was already skeptical of unification under the Kingdom of Italy from the get-go: after the Expedition of the Thousand, Giuseppe Garibaldi offered the South to Vittorio Emanuele II, prioritizing a unified Italy over his own political preferences for democratic and republican forms of government, an act that immediately disillusioned the Southern revolutionaries who had spilled their blood in hopes of achieving democratic self-government in the region. The only way to stop the impending ascendancy of a clientelist structure like the mafia, Mosca argues, is to institute redistributive measures, including government-financed development projects, that could attenuate economic inequality between the North and South.[40] Otherwise, he claims, Southerners will lose faith in the entire electoral apparatus, and think that their Red-Shirt revolution of the Thousand was fought only to replace their previous Bourbon monarchs with Northern capitalist ones (the House of Savoy).[41] In this context of disillusionment with plutocratic electoral outcomes, obedience to mafia structures of political authority makes sense because Southerners stood to gain materially from that clientelist arrangement. At the

very least, subjected Southerners are more inclined to respect local masters—
and not a foreign sect of Savoyard capitalists who can ignore demands for
economic redress.[42] This means that Mosca's solution is not only directed at
controlling wealth in government or patrolling the disproportionate power
of specific oligarchs; he insists that democratic measures to combat electoral
plutocracy require regulating geographical economic disparity. Half the battle
for political legitimacy of parliamentarism lies in equilibrating the extreme
economic inequality between Northerners and Southerners.

The other half of the battle lies in rejecting a particularly insidious delusion of the educated elite: that elections independently create popular representation or expressions of popular sovereignty. If anything, he writes, his
analysis demonstrates that "despite their claims to the contrary," parliamentary
government epitomizes the English "spirit of aristocracy" because it sepa-
rates "the rich . . . from the people."[43] For Mosca, English "political institutions
breed arrogance, hardness of heart, and a form of contrived gallantry" incompatible with popular government.[44] Exclusive reliance on electoralism causes
"the chic and the *bon ton* [to] become the arbiters of modern society," an
aristocratic orientation that has "unfortunately already begun to seep into
Italian political life" as a result of the Risorgimento's recent adoption of
Anglo-liberal ideals.[45]

Claims that parliamentary government is representative, despite obvious and
continued oppression of the poor by the rich, Mosca repeats, will only incite
a rather understandable uprising of the working class—both industrial laborers
and agricultural workers. These insurrections do not arise from plebeians' "jeal-
ousy" of the wealthy's riches "or delusions of their own grandeur," Mosca
claims. They develop as a result of a rightful "vendetta against those who have
commanded them, from the rancor that developed over a long period of
oppression." The rich, he asserts, must publicly admit that this "inequality
exists, that it must be remedied, and that the poor classes suffer from a social
injustice." Nevertheless, a commitment to political realism is a necessary but
insufficient condition to resolve the issue. Beyond honest acknowledgment
and intellectual sincerity, serious action in the form of redistribution must be
continually taken to relieve such gross disparities. If existing elites do not so-
berly enact concrete measures, Mosca warns, "working-class anger will foment"
and it will take only a "match to topple the current political class."[46]

The problem of the Mezzogiorno reveals why Mosca does not simply
argue that electoral institutions are a necessary but insufficient condition
for modern popular government. Somewhat parallel to claims made by the

60 DEMOCRATIC ELITISM

English Levellers (who notoriously exclude servants from their calls for an expanded franchise) and Sieyes's position in *What Is the Third Estate?*, Mosca claims that under the wrong conditions, the extension of suffrage can thwart the progress of the nation—in this case, unification.[47] Given the particularities of the Italian demographic landscape, he suggests, premature mass elections will seat Southern barons backed by Northern industrialists with an interest in protectionist policies, thereby engendering Southern mass protest against electoralism through nonparticipation. This is the same argument Gramsci later makes multiple times to develop the concept of hegemony.[48] As he will explain, this unexpected electoral alliance has two exponents. Tongue in cheek, he calls the first the program of the elitist Milanese newspaper *Corriere della Sera*, which he defines as "an alliance between Northern industrialists and some vague Southern rural democratic forces in regard to free trade."[49] The second is Giovanni Giolitti's "attempt to establish an alliance between the industrial bourgeoisie and a type of labor aristocracy in the North in order to oppress, and to subject to this bourgeois-proletarian formation, the mass of Italian peasants, especially in the South."[50]

Given these electoral formations, for both Mosca and Gramsci, the extension of suffrage in conditions of extreme regional inequality undermines trust in the integrity of elections (Southern masses will silently protest the unified Italian State through nonvoting) and other federal structures, such as courts and police.[51] This distrust can already be detected in the name of the Sicilian mafia: *Cosa nostra*, or "our thing." In contrast to depersonalized Northern capitalist exploitation, the Cosa nostra offers a more reliable local structure of political authority as a rival to the myth that universal suffrage would be a truly representative practice for the Southern population.[52] Mosca warns that regional economic disparity will entrench mafia dominance under the legitimating façade of leaders elected through mass suffrage, which is why as a parliamentarian Mosca votes against extension of suffrage in the 1890s Chamber of Deputies. Put differently, the myth of representation can thwart the ability of the ruling class to become as heterogeneous and diverse as the liberal electoral doctrine traditionally promises. To borrow the language of contemporary elite theory, instead of fostering competition, electoral processes translated "elite heterogeneity" into "elite cohesion" through the alliance between Piedmontese industrialists and Southern barons.[53]

Mosca's argument is not simply that the extension of suffrage would not meaningfully empower new citizens. Instead, he worries that given mechanisms of electoral corruption operating in the South—intense voter intimidation, extreme inequalities in campaign financing and information flows, and the impossibility that poor, illiterate voters would coordinate—extension of suffrage would disempower the enfranchised at a critical moment when Southern lack of faith in electoralism would forever compromise the Italian nation. Having grown up in a Sicily where less than democratic forms of persuasion were employed in the newly established electoral practices, he rejects the view that expansion of suffrage, however imperfect, offered even a modicum of ever-increasing democratic empowerment. In one history of the Mezzogiorno, an observer portrays common electoral practices:

> Some short distance from the polling station the road was barred by a group of sinister figures. Here each voter as he approached was seized, thoroughly bastinadoed and forced to drink a huge glass of wine. There followed a thorough search of his person, after which the government candidate's voting slip was put into his hand and he was led or dragged to the ballot box, where the president took the slip from him and put it in.[54]

Southern masses may be poor and illiterate, Mosca suggests, but it is an insult to their intelligence to expect them to view this type of electoral experience as an asymptomatic means toward democratic empowerment: seen from their perspective, it is just another form of oppression. Given this electoral façade, in which intense voter intimidation was militaristically underpinned by Piedmontese troops in the South, Mosca warns that Southerners will choose clientelist systems of patronage like the mafia in an act of resistance against the electoralism of the newly unified Italian state.[55]

Retrospective empirical analysis of the electoral climate may help us properly understand Mosca's opposition to universal suffrage. Valentino Larcinese analyzes the 1912 extension of suffrage, which increased the electorate from three million to more than eight and a half million but left electoral rules and boundaries unchanged.[56] The law increased the vote share of social reformers (Socialists, Republicans, and Radicals) by 2 percent but had no impact on their net gains in parliamentary seats. Similarly, "enfranchisement also had no impact on parliamentary representation of aristocracy and the traditional elites," and all other outcomes that could be measured, such as the Herfindel-Hirshman index of electoral competition, were unaffected—*with the exception of decreased voter turnout*. Larcinese concludes that in the Italian example, "de jure political equalization did not change political representation" despite the fact that the voting choices of newly enfranchised citizens differed, on average, from those of citizens who already had the vote. He documents the "elite's effort to minimize the political impact of the reform," suggesting that extended enfranchisement ironically helped coordinate elites and consolidate their power—or, to use Gramsci's words on this issue, helped solidify Piedmontese hegemony.[57]

In fact, for Gramsci the conceit of democratic representation reflects hegemony, or the conjunction of political, economic, and cultural domination, in its purest form: the ubiquitous idea that universal suffrage produces democratic results inhibited even the "popular masses in the North" from understanding that "unity had not taken place on a basis of equality, but as hegemony of the North over the Mezzogiorno . . . that the North concretely was an 'octopus' which enriched itself at the expense of the South, and that its economic-industrial increment was in direct proportion to the impoverishment of the economy and the agriculture of the South." The myth of democratic representation and the extension of the suffrage, Gramsci continues, concretized Northern domination because it convinced even the Northern urban masses that the poverty and illiteracy of the South was a result of its own political depravity, thereby undermining the potential for a proper working-class alliance between the urban and rural proletariat.[58]

As a twenty-five-year-old thoroughly exposed to the grand pretenses of competitive party politics, Mosca needed neither empirical data nor the owl of Minerva to envision this possibility coming to fruition. By 1883 the writing was already on the wall. Mosca warned that these kinds of electoral outcomes would paradoxically decrease voter turnout, embitter Southern masses, and encourage a mass mutiny to topple the Italian republic. If the Piedmontese elite did not immediately address economic inequality to elicit Southern popular support for the unified state, then any later redress of wealth inequality would further entrench plutocracy instead of combat it, thereby benefiting the elites and not the people. Put differently, once various Southern structures of criminalized clientelism (Mafia, 'Ndrangheta, or Camorra) are established, redistributive measures will only further line the pockets of Southern *baroni*, as indeed can be seen today.[59]

A few decades later, Gramsci will vindicate Mosca's warning that the ruling class's ineffectiveness in generating popular Southern support spells its own ruin. Wealth inequality needed to be addressed during the Risorgimento to engender Southern support for unification. For Gramsci, the ruling class had acted "absurdly" by expecting Southern support for Piedmontese capitalistic electoralism without any indication of economic redress at the time of unification: "One cannot ask for enthusiasm, spirit of sacrifice, etc. without giving anything return, even from the subjects of one's own country," he writes, "and the less one can ask these things of citizens from outside that country on the basis of a generic and abstract programme and a blind faith in the far-distant government."[60] Deploying Mosca's theoretical categories in a style reminiscent of Mosca's diatribe against the ruling classes, he writes:

> They said that they were aiming at the creation of the modern State in Italy, and they in fact produced a bastard. They aimed at stimulating the formation of an extensive and energetic ruling class, and they did not succeed; at integrating the people into the framework of the new State, and they did not succeed. The paltry political life from 1870 to 1900, the fundamental and endemic rebelliousness of the Italian popular classes, the narrow and stunted existence of a skeptical and cowardly ruling stratum, these are all the consequences of that failure.[61]

In Gramsci's formulation, Italian Fascism presented this very phenomenon of "popular rebelliousness" against the decrepit ruling classes: an "anticlerical," "anti-bourgeois," "rural reactionary" insurrection against the empty electoral promises of the Risorgimento.[62]

In the conclusion of the *Teorica*, Mosca more emphatically casts his plea to existing parliamentarians and heightens fear of the current order's waning stability. Given the plutocratic problems he elucidated in earlier chapters, Mosca predicts that in Italy "*pure* parliamentary regimes" will likely fail.[63] To avoid such a breakdown, it was necessary to have "radical reform of the entire political class"—a reform that rebuilds a political class committed to an authentic meritocracy and ensures "reciprocal control of its members" to the broader population, meaning that the broader population would have some real control over the political class.[64] Only through economic redistribution can *la classe politica* create adequate channels for contestation and genuine access to entry to the legislature for the lower classes.[65] Like Pareto, Mosca incessantly warns the current ruling class of the consequences to their own power if they do take the necessary measures toward self-imposed restraint: if the ruling class does not amend its ways, then either a violent insurrection will take hold of the peninsula, or the ruling class will be entirely replaced by a more competent, less corrupt cohort that may or may not advance the Italian unified state in an autocratic direction.[66]

But unlike Pareto, Mosca explicitly cautions against seeing his distrust of plutocracy as an attempt to thwart any trace of electoral institutions in a future political form. Although he has been accused of "wanting to destroy" parliamentary government without knowing how to "rebuild it," he says that his cynicism about the popular character of electoral regimes certainly need not be interpreted in that vein.[67] His assessment of the problems facing parliamentary government ought to encourage reform by "outlining the directions of a broad assignment that cannot be performed by a single man of action" or by a small coterie of individuals. This *compito* (task), he asserts, must be taken up with "the energy of an entire people—of an entire generation that will prepare and realize a better form of government" by keeping his admonitions of plutocracy in mind.[68]

On a broad scale, Mosca suggests constant monitoring of the minorities in power as the important first step in advancing the next generation's task to keep plutocracy at bay. If anything, his theory of "political history"—the forerunner to his theory of the ruling class—should attune the "entire people" to patrolling "the degree of coordination between the various political classes, the amount of resources under their control, the force of their collective action, the various elements that enter into these classes, and the different ways in which they impose their will, the rivalry and struggles between them, their mutual transactions and combinations."[69] By adopting such a vigilant attitude toward the various elite sects that make up the ruling class, Mosca claims, awareness of the composition, resources, and power of a particular ruling group can serve as a protective instrument against their corruption and, additionally, against less overt demonstrations of minority domination that manifest themselves under the legitimating color of electoral institutions. In this sense, the closing note of *Teorica* sounds like a clarion call for future democratic action against the plutocratic domination of parliamentary government—and not a conservative, antidemocratic attempt to thwart universal suffrage or other mechanisms of popular participation.

Richard Bellamy, one of the Anglo-American world's most astute readers of Mosca's political thought, recognizes that Mosca's (and Pareto's) chief aim in developing elite theories was to offer a "description of contemporary politics [that] revealed the manipulation of democratic procedures by economic interests."[70] But herein lies a consequential misunderstanding of the Italian School. Although Bellamy rightly acknowledges the Italian anxiety over plutocracy, for Mosca and Pareto these representative procedures are not inherently democratic, and moreover, even calling them such is politically toxic. Nowhere in *Teorica* does Mosca call liberal conceptions of freedom or electoralism "democratic." In his vocabulary, they amount to what people in his own time call "liberal," and he even explicitly blames English parliamentarism for confusing these two ideas. He shows that representative institutions are often antidemocratic because they covertly foster plutocracy; moreover, when they are disingenuously touted to be essentially democratic in character, they can delegitimize a popular regime. Taken in its entirety, *Teorica* presents the conflation of democracy and liberal elections as the absurdity of our epoch, which "future generations will immediately recognize but to which we are currently blind."[71]

The Soft Mosca: Elementi di scienza politica in 1896, 1923, and 1939

At the time of writing *Teorica*, Mosca was disturbed that both socialist and liberal doctrines exhibited excessive confidence in the progressive advancement against domination throughout human history, but he was particularly vexed by the way parliamentary institutions, through plutocracy, economically oppress the lower classes, stifling their ability to contest the ruling group and hold them accountable. He describes these tendencies as a chain reaction that threatens the stability of contemporary popular regimes. Yet precisely because of his uninhibited criticism of representative procedures, most scholars identify *Teorica* as evidence of Mosca's antidemocratic propensities.

Postwar scholars contend that Mosca minimized the antidemocratic, conservative posture of *Teorica* and reversed the resolutely elitist stance of his youth in his next major work, *Elementi di scienza politica (Elements of Political Science)*. By contrast, I demonstrate that Mosca's assessment of electoral institutions developed out of a cynical but still popular orientation against plutocracy, an orientation he maintained relatively consistently despite his moderated attitude toward liberalism in the 1920s. Contextualizing the evolution of *Elementi's* three editions (1896, 1923, and 1939) with respect to positivism, socialism, and liberalism helps make sense of Mosca's political pessimism and its later obfuscation.[72]

A dozen years after the publication of *Teorica*, Mosca had not yet tired of his methodological debate with Pollyanna positivists or his political disagreement with naive socialists. *Elementi* debuted in 1896 as a treatise in conversation with both nineteenth-century socialist philosophy and positivist dominance in the burgeoning social sciences because he saw these two movements as suffering from the same ailments of Enlightenment optimism. Here, the positivist invasion of the academy strikes him as more threatening than ever because he fears that their self-proclaimed "scientific" posture will lead to an anti-historical orientation—which, in the study of politics, would either latently justify elite domination or, at the very least, promote a quietist response to it.

The first chapter of *Elementi* therefore protests against the precursors of rational-choice-style theories, social Darwinism, and all racial theories—the reigning "scientific" approaches to social science of the day. Most clearly, Mosca finds the application of evolutionary theories to political science shockingly dangerous.[73] "No satisfactory law has been found on the basis of racial diversities," he says, "nor is it possible to ascribe the progress or the ruin of nations to organic improvement or organic degenerations or races."[74] Mosca views

66   DEMOCRATIC ELITISM

this approach to social theory formation as the crippling of political science by conservative forces, because its progressive epistemology legitimates existing structures of domination on suspect grounds of "scientific" claims to objectivity.

Mosca finds self-interest-based paradigms to be no more accurate but less insidious, because their superficiality will prevent them from taking a stronghold in the discipline: "The person who wrote that the human being lets himself be guided by self-interest alone stated a general maxim that is almost entirely devoid of practical value," he states, "since it can tell us nothing save at the cost of exceedingly minute analyses and distinctions."[75] Understanding human behavior in terms of arbitrary, *de minimis*, but quantifiable metrics of self-interest helps justify corrupt forms of elite power because it presumes that once these random units of interest are satisfied, domination no longer exists. And besides, "anyone who thinks that interest has to be something that can be expressed materially in terms of money and measured in pounds and pence," he continues, "is a person of too little heart and too little head to understand the people about him."[76] Ironically, fifty years later not only would interest-based paradigms and rational choice theories control political science, but Mosca would be considered one of the founders of such a "value-free" approach.

Elementi thus constitutes a more pronounced rejection of the dominance of positivism in social theory than the earlier presentation in *Teorica*. Mosca's polemic against the "inward" scientific paradigm closely anticipates later attempts to discredit the formation of objective criteria to demonstrate "truth" in fields of traditional hermeneutic inquiry. His work champions a return to the "old historical method" and contends that the most basic element of political science is actually a broad knowledge of the history of mankind as a whole. *Elementi* does not outline a new method required for the future "science of politics" but instead calls for a historical approach that allows for a multiplicity of interpretations to coexist within the discipline.[77] Although scientific objectivity and "value-free" investigations may sound more promising in the reigning epistemological environment, Mosca maintains that the historian's cynicism has always offered an effective antidote to such delusions and conceits.

Optimistic hubris also is the main problem with Marxist theory, and in this respect Mosca understands positivism and Marxism to be conjoined twins. At bottom, he writes, both Auguste Comte and Karl Marx are disciples of Saint-Simon, who believed that "control over society was to belong in the future to a scientific aristocracy . . . and that such a form of government would be a necessary consequence of the 'positive' stage which the human mind had attained in the nineteenth century." For Comte, the management of society would be left in the hands of a "scientific priesthood"; for Marx, it would find itself in the hands of the "whole collectivity"; but they shared a belief in the progressive development of the ruling class, or a Hegelian assumption that conditions of mass domination progressively improve throughout human history by a continual amelioration in the quality of the ruling class. Both doctrines, Mosca relates, propose that "an evolutionary process" in society would inevitably lead to a superior "system of political and economic management" that increasingly minimized and, in the case of Marxism, ultimately eradicated oppression.[78]

According to James Meisel, the entire first half of *Elementi* should be read as a Marxist response "aimed at the naïve optimism of the eighteenth-century Enlightenment." In particular, Mosca complained that Marxism had "inherited that [Enlightenment] confidence," and he sought specifically to contest the progressive premise of history conceived in terms of class struggle toward ever-increasing freedom against domination. For Meisel, Mosca's cynical retort that history is instead a graveyard of aristocracies highlighted his view that "forever new elite formations eternalize the cycle of domination" in order to remind readers that exploitation exists no matter which economic modality dominates a given historical period.[79] When seen in this light, the tenor of Mosca's opposition to Marxist theory becomes clearer: by contesting progressive assumptions about the necessary and continual advancement of freedom throughout history, Mosca sought to undermine the confidence of Marxist doctrine, and not its political ends, in order to better fortify theoretical instruments against domination.

Unsurprisingly, Mosca's interpretation of Marxist theory directly translates to his understanding of all variants of socialist philosophy. Put simply, for Mosca socialist optimism promotes a complacent attitude toward domination. The socialists dangerously assume too much, he writes, as they "are evidently counting on a moral progress which they say will be attained, in order to bring into existence a type of social organization which assumes that progress has already been attained, and which in all probability would be able to function only if that progress had been attained." Contrary to popular belief, this assumption that progress will be made against domination relaxes defensive strategies against elite control, he maintains, and as a result such a socialist form of organization "would only be repeating on a large scale . . . the mistake [of unwarranted confidence] to which we primarily owe the current evils of parliamentarism."[80]

As an alternative to this hopeful posture about the possibility of a socialist eradication of elite domination, Mosca's focus on *la classe dirigente* spotlights the recurring cycle of oppression in order to demonstrate that "the setbacks of one nation or another, or the catastrophes that threaten them, [should] not [be] so much ascribed to the ignorance of the masses or to the wickedness of men in power as to the incompetence and inadequacy of the ruling class," and consequently, the need for that class's reform or ouster. Whereas in *Teorica* Mosca uses the terms *la classe politica* (the political class) and *la classe dirigente* (the ruling class) somewhat interchangeably, in 1896 Mosca begins to prefer the more capacious *la classe dirigente* or *la classe governante* in order to designate a broad group that necessarily includes politicians but also highlights those who exercise formidable control over them in the parliamentary context. [81] He stresses that the reader must never forget that, in addition to the politicians, the ruling class also consists of "proprietors, capitalists, industrialists, employees, and professionals . . . that is to say, all those who do not live from manual labor."[82]

This means that, notwithstanding Mosca's advocacy for reform of the ruling class through co-optation of individuals from lower socioeconomic classes, he held that a ruling class can, and in some cases must be, entirely replaced—not just amended through selective addition of representatives of the lower class to the governing body. In fact, given the ruling class's ostentatious displays of incompetence and corruption, the entire replacement of the current ruling class is precisely what liberal defenders of representative government, he suggests, ought to be worried about.

To Mosca's Italian colleagues, there was no question that the first edition of *Elementi* sought to deconstruct the optimistic intellectual currents of the time in order to accentuate the problem of plutocracy. The 1896 version of the work was a finalist for the Accademia dei Lincei's prize for best book in the social and economic sciences.[83] In one reviewer's summary, Mosca's attention to *la classe dirigente* questioned the durability of electoral institutions, given "the social question," and proposed remedies for the contradiction between continued economic oppression and the "extension of social democracy."[84] At the end of the nineteenth century, at least within the Italian milieu, Mosca's anti-plutocratic aims were more than evident.

Mosca did not win the book prize for two reasons. First, and rather ironically given how he will come to be remembered, the reviewers found his methodology too historical to warrant consideration for a prize in the social and economic sciences. More importantly, the reviewers felt that *Elementi* was not a novel contribution to the literature. The committee decided that, although the problem of parliamentary plutocracy poses a "complicated issue currently prominent in the life of the people," the division of society between rulers and ruled was not a "felicitous innovation" or even a compelling "political law."

Everyone knows that plutocracy vexes the newly established parliamentary state, one reviewer remarks, but dividing society between "rulers and ruled neither supplements nor replaces the old Aristotelian regime classifications"; it is simply too obvious a presupposition to belabor.[85] Besides, another reporter notes, political thought has focused on the sovereigns of a given society since time immemorial.[86] To the Accademia dei Lincei, a theory dedicated to uncovering the particularities of a specific ruling class's power seemed gratuitous.

The 1896 edition of *Elementi* thus did not fare as well among the upper crust of the Italian intellectual community as Mosca had hoped, but it was far better received among the broader public. Throughout the first two decades of the twentieth century, Mosca's identification of *la classe dirigente* with a plutocratic elite (one that included, but was not confined to, the political sector) became increasingly popular, especially among socialists and early fascists. Professionally benefiting from its popularity, in the early 1920s Mosca decided to write a second edition of *Elementi* (1923) in which he expanded his treatment of *la classe dirigente* into a full chapter—a decision that, ironically, helped him win life appointments to the University of Rome and the Italian Senate. However, at the same time he became concerned by the destruction of liberal safeguards and consequently began to distance himself from Mussolini—culminating in a sensational denunciation of fascism, resignation from the Senate, and signing the Manifesto of Anti-Fascist Intellectuals in 1925.[87]

During the twenty-five years between the first two editions, fascism changed the Sicilian student of socialism. No longer interested in socialist or positivist philosophy, Mosca felt that there was a larger threat to society than liberal plutocratic domination: in a word, the experience of fascism softened his attitude toward liberalism. At the turn of the century Mosca had argued that parliamentary systems had "failed miserably" to inhibit the plutocratic transformations of liberalism, but in the 1923 publication, shortly after Mussolini's rise to power, Mosca attributed to the representative system the highest degree of "juridical defense" against elite domination ever attained in history.[88] Whereas in the 1890s Mosca had taken openness and discussion between elite sects for granted, later in the twentieth century he found it necessary to openly appreciate the importance of this feature of liberalism as a contrast to Mussolini's proposed authoritarian constitutional amendments in 1925. Mosca's experience with fascism thus led to a revision of his magnum opus in a way that obscures his original anxiety over plutocracy and liberalism. In fact, he worked meticulously with editor Arthur Livingston on the 1939 English translation, in which Mosca "insisted on deleting the study of the Roman question," the part of the text explicitly devoted to plutocracy.[89]

70   DEMOCRATIC ELITISM

And yet, even though Mosca's disdain for the liberal plutocratic nexus was far more explicit in 1896, his concern remains evident in the final 1939 edition of *Elementi*. I unearth his critique of liberal plutocracy in this version, with a focus on the ruling-class theory. On Mosca's pessimistic account of the inevitability of oligarchy, frank acknowledgment of plutocratic tendencies in liberal societies helps orient us toward the need for ever-increasing "multiplicities" of elites and the "democratic" renewal of leadership from below—the "indispensable" element to anything that can be likened to human "progress."[90]

Mosca's ruling-class theory contends that the composition of the ruling class changes when the management of the state requires capacities different from those made available by the status quo.[91] *Elementi* insists that efforts to track changes in the makeup of ruling classes should be only one variable, albeit a crucial one, among others in the study of politics. His endeavor at first appears to focus exclusively on a select group of elites, but over the course of the book it becomes clear that he intends his analysis of the ruling class to help others study the dynamics among all social classes at various historical junctures. The ruling-class theory does not fixate on inevitable domination by a minority: it constitutes one technique among others employed in his more comprehensive study of political change. When translated into English, the title of Mosca's treatise was transformed from its literal equivalent—"Elements of political science"—to *The Ruling Class*. With this change in title, one element traced in his treatise on political science—the law of the political class or, as it was subsequently translated, the "theory of the ruling class"—became his defining contribution. This furthered the perception that the ruling-class theory was Mosca's desired normative prescription as opposed to a heuristic for analysis.

Yet according to Mosca, the ruling-class theory does not create "labels for the various types of ruling classes," but instead bids us to "examine the contents of *our* bottles and investigate and analyze the criteria that prevail in the constitution of the ruling classes on which the strength or weakness of *our* states depend."[92] In this passage, Mosca instructs the reader to use the ruling-class theory as a tool for inward reflection on our own polities—as a way to candidly assess our own "strengths and weaknesses" without deluding ourselves about who maintains power in contemporary society. He suggests that honest investigation and sober self-analysis can prompt the desire to change the constitution of the ruling classes for the better, as opposed to simply enumerating, or "labeling" types of ruling groups to no constructive end. The ruling-class theory thus offers a useful heuristic that promotes candid confrontation with existing structures of domination; it does not simply serve to encourage a dispassionate assessment of irresistible political laws.

SOBER CYNICISM   71

Similar to Mosca's formulation in *Teorica*, in *Elementi* the rhetoric suggests that the ruling-class theory can even serve as a subversive tool in disrupting the domination of a particular ruling class. He reminds the reader that given the "various ways in which the ruling classes are formed and organized, [it] is precisely in that variety of type that *the secret* of their strength and weakness must be sought and found"—as if to say that identifying this "secret" helps undermine or eliminate an undesirable elite. The power of an organized minority over the majority is "inevitable," Mosca famously states, but "at the same time" the minority becomes "organized for the very reason that it is a minority."[93] Far from encouraging acceptance of uncontainable minority domination, the ruling-class theory implies that organization is the only resource minorities have against the far more formidable power of a numerical majority. No less of a revolutionary than Gramsci would explicitly elaborate this political law in his notebooks 8 and 13.[94]

When we add to this idea Mosca's view that the "democratic impulse"—that is, the constant "replenishing of ruling classes from the lower classes"—is the key to human advancement, then his drive to identify elite strengths and weaknesses reads much more like an exposé of minority domination that encourages democratic renewal of political leadership from below, rather than a celebratory promotion or resigned acceptance of elite rule.[95] Importantly, Mosca contrasts this democratic impulse with both the autocratic transfer of power from above, through inheritance or appointment, and the liberal principle, which transfers power between elite minorities through elections. Taken together, his arguments advocate the demystification of elite power as a potential corrective to the insufficiency of liberal institutions in checking plutocratic tendencies—institutions that, after the advent of fascism, Mosca ultimately endorses but admits are weak in the face of plutocratic tendencies that elude parliamentary regulation.

Despite having removed the chapter dedicated to Roman plutocracy, which had been featured in the original edition, Mosca weaves a critique of plutocracy into his accounts of the ancient, medieval, and modern civilizations he assesses. The book treats plutocracy as an unavoidable tendency throughout history that we must constantly be on guard against and seek to contain—a normative orientation confirmed by the condemnations, scattered throughout the text, of plutocracy in modern governments. He warns that electoral politics can never forestall or control plutocracy once these institutions are wedded to unrestrained capitalistic structures. The American context provides a paradigmatic example, he writes, where nothing can prevent the rich from becoming more influential than the poor because the rich will always

72   DEMOCRATIC ELITISM

effectively pressure the politicians who control public administration. For Mosca, America proves that liberal constraints do not "prevent elections from being carried on to the music of clinking dollars . . . or whole legislatures and considerable numbers of national congressmen from feeling the influence of powerful corporations and great financiers."[96] But the palpable pessimism in this critique of American plutocracy constitutes an encouragement toward reform—not a compulsion to compliance.

Thanks to James Burnham, much of the Anglo-American literature on Mosca's thought has focused on the inspiration it took from Machiavelli's "realistic" or "scientific" approach to studying politics and power.[97] But without appreciating Mosca's critique of plutocracy, the Sicilian's reading of the Florentine is severely impoverished. Mosca agrees with his predecessor's assessment that there exist two tendencies in every polity, one "aristocratic" and the other "democratic," and if one had to choose, the democratic element is more responsible for anything that can account for effective political procedures and human advancement.[98] Mosca also defends Machiavelli's view that rather than ignoring the tumults that transpire between these two elements, the institutionalization of the conflict between the "humors" offers the best guarantee that "the most severe and degrading poverty is avoided" and "that wealth is less the effect of birth and fortune [and more] the just reward for meritorious efforts and intelligent activity."[99]

Ultimately, however, Mosca finds Machiavelli's assessment wanting because Machiavelli is not pessimistic enough about the potential for plutocratic corruption of a ruling class. His verdict on Machiavellian thought offers the following suggestion:

> If some observer in our day were to note the ways in which private fortunes are made and unmade on our stock exchanges, in our corporations or in our banks, he could easily write a book on the art of getting rich that would probably offer very sound advice on how to look like an honest man and yet not be one, and on how to thieve and rob and still keep clear of the criminal courts. Such a book would, one may be sure, make the precepts that the Florentine Secretary lays down in his essay look likes jests for innocent babes.[100]

Here Mosca admonishes Machiavelli for focusing only on the fraud perpetrated by the political sect of the ruling class, and not emphasizing the part of the *classe dirigente* that can easily hide its rampant corruption through perfectly legal institutions like stock exchanges, corporations, and banks. This type of fraud bears the mark of a regime characterized by plutocracy, because the political class allows those who have "thieved and robbed" their way to "private fortunes" to steer "clear of the criminal courts."[101] Mosca suggests that the plutocratic moment of the Italian Risorgimento would make Machiavelli's infamous descriptions of political deceit and domination seem benign.

In H. Stuart Hughes's account, the second edition of *Elementi* (1923) "already shows his transformation from a critic of parliamentary democracy into its defender—a skeptical defender, indeed, but an extremely effective one."[102] Admittedly, Mosca's critique of liberal institutions was certainly attenuated during Mussolini's ascent to power, when Mosca became a staunch critic of the Fascist regime, and a staunch supporter of the openness and discussion between elite sects that liberal parliamentary institutions allow. Yet his anxiety over the ways parliamentary bodies become susceptible to plutocratic corruption, and over the increasing temptation to conflate of democracy and liberal elections, never disappears. Mosca always guarded against conflating parliamentary politics and democracy because he believed this conflation could cause disillusionment with liberal representative government itself.

Even in the third edition (1939), Mosca implores his reader to refuse the tempting association between democracy and election. Under the representative system, Mosca says, we must face the fact that "the voters" never "choose" their representative. "The truth is that the representative *is himself elected* by the voters," or to be more exact, "*his friends have him elected.*" The very structure of representation, he claims, prohibits "each voter [from] giving his vote to the candidate of his heart." "If his vote is to have any efficacy at all, each voter is forced to limit his choice to a very narrow field, in other words to a choice among two or three persons who have some chance of succeeding," writes Mosca, before problematically adding that "the only ones who have any chance of succeeding are those whose candidates are championed by groups, committees, *by organized minorities.*"[103] In this context, it becomes imperative to uncover the interconnections between the representative and "his friends," as this network of ruling-class sects exhibits the antidemocratic forces residing within electoral politics.

Although this depiction of representative government may sound resigned, Mosca insists that saving representative government from fascism requires direct confrontation with this reality. In an addition to the 1939 edition, Mosca does not renounce his earlier, more discernible position against the plutocratic tendencies of liberalism. In the closing chapter Mosca discusses the ways the representative system could be "restored" on a sounder basis, and intimates that his critique of parliamentarism constitutes an integral part of that effort—one that should continue to be "deeply pondered" in the present moment:

74   DEMOCRATIC ELITISM

> Fifty years ago the author of this volume opened his career as a writer
> with a book [*Teorica*] which was a book of his youth but which he still
> does not disown. In it he sought to lay bare some of the untruths that lie
> imbedded in certain assumptions of the representative system, and some
> of the defects of parliamentarism. Today advancing years have made him
> more cautious in judgment and, he might venture to say, more balanced.
> His conclusions at any rate are deeply pondered. As he looks closely and
> dispassionately at the conditions that prevail in many European nations
> and especially in his own country, Italy, he feels impelled to urge the rising
> generation to restore and conserve the political system which it inherited
> from its fathers.[104]

Mosca does not reject his youthful determination to identify the plutocratic
challenges facing representative regimes, because, he suggests, those are the very
same problems that have led Italy to adopt an authoritarian government
antithetical to the "political system . . . of its fathers." In my view, that paternal
heritage is broadly marked by the democratically republican ethos of local
government characteristic of the Italian city-states—an ethos most certainly antithetical to English liberal parliamentarism and the autocracy of
many European nations of his day.

In this respect Mosca and Pareto not only share a concern for the ways plutocracy transforms a representative institution into an autocratic form; they
are also united in a common effort to "lay bare . . . the untruths" of representative government that prompt this authoritarian invasion of parliamentary regimes in the first place. Far more diplomatic than Pareto, Mosca does not call
the threats inherent in the hypocritical, supposedly "democratic" assumptions
of representative systems "demagogic plutocracy" or even authoritarian dictatorship, but his subtlety here would not have been lost on an audience living
in Fascist Italy.

Italian Pessimism, Southern Style

Both *Teorica* and all three editions of *Elementi* present a view of representative government as involving small, self-perpetuating cliques that manage the
political process, where the representative is never elected by his constituents
but instead has himself elected through plutocratic manipulation managed by
various sects. In this respect, Mosca's and Pareto's critiques of socialism and
liberalism bear similar features: they both present plutocratic depictions of parliamentary systems, staunch opposition to the conflation of democracy and

elections, and a general pessimism regarding the current plutocratic elite's capabilities for government. In their own ways, they urge reform and/or supplementation of these electoral procedures or regional economic redress so that the Risorgimento does not become a mere organizational reshuffling that maintains structures of elite domination in purportedly "democratic" regimes. If preventative measures against plutocracy are not enacted, both the Ligurian aristocrat and the Sicilian statesman warn, parliamentary bodies will ultimately succumb to some form of authoritarianism, either through understandable mass insurrection (Mosca) or by the more subtle invitation of a demagogic plutocrat (Pareto).

While Pareto uses angry, vitriolic condemnations of the existing ruling class to issue his warning, Mosca deploys a more restrained approach. The Sicilian also finds current elites corrupt and deficient, but in order to dispel the comforting, illusory idea that representative institutions foster egalitarian outcomes, his ruling-class theory serves as an intellectual instrument that forces elites to acknowledge the plutocratic tendencies inherent in liberal government, and more importantly, actively encourages measures to combat those tendencies. Democratic replenishing of the ruling class with members from the lower strata will do the most to mitigate mass oppression and promote regime stability, Mosca contends, but this impulse will not develop naturally if electoral institutions remain unreformed. Such a replenishing of the ruling class can only occur if *regional* economic disparity between the masses and the elites—that is, between the North and the South—is addressed. Either the existing ruling class implements economic change to cultivate this democratic impulse by creating genuine access into the governing body, or it shall perish and a new form of minority domination over the majority will prevail.

This narrative has always been a familiar one in Mezzogiorno political thought. Mosca's skepticism comes from a history of millennia of successive different governments controlling his native Sicily. The governments varied structurally, but all involved the particularly oppressive command of the majority by a foreign minority. Moreover, in the mid-eighteenth and nineteenth centuries, it was commonly feared that the democratic pretenses of the Risorgimento were simply a cover for Northern plutocratic exploitation of the South. From the Southern perspective, Italian statehood had come to fruition because Giuseppe Garibaldi had harnessed the majoritarian power of the Southern revolutionaries to fight the Kingdom of the Two Sicilies, only to then offer their independence to the Kingdom of Savoy under the guise of "unification."

From this context arose the proverb "Everything must change for everything to remain the same." In Tomasi di Lampedusa's novel *The Leopard*, the line is

76 DEMOCRATIC ELITISM

originally spoken by Tancredi Falconieri, a member of the old Bourbon aristocracy who understands that in order to remain a part of the elite, he must join Garibaldi's Redshirts and marry the daughter of Don Calogero Sedara—a newly moneyed, dodgy businessman whose suspect political influence represents the ascendence of the liberal capitalist ruling class. These changes, however, would only be superficial—everything would really stay the same in the New Italy—and the basic structure of Northern elite domination of the Southern masses would go unaltered.

On the most basic level, then, the maxim expresses Southern suspicion of the democratic expectations promised in the Risorgimento's liberal republican ideals, and more generally, explains why the Southern masses were disinclined to support less than trustworthy [Northern capitalist] minorities who promised to give them emancipation or sovereignty through universal suffrage. In fact, Mosca admits that as a child he himself was hoodwinked into believing that his "democratic bordering on red" beliefs would be best served by liberal republican institutions imposed by the Savoyard constitutional monarchy. At university, Mosca realized that this confusing amalgamation of terms—liberal, republican, democratic, and so forth—all aimed to conceal the elite domination proposed in the Risorgimento's transfer of power.[105] Like so many *meridionalisi*—Cuoco, De Sanctis, Lampedusa, and Gramsci, among others—Mosca suggests that one way to remain vigilant against (Northern) elite domination is to arm oneself with a systematically pessimistic attitude toward it.

While Lampedusa's adage beseeches Southern Italians to remain on guard against the illusory democratic ideals of the Risorgimento in the twentieth century, Lampedusa added that "after all is said and done, Sicilians are also Italians."[106] A pessimistic orientation toward minority domination was characteristic of political thought in the Mezzogiorno, but the works of Pareto and Mosca attest to the fact that it also defines the Italian political disposition as a whole.

The Anti-fascist, Anti-socialist Mosca in Italy and the United States, 1924–1941

Mosca fought tirelessly against Mussolini's ascent to power and against any Fascist appropriation of his thought. Mussolini would identify Pareto as a theoretical patron of Fascism after allegedly attending his lectures as an exile in Switzerland, but he knew to stay silent where Mosca was concerned. In 1923, the year of Pareto's death, Croce wrote a glowing review of *Elementi*, which was reprinted as a foreword to what for twenty-five years was the only available edition of the book. In 1924, Mosca and Croce began to work closely together as the co-organizers of the Liberal Party to present a united front against Fascist gains in the Italian Parliament. From that point on, Mosca's protest against Mussolini came by way of speeches in support of civil liberties and the virtues of parliamentary government, along with a steadfast refusal to compromise with the regime. His anti-Fascism profoundly influenced more famous opponents of Fascism such as Gramsci, Gaetano Salvemini, and Piero Gobetti.[107] As seen above, Mosca was invested in modifying the translations of his work so that no part of it could be understood as supporting Mussolini's totalitarian politics.

Despite his best efforts to avoid this, Mosca was labeled "archconservative," "protofascist," and even "positivist" in the postwar period. It was a case of Sod's law: the more Mosca desperately tried to explain the direct relationship between his earlier political theory as a scholar and his later political practice as a parliamentarian, the more his anti-Fascist efforts were seen as a reversal of his position on the plutocratic dangers of electoral government—and worse, the more it appeared that his earlier critique of parliamentarism had enabled Mussolini's rise to power.

Part of the explanation lies with the terminological evolution of the labels "democrat," "liberal," and "conservative" during Mosca's own lifetime. Since the beginning of his career, Mosca had called himself an "antidemocrat" because of his opposition to any pure majoritarian government and accompanying institutions such as sortition. Of course, by today's standards rejection of pure majoritarianism would not disqualify anyone from being designated a democrat, but at the time democracy was still understood in majoritarian terms, and therefore it made sense for him to deny any association with it. Mosca also initially rejected identification as a "liberal" because to his mind the term was associated with the apparatus of Northern hegemony. After all, as Gramsci would later write, the Northern capitalist elite "succeed[ed] in establishing the apparatus (mechanism) of their intellectual moral and political hegemony . . . in forms, and by means, which may be called 'liberal'—in other words through individual molecular, private enterprise"—and, accordingly, no young man of Sicilian origin would willingly accept that label.[108] Mosca's rejection of democracy and liberalism, however, far outlasted their original Italian political significations, and it became easy for postwar scholars to assume that Mosca's denunciation of "democracy" and "liberalism" was a vestige of nineteenth-century reactionary conservatism.

In response to the accusation that his critique of electoral government identified him as an archconservative aristocrat, Mosca later came to accept the

78   DEMOCRATIC ELITISM

moniker "liberal." In clarifying his political identification during a famous 1904 interview, Mosca said that he called himself a "liberal" because he was dedicated to the idea that the "ruling class ought not be monolithic and homogeneous."[109] If this commitment to a pluralistic ruling class that engaged in free discussion and debate made him a liberal, he claimed, so be it. But he also explained that this did not change his position vis-à-vis electoral government. "When political power originates from a single source," he says, "even if this be elections with universal suffrage, I regard it as dangerous and liable to become oppressive." As he had explained in the *Teorica*, "there exist extremely important political forces that do not have the means to prevail in a popular election," and therefore "it is not useful that because of this they should be suppressed and unable to exercise any effective political action."[110] If liberalism strictly referred to elite pluralism and debate between diverse groups, then Mosca was a liberal, but that did not mean that he ever thought universal suffrage was sufficient to attain his desired representative, plural heterogeneity of the ruling class.

Far more importantly, Mosca's Senate resignation speech contributed to the now-ubiquitous view that the advent of Fascism triggered his nostalgia for the greatness of nineteenth-century European liberalism.[111] On December 19, 1925, Mosca reprimanded his milquetoast colleagues who had been wavering in their denunciations of Mussolini: "I never would have thought," he scolded, "that I would be alone in pronouncing the funeral oration for the parliamentary system." But perhaps it all makes sense, Mosca somberly continues:

> When I was in the Chamber of Deputies I remember being surprised at the common practice whereby, when a former Deputy died, his funeral oration was nearly always delivered by his successor in the constituency, who in many cases had been the one to unseat him; so it happens that an antagonist who had previously spoken ill of his opponents was then obliged to sing his praises. Similarly, I who have always been sharply critical of parliamentary government must now almost regret its fall. I admit that this system has been in need of considerable modification, but I don't think the time is right for a radical transformation, and now that the system is being renounced we should remember its merits.[112]

To many commentators the "emotional" funeral oration represents an about-face—a demonstration that Mosca recognized the light of liberal parliamentarism, as it were, and the Fascist dangers of emphasizing the plutocratic character of electoral government, albeit too late. Yet in his very next breath,

Mosca explains that Italy is faced with the totalitarian transformation of its constitution for the very same reasons he had warned against in the late nineteenth century. The First World War obviously caused the republican regime to "degenerate," Mosca says. But more than this, political elites made "two grave errors" that destabilized the state at precisely the wrong moment: (1) the introduction of universal suffrage before the war and (2) the introduction of proportional representation after it.[113] Borrowing Piero Gobetti's formulation, Mosca suggests that the Fascist turn to totalitarianism represented the "autobiography of the nation," an accretion of all the ills of Italian society through the Risorgimento.

Mosca's warning of the perils of universal suffrage and proportional representation within precarious parliamentary regimes cannot help but strike the modern ear as antidemocratic. Yet given Mosca's continued critique of elite incapacities, consistent commitment to pluralism of the ruling class, and insistence on the democratic renewal of the political class from below, it cannot be the case that in opposing universal suffrage and proportional representation Mosca yearned for a narrow elite class, nor could it be that he simply "changed his mind" about the perils of parliamentary politics. In the 1890s Mosca opposed the extension of suffrage because he believed that under conditions of extreme regional economic inequality and the history of the Bourbon plebiscite, the introduction of electoralism would lead to a consolidation of a patrimonial elite that would prohibit the substantive growth of democracy in the New Italy. In other words, Mosca argued that extension of suffrage would solidify the electoral seats of the landed aristocracy by purportedly "democratic" means. He especially worried that the introduction of electoralism and the consequent consolidation of the *baroni* would allow Northern elites to use elections as a pretense of legitimating authority, or "democracy." He warned that in this case elections actually functioned as a hegemonic instrument of Southern mass oppression, which would lead to a lack of faith in elections and democracy properly configured, thereby inviting Fascist and / or populist usurpation of the republic.

This argument need not be made by an antidemocrat—Gramsci will corroborate Mosca's prediction as the reason for the impossibility of democracy in Italy under existing conditions. Gramsci's appropriation of Mosca's ruling-class theory indicates that critiques of parliamentarism need not necessarily lead to fascism, and also that Mosca's "anti-socialist" preoccupations should be understood in a different light. After all, the parallels with Gramsci's thought suggest that Mosca might have always been an anti-socialist thinker, but for very different reasons than the ones previously assumed.

80   DEMOCRATIC ELITISM

Nevertheless, the perceived "reversal" of Mosca's youthful "antidemocratic" stance to a more hopeful anti-socialist, anti-fascist defender of liberal, electoral government would be decisive in shaping American political science and in launching a new understanding of democracy itself. At Columbia, where Livingston was a professor of romance languages, Mosca's thought was publicized by means of his association with the National Dante Society and his friendship with Walter Lippmann.[114] Through Livingston's role in the genesis and launch of the *New Republic*, Lippman informally popularized Mosca in order to underscore the danger of ever criticizing electoral governments.[115] In fact, Lippmann was invested in Livingston's edition of *Elementi*, and at one point it was hoped that Lippmann himself would write the introduction to the work.[116]

At the University of Chicago, Charles Merriam, the founding father of the empirical-behavioral school of American political science, would deploy Mosca's realistic, yet purportedly more sanguine approach to electoral government as a starting point for the discipline. Pareto, "the foe of democracy," was a completely untenable patron because he *seemed* to criticize universal suffrage (the irony here is that Pareto had always expressed unqualified support for it and Mosca had not), whereas for Merriam, Mosca presented the path forward for American political thought in the Second World War, on both methodological and substantive grounds.[117] Methodologically, Merriam set the groundwork for misunderstanding the historical character of Mosca's political thought, allowing for his "new science" to serve as the foundation for the development of a "value free" social science in the future.[118] Substantively, Mosca's purported reorientation and rejection of Fascism highlighted the dangers of critiques of parliamentarism amid battle with totalitarian enemies.[119]

Merriam trained the most preeminent cohort of political scientists who applied Mosca's "value-free" orientation to the quantifiable study of elections; these included Harrold Lasswell, Harold Gosnell, Harry Eckstein, Harold Laski, V. O. Key, Gabriel Almond, David Truman, Herbert Simon, Renzo Sereno, Edward Banfield, and others. Lasswell, Merriam's oldest student (and later his colleague), is of particular importance, not only because he became known as "Mosca's advance man" in the United States, but also because his development of "elite theory" in the 1930s spearheaded the psychological aspect of the behavioral revolution.[120] Lasswell considered Pareto far too abstruse to be used productively in a formal, value-free study of politics. Instead he acknowledged Mosca as a "realistic" exemplar, who boiled politics down to "a struggle of elites over who gets income, power, and safety."[121]

Merriam's younger pupils would go on to create a cottage industry of research on the "Italian case," specifically the Italian South, to contend that without a culture of enthusiastic and unqualified support of elections, there could never be democracy. Most famously, Edward Banfield's *The Moral Basis of a Backward Society* (1958) would specifically state as much in explaining why democracy could never work in Italy—because Southern Italians did not have a "civic" culture of revering the more local political and cultural institutions that undergird elections. Entirely ignoring the politics of the Risorgimento, Banfield claims that feudalism had generated Southern Italians practices of clientelism, thereby suggesting that there was no hope that ordinary Mezzogiorno citizens could understand the long-term benefits of investing in salutary popular participation. This idea was essentially reproduced in Gabriel Almond and Sidney Verba's *The Civic Culture* (1965) and Sidney Tarrow's *Peasant Communism in Southern Italy* (1967) vis-à-vis the concepts of "parochialism" and "clientelism," respectively.[122] Italy became a primary site for research on how to advance democracy understood in terms of free and fair elections in comparative politics, inspiring canonical texts such as Frederic Spotts and Theodore Wiser's *Italy: A Difficult Democracy* (1986), Joseph LaPalombara's *Democracy, Italian Style* (1989), and Robert Putnam's *Making Democracy Work: Civic Traditions in Modern Italy* (1993). Although Banfield, Almond and Verba, and Tarrow all understood themselves to be Tocquevillians who, in contrast to Dahl and Lipset, drew attention to the conditions that accompany elections, they all still defined democratic "culture" by the activities that supported investment in electoral outcomes, completely ignoring the plutocratic critique of elections that shaped Italian unification and its aftermath.

Even for James Meisel and Stuart Hughes, Pareto's most sophisticated readers in the United States, Mosca was clearly the Italian theorist to be salvaged for the political thought of the postwar period. Both Meisel and Hughes were aware of the controversy of precedence between the two Italians and lamented that as international "fame continued to shine down on Pareto," Mosca's anti-fascist investment in Italian politics rendered him increasingly obscure to an outside readership.[123] Yet, perhaps partly because of this perceived injustice, Meisel's and Hughes's work championed Mosca's thought over the work of the desperately pessimistic Pareto because they understood the mature Mosca to have changed his tune about the promise of parliamentary government. Hughes's rendition of Mosca would influence more humanistic government departments from Harvard to Berkeley, while Meisel's liberal-leaning recuperation of Mosca would reach such thinkers as Louis Hartz and

82   DEMOCRATIC ELITISM

the burgeoning behavioralist school at his own institution, the University of Michigan. In his review of Meisel's work, Louis Hartz claims that Meisel's depiction of Mosca's thought demonstrates that the "line between 'elitism' and democracy is more difficult than we usually like to concede," already encouraging the development of democratic elitism as a regime type.[124]

Pareto earned a legacy in the international realm of economics and sociology, but Mosca became the father of American political science.[125] Yet it is safe to say that Mosca would have never accepted this progeny: his illegitimate American heirs betrayed the two erroneous assumptions he spent his entire life combating. They used his work both to advance a behavioral, empirical orientation in the study of politics and to encourage the conflation of elections and democracy. For the Americans, Mosca's political evolution demonstrated that any critique of elections invited totalitarian usurpation. Mosca, meanwhile, had always claimed the very opposite: namely, that the failure to recognize the danger of plutocratic capture of elections and the necessity of explicit economic redress for this danger would almost certainly ensure a totalitarian revival through mass insurrection.

CHAPTER 3

The Edge of Fatalism

Michels and the Iron Law of Oligarchy

The hardest thing to translate from one language into another is the
tempo of its style, which is grounded in the character of the race or—
to be more physiological—in the average tempo of its "metabolism."
There are well-meaning interpretations that are practically falsifications;
they involuntarily debase the original, simply because it has a tempo that
cannot be translated.... How could the German language ... imitate
Machiavelli's tempo ... who ... allows one to breath the fine dry air
of Florence?

—Friedrich Nietzsche, *Beyond Good and Evil*

Although Robert Michels began his career as a card-carrying socialist passion-
ately committed to the most revolutionary forms of syndicalism, the German
sociologist famously went on to embrace Fascism in the 1920s. Many attribute
this turn to his disillusionment with socialism as a result of his engagement
with Pareto and Mosca.[1] Scholars often treat Michels's renowned "iron law
of oligarchy" as the natural development of the Italians' anti-socialist and antidemocratic elitism, furthering the perception that his personal affiliation with
his Italian colleagues ultimately pushed him toward Fascist conclusions.[2]

A superficial reading of Michels's biographical record seems to indicate
that his arrival on the peninsula corrupted his socialist commitments and inspired his eventual defense of Mussolini's dictatorship. While in Germany,
Michels was an active member of the Social Democratic Party (SPD), but
after a mere four years working with the Italian revolutionary syndicalists in

84 DEMOCRATIC ELITISM

Turin—where, incidentally, he met Pareto and Mosca—he dramatically abandoned his German socialist affiliations in 1906 and then his Italian socialist and syndicalist ones in 1907 and 1909, respectively. In 1911 he published his masterpiece, *On the Sociology of the Party System in Modern Democracy: Investigations of the Oligarchic Tendencies of Group Life*, which struck his intimates as an SPD insider's devastating betrayal of Marxism.

Commentators often link Michels's alleged disdain for the epistemic shortcomings of the masses to Pareto's supposed predilection for crowd psychology.[3] Yet although Michels made pilgrimages to Pareto's retirement home in Céligny, their relationship developed after Pareto's health had already deteriorated, and Michels developed stronger professional ties with Mosca.[4] Scholarship has thus focused primarily on Michels as "Mosca's young man" and on the Sicilian's "decisive" influence on him.[5] The consensus is that Michels's conversion to Fascism should be seen in light of his flattering account of the Italian professor's brilliance in *Corso di sociologia politica* (*First Lectures on Political Sociology*), Michels's introductory lectures delivered at the University of Rome in 1927, where Mosca then held the chair of public law.[6] In these lectures Michels first suggests that "only charismatic leadership could transcend organizational leadership and engender mass support for great tasks."[7] By implication, it seems to many that Mosca's theory of the ruling class and its focus on minority organization emboldened Michels to move in this plebiscitary, authoritarian direction, for which he was promptly rewarded: in 1928 he accepted Mussolini's offer to join the openly Fascist faculty of political science at the University of Perugia.

Michels did inherit some of the Italians' precepts, but not on the grounds traditionally supposed. This chapter contextualizes Michels's work by tracing both its continuities with his predecessors and, ultimately, its deviation away from their orientation. Much like Pareto and Mosca, I argue that Michels's 1912 Italian articulation of the "iron law of oligarchy" (on which the 1915 English translation is based) sought to restrict the growth of plutocracy and contain the oligarchic propensities of modern popular government by revealing the composition of electoral institutions—in Michels's case, by revealing the internal organization of electoral party structure. In line with the Italians, his account of oligarchy reveals how parties breed plutocratic manipulation of popular interests through unequal access to economic resources. From Mosca, Michels acquires cynical suspicion toward the organizational aspects of representative polities that generate minority domination. Like Pareto, Michels's vitriol is aimed, not at the cognitive deficiencies of the masses, but instead at elites' behavioral role in electoral systems—a role that is central to his understanding of the "technical indispensability of leadership."[8]

THE EDGE OF FATALISM   85

All three theorists of elitism, thus, distrusted electoral politics. For Pareto, Mosca, and Michels, a commitment to democratic outcomes demands continual contestation of elite power through the ruthless exposure of majority domination by elite minorities. Michels's *Zur Soziologie des Parteiwesens in der modernen Demokratie* (*On the Sociology of the Party System in Modern Democracy;* henceforth cited as *Sociology of the Party*) (1911) offers one permutation of the Italian orientation toward democracy, and the following discussion previews the way American political scientists would later inappropriately interpret Michels's pessimism and its implications.[9]

This is not to say, however, that Pareto, Mosca, and Michels had identical postures toward plutocracy, oligarchy, and elites. Pareto and Mosca aimed to spur elites to correct the plutocratic corruption that was rampant in the Italian version of liberal electoralism. By contrast, the focus on plutocracy becomes sublimated in the German scholar's work, and Michels's broader interest in oligarchy outside of Italy renders his pessimism more fatalistic than the angry or sober warnings of his more strictly Italian counterparts. Moreover, Michels does not forcefully reject the modern conflation of democracy and elections, which makes his conception of what constitutes salutary popular government radically distinct from Pareto's and Mosca's views.

This reconsideration of *Sociology of the Party* reveals that upon closer inspection the schism between the Italians and Michels makes a great deal of theoretical and historical sense.[10] On a theoretical register, the competing Weberian and Mosca-Paretian impulses in Michels's early training result in tensions that ultimately render his research incommensurable with the Italian prognosis of the problems with representative politics. And from a historical vantage point, Pareto and Mosca were both committed to realizing the unified Italian state as a lasting project and insisted that combatting the Risorgimento's parliamentary plutocracy was key to generating a salutary popular government in Italy. As a German émigré, Michels was less invested in the fragile project of the Italian State and its plutocratic propensities, and therefore more susceptible to the political risks of equating democracy with elections.

In the postwar period, American political science will identify Pareto and Mosca as protofascist thinkers whose influence on Michels was responsible for his becoming Mussolini's acolyte. Consequently, these political scientists saw Michels's Weberian-inspired orientation as a more productive resource for democratic theory. Below I offer a different reading. Instead of identifying the continuities with his Italian predecessors as the source of Michels's later authoritarian proclivities, I propose that Michels's eventual embrace of Fascist precepts is best accounted for by his distinctly Weberian appropriation of the Italians' pessimistic concerns vis-à-vis "the problem of democracy," his more

86 DEMOCRATIC ELITISM

subtle emphasis on plutocratic oligarchy in representative regimes, and his acceptance of the view that modern democracy is synonymous with electoral government. The difference in emphasis, nuance, and tone between the Italians and the German may also reveal why it became tempting for postwar American political scientists to understand Pareto's and Mosca's focus on elites as a dead end for democratic theory and participatory politics, but Michels's thought as a generative resource for it.

German Idealism and Disenchantment: The Sources of Sociology of the Party

Before turning to his most renowned text, it is worth disentangling the conflicting impulses of Michels's early intellectual formation. Michels began working on *Sociology of the Party* in a series of essays published for the journal *Archiv für Sozialwissenschaft und Sozialpolitik* (*Archive for Social Science and Social Policy*) under the tutelage of Max Weber. At the time Weber was a meticulous reader of Michels's writings, working through "two chapters" and a "rough draft" of a projected "book"—the first version of *Sociology of the Party*—and two separate articles.[11] In fact, the deceptively simplistic "iron law of oligarchy" was the conclusion of two related but distinct theses developed in the preliminary pieces written five years before the original publication of *Sociology of the Party*, in 1911. These expositions may be summarized as follows:

1) A sociological analysis of the way electoral institutions, which Weber and Michels treat as synonymous with "modern democracy," transform the internal organization of the most revolutionary, democratically organized political parties explicitly posited in the *Parteienforschung* (party research) tradition of Weber, Moisei Ostrogorski, and James Bryce.
2) A fatalistic reflection of the necessarily plutocratic organizational tendencies of liberal representative governments, based on a suspect analogy between the modern political party and the modern state— an idea *partially* indebted to Pareto's and Mosca's theories of elitism.

Michels could have never offered his trenchant *Parteienforschung* analysis of the transformation of internal party structure had it not been for his experience as a "militant" insider of the SPD.[12] Scholars have long described Michels's defection from socialism, which he had previously termed the "ethics" of life, as the initial source of his "disillusionment" with the possibility of democracy in modern industrialized societies.[13] Whereas even in their youth, Pareto and Mosca maintained a pessimistic posture toward socialism precisely to defend themselves against the fatalistic dangers of such disillusionment, the young Michels indulged in the most faithful commitment to the emancipatory promises of democratic politics only to experience the most devastating disenchantment. His initial loyalty to the principles of socialism cost him not only the support of his most important aristocratic patrons, but also a permanent position in the German academy. Michels would later identify his "idealism of the purest kind" and subsequent disillusionment as the "determinate influence on his study of political parties."[14]

At precisely the moment in which his disenchantment with democratic socialism began to unfold, Michels encountered Weber, his most formative intellectual benefactor.[15] In the 1904–1905 edition of the *Archiv für Sozialwissenschaft und Sozialpolitik*, Weber published a call for a social scientific study of the SPD. In Weber's estimation, the SPD was the most "crucial actor" in German democratic politics, yet the basis of the party's claim to legitimacy—its representative connection to the German masses—was waning. Weber called on a social scientist to conduct a dispassionate research study "of this inexorable development" that would explain the "Americanization" of the SPD and to investigate its "devastating consequences," particularly through an investigation of the declining proletarian influences on the electors.[16] Weber specifically enlisted Michels for the job, complaining that a "cool, disinterested 'anatomy' of the Party is missing, one that does not immediately ask 'cui bono?' [Whose good?], and it can be produced neither by an outsider nor by someone directly involved as a 'Party' participant in the internal Party struggle."[17] As a former citizen of Cologne and ex-Socialist candidate for the Reichstag, Michels was the perfect candidate for the charge.

A few months later Michels formally proposed a project, following Weber's research program, studying the structure of the SPD based on his privileged vantage point as an ex-party insider.[18] The first iteration of the project, published as "Die deutsche Sozialdemokratie," (German social democracy) self-consciously adopted the criteria of confirmation from Weber's version of social science.[19] Paraphrasing Weber, Michels urges that any scientific critique "must turn to consideration of the organizational basis and tactical method that give direction to Party politics and that reciprocally condition and limit the spheres of power of Social Democracy's various ranks."[20] Here Michels elaborates Weber's stated view that the SPD will "inevitably" move toward the machine type and begin to treat politics as the art of achieving tangible, material success.[21] As Lawrence Scaff documents in his meticulous

88   DEMOCRATIC ELITISM

reconstruction of their correspondence, in this phase Weber repeatedly urged Michels to "[rethink] the meaning of 'democratic rule' under modern conditions," a theme that would later emerge in *Sociology of the Party* as "the problem of democracy."[22]

In his next iteration of the project, "Die oligarchischen Tendenzen der Gesellschaft," (The oligarchic tendencies of society) Michels emphasizes the transformation of proletarian electors into professional politicians vis-à-vis "the problem of democracy."[23] Here Michels's fatalistic picture of democracy begins to coalesce: "Ideal" or "pure" democracy, he writes, consists in "popular sovereignty" of the masses understood as the supremacy of leadership; as the supremacy of the general will in the tradition of Jean-Jacques Rousseau.[24] Applying Weber's famous "ideal type" analysis, Michels posits "real," "ideal," or "pure" democracy as the leadership of the people understood as a homogenized whole in nonrepresentative terms. As such, the fact that parties exhibit oligarchic tendencies meant that such institutions necessarily result in "false democracy."[25] Michels thus articulates a binary between "real" democracy, in which the people as a whole exercise sovereign leadership through executive decision-making, and a "false" democracy predicated on representative practices that bifurcate the people into sects, ultimately culminating in oligarchic domination. If leadership in popular government now required political parties, then democracy, at least in its true form, could never really exist in such modern circumstances.

In this early moment of his intellectual formation, Michels's vision of democracy and his consequent critique of political parties actively compete with the Italian critique of electoral government. For Pareto and Mosca, modern representative institutions are not democratic, nor should regimes based on this electoral mechanism be called "modern democracy," but not because there actually exists such a thing as an "ideal democracy" executed through popular sovereignty of the general will. As we saw in Chapters 1 and 2, unlike Rousseau and Michels, Pareto and Mosca argue that popular sovereignty understood through the concept of a general will is not only chimerical but also a dangerous threat to other institutional means of contesting elite power beyond the electorally mandated, plebiscitary invocation of a demagogic plutocrat (Pareto), or worse still, a legitimate popular insurrection that entirely destroys the state apparatus (Mosca). From the Italian perspective it made no sense to suggest there was a more "real" democracy based in the articulation of a general will—and even if there were, this regime would never constitute an "ideal" form of modern popular government for it categorically denied the pluralism of a polity. The idea that the "failure" of democracy was owing to the inability

THE EDGE OF FATALISM   89

of electoral institutions to champion the will of a cohesive, singular people was a large part of the problem: for Pareto and Mosca, Michels's vision of "pure" democracy was far from both the real and the ideal.

Michels emphasizes this very distinction by leveling an attack on Pareto and Mosca's theories, continuing his openly antagonistic posture toward the two Italians and his defense of their syndicalist / socialist interlocutors, originally published in December 1907 as "L'oligarchia organica costituzionale: Nuovi studi sulla classe politica" (Organic constitutional oligarchy: New studies on the political class).[26] Taking Mosca's *Piccola polemica* (A short polemic) (1907) as emblematic of the Italian position, Michels contends that while the idea that "the political class constitutes an indispensable and valuable element in the social life of the people" is true "up to a certain point," much of the substance of the Italians' conceptual contributions were "inadmissible." For starters, Michels questioned whether Pareto and Mosca were conducting rigorous social "scientific" theory beyond the theoretical contribution that had already been advanced by socialist and Marxist critiques. The only difference between these Italian "conservatives" and the Marxists, Michels complained, was normative: the Italians did not view minority domination as a sickness or disease to be contained—for how could they? Pareto and Mosca did not even believe in the "democratic" concept of popular sovereignty.[27] Just like his successors, Michels already misunderstands their critique of popular sovereignty and the general will as necessarily antidemocratic precepts.

In the conclusion of his polemic against Mosca, Michels announced that his future work would conduct a "closer inspection" of the oligarchic effects of organization, based on the internal structure of the party. In a letter of 1907 Mosca graciously responded to Michels's criticisms, claiming that he looked forward to his next writing with "great interest."[28] And after reading Michels's German edition of the "Die oligarchischen Tendenzen der Gesellschaft" in 1908, Mosca remarked that Michels had "played the game of critique well," and that he was intrigued by the idea that organization necessarily breeds oligarchic domination through material consolidation.[29] Yet Mosca expressed reservations about the idea that an analysis of the party could be analogized to the level of the state.[30] After all, Michels was analyzing the structure of parties, not their function. Plenty of political parties did not aim to reproduce socialist or democratic results: the idea that we should expect to find democracy inside the party was *a priori* unconvincing. This finding could only be the case if popular government required the supremacy of mass leadership in executive decision-making—a claim Mosca rejected. In response to Mosca's critique, Michels subsequently narrowed the scope of his main argument for the 1912

Italian edition of *Sociology of the Party*, such that his new thesis focused on the "effects of democracy on the internal life of parties *that profess themselves to be democratic.*"[31]

Michels spent the better part of 1906 attempting to secure a permanent university position in Germany. Despite Weber's protracted intervention, the attempt failed on account of Michels's Socialist Party membership and two amusing alleged "infractions" that became known only later.[32] Michels decided to return to Turin, where he had studied abroad, for a clean slate and a better chance at climbing the academic professional ladder. It was at this point that Michels changed his mind about the value of the Italian School of Elitism and their theoretical contributions, but he never relinquished the Weberian idea that electoral representative institutions could be equated with modern democracy.

Plutocracy: Organization and Property

Michels had clearly been working on *Sociology of the Party* with a specific research agenda and many of his theoretical ambitions in place well before his move to Italy. Yet upon arriving on the peninsula, his concerted effort to enter the Italian academy—and in particular, his intellectual encounter with Pareto and Mosca—led him to double down on plutocracy as a political problem and elite contestation as a theoretical solution.[33]

Sociology of the Party studies the composition and functioning of electoral politics through a socialist lens. In this text, Michels takes the most radical, left-wing parties of the movement as case studies to prove that in electoral governments, no party can qualify as democratic because of the bureaucratic organization that representative politics require. Having argued that a political party functions as a "state in miniature" Michels closes the work by positing his infamous "iron law of oligarchy," which can be summarized, he states, as follows: "It is organization that gives birth to the domination of the elected over the electors, of the mandatories over the mandators, of the delegates over the delegators. Who says organization, says oligarchy."[34]

Before Michels ever mentions this iron-clad law, he must explain which particular features of electoral politics necessitate a type of organization that breeds oligarchy. Much like Pareto and Mosca, Michels contends that representative institutions compel organization predicated on money, which consequently fosters plutocratic domination of the party. He takes pains to prove that in the German, French, and Italian Socialist parties, significant capital is required in order to develop the bureaucratic apparatus essential for organization, and therefore "the danger of plutocracy arises from the fact that members of parliament must necessarily be men of means." In explaining the "financial power of leaders and the party," he describes the inner workings of the vicious plutocratic cycle that pervades party structure: the party's success depends on its cohesion developed through advanced bureaucracy, which depends on the growth of the party treasury, which in turn enriches the deputies, consequently inclining any such organization to be controlled by the wealthy.[35]

In representative systems, Michels contends, plutocracy develops more subtly and through more varied channels than in other oligarchic forms. There are obvious reasons for such plutocratic domination. As one might expect, in democratic parties where the organization is "not well supplied," he explains, there frequently "arises within the party a peculiar form of financial authority, since the comrades who are better endowed with means gain and retain influence through the pecuniary services which they render." This dependence on wealthy officials promotes a state of affairs that, for him, is "eminently calculated to favor the predominance of [wealthy] deputies, who become the financial props of party administration, and thus are persons of importance whom the rank and file must treat with all possible respect."[36]

Dependence on and reverence for the wealthy appears both inside and outside of the internal apparatus to include other well-intentioned "patricians" who transcend the official party leadership. To take one crucial example, Michels asserts that "a plutocratic supremacy" develops in the press, or the communication channels of those parties that, "lacking means for the independent maintenance of their own organs, are forced to depend upon the pecuniary assistance given by well-to-do comrades" outside of the elected deputies. Even the most well-meaning philanthropic assistance to democratic aims often mutates into dependence on plutocrats, because "the principal shareholders in the newspapers," for instance, "possess a natural right of controlling its policy"—a feature that does not always benefit the egalitarian outcomes that the philanthropic assistance was initially intended to serve. During the Dreyfus affair, *L'Humanité*, the French socialist newspaper of the time, "was supported by a syndicate of wealthy Jews," but Michels suggests that for every beneficial act of philanthropy there is an equivalent one in which sinister interests prevail.[37] Following Lipset, many later commentators will take Michels's point here as merely being about officials controlling "the means of communication," eliminating the plutocratic basis for the officials' power over these communication channels in the first place.[38]

92   DEMOCRATIC ELITISM

This chain of dependence constitutes the most overt development of plutocracy within the party, a characteristic attribute of the socialist parties in France, Holland, and especially Italy, whose Socialist Party is particularly "poor" and primarily composed of "manual workers." And while the Germans fancy themselves as superior in this regard, Michels claims that the SPD can exercise more independence than its European counterparts only because of the atypical wealth of their party membership or the "well-to-do" members' ability to "contribute to the flourishing conditions of party finances"—that is, to fund the party treasury directly, without need for alms from outside private interests. At any rate, Michels goes on to show that this peculiar condition pushes toward plutocracy just the same. In Germany, "the financial superiority of the rich comrade over the poor one is often replaced by the superiority of the rich branch" over poor representation, he says, such that the party membership begins to look like a mini "aristocratic" regime far more quickly than its less-effective arms in France, Holland, or Italy.[39]

Michels acknowledges that insiders attribute the aristocratic composition of the SPD to the fact that parties will "retain their essentially plutocratic character because elected officials are usually unpaid." Remuneration may alleviate the influence of independently wealthy deputies or well-intentioned philanthropists, but Michels insists that it does not undermine the party's inherently plutocratic composition, as evidenced by the French and German examples. When a change in state law created salary funds for elected officials, the French Socialist Party began paying its deputies the relatively high rate of 600 francs annually with the stipulation that 120 francs per annum be paid as dues to the treasury to keep the party afloat, in order to maintain a party bureaucracy that does not directly depend on the pecuniary services of individual members. This measure prompted a "mass exodus" of deputies out of the party and the creation of a competing party because officials wished to "escape this heavy tax, and to preserve intact for themselves the fine round sum paid as salary by the state." Although the congresses were still marked by "interminable discussions" about how to address this issue, Michels writes, "it has not taken long to discover that to despoil the deputies of a portion of their salary does not after all constitute the most efficacious means of preventing the formation within the party of an oligarchy of plutocrats."[40]

Here Michels describes yet another element of the electoral predicament: on the one hand, elected officials must be adequately paid so that working-class members can join the governing body while avoiding direct dependence on wealthy private citizens, either among or outside of the deputies themselves.

THE EDGE OF FATALISM   93

On the other, remuneration does not protect the egalitarian elements of the organization that the party intends to preserve. Michels observes: "The non-payment of the party leaders or their remuneration on a very moderate scale does not afford any safeguard for the observance of democratic principles on the part of the officials."[41]

Even if the pitfalls exemplified by the French case can somehow be avoided, the German experience proves that plutocracy always infiltrates the party apparatus. Before 1906 the SPD paid the salaries of its deputies and did not encounter the same problems as the French, Michels says, by virtue of their "unshaken fidelity" to the ideals of the movement, a fidelity prompted by "the characteristic love of the German for his chosen vocation." Nevertheless, the SPD's bureaucratic development facilitated plutocratic control of the party just the same, albeit through different channels. An "increase in the financial strength of the party, which first renders liberal payment of the officials possible," he states, "contributes greatly to nourish the dictatorial appetites of the members of the party bureaucracy, who control the economic force of the party in virtue of their position as administrators."[42] In other words, if the party structure does not start out plutocratic, it will eventually acquire that characteristic due to increased financial power and bureaucratic advancement of the party's leaders.

Although the SPD proudly proclaims that they "have not yet lost contact with the masses," Michels says that their connection to the masses has nothing to do with egalitarianism or even representation, but actually resembles the plutocratic features of the Catholic Church.[43] As he describes it, the Church and the SPD matured along the same lines of plutocratic and hierarchically organizational expansion:

> As the wealth of the Church increased, there increased the independence of the clergy, of the ecclesiastical employees, vis-à-vis the community. As representatives of the community they were in charge of the goods. Consequently, all those who had need of these goods, or wished in any way to speculate upon them, were dependent upon the clergy. This applied not only to mendicants and to all kinds of receivers of alms, but also to those whose aim it was to swell the ranks of the clergy, or to succeed to the positions of these, all aspirants to sacerdotal honors. For the administration of the funds and for the conduct of affairs, Christianity needed a graded corps of employees. This was the origin of the hierarchy which changed the inner meaning of Christianity and perverted its aims.[44]

94 DEMOCRATIC ELITISM

For Michels, herein lies the precise "danger encountered by all democratic parties which possess an elaborate financial administration"—a danger that was especially visible in the case of the German SPD. Just like the medieval church, an electoral party needs ample "funds" to advance its political ambitions, because it requires "employees," or people, to advance those aims.[45] And yet, the more advanced the party becomes in providing the means for furthering its ambitions, the more the hierarchy in place to achieve its political ends perverts those commitments. Put differently, the hierarchical organization mandated by representative politics opposes the egalitarian aims of democratic socialist movements. As a party increases in wealth, it puts a select minority in charge of its resources.

To be clear, these employees do not stay part of the petty bourgeoisie for long. They quickly develop into a plutocratic sect because their loyalties do not remain with their previous comrades, whom they claim to represent, or even with the principles of the movement. Instead, their interests become intrinsically attached to the survival of the party.[46] More incisively, Michels says, the deputies come to believe that their own interests and the party are one and the same—all of a sudden, just like Louis XIV, they begin to the believe that "Le Parti, c'est moi."[47] Henceforth entrain all the characteristics typical of a plutocratic caste. Nepotism, for example, develops within one generation, as the children of the new deputies often succeed their fathers in their roles, thanks to the "bourgeois upbringing" that their parents were able to buy with their party salaries. This phenomenon accelerates exponentially, Michels claims, to the point where "a constituency comes to be regarded as family *property.*"[48]

Michels here describes a classic Catch-22: no matter which preventative measures are established, plutocracy develops out of electoral systems in which the political party constitutes the mechanism of representation. Most often, party revenue comes from direct contributions of the wealthy patrons, which creates dependence and entrenches the patrons in positions of leadership. If the treasury is supplied through the state or other means, the hierarchical structure needed to advance its political aims creates a minority cut off from the majority by access to its resources. The plutocratic-electoral nexus, Michels laments, "brings into existence strict relationships of dependence, of hierarchical superiority and inferiority, engendered by the invisible force of the great god Money."[49]

Adopting Pareto's and Mosca's reprimand to their own peers, Michels scolds the SPD for claiming exceptionalism in their democratically organized party structure. In some sense they are the greatest offenders, he intimates, as they have adopted the same plutocratic means of oppression that the Catholic

Church deployed at the apex of its financial power. With the bureaucratic apparatus at its fingertips, Michels accuses party leaders of having "for years ... employed numerous methods of oppression, such as the threat to give no aid either in men or money on behalf of the electoral propaganda of a candidate from whose views they dissent," despite the fact that the "local comrades give this candidate their full confidence." The SPD's claims to superiority are particularly appalling to the working-class masses in light of the party's constant touting of their motto, "Ni Dieu ni maître" (Neither gods, nor masters.) To everyone outside of the SPD leadership, including Michels, it is obvious that the "great god Money" clearly triumphs.[50]

Michels thus emphatically underscores the "financial power of leaders" in a way that attests to the systemic plutocracy inherent in the electoral party structure. Far from being tangential, the idea that electoral organization depends on the development of a plutocratic sect is the basis for his contention that organization generates oligarchy; it is the reason he insists that "who says organization, says oligarchy." While the dictum itself seems to focus only on oligarchy, Michels insists that parties are particularly prone to oligarchy because of their need to raise money.

In his classic 1953 study on the iron law of oligarchy published in the *American Political Science Review,* C. W. Cassinelli argues that the term "oligarchy" is too narrow for the phenomenon that Michels sought to describe. Cassinelli suggests that Michels must have meant something else far less aristocratic than it sounds, and certainly did not mean to propose an affinity between plutocracy and representative government. The "term 'oligarchy' is not especially fortunate," Cassinelli writes, "since its ordinary connotation is more narrow than the one that must be given it in the present discussion, and since it is ordinarily ambiguous, referring both to rule by the few and to rule by the wealthy."[51] Michels was indeed clearly referring "both to rule by the few and to rule by the wealthy," but like so many Anglo-American political scientists, Cassinelli would not entertain the notion that representative government instantiates the necessarily plutocratic features that, for Michels, party organization requires.

Oligarchy: Organization, Minority Domination, and Elite Competition

Through the work of postwar political scientists, who were intent on advancing democracy understood as representative government, Michels came to be identified as a theorist of oligarchy and not of plutocracy.[52] This characterization is somewhat unfortunate, but it points toward one reason Mosca and Michels

96   DEMOCRATIC ELITISM

have been so often coupled in the last century. Both the Italian and the German identify plutocracy as the means by which a minority group exerts oligarchic power in electoral government; but unlike Pareto, they subsume plutocracy into their respective accounts of oligarchy, an element that prompts later interpreters to entirely neglect their worry over the particularly plutocratic threats of representative politics.[53]

Michels thus assumes Mosca's cynical orientation toward how electoral institutions, through economic inequalities, structure organization such that a minority always rules. However, Mosca and Michels disagree about the causal direction of this relationship. In Giorgio Sola's pithy formulation, "For Mosca, oligarchy adopts an organization in order to consolidate and impose its power; for Michels it is organization that generates oligarchy, in order to ensure its survival in a hostile environment and achieve the goals it proposes to achieve."[54]

For Mosca, elites organize because they recognize, subconsciously or otherwise, that they are a minority and decide that they must preemptively combat the majority's numerical superiority. In Mosca's analysis, existing minorities in representative polities use organizational tactics provided by the electoral system in order to consolidate their power. Michels, however, identifies a different starting point with more far-ranging implications: Not only does oligarchy spring from organization, he argues, but so do all forms of democratic action. Michels identifies organization as the source of both oligarchy and democracy.

According to Michels, proletarian interests require the organizational oligarchy mandated by representative politics because existing plutocratic interests are too strong a force to oppose. "In the hands of those who are economically stronger," Michels states, "the working class is defenseless." In order to fight those economically superior forces, the masses must "acquire the faculty of political resistance and attain social dignity only by combination to form a structural aggregate"—that is to say, only by organizing their numerical majority and by combining into a cohesive group. And yet again, when the masses come together to develop and coordinate that structural aggregate against the economically superior minority, he writes, they are themselves ensnared into the same trap of domination: "Yet this politically necessary principle of organization, while it overcomes that disorganization of forces which would be favorable to the adversary, brings other dangers in its train. We escape Scylla only to dash ourselves on Charybdis. Organization, in fact, is the source from which the conservative currents flow over the plain of democracy, occasioning there disastrous floods and rendering the plain unrecognizable."[55] For Michels, at least within representative government, organization is *"the only weapon* of the weak against the strong"; it constitutes *"the only means* for creation of a collective will." But once the working classes have organized, he says, then, failing to recognize "the real fount of the oligarchical evil in the centralization of power within the party, they often consider the best means of counteracting oligarchy is to intensify this very centralization." For this reason, "as democracy continues to develop, a backwash sets in," and "with the advance of organization, democracy tends to decline."[56] In this tautological paradigm where organization constitutes the "real fount" of oligarchy and democracy, minority domination may indeed seem a force so formidable that it cannot be resisted.

Michels nevertheless offers some qualified hope, as he eventually concludes that the chances for success in the battle against elite domination "will depend upon the degree to which this struggle is carried out upon a basis of solidarity between individuals whose interests are identical."[57] But given Michels's brutal account of the organization of leadership both within the oligarchic consolidation of power *and* within nascent democratic action that aims to combat this consolidation, "identical" sounds like too high a bar. Whereas Mosca proposes to keep interests aligned by alleviating gross economic inequality, Michels remains silent on this score, and his pessimism seems to suggest more determinism than he will ultimately claim there is.

Beyond his elaboration of the relationship between organization and oligarchy, Michels also adopts Mosca's interpretation of class struggle and the need for "multiplicities" of elite groups to combat the plutocratic effects of representative government. Thanks to Mosca, Michels writes, we are encouraged to think of class struggle, not in terms of progressive development between the minority and the majority, but instead as the "eternal struggle" that really comes down to a "battle between an old minority . . . and a new and ambitious minority, intent upon the conquest of power, desiring either to fuse with the former or to dethrone and replace it." But Mosca, Michels acknowledges, demonstrates that this battle need not imply entirely defeatist consequences, for at least within electoral institutions this contestation of a corrupt, decaying elite group by an invigorated one "prevents the formation of a single gigantic oligarchy, [resulting] merely in the creation of a number of smaller oligarchies, each of which is no less powerful within its own sphere"—an early iteration of what will become Dahl's polyarchy.[58]

As discussed in Chapters 2 and 4, Mosca insists on the need for "multiplicities" of elite groups in representative bodies. For Mosca, "the democratic impulse" attests to the replenishing of the ruling class with lower-class membership, and the circulation of power between minority groups constitutes "the liberal principle." Mosca claims that in representative government, power can be transferred in the autocratic way, top-down, with the members of the ruling class selected by inheritance or co-optation by those who are already in power. Alternatively, power can be transferred in "the liberal way," in which power is delegated by the governed to the governing classes by way of elections. The two systems, he says, "may be fused and balanced in various ways, as happens in representative governments today," where the president is chosen by the citizens and in turn has the power to appoint federal government officials and the Supreme Court magistrates.[59] In contrast to these two methods, the "democratic impulse" creates genuine opportunities for lower classes to swell the ranks of leadership by means other than elections. In Mosca's vision, both mechanisms can exist in modern popular government, but representative systems, without supplementation, do not facilitate the democratic impulse.

Michels deploys Mosca's thought here with a more concerted emphasis on the "prolonged struggle for dominion between [equal] factions within the party," and by implication, the competition between sects outside of the parties on the state level.[60] The competition between elite factions *within and between* parties results in a seemingly proto-Schumpeterian conception of democracy: under electoral schemes, Michels writes, "the democratic system is reduced, in ultimate analysis, to the right of the masses, at state intervals, to choose masters to whom in the interim they owe unconditional obedience."[61] The struggle between parties is not a struggle "of principle," he states, but "simply [one] of competition."[62]

Here Michels makes a crucial change to Mosca's doctrine. By adopting Mosca's focus on "multiplicities" of minority groups but eliminating the democratic institutional focus on elite contestation specifically *from below*, Michels omits an important feature of Mosca's counter-oligarchic vision and his eventual defense of representative government. Mosca maintains that the "democratic impulse" underscores the need for integrating lower classes into government in some form beyond the mere exercise of their electoral power. Alternatively, Michels removes the focus on the majority's access to positions of leadership and replaces it with the contest *between* elite sects. Competition between elites, both Mosca and Michels argue, is endogenous to representative systems, which of course we can all admit is better than no competition at all. But Michels at times is willing to call this competition "democratic," whereas Mosca would have entirely rejected that label to describe elite circulation within representative polities.

THE EDGE OF FATALISM   99

Michels thus weaves two features of Mosca's thought (oligarchic organization and multiplicities of elites that liberal institutions engender) into his own theory of competition between elites in representative regimes. The competitive feature of the electoral system attracted many postwar political scientists to Michels's thought. Commentators would later argue that Michels honestly directs us, not just toward the silver lining of electoral organization as Mosca would have it, but to the essence of modern democratic politics.

To take one portentous example, in a 1965 issue of the *American Political Science Review*, John May offered Michels as a theorist of "democratization." May maintains that even though Michels proposes that "organization precludes democracy, and can destroy democracy," the most important feature of his thought attunes us to how organization can "facilitate democratization."[63] While May admits that "Michels does not deal explicitly with the possibility that organization can facilitate the democratization of groups within society," he claims that the idea can be "inferred" because Michels proves that "increments of organization necessitate delegation and dispersal of authority." In this respect, May attributes "delegation" and "dispersal of authority" to Michels's account of democracy, not of representative government or electoral politics. Michels's theory, May continues, might never bring about "the equalization of resources among members and the conformity of leaders' policies to followers' wishes," but it will result in the "mitigation of informal dictatorship," which is what democracy, for May at least, must mean in the modern era.[64]

In this fashion, during the immediate postwar period, political scientists treated Pareto and Mosca as irredeemable Fascist theorists, and Michels as one who could be reconstructed for democratic purposes. Michels seemed to be a more attractive exponent of the Italian School of Elitism because his critique of electoral institutions does not assert the antidemocratic character of representative government as forcefully as the Italians do. Not only did Pareto and Mosca avoid conflating modern democracy with elections; they believed that insisting upon the substantive difference between the two would inspire opposition to existing elite rule and promote more egalitarian outcomes than could be otherwise expected. Similarly, Michels often states that representative institutions *only appear* to advance popular participation while actually perverting it, and he even adopts the Italians' hope that ruthless exposure will promote the asymptotic fulfillment of popular sovereignty. And yet, crucially, he does not distinguish between democracy and representation as thoroughly as his predecessors did. In fact, Michels simultaneously brings to light the "myths of popular representations" that plagued Pareto and Mosca's thought while confusingly calling it "modern democracy" just the same:[65]

> In modern day democracy it is held that no one may disobey the orders of the oligarchs, for in so doing the people sin against themselves defying their own will spontaneously transferred by them to their representatives, and thus infringing [upon] democratic principles. In democracies the leaders base their right to command on the democratic omnipotence of the masses.... In practice, however the election of leaders, and above all their re-election, is effected by such methods of coercion so powerful that the freedom of choice of the masses is considerably impaired.[66]

Some political scientists—Lipset, for example—admitted that representation was completely alien to Michels's conception of "applied democracy."[67] Nevertheless, Michels exhibits fewer reservations concerning representation, describing it as "modern-day democracy" or "what we know as the era of democracy," thus prompting American political scientists to glean a credible, new theory of democratic politics—one that fused electoral practices, representation, and popular participation—based on Michels's thought.[68]

Elites: "The Chiefs" and the Technical "Indispensability" of Leadership

Michels transforms Mosca's key concerns over the plutocracy-elections nexus into a vision of "modern democracy" redefined as elite competition; as a result, appropriations of *Sociology of the Party* for contemporary democracy proliferated in the postwar Anglo-American world. Virtually all of these reconstructions, however, eschewed Michels's purported elitist disdain for mass incompetence, and they distanced themselves from his unfortunate reliance on the "social psychological" propositions fashionable in his time.[69] David Beetham argues that Michels's Fascist sympathies can be linked at least partially to the prevalence of such theories in *Sociology of the Party*.[70] Robert Nye's criticism of Michels's use of crowd psychology to disparage the masses or the mob is also cited regularly in the literature.[71] All such accounts link Pareto and Michels to crowd psychologist Gustave Le Bon, from whom both Pareto and Michels directly inherited their supposed disdain for the masses' epistemic incapacities for politics.[72]

Political scientists' relentless emphasis on Pareto's and Michels's interest in crowd psychology and the incompetence of the masses is strange because both theorists primarily feared *elite* incompetence and incapacity for government. Both of their descriptions of mass psychology, moreover, are contingent on elite behavior. In *Sociology of the Party*, Michels continually accuses political leaders of engaging in deliberate and dishonest machinations to oppress the masses. More like Pareto than Mosca, Michels's critique exhibits an aggressive, rhetorical orientation toward existing elites. His vitriol for "the chiefs" is no less cutting than Pareto's, stressing that leaders sow disunion within the parties and betray democratic aspirations.[73]

Michels constantly highlights how even when party leaders start with the best motivations, they intentionally discourage the masses from participating by confusing them, but not in a way that supposes that the masses have cognitive shortcomings.[74] On the subject of simple voting, Michels states: "To justify the substitution of the indirect vote for the direct vote, the leaders invoke, in addition to political motives, the complicated structure of the party organization." Even the referendum's disuse and ineffectiveness, he claims, is the fault of the leaders who undermine them: "It is easy for the chiefs to lead the masses astray by clever phrasing of the questions, and by reserving to themselves the right of interpretation in the case of replies which are ambiguous precisely because the questions have been ambiguously posed." In this case, the masses fully recognize the ambiguity of the questions they are being asked to answer, Michels says, because the questions were purposefully written to be deceptive. The "disunion" that subsequently ensues in the parties, therefore, "is almost always the work of leaders."[75]

Michels explicates another dimension of minority domination, explaining the reasons for political passivity among the masses and absolving the latter for adopting such an orientation. He complains that the chiefs ignore all "legal, logical, and economic bonds which unite the paid leaders to the paying masses"—thereby rejecting the age-old idea that leaders are held accountable through electoral competition. The masses, he continues, "are sulky, but never rebel for they lack power to punish the treachery of the chiefs."[76] Put differently, it is not that the majority are epistemically incapable of knowing that they are being exploited; instead their oppression and powerlessness inhibit them from doing anything about it.

Michels does not merely absolve the masses for their passivity in rhetorical asides. Besides charging elites with corruption and dishonesty, two crucial aspects of his argument undermine the unfavorable view of the masses that later interpreters attribute to him. Firstly, he declares that the chiefs are in no way genuine *aristoi* (the best) or even intellectually superior to the crowd: the "reverence paid to leaders" is mostly an expression of "respect" rather than an estimation of their "true intellectual worth." Secondly, he maintains that the masses are politically passive, not because they are stupid, gullible, or incapable, but instead because their oppression makes them grateful to those "who speak and write on their behalf." For Michels, this gratitude serves as an understandable palliative for their oppression, offering them a semblance of hope amid otherwise bleak prospects for emancipation. More importantly, in a world where "megalomaniacal" leaders desirous of flattery have the power to substantively alter their constituents' quality of life, Michels opines that mass gratitude bordering on cult veneration makes perfect sense. After all, the chiefs will distribute favors to the masses only if they are compensated with the "hero-worship" that in a rather "comical" sense such party leader and demagogues presume themselves to deserve.[77] Michels suggests that while the masses may be somewhat complicit in their own subjection, this complicity certainly does not indicate any significant cognitive deficiency, nor does it make them responsible for it. They fawn over the emperor's absent clothing and hope for the best.

Contrary to how we remember Michels's text, *Sociology of the Party* does not merely seek to confirm early twentieth-century crowd psychology theories and apply them to the masses of the political sphere. Even Michels's references to Le Bon in no way validate the crowd psychology of the masses; instead they point to the psychology of leaders who become more delusional than members of a mob through their struggle for power. Michels cites Le Bon approvingly in order to psychologize about *leadership* and to explain how modern political leaders, who begin on equal footing with the masses, develop "autocratic" personalities as they become professional politicians. In Michels's words, "Le Bon writes with good reason: 'The leader has usually been at one time the led. He himself has been hypnotized by the idea of which he afterwards becomes the apostate.'"[78]

In fact, the guiding question of the work asks how leaders—who arise "spontaneously" and initially serve an "accessory" and "gratuitous" function—become, over the course of time, "irremovable."[79] Devoting much of its energy to deconstructing the psychology of leaders, the book not only undermines assumptions of their formal superiority, but also rationalizes the gratitude of the led without suggesting the latter's cognitive incapacity or responsibility for their own subjection.

Michels develops these two ideas of elite delusions of grandeur and resigned mass gratitude consistently throughout the text, so much so that when he finally presents the "iron law of oligarchy" at the end of the book, they are built into his presentation of this so-called law:

THE EDGE OF FATALISM 103

> Now, *if we are to leave out* consideration of the tendency of the leaders to organize themselves and to consolidate their interests, *and if we leave out* of consideration the gratitude of the led towards the leaders, and the general immobility and the passivity of the masses, we are led to conclude that the principal cause of oligarchy in the democratic parties is to be found in the technical indispensability of leadership.[80]

While Michels concedes the existence of a certain passivity on the part of the masses, it sets in only after leadership has been consolidated and the led experience a modicum of gratitude. As a whole, *Sociology of the Party* develops the first two "considerations" (megalomania and gratitude) from the above quote at the substantive expense of the third (passivity). It is both somewhat odd and perhaps telling that Michels, in his explication of the iron law of oligarchy, asks the reader to set aside two critical considerations that his entire book accentuates: namely, how exactly leaders collude with each other despite their expressly conflicting political agendas, and how the masses tend to express unwarranted gratitude for this so-called leadership. If we take the iron law of oligarchy at face value, then the technical indispensability of leadership, and hence oligarchy, can be granted only by "leaving out" the "considerations" that he says decisively affect organizational structure in modern society. The widespread contention that mass passivity—rather than elite corruption—was the major object of Michels's disdain is a striking perversion of his actual sentiments and general attitude.

More than any other text, Seymour Martin Lipset's 1961 introduction to *Political Parties* (as *Sociology of the Party* was known to its English readers) facilitated this perversion by refocusing Michels's critique away from elites and by ascribing positive normative assessments to Michels's account of oligarchy. Lipset contends that Michels chose to investigate socialist organizations only to prove that even the most democratic-leaning organizations are hypocritical, and "as such found it difficult to believe in any sustained democratic ideologies or movements, even as lesser evils." As a result, Michels's "view of society and organization as divided between elites and followers," according to Lipset, "led Michels to accept the idea that the best government is an avowedly elitist system under the leadership of a charismatic leader."[81]

While Lipset may have anachronistically projected this view onto the early Michels because of the latter's eventual association with Italian Fascism, this is, at least according to the letter of *Political Parties*, completely inappropriate. Not only does Michels claim that "we must choose democracy as the least of

104 DEMOCRATIC ELITISM

evils" and demand that humanity "recognize the advantages which democracy, however imperfect, presents over aristocracy"; he also extols the virtues of democracy and its contribution to individual development and human flourishing.[82] In fact, the young Michels explicitly warns against the interpretation that Lipset would arrive at when he claims that he

> does not wish to deny that every revolutionary working-class movement, and every movement sincerely inspired by the democratic spirit, may have a certain value as contributing to the enfeeblement of oligarchic tendencies. . . . Democracy is a treasure which no one will ever discover by deliberate search. But in continuing our search . . . we shall preform work which will have fertile results in the democratic sense.[83]

"The error of the socialists," Michels continues, lies in their "rosy optimism and immeasurable confidence regarding the future," but that does not mean that we must abandon the desperate enterprise of seeking the "treasure" of democracy that lies "buried" in the "bosom of the democratic working-class party." For Michels the cynical orientation toward electoral procedures ought to encourage a focus on its two main panaceas: concentrated efforts to improve lower-class "social education" and "economic" status, so that the masses "may be enabled . . . to counteract the oligarchical tendencies of the working-class movement."[84] At the time of writing his first book, Michels uses political pessimism in order to preserve the "treasure of democracy" in a way reminiscent of the Italians' efforts, as his theory seeks to equalize access to education and material wealth.[85]

Lipset ignores these efforts, or what I call the Italian disposition, which Michels explained more pointedly than any of his peers: the inclination to honestly expose the deficiencies of elite rule in order to encourage a greater striving for democracy and popular sovereignty. On a basic level, to deny the influence of leaders, Michels writes, is "to strengthen the rule of the leaders, for it serves to conceal from the mass a danger which really threatens democracy." He reminds us that "nothing but a serene and frank examination of the oligarchical dangers of democracy will enable us to minimize these dangers, even though they can never be entirely avoided."[86] Lipset commits the exact "error" against which Michels warns in the closing chapter of *Political Parties*—that is, Lipset reads Michels's work as a justification to "abandon the desperate enterprise of endeavoring to discover a social order which will *render possible the complete realization* of the idea of popular sovereignty." Despite the tragic plutocratic qualities of parliamentary regimes, Michels emphasizes that his efforts aim to "throw light upon certain . . . tendencies which oppose the reign of democracy" so that these tendencies can be better combated, not passively accepted as faits accomplis.[87]

Italian versus German Pessimism: Michels and Weber

Pareto, Mosca, and Michels—also known as "the Modern Machiavellians"— offer biting critiques of elites, plutocracy, and oligarchy, frankly exposing elite domination so that democratic theory and practice might better control and contain it.[88] All three democratic theorists of elitism quite self-consciously employed a pessimistic disposition, but not because they were encouraging quietist acceptance of incontestable structures of hierarchical power. Rather, their pessimism is intended to motivate a kind of strategic vigilance against the plutocratic hierarchy that they diagnose as pervading liberal governments— and, more generally, strategic vigilance against the continuous threat of democracy devolving into oligarchy as a result of the consolidation of leadership.

In recent years Jeffrey Green has derided contemporary liberal thinkers' "excessive sunniness . . . regarding the problem of plutocracy," and thereby revives a new variant of Italian pessimism.[89] Green, too, understands plutocracy as an integral component of liberal-democratic states, and consequently argues that we ought to not only strive to "reduce plutocracy" but also develop strategies that "retrospectively respond" to it.[90] I contend that adopting such a pessimistic disposition in itself is one such retrospective response, for it serves as an offensive / defensive strategy against the liberal plutocratic nexus that Pareto, Mosca, and Michels detail with refreshing honesty.

However, not all pessimistic dispositions are the same, or directed toward identical ends. This difference in literary expression can already be seen in a comparison of Pareto and Mosca, on the one hand, and in Michels, on the other. For starters, Michels, a German in Italy, explicitly states the purpose of his pessimism in a way that his Italian counterparts would have never dreamed of admitting, for fear of undermining the force of their own pessimism. Moreover, the Italian disdain for equating democracy and representative regimes does not translate into the German's political concerns. As suggested by the title of his book, *On the Sociology of the Party System in Modern Democracy*, for Michels the distinction between "modern democracy" and electoral institutions is a terminological issue. At the very least, for all intents and purposes modern democracy should be seen as distinct from the "applied democracy" of the past, and therefore the "frequent repetition of election is an elementary precaution on the part of democracy against the virus of oligarchy."[91] For the Italians, frequent repetition of elections is of course necessary, but the conflation of democracy and electoral regimes directly undermines the legitimacy and durability of popular government. The equation cannot be a matter of mere semantics, because it raises unrealistic expectations of what elections on their own can achieve.

In addition, Michels's broad focus on oligarchy, as opposed to a localized critique of its specifically plutocratic strain, pushes more extreme conclusions that seem to border on encouraging resignation. Chapters 1 and 2 revealed that despite the Italians' reputation for preferring abstract principles and generalizable political laws, both Pareto and Mosca, like Machiavelli, allow the reader "to breathe the fine dry air" of the Italian peninsula during the Risorgimento. Pareto's and Mosca's concentrated focus on the plutocratic challenge facing Italian parliamentarism suggests remedies that can be implemented to alleviate plutocratic corruption, at least if one is attuned to the highly corrupt electoral environment in which the Italians were operating. Their pessimistic warnings, whether of the angry or the sober variety, exhibit no fatalistic valence; even in the face of Fascist authoritarian threats, they still doggedly aim to inspire new defensive strategies against such corruption and establish the unification of Italy on stronger popular, egalitarian—dare we say democratic— grounds. By contrast, Michels's more muted emphasis on plutocracy and his equation of electoral systems with "modern democracy" obfuscates the reforms to oligarchic domination, institutional or otherwise, that he poses at the end of the work. Without the overt goal of attenuating plutocracy in the Italian post-unification process, the elements that encourage democratic reform become a lost afterthought in his analysis. Although Peter LaVenia makes an argument antithetical to the one presented here, he accurately maintains that "the use of Mosca's and Pareto's theoretical observations did not rank him as their follower, either."[92]

In the mid-1920s Michels veers ever further from Pareto's and Mosca's presuppositions about the constitution of a ruling class. Unlike the Italians, Michels comes to believe that, in any case, it is impossible for ruling classes to be replaced, that "absorption" is always a more accurate description of the process, and that even still, charismatic authority is the only authentic bridge between mass participation and political leadership in modern-day polities.[93] Even in *Sociology of the Party*, Michels accepts Pareto and Mosca's point about replacement of the ruling class only with "considerable reserve," and therefore easily forsakes it in favor of the model of charismatic authority at the advent of Mussolini's ascent to power.[94] In 1924–1925 Michels writes an entirely new edition of *Sociology of the Party* in which he abandons his earlier focus on the two panaceas of representative government, instead highlighting the connection between plebiscitary politics and true democracy. To this day, the standard English translation has always been the 1915 *Political Parties* edition based on the 1912 Italian translation, which means that it is unlikely Anglo-American political scientists knew that Michels later made radical changes and amendments to his work.

Given these differences between Italian and German expressions of political pessimism, Michels might have been more susceptible to abandoning the defensive postures of Pareto and Mosca, and therefore less wary of charismatic leadership manifesting itself in an autocratic regime. Although the conventional narrative suggests that Michels became a preeminent *fasciste* thinker by way of the Italian influence, it might just as well have been that his ultimate embrace of Fascist ideology was prompted specifically by ideas of Weber, his real *Doktorvater*, who presents plebiscitary democracy and executive authority based on personality in a far less critical fashion than the Italian theorists of elitism.[95] As Wolfgang Mommsen explains, over time—incidentally, right before Michels began to curry favor with Mussolini—Weber came to believe that the exogenous force of"'plebiscitarian democracy' . . . served as a counterweight to the bureaucratization of the apparatuses of power."[96] This evolution from proponent of bureaucratization to skeptic led Weber to advocate a "plebiscitary democracy" in which a popularly elected, charismatic leader should be given substantial executive power to break out from the "iron cage of modernity" to escape the "iron clad law of oligarchy."[97]

Above all else, Pareto and Mosca feared invocations of charismatic authority as a legitimating justification for political rule. Their cynical approach toward the democratic possibilities of electoral institutions aimed to encourage reform of the plutocratic tendencies that might lead to authoritarian transformation, regardless of whether this transformation resulted in an autocratic, Byzantine, demagogic, or Fascist form. The originality of their contribution was to connect the intrinsic plutocratic threats of electoralism to demagogic usurpation *through* the problematic conflation of elections and democracy. Put differently, their main theoretical lesson was that equating elections and democracy will only precipitate demagogic usurpation of electoral institutions—a warning that Michels, a German émigré somewhat alienated from the plutocratic context of the Risorgimento, could not appreciate or heed. As H. Stuart Hughes aptly put it, "there is a quaint justice in the fact that it was [Michels], the least original among the trio of neo-Machiavellians, who found Fascism the least troubling."[98]

108   DEMOCRATIC ELITISM

The historical records also give us some speculative reasons to believe that Michels's defense of charismatic authority and his foray into Italian Fascism displeased Mosca, who ultimately distanced himself from his brilliant German "pupil."[99] In July 1932 Michels wrote to Mosca proposing himself as the natural heir to Mosca's academic chair at the University of Rome.[100] After a long list of the reasons he was the obvious successor, Michels enumerates the ways he has furthered Mosca's academic agenda and scientific methodology throughout the course of his career. Yet despite this nearly sycophantic praise, Mosca politely dismisses Michels's request for support and claims that he holds less power in the appointment process than Michels presumes—a clear slight to Michels, who knew, just like everyone else did, that Mosca's vote would be decisive in selecting his successor.[101]

Ettore Albertoni notes, "It was Michels himself who always referred to Mosca as one of his mentors"—and never the other way around.[102] Although he may have initially been hopeful about the potential of Michels's early work, Mosca most certainly did not condone the way Michels turns his critique of representative government and distrust for elites into a defense of Mussolini's dictatorship.[103] Indeed, as early as December 1925 Mosca had made his hostile position on Mussolini quite clear in his Senate resignation speech.[104] Presumably, it took a significant amount of gall and self-delusion for Michels to think that Mosca would entertain the idea of endorsing a Fascist faculty member to assume his university chair and informal stewardship of the Italian School of Elitism.

It also seems that Mosca disapproved of the way Michels deployed the pessimistic posture of the Italian School. In response to James Meisel's postwar appellation, both Albertoni and Francesco Tuccari have recently argued that Mosca rather quickly abandoned the hope of adopting Michels into his school of thought and soon came to view him more as a rival—and certainly not as a disciple.[105] Perhaps Pareto's and Mosca's pessimistic "tempo"—a style that seeks to constrain plutocracy through relentless criticism of elites—cannot be easily "translated" outside of the Italian context, shaped by democratically inspired antagonism toward liberalism's plutocratic tendencies. Without this background, the tone in Michels's study of oligarchy may seem to encourage resignation to elite rule despite his initial explicit pronouncements to the contrary in *Sociology of the Party*.

In this sense Michels's cynical attitude drove Italian pessimism to the edge of fatalism. His analysis of the oligarchic elements of representative government and their relationship to democracy danced on the line between exposure of minority domination and insistence on its inevitability. But there are certainly far more types of pessimistic posture than the angry, sober, or nearly resigned ones of Pareto, Mosca, and Michels. As we shall see, Schumpeter's attitude toward elites is just as pessimistic as his Italian and German predecessors. But his sardonic irony exhibits a completely different tenor of distrust for elites, manifesting itself in a different kind of disappointment in them that necessitates different prescriptions for confronting the problems that electoral government and representation pose to democracy.

The Modern Machiavellians Reconsidered: 1912–1943

Michels's *Sociology of the Party* is the product of competing German and Italian heritages that managed to displease both sides of its ancestry. Even though Weber supported the turn to charismatic authority, in the end he judged Michels to be an overly "moralistic ideologue" who ultimately confused "the problem of democracy" with "the problem of bureaucracy" and "the problem of domination."[106] And yet, to put it in Wilfred Rohrich's formulation, the scholarly consensus has always insisted that "Weber stands in the background as the questioner, as the *Realpolitiker* whose questions determine the direction of many an answer" in all of Michels's writings.[107] On the Italian side, Mosca snubbed his presumed heir apparent, rejected many of his substantive conclusions, and famously ended up on the opposite side of the political landscape. Nevertheless, despite the vast scholarship on the strong theoretical connections between Weber and Michels and the documented record of Mosca's politically fraught relationship with Michels, Michels earned his place as the third founding member of the Italian School of Elitism. This peculiar lineage can be explained by the intersection of two historical contingencies: (1) Michels's ultimate rejection of Weber and self-proclaimed identification with Pareto and Mosca, and (2) the suspect but eventually decisive development of the "Machiavellian" realist tradition in American political science.

From the outset, Michels was primarily responsible for generating confusion about his intellectual commitments and political identifications. Between 1907 and 1925, Michels found himself in a precarious professional position and was justifiably concerned about the reception of his work. Consequently, he significantly revised a myriad of different editions and translations of *Sociology of the Party*, continually altering the avowed sources of his thought in a way that made it more amenable to a wider range of audiences. As his prospects in the German academy dwindled, and as it became increasingly clear between 1907 and 1911 that his comrades and supporters from Turin such as Antonio Labriola and Achille Loria could offer him no more secure academic patronage, these alterations increasingly indicated that Michels took himself to be faithfully following in the footsteps of the more internationally established and critically acclaimed scholars Pareto and Mosca.[108]

In the space of three years, Michels inverted the acknowledgments of *Sociology of the Party* from a focus on its Weberian foundations to an emphasis on the Italian influences. In 1911 Michels dedicated the German edition to his "dear friend" and "kindred soul" Weber, "that upright man who does not shy away from vivisection if it is in the interest of science."[109] But that very same year Michels began to make "ample and significant changes" such that the 1912 Italian translation replaced his dedication to Weber with one to "our" Gaetano Mosca.[110] In this introduction, Michels described himself as following the roads paved by Pareto and especially Mosca while significantly diminishing Weber's role in the production of the manuscript.[111] Similarly, in his 1913 letters to Gustave Le Bon, director of the Bibliothèque de philosophie scientifique for Flammarion, in which the French translation of *Sociology of the Party* appeared, Michels professes to make "radical revisions" on crowd psychology, resulting in an almost entirely new manuscript.[112] Nearly every audience had its own version of the book, with one crucial exception: the 1915 translation by Eden and Cedar Paul was based on the 1912 Italian edition, and not the original German edition, which obscured many of the underlying Weberian motivations and paradigms of the work. What is more, in the 1915 dedication, Michels's acknowledgments of Weber became even more guarded, and his ties to the Italian School more pronounced, suggesting to American audiences that the Italians were the more important progenitors of Michels's thought.

In the same year, political disagreements about the war and a messy quarrel over Michels's publicist activities in Switzerland put an end to the ten-year friendship between Weber and Michels. The sensational rupture between Michels and his advisor pushed the jobless Michels to identify intellectually more with his Italian interlocutors. Michels's efforts were not in vain, and he eventually assimilated into the upper echelon of Italian society. In 1933 Michels's daughter Manon married Luigi Einaudi's son Mario, entrenching Michels's family in the crème de la crème of the Italian intellectual class. This union generated a crucial connection to the liberal Italian elite despite Michels's association with the Fascists. After the war this connection certainly helped obscure the fact that Michels had died (in 1936) a committed Mussolini supporter.

Even still, Italian intellectuals were hesitant to embrace Michels as a part of their tradition of political thought. Fate would have it that American political science became responsible for "embroiling" Michels in the Italian School of Elitism through its identification of Mosca, Pareto, and Michels as "the Modern Machiavellians."[113] While *Sociology of the Party* had been circulated in the Anglo-American world as early as 1915, Pareto and Mosca had not been available to English-speaking audiences until the 1930s.[114] In 1939, as James Burnham, a New York University political theorist and the chair of the philosophy department, was writing *The Managerial Revolution* (1941) on the Lower East Side, on the Upper West Side, Arthur Livingston finished his translations of Pareto and Mosca, which he famously described in the introduction to *The Ruling Class* as an "enterprise for making monuments of Italian Machiavellian thought available to English-speaking scholars."[115] In his next work, *The Machiavellians: Defenders of Freedom* (1943), Burnham seized upon Livingston's epithet for Mosca and Pareto and assimilated Michels into this "neo-Machiavellian" category. These Machiavellians, he suggests, offered the proper "realist" methodological and theoretical orientation to fight the managerial revolution against the technocratic stifling of political liberty.

Burnham places Michels in the company of his fellow political "realist" contemporaries Mosca, Pareto, and Georges Sorel. Burnham sees these figures as being like Machiavelli in that they take the facts "as they are" and do not assume the desirability of any ideal goal such as justice or peace in a political community. Strangely enough, Burnham claims that Michels (and even Pareto) should be considered Machiavellians more by way of the Frenchman Sorel's "realistic" justification of political violence than by way of the strictly Italian influence. Be that as it may, *Sociology of the Party* was essential to the modern variant of the Machiavellian tradition because it squarely faced the "the problem of democracy" or "the limits of democracy." In Burnham's eyes, *Sociology of the Party* is a book about democracy—not about parliamentarism or electoral party structure or its transformation—but democracy itself in its purest, most "ideal form." More specifically, he argues, Michels's work reveals the "unrealizability" of democracy based on an analysis of the principles of organization: it is simply "impossible for a large group . . . to make a quick decision; there is just no way for all the members to participate."[116] According to Burnham, these Machiavellian realists accepted that democracy understood as a mass decision-making apparatus could never exist and consequently reoriented their political expectations around that fact.

Burnham's reading crystallizes a moment of the closing of the American mind. Without the strong separation between "election" and "democracy" that Pareto and Mosca had emphasized, American readers succumbed to the temptation to collapse the oligarchic transformation of electoral party structure and democracy. In Burnham's view, the transformation of electoral party structure almost came to be seen as the essential quality of democracy itself. Moreover, the idea that "traditional," "ideal democracy" is synonymous with popular sovereignty expressed through an electoral mandate severely restricted any other conception of what "real" democratic contestation of elite power may entail.[117] Burnham acknowledges in the closing pages of his chapter dedicated to Michels that he did not suggest abandoning "the struggle for democracy" despite its unrealizability, but the finitude of the iron law of oligarchy suggested that the struggle will always be in vain.[118]

However, Burnham identifies not Michels but Mosca as the modern Machiavellian par excellence. According to Burnham, Mosca ultimately became the greatest defender of parliamentarism, which for Burnham epitomized the Machiavellian defense of liberty. In light of Michels's pronouncement of the unrealizability of democracy understood as popular sovereignty, Mosca's experience supplied the next best thing: a renewed appreciation for the "favorable" qualities of representative politics in moments of their demise. Eventually, Burnham writes, Mosca realized that parliamentarian government constitutes the societies of "the least evil," and consequently became nostalgic for them in comparison to autocratic Fascist regimes that threatened the Italian's republic's existence.[119]

Burnham was quite alive to Mosca's pessimistic prediction for the fate of liberal parliamentarism: "From his favorable judgment [of parliamentarism], however, Mosca did not conclude that the 19th century form of parliamentary government was necessarily going to last." Burnham cautions that for Mosca, "though a small reserve of optimism was permissible, pessimism was on the whole called for by the facts."[120] By implication, Burnham understandably argues that the focus should be on the virtues of liberal electoralism in the face of such threats. Crucially, though, he misunderstands the actual "realist" lesson to be gleaned from Mosca's pessimistic realism: Burnham emphasizes appreciating electoralism now that it is almost too late, whereas Mosca had implored elites to tame electoralism *before* it is too late—that is to say, well before electoralism's plutocratic proclivities invite authoritarian usurpation. Instead of searching for realistic means of cultivating elite and autocratic contestation, Burnham beckons his reader to settle on liberal electoral politics as "the least of all evils" in the "the new age of catastrophe" that awaited the end of the Second World War.

Burnham repeats in the closing lines of the work, "The present war . . . is a stage in a world social revolution." "The real struggle is not to recapture the past," he continues, "but to conquer the future. It may be well that those who understand this will emerge the victors." The future lay with the modern Machiavellians, for they "did not waste their time on the myth of democracy defined as self-government." Instead they were "very profoundly concerned with the reality of democracy defined as liberty." For Burnham, the victors of the war would be those who defined liberty, and hence democracy, "as the right of [elite] opposition, the right of [elite] opponents of the currently governing elite to express publicly their opposition views and to organize and implement those views."[121]

In the American political imaginary, "pessimism," "realism," and even Machiavellianism thus morphed into an optimistic ode to elite contestation through electoral institutions. The stage was set to redefine democracy as liberal election, the "next best thing" to democracy understood as self-government. Ironically, in the process this new optimism about the democratic possibilities of liberal representative politics was rebranded as a plausibly "pessimistic realist" orientation, an orientation that surely enough "conquered the future" with a new definition of democracy as free and fair elections.

CHAPTER 4

Sardonic Irony

Schumpeter and the Alternate Theory

Whoever has [a sense of possibility] does not say, for instance:
Here this or that happened, will happen, must happen; but he invents:
Here this or that might, could, or ought to happen. If he is told that
something is the way it is, he will think: Well, it could probably just as
well be otherwise.

—ROBERT MUSIL, *The Man without Qualities*

As fate would have it, the Italian School found its progeny in the German émigré Robert Michels. While Michels initiated and sustained the corruption of the Italian theories of elitism on the continent of their birth, another Central European figure—the world-renowned economist, political theorist, and sociologist Joseph Schumpeter—would ferry the pessimistic posture of elite theory directly to the United States, there subjecting it to a more pronounced perversion.

Schumpeter spent the first fifty years of his illustrious career across Europe in myriad professional roles: as a lawyer in London and Cairo; as president of the Biedermann Bank; as a politician, serving first as a civil servant for the German Socialization Committee and then as finance minister for the Republic of Austria-Germany; and, most notably, as professor at the Universities of Graz, Vienna, and Bonn. At Harvard he was a visiting professor in 1927–1928 and 1930–1931, and after a brief stint in Japan at the Tokyo College of Commerce, he returned to Cambridge. He became a permanent faculty member at Harvard in 1932, suitably poised to transport interwar European pessimism to the new world—a world that would soon enter the next transatlantic conflict. Written between 1938 and 1941, just before Germany's invasion of the Soviet Union and the United States' declaration of war, Schumpeter's seminal work *Capitalism, Socialism and Democracy* urged its sleepy American readers to equip themselves with the instruments of elite theory in the face of impending totalitarian usurpation. There was no time to entertain fanciful nineteenth-century delusions that representative democracy was a government of robust citizen participation, he worried, when Hitlerite Germany and Stalinist Russia threatened to imminently eradicate from the map all traces of political liberalism.[1] The pessimism of elite theory was urgently required in light of such dire circumstances.

Capitalism, Socialism and Democracy was a watershed contribution to elite theory at a major turning point in the history of the twentieth century. Schumpeter has thus long been classified as the heir of the Italian School of Elitism and as its conduit into American social science. In this foundational text of political science, the Austrian economist explicitly appropriates many of the Italians' substantive concerns and methodological inclinations: democracy's inherent susceptibility to oligarchic and demagogic threats, disappointment in the capacities of elites to advance liberal politics, attention to the symbols and myths that accompany twentieth-century democratic and socialist movements, and a commitment to a historically and sociologically oriented methodology alongside advances in more empirically driven econometrics.

Like the Italians, Schumpeter is mistakenly remembered as a resolutely "empirical" political theorist who hoped to direct the practice of social science in a more econometric direction. Perhaps Schumpeter's inappropriate reputation for such a strictly "empirical" approach is maintained partially because he ruffled feathers when he insisted upon teaching econometrics at Harvard, whose economics department was then far more influenced by the theoretical and historical tendencies of the discipline.[2] Much like Pareto's and Mosca's orientation toward the emergence of scientific paradigms in the study of social inquiry, Schumpeter envisioned a social science committed to methodological pluralism with equal emphasis on historical, sociological, and economic orientations.[3] John Medearis rightly describes the capacious "scope and ambition" of Schumpeter's methodological project as "a social science of transformation."[4]

Schumpeter approaches the political and methodological concerns of his Italian predecessors with similarly undiluted pessimism, but his pessimism is considerably more cynical in nature and sarcastic in expression. Throughout the text he articulates disappointment in and contempt for his own class—specifically, in the intellectuals and politicians who have not lived up to their responsibilities as elites (that is, as genuine *aristoi*), having failed to articulate coherent theoretical positions and political aspirations relevant to the historical moment. Given Schumpeter's claims in the rest of the work, combined with the palpable scorn he vents toward elites, I argue that the infamous Part 4 of the text should be read as Schumpeter's sardonic challenge to elites to rewrite "democratic" theory if they desire to preserve their place in the current global hierarchy—an outcome he severely doubts them capable of achieving. In this respect, Schumpeter adopted a different pessimistic tone, one I call sardonic irony, but it is still a posture that aims to encourage a corrupt and decaying ruling class to reform itself.[5]

Notwithstanding these continuities with the Italian School, *Capitalism, Socialism and Democracy* also amounted to a definitive break in the tradition. Precisely because the Italians had lost faith in cosmopolitan liberal elites and their epistemic capacities for government, Pareto and Mosca explicitly warned against the practice of conflating democracy with elections as a way to manage popular expectations of the democratic possibilities contained within liberal representative government. And although at the end of *Sociology of the Party* Michels resigns himself to electoral politics as a second-best alternative to democracy in the face of the iron law of oligarchy, he never went so far as to fully endorse a conflation of the two. Instead Michels took a different position: because ideal democracy in contemporary mass polities is structurally impossible, the possibility of contestation provided by electoral competition could be understood as a feasible alternative, however disappointing.

In contrast to both the Italian and the German orientation, the Austrian elite theorist challenged his readers to baldly equate electoral procedures and democratic governance, with no suggestion that electoral competition is an imperfect or second-best alternative. Instead, Schumpeter proposes to define democracy as electoral competition by entirely forsaking the tenuous connection between popular sovereignty and representative practices. His alternative to representative democracy, "the theory of competitive leadership," proposed identifying democracy simply as an electoral method in a way that utilized the approaches of his Italian predecessors to invert their most sacred lesson: democracy, he dared, can just as easily be understood as its opposite if we define it as such.

Schumpeter's sardonic dare to identify democracy as competitive elections simultaneously inherited and transformed the major precepts of elite theory, but not for the reasons that would later be claimed by postwar political science.[6] In order to trace and isolate these lines of continuity and rupture, in the following discussion I reconstruct the nature of the "alternate theory" of competitive leadership in relationship to the substantive and affective positions espoused by the original members of the Italian School. In a cynical manner reminiscent of all his precursors, and of Michels in particular, Schumpeter contests socialist claims to having a monopoly on democratic legitimacy while replacing the Italian fear of plutocracy with an anxiety over autocracy. His attack on the "classical democratic doctrine" follows in the footsteps of the Italians, who sought to dismantle the concept of popular sovereignty expressed through representative practices, yet the Austrian economist emphasizes the manufactured element of the "people's will" as opposed to the Italian economist Pareto's focus on its simultaneously irrational and creative potential. Like his predecessors, Schumpeter most famously champions an "empirical" and "realistic" approach to politics; but crucially, unlike Pareto and especially Mosca, he wryly contends that realism consists, not in lowering our democratic expectations of liberalism and representative institutions, but instead in lowering our majoritarian and participatory expectations of democracy. In the end Schumpeter poses his redefinition of democracy neither as a desperate, sober warning nor a resigned plea to analytically distinguish the categories of democracy and competitive elections, but instead as a sardonic challenge to conflate them on the grounds of historical expediency.

"The Setting of the Problem" Anew: Plutocracy versus Autocracy

At the beginning of the millennium, Ian Shapiro hailed *Capitalism, Socialism and Democracy* as "the most influential twentieth-century approach to the democratic management of power relations."[7] Arguably no text has been deployed more consistently across the various subfields of political science than part 4 of this work, and it remains the third most cited book in the social sciences, behind Marx's *Capital* and *The Wealth of Nations* by Adam Smith. Specifically, the third chapter of part 4 presents the alternate theory—the "theory of competitive leadership"—which defines democracy as "an institutional arrangement for arriving at political decisions in which individuals acquire the power to decide by means of competitive struggle for the people's vote."[8] This definition remains the standard conception of democracy operating in the social sciences and even in popular discourse, most often identified by its contemporary shorthand "free and fair elections." Admirers and critics agree that this model became the essential core of the elite theory of democracy.[9]

Before the alternate theory makes its official appearance, the first chapter of part 4 begins by establishing the reasons we desperately need a renewed doctrine of democracy in the first place. Schumpeter shares the Italian School's desire to dispel the Marxist fairy tale that elite domination of the masses, or the "exploitation of man by man," will end with the public ownership of the means of production. Prior to 1916, he says, this assignment would have scarcely been possible. Not long ago, he writes, socialists could call themselves "the exclusive sellers of the genuine [democratic] stuff, never to be confused with the bourgeois fake," and no one would bat an eyelash when socialism and democracy were linked. Attempts to disentangle their relation—such as the efforts of Pareto, Mosca, and Michels—were understood by "most people" as either reactionary bids to turn back the clocks and erase the historical developments that advanced the "dictatorship of the proletariat" or as the cathartic exercises of disillusioned ex-socialists.[10] Whether intentionally or inadvertently, Schumpeter resumes the task of divorcing socialism and democracy and thus sets "the problem" in a way that casts himself as a successor of the elite tradition.[11]

Yet times have changed, Schumpeter continues, and the intellectual and empirical developments of the past twenty years have generated an "obvious" opportunity to sever the socialism/democracy nexus. As far as the theoretical element is concerned, many of Marx's reputable disciples have insisted that their "prophet" would have prioritized socialization of the economy over observance of democratic procedure—and Schumpeter asserts that we should take their word for it. Beyond this first step of facile theoretical disconnection, he contends that "the record of the socialist parties" has created the grounds for contesting the previously presumed inextricability of socialism and democratic governance.[12] In the most significant cases, he says, socialist parties have opted to suspend democratic procedures with the purported aim of "realizing true democracy"—with frighteningly autocratic results. The case of the Soviet Union looms large in this picture, especially in the opening pages of the chapter, which remind the reader that "any argument in favor of shelving democracy for the transitional period affords an excellent opportunity to evade all responsibility for it. Such provisional arrangements may well last for a century or more and means are available for a ruling group installed by a victorious revolution to prolong them indefinitely or to adopt *the forms of democracy without the substance*."[13] Interestingly enough, just a few pages before Schumpeter presents his own procedural conception of democracy, he admits that democratic "forms" or procedures can easily subvert democratic "substance" or outcomes. Although many denied that the USSR embodied "true" socialism, given the existence of socialist political parties that have adhered to democratic norms, Schumpeter contends that insisting on Russia's aberrational quality amounts to recognizing that "there are forms of socialism which do not command the allegiance of all socialists and which include non-democratic ones."[14] For Schumpeter, the existence of Soviet Russia has proved that socialism understood as the public ownership of the means of production need not be democratic, despite nineteenth-century fantasies to the contrary. Whereas previously this idea could only be sustained as mere speculation, he claims, the Russian Revolution and its aftermath have rendered it an empirical fact to be deployed in the service of separating socialism from democracy in the popular imaginary.

In addition, Schumpeter maintains that we do not have a clear sense of how any one of the more democratically inclined socialist parties would behave if they had the opportunity or motivation to initiate an immediate transition to a system of full-scale public ownership. Even the most successful "test cases," such as the German Social Democratic Party (SPD), have proven that the socialist parties that chose to defend democratic procedure and put down their more committed communist rivals have seriously jeopardized their claims to socialist legitimacy—"the seceding dissenters," he confirms, "have more, not less, claim to the badge of socialism than those who stayed."[15] On this point Schumpeter agrees with Michels, who goes unnamed but remains palpably present in the discussion. The performance of the SPD has not been an unqualified success in connecting socialism to democracy; if anything, Michels's study proved that 'the sell-out' aspect of the SPD's reputation has cast even further doubt on their compatibility.

Despite this initial point of agreement, Schumpeter's position thereafter deviates from those of his Italian and German predecessors. He contests the view that the SPD's oligarchic hierarchies reside in the plutocratic tendencies of liberal representative politics or even more specifically in the organizational structure of the modern party system. Liberal capitalism does not necessarily generate more acute plutocratic consequences than other economic organizations, he submits, and even if it did, one would still have to account for the SPD's having flourished in the most "unplutocratic" of environments possible.[16] Contra Pareto and Mosca, then, according to Schumpeter we cannot blame the inherent plutocratic propensities of electoral procedure for the rise and success of socialist ideology. On the other hand, he rejects the view that the organization of political parties encourages its members to embrace the "comfortable armchairs of officialdom." Contra Michels he laconically describes this eventuality as "a common human failing" that exists outside of modern party structure in all governments, including the most "responsible" ones in history.[17] Rather, for Schumpeter the issue arises out of the age-old but recently renewed Platonic anxiety about our commitments to majoritarian politics and

120 DEMOCRATIC ELITISM

the autocratic possibilities that arise whenever majority rule exists to any meaningful extent.

To underscore that we may not be as committed to majoritarian principles as we pretend, Schumpeter superciliously proposes a "mental experiment" that "has some bearing on modern issues."[18] He asks whether we would approve of a community that uses majoritarian procedures to legitimate the slaughter of Jews over a patently nondemocratic (that is, liberal) constitution that tends to better avoid such results. To restate the question, he asks whether the reader would prefer a democratic government with majoritarian norms that may invite genocidal persecution to a patently nondemocratic regime that tends to foreclose the possibility. As Carole Pateman later describes it, the mental experiment poses a peculiar "straw man" between the mere logical possibility of majoritarian persecution of minorities engendered by seemingly democratic processes or a presumably liberal constitution with more robust built-in institutional safeguards to avoid it.[19]

While Schumpeter makes the case of Soviet autocracy explicit, he uses the mental experiment to raise the issue of Weimar Germany's collapse through majoritarian support of demagogic usurpation. Moving to the more historically removed examples of Nero's persecution of the early Christians and Maria Theresa's treatment of Catholic witch-hunting, he underscores that such instances of minority oppression were initially driven by the prejudices of the majority and autocrats' willingness to use such impulses to further consolidate their power.[20] More than anything else—and certainly more than plutocracy—he suggests that we now ought to fear autocratic governments that deploy majoritarian and seemingly democratic practices to ends that undermine the "substance" of democracy itself, and even undermine other, more preferable forms of government, including oligarchy and monarchy. After all, he writes, the most famous trial in history attests to the fact that autocracy and democracy can go well together: Pontius Pilate was, from the standpoint of the Jews, "a representative of autocracy who yielded to democracy."[21]

For some postwar readers, Schumpeter's mordant straw man exposes his hatred of the socializing tendencies of his day.[22] Yet this view projects a Cold War anxiety onto Schumpeter, who, writing at the apex of the Nazi-Soviet coalition and nadir of the Allied campaign, did not express one. Despite his stated preferences for a mitigated, "plausible" capitalist economy, at this point in the late 1930s Schumpeter does not fear socialism as an economic framework because he perceived a far more dangerous threat. He repeatedly stresses that the anxiety around the socialization of the economy is distracting from the real problem at hand: that liberal governments are losing an existential war against a totalitarian enemy whose partners exhibit both private and public ownership of production. As he insists throughout *Capitalism, Socialism and Democracy*, a dispassionate, objective, or empirical assessment of capitalism and socialism reveals that there are political and economic virtues to each respective framework, but we might never live to apply either structure in the West if we lose the fight against fascist totalitarianism.

When a new form of totalitarian autocracy (as opposed to the socialist global encroachment) is prioritized as the text's main theoretical preoccupation, it is easier to appreciate the mental experiment for what it really is: an invitation to reconsider liberalism in light of the recent emergence of totalitarian governments with majoritarian approval. Because democracy, however defined, relies upon the implementation of some kind of majoritarian procedures to be understood as legitimate, Schumpeter states that this regime typology must always be put in the service of other "hyper-rational values." Pledging allegiance to democratic procedures and the majoritarianism they require only makes sense, he continues, "when it can be expected to work in ways we approve."[23] Given the contemporary political catastrophe, Schumpeter, through his mental experiment, urges readers not to take for granted the anti-majoritarian features of liberalism which may often help preclude minority persecution as one such attractive "hyper-rational value." Put differently, if we are to take seriously the majoritarian basis of democratic governments, he pleads, then we might not want to do away with our commitments to liberal norms and representative practices just yet.

Foregrounding the particularities of the late 1930s historical moment brings Schumpeter's polemical reconsideration of liberalism into sharp relief. When his book is read in its entirety, the fear of global totalitarian usurpation cannot be ignored. The ostensible point of the entire book, and the explicit thesis of the first three parts, is that liberal capitalism will imminently self-destruct because liberal values are "crumbling"—that is, they have fallen out of favor with all social classes, including the bourgeoisie itself.[24] This loss of faith has been a long time coming—Schumpeter details throughout the book the myriad circumstances that have prompted the public's rejection of liberal capitalism and permitted autocrats the opportunity to contest and usurp liberal practice. After posing a reconsideration of liberalism's virtues in part 4, in part 5 Schumpeter resumes his critique of liberal intellectuals, politicians, and economic elites who have been unable to govern efficiently amid the rise of demagogic threats to representative government. Read in conjunction with the rest of the

122 DEMOCRATIC ELITISM

work, the mental experiment calls for a more balanced reassessment of liberalism's virtues by contrasting it with the totalitarianism that gained majoritarian approval in Germany and Eastern Europe.

Yet whereas the Italian School had worried about the oligarchic conditions that allow for demagogic usurpation of parliamentary politics, Schumpeter narrows the concern to the existence of demagogic usurpation itself. He rejects the anxious Italian assumption that plutocracy creates the groundwork for demagogic autocracy because, even if it were the case, that moment has already been superseded by a more imminent threat. As an inheritor of the Italian School, he too aims to decouple socialism and democracy, but he recasts the poignant political concern of elite theory as the issue of democracy's susceptibility to autocratic threats *independent of the contribution electoral governments may make in creating the environment for such usurpation.* Instead of divorcing democracy from parliamentary politics, he proposes that we honestly reevaluate and recommit to liberal outcomes as the "hyper-rational" value we identify as the end of democratic procedure, despite the many obvious shortcomings of electoral government.

Part 4 advances this proposition through a sardonic polemic, but elsewhere Schumpeter admits that he aims to combat fascist, and not necessarily socialist, assaults on political or economic liberalism. The concluding chapter of the book begs Anglo-American readers to sever the connection between socialism and democracy and squarely face the problem posed by increasing majoritarian support for totalitarian government. The problem with Russia, he says, "is not that she is socialist but that she is Russia." Lest we all forget, he continues, Stalinist Russia is above all a "fascist," "military autocracy" because, just like Hitler's Germany, "it rules by means of a single and strictly disciplined party and does not admit freedom of the press. . . . We may understand, and condole with, the American intellectual who is so circumstanced [as to call Stalinism] democratic socialism . . . although we may resent the insult to our intelligence that is implied in his expectation of being believed."[25] Schumpeter thus pities American intellectuals who have so little experience with socialism that they are willing to justify Stalin's Russia on democratic terms, but most of all he resents those intellectuals' delusional ignorance of fascism and lack of appreciation for the liberal values that currently protect them. In a word, he begs his audience not to take political liberalism for granted.

Some scholars have recently emphasized that this fear of totalitarian autocracy, and not the postwar fear of socialism, permeates *Capitalism, Socialism and Democracy*—including Schumpeter's famed attack on the classical democratic doctrine. As JanaLee Cherneski puts it, Schumpeter uses the classical theory of democracy to warn against fascist invocations of "the people," to preserve political liberalism, whichever economic (capitalist or socialist) instantiation it took in the future.[26] Yet somewhat understandably, once totalitarianism had been defeated, American political scientists faced a radically different political landscape and therefore drew a different lesson from Schumpeter's attack on classical democratic doctrine: the critique of the masses' epistemic capacities for governance.

The Classical Doctrine and the People's Will: Irrational versus Manufactured

Most politically oriented treatments of *Capitalism, Socialism and Democracy* ignore this preliminary discussion on socialism and take part 4's critique of the doctrine of popular sovereignty as their starting point. In the second chapter, Schumpeter describes the flaws of the classical justification of democracy in the section somewhat facetiously titled "Human Nature in Politics"—a nod to English socialist Graham Wallas.[27] In tribute to Wallas's social psychology, Schumpeter explains why there can be no such thing as a "people" or a "people's will" in modern mass government: in the aggregate, human nature does not allow for a "people" adequately united through shared interest, nor for a "people's will" cohesive enough to instigate decisive action. The theory of popular sovereignty is inadequate, he contends, because it does not match the failure of public will formation under liberal politics, and we can never hope for liberalism to formulate a popular will if human cognitive shortcomings are honestly taken into consideration.

Some readers understand the political psychology expressed in this section to convey a candid truism that intellectual sincerity cannot deny, while others bristle at the limited capacities Schumpeter attributes to average voters. But both types of reader agree that herein lies Schumpeter's judgment on the "rabble" or the "stampede"—that is, his unfavorable view of mass epistemic capacities, the genesis of his critique of the classical theory of democracy, and the inspiration for his own "alternative theory" of competitive political leadership.[28] His vitriol for the rabble also constitutes yet another basis of the presumed connection between Schumpeter and his predecessors Pareto, Mosca, and Michels on the grounds of their presumed elitist disdain for mass epistemic faculties.[29]

In particular, the critique of the notion that there is a people's will and its inability to be faithfully represented through delegation forcefully calls to mind Pareto's aggressive attacks on human rationality and the concept of a singular,

124 DEMOCRATIC ELITISM

decisive will, especially one shared by a heterogeneous mix of socioeconomic classes. In these pages Schumpeter cites Pareto as the authority who instantiated the studies of human psychology that dispel the possibility of rational collective action.[30] Although Schumpeter distinguishes between mass psychology of the Paretian variety and Gustave Le Bon's investigation of crowds, he attaches Le Bon to Pareto, enacting a chain of continuity in what will become the standard genealogy of elite theory in American political science and democratic theory.[31]

Revisiting Pareto's account of human irrationality vis-à-vis his criticism of popular sovereignty helps us compare it with Schumpeter's position. In his quintessentially misanthropic fashion, Pareto often underscores the irrationality of human behavior and the tragic stupidity of humanity, both individually and collectively. Pareto was certainly not the first to question the rationality of human behavior, but unlike his pessimistic contemporaries such as Nietzsche and Freud, he infelicitously attempts to "scientifically" classify the sentiments, or the "residues" guiding our conduct. Recall that his account divides human sentiments or residues between the "instinct of combinations" (Class I) and "the persistence of aggregates" (Class II) and their various *combinazioni*, or combinations. In addition to these two categories, Pareto identifies the actions that result from the active combination of these two sentimental proclivities as Class III, or "the need of expressing sentiments by external acts."[32]

Although these residues are "irrational" in that the sentiments or perceptions are elicited through associations that do not result from the application of what Pareto terms "logico-experimental" reasoning, they are by no means mistaken or fruitless for the purposes of political decision-making. Even seemingly preposterous superstitions can generate productive politics, Pareto says, such as preventing crime or generating solidarity.[33] He angrily taunts so-called social "scientists" who allow their misguided glorification of rationality to advance behavioral paradigms with no explanatory power; his contemporaries, he continues, fail to understand that it is to society's benefit that Class I residues are not motivated by a specific aim or interest. In particular, he rejects the Darwinian view that sentiments and irrational behavior are subject to the disciplining feedback of experience and thus to the alleged law of the survival of the fittest, resulting in the most opportune sentiments.[34] He sees Darwinian theories and the Spencerian varieties of individual and collective survival as illogical, inasmuch as combinations are sustained by customs and habits (or Class II residues) irrespective of whether they advance fitness, health, or even survival.[35]

Self-interest paradigms cannot even explain basic practices such as the domestication of animals, Pareto laments, because such behavior derives from the "instinct of combinations, which impels human beings to put things and acts together without pre-established design."[36] We are political animals, able to construct sustainable communities precisely because of our irrational sentiments. Pareto offers the following example to make his point: Why will a child care for a fallen bird for no reason other than simply the pleasure of doing so? Basic human behavior indicates that irrational sentiments constitute one of the main sources of human ruin *and* creative generation.

In a more Nietzschean, anti-Spencerian fashion, then, Pareto advances human irrationality as both the destructive and the productive driver in the maintenance of political communities.[37] He stresses the irrationality of human behavior and its inability to follow the dictates of self-interest, but not that this irrationality should be discounted or reductively regarded merely as mass deficiency. For Pareto, the disparagement of irrationality is a moralizing and unscientific judgment as opposed to an objective understanding or dispassionate assessment of the role that mass irrationality plays in politics, which constitutes the heart of his criticism against the purported "scientists" of his day.

Parallel to Mosca's historically oriented approach to social science described in Chapter 2, we should understand Pareto's attempt, however unsuccessful, to classify sentiments "scientifically" in a Vichian epistemological register— that is, as an effort to reject mechanistic and linear models of causality and eschew moralistic thinking in political discourse as opposed to science understood strictly as the Cartesian insistence on empirical validity.[38] For Pareto, this reliance on causal reasoning explains the great "error" of Marx's historical materialism—that is, of having "exchanged the interdependence [of economic and social phenomenon] with the relationship of cause and effect."[39] Pareto dedicates the first volume of the *Trattato* to developing his view of equilibrium analysis as an alternative to causal reasoning. As Alasdair Marshall and Joseph Femia have both insisted, Pareto's "scientism" consisted in "[abandoning] reductionism in favor of an assumption of complex variable interaction" in order to offer heuristics that were of course vulgar generalizations but still useful in contesting the reductive approach of cause-and-effect reasoning.[40]

Amusingly enough, Pareto also suggests that mass irrationality or, at best, mass inertia in the face of elite incompetence often accounts for the maintenance of a particularly corrupt ruling order.[41] Of course, there could be no singular, rational popular will because there could be no singular, rational will in individuals themselves—yet this was not always a pernicious political precept, given that in some circumstances regime stability is preferable to civil

126   DEMOCRATIC ELITISM

war. Moreover, for Pareto the problem with the idea of popular sovereignty is not so much that its construction unrealistically hinged on presuppositions of human rationality that did not exist, although of course that presented a logical obstacle. Rather, it is that nothing akin to the fictitious concept of popular sovereignty could be attained through representative practices. As we saw in Chapter 1, for Pareto electoral contests were always too easily subject to plutocratic capture, thereby invalidating the presumption of the people's effective "rule."

Schumpeter rehearses Pareto's claims about the lack of rationality in the individual will through a similarly "realistic" assessment, but one that turns more on the empirical existence of the "people" and its "will." For the theory of popular sovereignty to make any sense, he writes, "we remain under the practical necessity of attributing to the will of the individual an independence and a rational quality that are altogether unrealistic. If we are to argue that the will of the citizens per se is a political factor entitled to respect, it must first exist. That is to say, it must be something more than an indeterminate bundle of vague impulses loosely playing about given slogans and mistaken impressions."[42] In order for the classical doctrine to be plausible, a "people" and its "will" requires a more definite expression than an amorphous conception of popular opinion and / or popular judgment can provide. This passage recalls Pareto's position on the relationship between individual and mass irrationality vis-à-vis the formation of a potential popular will. Yet Schumpeter thereafter makes a related but distinct point that constitutes the majority of the discussion of "human nature in politics": not only are individuals irrational, as Pareto insists, but more problematically for democratic theory the people's desires and preferences are manufactured.

Schumpeter thus makes a two-pronged attack on classical democratic doctrine in which the secondary prong offers the most penetrating critique. In line with the Paretian tradition, he sees the lack of individual rationality as posing a major blow to the possibility of a cogent collective will. But more importantly, even if such a rational and definite will could be constructed, he argues, such individual wants and desires are "so amenable to the influence of advertising and other methods of persuasion that producers often seem to dictate to them instead of being directed by them." While there is always an appeal to reason in the sale of a product, an idea, or a political position, the real worry, he writes, is that "mere assertion, often repeated, counts more than rational argument and so does the direct attack on the subconscious which takes the form of attempts to evoke and crystallize pleasant associations of an entirely extrarational, very frequently of a sexual nature."[43] The prevalence of advertising raises the concern that the people's will, even if it were to exist, would not actually be its own as opposed to an elite manipulation.

The argument runs deeper than the probability of advertising influencing individual choices. More drastically, Schumpeter contends that even in the decisions of everyday life both political and economic consumers have far less agency than classical textbooks of economics would have us believe.[44] In part 2, and then again part 4, he insists upon the Marxist precept that producers, and not consumers, generate demand. Against the marginalist, neoclassical, Austrian, and even some socialist economic schools of thought, he maintains that consumers do not go about instructing producers on their needs and desires through the market, which in turn disciplines producers into making such commodities or offering such services. For Schumpeter, that idea would presuppose that consumers know what goods and services they want that have yet to be invented or innovated.[45] Instead, producers "teach" economic and political consumers to want new things, by inventing those new commodities in the first place and then persuading consumers, often through relentless advertising, that they need them.[46]

By extension, Schumpeter maintains that individuals do not construct their voting preferences independent of institutional structures. Instead, the people's preferences and desires are highly manipulated to the point of bordering on elite—that is, on the producer's or politician's—construction. This manipulation becomes more acute in the political sphere because individual desires are further removed from the disciplining aspects of economic needs that force a housewife to become familiar with "foods, familiar household articles, wearing apparel," and therefore they are not forced to exert as much effort in exercising a discerning political judgment. Ironically, later supposedly "Schumpeterian" economic conceptions of democracy posited by Anthony Downs and John Zaller will treat voters as consumers who choose candidates in order to maximize their preexisting values, interests, opinions, and preferences. Schumpeter preemptively invalidates this view by insisting that voters are not an exogenous source of demand.[47]

Schumpeter's attack on the classical doctrine of popular sovereignty transforms Pareto's critique of collective agency by shifting the focus from human irrationality to the manipulation and even construction of collective agency by economic and political elites. This critique of the "classical democratic doctrine" will form a founding pillar of the behavioral revolution—a generation of postwar political scientists who relied on psychologizing the masses' epistemic incapacities for politics beyond the moment of electoral decision. Although some behavioralists would follow Walter Lippmann's and Edward Bernays's unflattering characterizations of public opinion and propaganda developed in the interwar period, early articulations of the "realist view of democracy" were predicated on empirical studies that paid homage to Schumpeter's political thought, attesting to the politically disorganized, passive state of the great majority of people.[48] Sheldon Wolin later summarizes his era as having a Schumpeterian zeitgeist in which "the findings of empirical political and social science have seriously weakened the democratic faith in the qualities and capacities of citizens. The voter is presented in a highly unflattering light: poorly informed, prejudiced, and apathetic."[49]

The Alternate Theory: Realistic Liberalism versus Realistic Democracy

Throughout the first two chapters of part 4, Schumpeter stresses the realism of his approach. An honest treatment of the masses' cognitive shortcomings with respect to politics is necessary only insofar as it raises for Schumpeter the same larger concern that preoccupied the Italian School. Without naming the Italian theorists, Schumpeter puts himself in their company when he argues that the main problem with the classical doctrine of popular sovereignty is that it generates dangerously unrealistic expectations. In line with Pareto and Mosca, Schumpeter fears the consequences of a theory of popular sovereignty that promises democratic (majoritarian) outcomes through liberal (representative or parliamentary) electoral institutions. He restates the concern by identifying the central issue as the cognitive dissonance involved in understanding democracy as popular sovereignty amid liberal institutions; namely, the situation when citizens and theorists simultaneously hold an expansive normative-theoretical conception of democracy along with a narrower procedural understanding of parliamentary or representative government.

To dispel the cognitive dissonance, Schumpeter elaborates the ways that liberal capitalism creates an environment in which elites compete among themselves for political rule and then dishonestly call this system "democracy," as if parliamentary and representative institutions expressed popular sovereignty in a meaningful way. Much like his predecessors, he portrays the "classical" democratic doctrine of popular sovereignty—the idea that elections are a direct expression of the general or people's will—as an elite ruse that elides the difference between electoral and legislative power and consequently inhibits even a modicum of popular control and elite accountability once the electoral moment has passed. By emphatically stressing the ways in which "classical" democratic theory does not match the practice of electoral politics,

Schumpeter aggressively reveals the facticity of elite domination and the illusory democratic dimension of modern representative governments.

The problem with this ruse, according to both Schumpeter and the Italian theorists, is that its lack of credibility has become too apparent; the distance between liberal practice and democratic ideals renders adherence to electoral politics unconvincing and unappealing even to those who historically are the most committed to capitalism and liberal democracy: the bourgeoisie. At least, Schumpeter says, the masses are coherent in their consistent disdain for liberal capitalism; these institutions no longer speak to the "hearts and minds" of the general public, for reasons that transcend the desire for pecuniary gain. In this regard, he expresses more vitriol for the cognitive incapacity of the elites than of the masses: the masses admirably exhibit a certain consistency in calling for institutions that are morally and ideologically compatible with their values. Elites incoherently advance a theory and practice of democracy that contradicts their professed commitment to a socialist future and their own pecuniary interest in preserving liberal capitalism.[50] Elites, he complains, are intellectually ill-equipped to navigate a smooth political transition to socialist institutions, despite the overwhelming commitment that all social classes (including the elites themselves) have expressed for this economic framework.[51]

Yet whereas the Italians call for lowering popular expectations of what representative government can possibly achieve, and consequently warn intellectual and political elites against the prosaic conflation of democracy and electoral practices, Schumpeter redirects the critique of popular sovereignty toward a different solution. He enjoins future political theorists to close the cavernous gap between classical theory and modern practice by adopting an alternative "theory of competitive leadership," a conception that evacuates the historic majoritarian and participatory expectations of democracy and redefines it as leadership selection through liberal election of governors.

In this section, Schumpeter justifies redefining democracy as electoral practices through a practical appeal to expediency given the current threats to political liberalism. And although it may be tempting to understand the alternate theory exclusively as Schumpeter's ideal political model, his candor offers it more as a description of how "democracy" operates under liberal capitalism rather than as a prescriptive best case or as a reliable account of democracy in a dawning socialist age. Indeed, he explicitly argues no more than this: because his alternate account more accurately depicts the way that "democracy" has operated historically, it is the most plausible option in any attempt to foster and maintain what we now call "democracy" given current political and economic tendencies. Taking into account the information that

130 DEMOCRATIC ELITISM

we have concerning liberal capitalism, Schumpeter claims, his alternate theory is a more honest depiction of the purported "democracy" that we practice and uncritically celebrate.[52] He simultaneously describes present political practice and, consequently, suggests a change in theory to align with the actual workings of representative institutions if elites are committed to preserving their place in the current precarious social hierarchy and protecting their way of life from totalitarian usurpation.

Schumpeter identifies the many ways in which redefining democracy as the practice of electoral politics will offer a plausible theory that is "much truer to life" in liberal polities.[53] Most obviously, by aligning democratic theory with liberal practice, we can distinguish such practice from autocratic alternatives where the ruling party is installed and maintained by force. More complex Aristotelean typologies are unnecessary when the only relevant distinction, at least to Schumpeter's mind, is a criterion to differentiate nonviolent and therefore *more* popular monarchic, oligarchic, and democratic forms of government from autocratic ones like the Soviet Union and Nazi Germany—a criterion that conveniently permits classifying British constitutional monarchy and American federalism as the same regime type.[54] In a word, he rejects any effective distinction between democracy, oligarchy, and monarchy and reduces these forms of government to a single type in order to contrast them with coercive tyranny. Considering the siege against all governments that refrain from employing violence to generate submission, defining democracy as the competitive selection of leaders offers a more honest account of what "sponsors of the democratic method," or proponents of liberal government, "really mean by the term."[55] As we shall see in Chapter 5, Adam Przeworski will celebrate this minimal criterion against violence as the essence and "miracle" of democratic life.

Redefining democracy as competitive elections also appropriately recognizes the role that leadership plays in parliamentary politics while eliminating the concern about the "manufactured will" discussed above. According to Schumpeter, the issue is not that leaders play a large hand in shaping popular opinion and judgment in liberal policies; rather, the problem has been the democratic expectation that in representative governments popular opinion directs the leader's administrative and legislative decision-making to a meaningful extent, or at least as much as it would in regimes governed through more majoritarian and deliberative institutions. By focusing on leadership selection, he explains, the manufactured feature of popular opinion can be discussed openly as opposed to pretending that it does not exist.[56]

By redefining democracy as the *modus procedendi* of liberal politics, Schumpeter continues, we can properly specify the character of the "negative" liberty practiced in representative governments without inducing another dimension of cognitive dissonance. Instead of failing to meet the robust standards of civic participation historically demanded by all varieties of the classical democratic doctrine, the theory of competitive leadership circumscribes freedom to its practice in liberal regimes—that is, as an exercise bounded by the confines of freedom of discussion led by a free press and nothing more than that. In liberal practice, freedom of speech and conscience is far from absolute, but when compared with the heavily censored culture of fascist dictatorship, the middle ground permitted and sustained through electoral competition should not be taken for granted either.

Most famously, Schumpeter suggests aligning our political theory with our capitalist orientation toward market economics. As it currently stands, part of the cognitive dissonance experienced by citizens of representative governments is generated by the fact that we expect democratic (majoritarian) responsiveness out of our liberal political arrangements but maintain a different orientation toward our economic organization. Yet economics has made considerable advancements since the eighteenth-century delusions of free-market competition, he claims, and most experts are coming around to the idea that competition is never perfect—that is, it is neither fair nor efficient. Although in principle there are no formal barriers to marketplace entry, we should all accept that monopoly practices, the benefits of incumbency, and even the most innocuous elements of insider advantages, he says, cannot coincide with what we call "fair market competition."[57]

By likening political and economic competition, Schumpeter maintains that we can finally be honest about the fact that while electoral contests may be free to the extent that anyone can in principle enter a race, this does not require us to pretend that the race is a fair one. Experience with capitalism precludes us from expecting that market competition is fair; congruently, we ought not to expect that electoral competition can provide anything other than "unfair" and even "fraudulent" results. If we were to exclude unfair and fraudulent competitions in our definition of democracy, Schumpeter claims, we would be left with a "completely unrealistic ideal."[58] But unfair and fraudulent outcomes, he repeats, must still be appreciated over those routinely generated by violent coercion.

Finally, by calling democracy a form of electoral competition, we eliminate all expectations that legislative and administrative decisions are responsive to majoritarian preferences in a regime type that has historically been identified first and foremost by majority participation and / or majoritarian outcomes. Confining majoritarian decisions to one small area of politics will assuredly result in anti-majoritarian consequences, Schumpeter suggests; it will be another example of democratic "forms" or procedures that subvert democratic "substance." But in the climate of majoritarian-approved autocracy, that might be its very virtue. This redefinition, he caustically writes, ensures "the standing of the majority system within the logic of the democratic [that is, electoral] method, although we might still condemn it on the grounds that lie outside of that logic."[59]

On the face of it, Schumpeter reproduces many features of the anti-Aristotelianism Mosca expressed during his fin de siècle period at the University of Torino. In "Il principio aristocratico ed il democratico," Mosca makes it the mission of elite theory to replace Aristotelian typologies through a radical simplification. As opposed to reducing everything outside of coercive tyranny to democracy, he renders all regimes aristocracies, by which he means the control of an elite minority. Following Machiavelli, he insists, the main dictate of any "realist" approach emphasizes that a minority always exercises either formal or de facto rule.[60] Given that this dominating minority arises in every polity, he suggests that the institutional organizations of monarchy and democracy are better understood as means by which this minority is controlled. Mosca thus grounds his realism in not losing sight of the fact that all regimes are characterized by minority rule.

Like Schumpeter, Mosca also recognizes the majoritarian basis of "pure" ancient democracy and entertains a reinterpretation fit for the modern world. He claims that if one is committed to the primary realistic premise of elite theory—that every government exhibits some form of minority domination—then the possibility of absolute majoritarian rule could never really exist. Consequently, he charges Pareto with committing a logical error in his dual commitment to elite theory and endorsement of majoritarianism in *Les systèmes socialistes*.[61] However, if we instead define democracy more along the lines of Aristotle's conception of *politeia*, he writes, then we are left with a definition of democracy that requires "the formal and de facto [*in diritto ed in fatto*] accessibility of members of any socioeconomic group into the governing class and the disappearance of every single privilege related to birth in the fight for social preeminence."[62]

However, according to Mosca, the true theorist of elitism can "neither affirm nor deny" such an adaptation of democracy as *politeia* because it raises the recurring problem of the history of political thought and the "fulcrum around which the history of the present currently unfolds": the contest between the "haves" versus the "have-nots." In both antiquity and modernity, the main source of regime decay has always been found in the discrepancy between formal political equality and economic inequality, which generates an incessant battle between the rich and the poor. When the "have-nots" periodically assume possession of the state (meaning that oligarchy constitutes the de facto status quo), they are often "guided by one of the rich," or Pareto's "demagogic plutocrat," to "diminish economic inequality through confiscation of private property."[63] Unlike Schumpeter, Mosca sees the problem of autocracy as inseparable from the oligarchic conditions of the status quo ante that allow for the demagogic plutocrat's usurpation of the state.

If every regime must be considered the rule of a particular minority, Mosca again proposes we understand aristocracy and democracy, not as distinct typologies, but instead as principles that give shape to the constitution and power of a ruling class. When seen in this light, the democratic principle arises from the renewing of the ruling class from lower socioeconomic groups and, incidentally, constitutes the well-spring of all periods of human flourishing. By contrast, the aristocratic principle resides in the natural, "constant" tendency of the minority to combat this principle and preserve political power in the hands of their children and their own class. For Mosca, justice can prevail only when the democratic principle has "removed every single hereditary disparity or disadvantage," not only in principle but also de facto, in the fight to enter the ruling class.[64]

Mosca's merit-based interpretation of the democratic principle has led many to see his liberal credentials as tending in a conservative direction. This may very well be the case, but crucially, far from stating that formal political equality is sufficient to create the conditions for democracy as *politea*, he insists that this so-called meritocracy will never come close to fruition in conditions of economic inequality. This is not to say, however, that he thinks his elite theory should be understood in a "fatalistic or Sisyphean" register. Rather, the point of elite theory is to "teach" dominating minorities, first, that it is necessary for them to honestly recognize their own capacities to direct the social body and, second, that they themselves benefit when they, as a minority, place limits on themselves in order to allow the democratic principle to prosper.[65]

How can elites apply the lessons of elite theory when it is their involuntary, aristocratic instinct to combat democratic and socioeconomic restraints to their power? In "Stato città e stato rappresentativo," Mosca suggests that against the current trends in political theory that focus on the differences between antiquity and modernity, we should focus on the continuities. Then and now, the

134 DEMOCRATIC ELITISM

main obstacle to individual and political flourishing has been economic inequality, which is why, according to Mosca, Aristotle insisted that elites ought to develop and continually affirm an economic organization that privileges the *ceto medio*, or a middle class.[66] The existence of a large middle class means that conditions of economic equality are more prevalent than they would be otherwise, and in the context of Risorgimento Italy this middle class must be externally generated and not expected to arise naturally. Of course, Mosca at the time might have also defended courts and other technocratic institutions of cabinet government that could be used to combat the corruption of Northern financial elites and Southern barons. But he also thought that the source of the problem resides in a political structure that does not explicitly attend to regional economic inequalities.

Above all else, realism requires maintaining an awareness of the crucial distinctions between the liberal, the representative, and the democratic. At this point in his career, Mosca is willing to entertain the idea that "liberal" refers exclusively to the free discussion and critique of the governing class permitted informally through the press and formally through deliberative parliamentary institutions.[67] Against seventeenth-century doctrines, he rejects the view that "representation" refers to an instrument of democratic authorization; instead, he argues, it indicates a feudal mechanism that allows for smaller, heterogeneous bodies to assimilate under a singular governing body without denoting a democratic transfer of power. And these two doctrines, however important they may be, he says, are not responsible for the renewed flourishing of popular government or anything close to what we may term modern democracy. The resurgence of such a concept can only be understood as a revival of the "Greek and Roman conception of liberty," which problematically, he states, has manifold manifestations.[68]

At bottom, Mosca proposes that democracy must "convincingly" refer to a robust "public right" to "a form of political organization in which the law is a voluntary expression of those to whom it is supposed to serve, continually applied through functionaries selected by the people constrained to circumscribe their actions to the limits of preestablished laws."[69] While this idea sounds tantamount to an endorsement of parliamentary government, his central contention is that democracy must indicate something *more* than, and not equal to, liberal and representative institutions in order to effectively circumscribe elite power. Mosca may reject Pareto's more unequivocal defense of majoritarianism, but his preoccupation with economic inequality and desire to distinguish democracy from representative practices still makes it clear that he is not equating democracy with electoral procedures. Moreover, as we shall see below, Mosca is far more willing to allow democracy to retain some of its majoritarian connotations even though he rejects majoritarian institutionalism in its purest form.

The substantive differences between Pareto and Mosca attest to the variety of positions contained in elite theory. Nevertheless, the Italians' approach to realism shares critical commonalities that contrast sharply with the Austrian's deployment. The Italians advocated realistically lowering the expectations of liberal parliamentarism so that it might be supplemented by democratic institutions, principles, and theories that shore up the discrepancies so obvious in the doctrine of popular sovereignty. Schumpeter employs the opposite approach utilizing the same appeal to realism. Instead of lowering our aspirations for the democratic outcomes of liberalism and representative government, he asks us to eliminate our majoritarian expectations of democracy, in terms of both participation and outcomes. His competitive theory of leadership, Schumpeter stresses, deflates expectations of democracy so that we may define democracy simply as the practice of liberal electoral politics.

Democracy as Its Opposite

By abandoning the notion that electoral competition produces democratic outcomes, Schumpeter self-consciously invents a new definition of democracy. As we saw above, this new definition drastically reduces democracy to the minimal criterion required to distinguish practically any form of government from violent or coercive tyranny. As a result of this reductive approach, postwar scholars from Pateman to Przeworski would later name Schumpeter's invention the "minimalist" theory and would accordingly celebrate or malign it based on the fact that its parsimonious terms better corresponded to the empirical realties of liberal practice.

The alternate theory indeed reduces the criteria for democratic governance to a bare minimum, but in some ways the moniker "minimalist" obfuscates the novelty of Schumpeter's intervention. His presentation of his alternative conception of competitive leadership urges a redefinition of democracy in which we understand it in terms of liberal practice, a practice traditionally understood as democracy's opposite. In this sense, the alternate theory presents not so much a reduction as an elaborate reorientation that dramatically contests its historical meaning. Put differently, Schumpeter's theoretical invention does not merely strip democracy down to its barest essentials but rather entirely converts our conception of democracy into its historical antithesis: elections.

Schumpeter's caustic and sardonic proposal to define democracy as its historical converse is not an esoteric or latent suggestion submerged between the

136   DEMOCRATIC ELITISM

lines. He explicitly acknowledges that his theory rooted in the practice of liberal politics embarks upon a novel conception of democracy decidedly divorced from the historic attachments to the "rule" of the "people." In the final chapter of part 4, titled "The Inference," Schumpeter candidly explains that if we are to accept his proposal to redefine democracy along the lines of electoral practice, then the following is also the case:

> Democracy does not mean and *cannot* mean that the people actually rule in any obvious sense of the terms "people" and "rule." Democracy means only that the people have the opportunity of accepting or refusing the men who are to rule them ... by free competition among would-be leaders for the vote of the electorate. Now one aspect of this may be expressed by saying that *democracy is the rule of the politician.* It is of the utmost importance to realize clearly what this means.[70]

As opposed to engaging in a rhetorical sleight of hand, Schumpeter bluntly asks the reader to appreciate that accepting his proposal means that democracy will no longer signify the rule of the people, but instead will mean the rule of the leader or politician. Moreover, his redefinition does away with any discussion of representative ties between the politician and his constituency. If we are to adopt his radical redefinition, he says, then we will "immediately cease to wonder why it is that politicians so often fail to serve the interest of their class or of the groups with which they are personally connected," and we will consequently cease to expect this type of legislative responsiveness from the newly defined "democratic" government.[71] His doctrine therefore advances a novel conception in two different registers: first, it discards the etymological expectation of a people "ruling" in any immediate institutional sense of the term; and second, it denies any representative connection between the governors and the governed that enables the democratic transfer / translation of that people's rule.

Identifying democracy as the rule of the politician without the slightest pretense of representative ties between politicians and constituents continues to strike many commentators as a defense of a strong leader characteristic of plebiscitary politics, or at the very least as a celebration of the feudal knight or valiant entrepreneur as the archetype of political life.[72] Many postwar and contemporary readers would justifiably bristle at a theory of so-called democracy that advances a plebiscitary model that could just as well describe the demagogic usurpations that Schumpeter fears.[73]

Yet it is difficult to understand the presentation of the alternate theory as anything that runs along the lines of traditional advocacy or endorsement. Far from endorsing hopeful celebrations of the new doctrine or even the rule of the politician, Schumpeter insists that a reconsideration of liberal practice must be include a clear-eyed view of its inherent flaws. His pessimism does not permit him to acclaim the redefinition of democracy as competitive elections. In the spirit of realism, he belabors the fact that, empirically speaking, electoral / representative governments offer the most disappointing of trajectories:

> Nothing is easier than to compile an impressive list of failures of the democratic method, especially if we include not only cases in which there was actual breakdown or national discomfiture but also those in which, though the nation led a healthy and prosperous life, the performance in the political sector was clearly substandard relative to the performance in others. But it is just as easy to marshal hardly less impressive evidence in favor of the politician.[74]

In sum, the democratic method, now redefined as electoral procedure, has a terrible track record in terms of its historical chances of existential survival. Schumpeter states that even flourishing, healthy polities that champion electoral procedure as the sine qua non of political life usually have "substandard" political practices compared to their economic, cultural, and social patterns.

Moreover, as the last sentence of the passage above indicates, the redefinition of democracy along the lines of the alternate theory means accepting the fact that electoral competition will necessarily produce, at best, mediocre leadership unable to optimally govern the polity. Schumpeter describes how competition for votes warps the political sphere long after the electoral moment has passed, rendering politicians just as, or even more, incapable than the masses of distinguishing between short- and long-term interests, or at least incapable of acting upon the latter. The politician generated by electoral practices, he says:

> might be likened to a horseman who is so fully engrossed in trying to keep in the saddle that he cannot plan his ride, or to a general so fully occupied with making sure that his army will accept his order that he must leave strategy to take care of itself. And this remains true (and must, in the case of some countries such as France and Italy, be frankly recognized as one of the sources from which anti-democratic felling has spread) in spite of the acts that may be invoked in extenuation.[75]

As opposed to glorifying the politician as a feudal knight or eco-entrepreneurial actor, Schumpeter contends that the prime minister or presidential executive

138   DEMOCRATIC ELITISM

decided by unmitigated electoral matches will provide an abominable caricature of irresponsibility and a lack of competence. Like his predecessors Pareto
an Mosca, Schumpeter even blames the prioritizing of electoral competition
and its resultant disappointing quality of political leadership as the source of
"anti-democratic feeling"—that is, anti-parliamentary feeling—in countries like
France and Italy, which is hardly a rousing endorsement of the alternate conception based on electoral competition.

Schumpeter thus takes a far more cynical approach toward the incompetence and mediocrity of leadership that electoral politics engender. In this
regard it is helpful to evaluate Schumpeter's and Mosca's respective treatments
of elite leadership vis-à-vis majoritarianism. In the 1923 edition of *Elementi*,
Mosca elaborates his earlier development of democratic and aristocratic principles and urges the ruling classes to constrain themselves in the following three
ways: First, as previously mentioned, the ruling class must be constantly replenished by the lower socioeconomic strata through externally imposed political
and economic measures. Second, ruling minorities, he says, must feel morally
and intellectually attached to their constituents, or so thoroughly enmeshed with
"the small groups of people" that they "directly assist" them through constant
interaction with them in their regional localities, as opposed to those parliamentarians spending most of their time in some distant capital.[76]

Third, and "more than anything else," Mosca claims, the governing class must
assume the "conscience of the majority," such that majoritarian thinking becomes "preponderant in determining the ruling classes' thinking and feeling."[77]
This means that "true" aristocrats or "real" elites, in Mosca's estimation, are
those who are able to "suppress their own interest and those of the small
consortium of sects that gather around them" and instead "exhibit loyalty to
their subordinates."[78] Although it may strike some as utopian thinking, Mosca
continues, this idea actually contains the heart of his political realism: Loyalty
to subordinates, he writes, comes from candor about elite capacities and limitations in governing, and additionally from the recognition that suppressing minority interests in favor of the majority confers legitimacy and longevity on an
existing ruling class.[79]

Mosca may express anxiety about adopting certain Athenian practices, but
he ultimately underscores that political realism requires elite candor about their
interests, capacities, and limitations in the service of loyalty to *majoritarian*
needs and desires. In a poignant moment of exasperation, he writes in 1928
that he has spent his life studying the inevitable tendency toward minority
domination precisely because "it is *fatal* [to the state] when the few command
and the many obey" (*è fatale che i pochi comandino ed i molti obbediscano*)—not

that we should accept such an arrangement and lower our expectations of democratic leadership.[80]

By contrast, as opposed to warning elites that their rule depends on their responsiveness and loyalty to majority needs, desires, and concerns, Schumpeter sardonically submits altogether eliminating the majoritarian expectations of democratic leadership—however fantastical the idea may seem. After all, he caustically suggests, if constituencies learn to expect nothing from politicians, current political elites might still stand a chance.

Yet Schumpeter also underscores that this rather creative proposal borders on the absurd. The discussion on the failures of electoral politics and the incompetence of liberal politicians ends by foreshadowing the necessary, preexisting conditions that electoral schemes need to use if they are to produce adequate leaders. He subsequently delineates five conditions that might save the electoral method from utter failure: (1) candidates of "good quality"; (2) limits on the range of political decisions elected leaders will make; (3) a well-trained and evolved bureaucracy; (4) democratic self-control; and (5) tolerance for diversity of opinion. Strangely enough, he also claims that these external conditions cannot be generated by the electoral system itself and stresses how extremely difficult they are to sustain even within polities experienced with the required norms, such as toleration of diversity of opinion and a highly evolved, well-trained bureaucracy.[81] Much could be said about the supplemental criteria that he claims are required to adequately restrain electoral competition for office so that it does not deconstruct the political apparatus from within; however, for our purposes the point here is that, according to Schumpeter, democracy understood as its antithesis cannot survive without criteria external to elections that he describes as being somewhat impossible to instantiate and unlikely to be sustainable.[82]

Along with his equivocal endorsement in its presentation, outside of part 4 Schumpeter explicitly undermines every component of his alternate theory, thereby suggesting the somewhat farcical nature of his proposal.[83] The theory's first premise demands that democracy be considered as a procedure, but his more pervasive claim is that democracy is a transformative ideal.[84] The theory contends that there is no such thing as "the people" or "the people's will," and that therefore sovereignty should be redefined exclusively in terms of electoral outcomes. Yet throughout the text Schumpeter creates an analogous category of social consensus through his articulation of "hearts and minds" and "things and souls"—a collective entity that exhibits a clear and definitive will to do away with capitalist institutions.[85] The greatest issue with liberal capitalism, Schumpeter argues, is that these institutions do not adequately address the values,

140 DEMOCRATIC ELITISM

desires, and preferences of an increasing majority of individuals. He also belabors how this notion of popular sovereignty as popular judgment has the power to profoundly direct social, economic, and political change.[86] His proposition to liken elections to the economic market seems at best disingenuous, considering his biting critique of the uncompetitive, plebiscitary nature of elections that liberal capitalism has hitherto engendered.[87]

In other words, by proposing the theory of competitive leadership, Schumpeter sardonically challenges his readership to redefine democracy on the basis of how we practice politics in liberal representative governments. The tone is sardonic because his own presentation of the theory in and outside of part 4 details why democracy and liberal government have proven incompatible. Yet this change in democratic theory must occur, he writes, because "the friction" between democratic ideals and liberal representative practice imposes on the masses and elites a burden so great that the entire system might collapse.[88] Schumpeter's audience consists of the politicians and intellectuals he identifies as the elites who are responsible for causing democracy to deviate from its classical principles and practices, so he urges these elites to call a spade a spade and describe the system accurately—without resorting to the fallacious theoretical constructs they currently rely on to legitimate it. He suggests that while it might not serve as a lasting solution, his alternate theory could potentially stave off the imminent rejection of capitalism and liberal institutions altogether.

I call this challenge the Schumpeterian "dare" to forsake hypocrisy over liberal theory and practice. The dare, directed at "elites" widely construed, is carried out via irony and other rhetorical cues and consists of three substantive parts: (1) a challenge to redefine democracy such that popular sovereignty can only be measured at electoral moments; (2) the application of economic language to the political sphere such that our orientation toward capitalism and representative government is entirely consistent; and (3) the encouragement of more empirically grounded political studies, despite his ambivalence over the complications posed by such endeavors.[89] In Schumpeter's recounting, the task of adopting the alternate theory of competitive leadership does not consist in a simple or straightforward theoretical adjustment between our current conception of democracy and the modus operandi of representative government. Rather, his presentation reveals that the task of redefining democracy as elections asks elites to courageously embark on a hazardous and uncertain path forward and invent something entirely new. Who knows, Schumpeter acerbically insinuates: given their past performance, such an undertaking might be easier than encouraging simple reform of liberal politicians and representative practices.

Sardonic Irony, Pessimism, and Invention

Schumpeter's sardonic theory of competitive leadership exudes what Marjorie Perloff calls "Austro-Modernism": a profound skepticism about the power of government to reform human life and the power of language to convey meaning, primarily through the use of irony. For Perloff, the Austro-Modernists—Franz Kafka, Ludwig Wittgenstein, Robert Musil, Joseph Roth, Karl Kraus, Elias Canetti—all mourn that language no longer transmits transparency and meaning.[90] I would include Schumpeter in this heritage in that he too makes a mockery of words like "democracy" and of the ease with which one can redefine such words to indicate their very opposite.

And yet notwithstanding his laconic mockery and pessimistic orientation toward modernity, Schumpeter's sardonic irony does not necessarily indicate a fatalistic streak. In the preface to the second edition of *Capitalism, Socialism and Democracy*, Schumpeter denies charges of defeatism about the fate of liberal capitalism and invites his readers to do something about liberalism's "[sinking] ship." In response to impending totalitarian usurpation of liberal representative governments, elites "can sit down and drink the water or rush to the pumps," meaning that they can either fatally accept such usurpation or decide to do something about it. His prediction of a failure of liberal capitalism and the destruction of the contemporary ruling class does not mean that their collapse will necessarily occur. "What normal man will refuse to defend his life," he writes, "merely because he is quite convinced that sooner or later he will have to die anyhow?" This call to action, Schumpeter says, applies to both "sponsors of private-enterprise society and sponsors of democratic socialism." Both socialist elites and liberal elites, he continues "stand to gain if they see more clearly than they usually do the nature of the social situation in which it is their fate to act."[91]

Schumpeter begins his text with a thinly veiled plea for elites to act in response to the analysis in his book. After all, he says, "analysis never tells us what *will* happen to the pattern but only what *would* happen if they continued to act as they had been acting in the time interval covered by observation and if no other factors intruded."[92] To put it using Robert Musil's words, anyone who has a sense of possibility does not merely say what will happen; in saying what will happen he might also be inclined to think that if democracy currently contains some fantastical conception of popular sovereignty understood as rule of the people, surely it could just as well be otherwise.

Schumpeter thus employs the "modern Machiavellian" method so aggressively that he transforms the purpose that, in the hands of his Italian antecedents, it was intended to serve. His juxtaposition of the ideals of the classical doctrine and of the realities of the alternate account exposes the brutality of elite domination; that is, he details the facts of minority rule in liberal capitalist society such that it seems to be a force too strong to oppose. This pessimistic honesty produces the opposite effect of what the Italian theorists intended. They sought to expose elite domination so that neither elites nor masses could delude themselves into thinking that it was acceptable and, most importantly, so that no one could ever be induced into thinking that such elitism could be considered democratic. Schumpeter, however, radicalizes this exposé to such an extent that elite power seems insurmountable, and even preferable when considered against the authoritarian alternatives. Unlike the efforts of the Italians, the result of Schumpeter's exposé challenges democratic theory to embrace empirical studies and reject participatory and egalitarian aspirations—at least in the liberal capitalist present—lest authoritarianism overtake the Western world. He portrays minority domination in such a cynical light that the only option seems to be to surrender to liberal elite rule, compelling readers to take Schumpeter up on his dare and identify elite domination as part and parcel of modern democracy on the premise that elite domination is always better than totalitarian autocracy.

Postwar scholarship did just that. As Nils Gilman puts it, readers accepted the alternate theory of democracy at face value "while occluding those elements that were pessimistic about the future or critical about modernity."[93] In response to Schumpeter's dare, American political scientists reinterpreted nonvoting and political noninvolvement as an expression of support for the political system and began to understand "Schumpeterianism" as the equation of democracy and liberal competitive elections. A few scholars were attuned to Schumpeter's sardonic irony, but the majority took (and continue to take) Schumpeter's dare very seriously—in fact, too literally. This may explain Schumpeter's own dismay over his "little volume's" success.[94] I speculate that he believed his irony was vulgarized and misunderstood. Paradoxically, however, the dare's vulgarization seems to have procured the ends Schumpeter ultimately desired: popular rejection of liberal capitalism became a thing of the past. When seen in this light, the irony is not merely that the most criticized aspect of liberalism in Schumpeter's time, the limitations of electoral procedure, offered the only means of defending representative government from autocracy. Perhaps the greatest historical irony is that, for a variety of highly contingent circumstances, Schumpeter's reinvention of democracy as competitive elections actually did offer a theoretical path to save liberalism from itself.

Schumpeter thus radicalizes Italian pessimism and alters its ultimate purpose. Yet ironically, his successors managed to reverse the actual methodological and substantive relationship between Schumpeter and the Italian School, such that Schumpeter came to represent a more genuinely democratic alternative to the Italian theorists. To name just a few iconic examples, Norberto Bobbio, Harold Lasswell, and Giovanni Sartori transformed Schumpeter's theory of competitive leadership into the "elite" or "minimalist" theory of democracy and, in doing so, argued that Schumpeter was less "elitist" than the Italian theorists.[95] As late as 1997, Bernard Manin echoes these views when he states that "the epithet 'elitist' ill befits [Schumpeter's] theories" because "it mistakenly connects them to the elitist conceptions of Gaetano Mosca or Vilfredo Pareto."[96] Although Manin remains vague about why, exactly, Schumpeter should be considered, not an elite theorist, but instead a reconstructed democratic theorist, he clearly participates in the intellectual tradition of distinguishing the anti-elitist Schumpeter from the substantially elitist Italian School, despite substantial evidence to suggest that, if anything, the reverse is in fact the case.

Pareto, Mosca, and Michels clearly held pessimistic views of political leadership and expressed a lack of faith in the ability of liberal institutions to combat plutocracy. And yet, they later were cast not only as enemies of democracy but also as the forefathers of an intransigently elitist theory who would have rejected any reformation of democracy capable of combating elitism or plutocracy. This perversion of their contributions is bizarre. Nevertheless, all four European intellectuals engaged elite rule because of their suspicious views of elite leadership, and, more specifically, the quality of political leadership engendered by electoral institutions. The Italians worried that liberal elites perverted the democratic process; Schumpeter expressed suspicious views of their competence in organizing politics for the future. On this score, all four "elite theorists" consistently expressed anti-elitist pessimism, yet the tone of their respective pessimisms resulted in different conclusions that cannot be divorced from their expressed political prescriptions.

CHAPTER 5

Hopeful Panic

The American Reception

If God did not exist, it would be necessary to invent him.
— Voltaire

We all need enemies. Considering the geopolitical climate of the "Second Thirty Years War," it is somewhat understandable that the burgeoning discipline of political science refashioned the Italian investigations of elite domination into protofascistic celebrations of oligarchic power against "mass society." After all, the Italian School of Elitism was composed of two Italians and a German-born naturalized Italian, and therefore, on the face of it, these controversial figures could be treated as convenient representatives of Axis political philosophy. Given their vitriolic indictments of electoral government as invitations to plutocracy, it makes sense that the Allied victors would refer to the Italians to warn of the totalitarian dangers posed by any expressed ambivalence toward liberal or electoral democracy. At the very least, the prewar and interwar receptions of Pareto, Mosca, and Michels, combined with Michels's conversion to fascism, seemed to confirm that critiques of electoral politics ultimately, whether intentionally or not, lean in fascist directions and should be avoided at all costs.

That could have been the end of the story. Given the apex of its vogue at the turn of the century and its ideological vilification thereafter, Italian elitism could have easily been relegated to the history of fascist conservatism. Yet, surprisingly, the Italian School of Elitism did not disappear from the political science scene on either side of the Atlantic. After 1945, Pareto, Mosca, and

Michels continued to hold a central place in all subfields of political science, constituting the epistemological foundation of the behavioral revolution of the discipline and, ironically enough, even of contemporary democratic theory. Stranger still, as mentioned above, American political science determined that Pareto and Mosca exhibited fascist theoretical leanings but that Michels, the only committed fascist of the three, was a productive resource for future democratic theory.

The history of political science and its behavioral turn can be understood by connecting the two overlapping misappropriations of the Italian School of Elitism. In the first half of the twentieth century, the distortion of the Italian School turned on their presumed disdain for the masses and the "elitist" connection to electoral and democratic politics. In the second half of the twentieth century, the distortion focused on the extent to which the Italian School provided the foundation for an adequately scientific and "realistic" approach to the study of elites and the study of politics writ large, based on an empirical and anti-historical approach. Pareto, Mosca, Michels, and Schumpeter provided the standards for determining how any social science inquiry could properly qualify as scientific and / or "realistic."

In other words, somehow the Italians simultaneously became both the genesis and the antithesis of empirical political science. Political scientists' debates about which theories could be considered more properly scientific *and* democratic hinged on the presumed methodological similarity and normative distance from the Italian position. By making the Italians out to be the fascist enemies of democracy who nevertheless were responsible for redirecting political science in an empirical direction, a new defining question presented itself: How could the discipline maintain a plausibly scientific and objective approach but nevertheless remain enthusiastic about the prospects of electoral democracy over authoritarian communist alternatives? As a result, proponents and critics of the behavioral revolution condensed the argument space to which theories presented the more realistic position vis-à-vis mass political participation, given a world where democracy and elections were synonymous, thereby assuming the very presupposition that the Italians had sought to contest.

This falsification occurred through a variety of political, historical, and economic contingencies that will be elaborated below. But it is important to stress that these two distinct misappropriations—that is, (1) the political misunderstanding of the Italians as elitist or resolutely antidemocratic theorists, and (2) the reduction of their scientific approach to a positivist, anti-historicist or causally oriented empirical method—coalesced in the postwar period because of incommensurable ways of seeing the world. Unfamiliar with the

146   DEMOCRATIC ELITISM

rampant plutocratic corruption during the Risorgimento and the type of methodologically pluralist, anti-Cartesian "new science" that pervaded the Italian
peninsula, neither Anglo-American nor continental political science could appreciate the scope and direction of this specific variety of the pessimist tradition. It became existentially necessary to caricature members of the Italian
School as fascist positivists so that by rejecting them one could signify an
embrace of an optimistic orientation toward electoral democracy while still
maintaining the supposedly rigorous commitment to objective neutrality
that scientific standards demand. The discipline was then consumed by a
contest over which camp of political science could be simultaneously more
scientific and democratic, not by an absolute standard but by relative measure
against the mythically elitist, albeit supposedly more empirical, Italians. In
this respect both camps seemed more democratic and progressive than that
fictitious standard. Inventing the Italian straw man allowed for the discipline
to unite under an effort to impose a style of causal scientific criteria to the
study of politics while continuing a more circumscribed debate about democratic elitism, the new reigning definition of democracy that reduced it to
competitive elections.

The preceding chapters have traced how the Italians were misunderstood
before World War II in a way that shaped the empirical orientation of both
American and European political science thereafter. The subsequent discussion reconstructs how this evolution from purportedly "fascist" Italian thought
to "minimal" Schumpeterian democratic theory took place after 1945, with specific reference to the behavioral revolution. As we have seen, the distortion of
the Italian School was taken up by political scientists of all stripes, from international relations scholars to those working in American and comparative politics. I focus here on political theorists C. Wright Mills, Robert Dahl, Peter
Bachrach, Carole Pateman, Quentin Skinner, and Adam Przeworski—not only
because they are the most famous exponents of their respective movements, but
also because of their enormous influence on the development of democratic
theory and their massive contributions to the construction of the category
known as democratic elitism.

In what follows I analyze the reception of Schumpeter's *Capitalism, Socialism
and Democracy* and the transformation of the Italian School's legacy within
postwar political science. I contend that American political science heeded
Schumpeter's sardonic challenge to redefine democracy as electoral processes
by distorting the Italians as fascist or elitist positivists, and in so doing, solidified competitive elections as the hegemonic definition of democracy. Those
who should have been sympathetic to the Italian anti-plutocratic orientation,

such as C. Wright Mills, made Pareto and Mosca to be obstacles to a democratically inspired assault on the American elite "establishment." Epitomized by Dahl, pluralist political scientists who were presumed to have inherited the Italian School's methodological presuppositions optimistically reinterpreted nonvoting and noninvolvement by citizens as expressions of support for representative government and began to celebrate "Schumpeterianism" as the salutary equation of democracy with competitive elections, a disposition I describe as "hopeful ambivalence." Political theorists of the left, or participatory critics of pluralism such as Bachrach and Pateman, responded with panic, thereby reifying the institutional choices and empirically oriented research promoted in the postwar mainstream against which they were protesting. Even outsiders to the debate, such as the Cambridge School, formalized the pluralist versus participatory positions as the binaries of the new empirical political science, as Quentin Skinner's intervention attests. Finally, through an analysis of Przeworski's work, I show how the response to Michels and Schumpeter coalesced into an inappropriately sanguine "minimal" theory of democracy.

The point of these outlines is not merely to describe how American political science misinterpreted the Italian School, but also to illuminate examples of an unconscious and pervasive interpretive tendency that has had consequential ramifications. Misconstructions abound in the history of political thought, and the case of the Italian School of Elitism is certainly no exception. However, this hermeneutic injustice of the elite theory lineage is particularly important as it constitutes the founding myth of our discipline and continues to shape its self-understanding as the ontological foundation of realist theories of democracy. In presenting sketches of key figures of American postwar political science, the task is to understand why, exactly, casting the Italian School as conservatively authoritarian became central to the discipline, on what grounds this suspect genealogy of democratic elitism was generated, and how freeing ourselves from such an attachment may change our orientation toward the reigning realist definitions of democracy in terms of free and fair elections.

Rebellious Optimism: Early Pluralism and the Power Elite

Throughout the forties and early fifties, American political science followed in the footsteps of early pluralists such as Harold Laski, Charles Merriam, Walter Lippmann, Arthur Bentley, and Pendleton Herring. In a renewed response to Weber's and Michels's preoccupations concerning bureaucratization, midcentury authors reinvigorated a Madisonian / Tocquevillian vision of

148   DEMOCRATIC ELITISM

competing factions and coexisting associations to develop the pluralist "interest group" approach. Earl Lathan, John Galbraith, David Reisman, and David Truman, to take just a few of the most famous expositors, advanced theories of checks and balances between competing "interest" or "pressure" groups and associations as the stabilizing democratic force within representative governments.[1] Although it was occasionally acknowledged that any particular interest may be led by an elite, the early pluralists underscored the concept of competing associations such that the group, and not the individual, became the major unit of analysis for democratic theory. According to one political scientist surveying the field in 1942, "the modern expression of democracy by the people and for the people" manifested itself in the idea of a balance between competing pressure groups, a conception that continued to proliferate through the early fifties.[2] As Irving Howe put it in 1952, pluralism remained the narrow focus of American politics.[3]

Along with Floyd Hunter and E. E. Schattschneider, C. Wright Mills's *The Power Elite* offered one of the first, most sensational repudiations of the early pluralist approach, or what Mills refers to as "the theory of balance." For some time, at least at the beginning of its reception, it seemed obvious that Mills's intervention shared both the Italians' general orientation toward the tendency of elite cohesion and their particular attention to the transformation of the economic elite in the twentieth century. For Mills, the "power elite" are those individuals who are "in command of the major hierarchies and organizations of modern society" as a result of their positions within "pivotal" institutions.[4] Avoiding the word "plutocracy," Mills articulates a structural triangulation between military, political, and economic elites, with acute emphasis on the ways the former two sects act at the behest of "the very rich," the "corporate rich," and the "CEOs." Much like E. E. Schattschneider's response to the early pluralists, Mills sketches a history of the American republic in which the landed, Protestant well-to-do evolved into the Ivy-educated, Protestant class of the corporate rich. Mills contends that the American conflict system of partisan pressure politics was always inherently biased toward the plutocratic factionalism of an elite minority.[5]

Despite the context of general material prosperity that made current plutocratic domination more palatable and a "conservative mood" of the American intelligentsia more understandable, Mills urges readers to reconsider the category of elites as a heuristic that exposes the realities of minority domination. In a manner reminiscent of the Italians' approach to transparency, he insists that avoiding the facticity of elite domination is "politically irresponsible because it obfuscates" any serious attempt to locate responsibility for "the consequential decisions of men who do have the access to the means of power."[6]

Along with this theoretical focus on elite cohesion, Mills follows the Italians in articulating his commitment to a methodologically pluralistic approach to the social sciences that uncovers elements that go undetected by traditional causal approaches. Much like the Italians, he also rejects extreme forms of empiricism, which, to his mind, tend to produce a "paste-pot eclecticism which avoids the real task of social analysis." The "impossibility of rigorous proof" of his thesis, he writes, forces him to eschew overly formalistic empirical analysis, but he wishes to make "sense of the facts we know or can readily find out" by use of his concept of the power elite.[7]

Yet Mills not only fails to connect his work to the Italian predecessors, he also renders them as the antithesis of his own approach. In an early footnote he contrasts his definition of the elite with that of Pareto, claiming that from the Italian's point of view, "the elite are simply those who have the most of what there is to have," whereas in his perspective, the elite "could not 'have the most' were it not for their positions in the great institutions."[8] He calls Pareto the founder of the "statistical idea of choosing some value and calling those who have the most of it elite," lending to Pareto's definition an air of the "abstracted empiricism" that Mills seeks to refute.[9] Although this definition may have been used in the 80 / 20 rule and other such applications, it does not capture how Pareto actually employs the concept sociologically. Even when defined as an idealized analytic category, he distinguishes between the label "elite" and the capabilities and possessions of the elite. Like Mills, Pareto sought to understand the ways in which society's institutional structure *justified* the conjunction of title and position of a select minority of individuals in a manner that superseded the superficial Marxist understanding of who constitutes the categories of possessor and dispossessed.[10]

Mills also ostentatiously rejects Mosca's purported contention that in any society there is always a "certain quota of men who when provoked will always resort to violence," thereby suggesting that Mosca was primarily concerned with a Weberian definition of the elite as those who have a monopoly on the means of violence.[11] This reconstruction contradicts the thrust of Mosca's conception of the ruling class. Recall that for Mosca, different institutions achieve historical salience in different epochs. In some periods the most critical institutions are military in character; in others, religious; in still others, economic, political, and so on. In all periods, Mosca maintains, those who control one or more of the relevant institutions are also the holders of great power—and both Pareto

150   DEMOCRATIC ELITISM

and Mosca agreed that it was futile to argue against or moralize about this universal law.

It is precisely this universalist characterization that perturbs Mills. In a rather obvious but latent refutation of the Italian theorists, he proclaims, "It is not my thesis that for all epochs of human history and in all nations a creative minority, a ruling class, an omnipotent elite, shapes all historical events." Similarly, he adds, he also contests the "Schumpeterian" view that within this perennial category of elites or supranormal men one can always discover the sources of innovation.[12] Mills thus recoils from the seeming finality contained within any study of elites that amounts to a generalizable tendency. Instead, he offers a more historically circumscribed argument about the ramifications of large-scale industrialization and bureaucratization strictly in the context of the American example. Far from proposing any scientific law, he says, "What I am asserting is that in this particular epoch a conjunction of historical circumstances has led to the rise of an elite of power ... and that given the enlargement and the centralization of the means of power now available, the decisions that they make and fail to make carry more consequences of more people than has been the case in the world history of mankind."[13] In other words, the rise of the contemporary American power elite results from a series of historical contingences—increased industrialization, nationalization, bureaucratization, and the centralization of economic, military, and political institutions that has eliminated the possibility of local governance. According to Mills, the associational politics of competing group interests is not a complete chimera; such political practices were performed on a local scale in the eighteenth and nineteenth centuries, which made Madisonian or Tocquevillian theories of balance plausible. Yet this golden age has been surpassed by the centralization that mass industrialization necessitated. Pluralists like David Riesman, he complains, hang on to this "old model of power as an automatic balance, with its assumptions of a plurality of independent, relatively equal, and conflicting groups of the balancing" simply to justify their own privilege. In the end, liberalism, which rests on the idea of a "social balance" among competing interests, "has become irrelevant, and in its optative mood, misleading."[14]

Despite his charges of sinister intentions that lie behind romantic pluralism, Mills is no pessimist about the future prospects of democracy.[15] Most obviously, his conception of the power elite, although institutionally driven, is not intrinsically tied to a critique of electoral structures that encourage elite cohesion. Instead he argues that changes to the social structure have increased the cohesion of elites while simultaneously inhibiting cohesion among the middle and lower classes, rendering politics an affair that transcends the national scale by bypassing electoral channels. Mills's main preoccupation is to illustrate how the power elite is not primarily political; his analysis helps us recognize, for example, that the question of racial inequality "is really in the hands of corporate executives who hire housing contractors who build, and of bankers who extend loans," thereby remaining rather neutral on the inherent structural tendencies of electoral politics.[16] Electoral corruption is not the heart of Mills's critique, and therefore Mills remains more open to the potential for salvaging American democracy on electoral grounds.

Although he rebelliously rails against the power elite and the American "establishment," Mills remains hopeful that there can be a redirection of one subset of the class: the intelligentsia. The future of American democracy, he contends, lies in the development of a counter-elite composed of unaffiliated, free-thinking intellectuals. "Once upon a time in the United States, men of affairs were also men of sensibility," he writes; "to a considerable extent the elite of power and the elite of culture coincided." He laments the fact that Washington "relaxed with Voltaire's Letters and Locke's 'On Human Understanding' [while] Eisenhower read cowboy tales and detective stories."[17] Mills urges intellectuals to somehow cultivate a more sophisticated cultural sensibility and use the tool of critique to contain the amorphous ambition of the men of affairs, thereby redirecting the course of politics against the power elite.[18]

Mills's aversion to the pessimism of the Italian theorists, both in their critique of electoral institutions and their unwillingness to elevate some subset of the elite, may have encouraged his misconstruction of their overly empirical methodological orientations. He establishes a methodological antagonism between the Italian formalistic empirical orientation and his historically focused conceptualization, even though he is far closer to their approach than he appreciates. Nevertheless, critics capitalized on Mills's rejection of empiricism and defended the purported strict formalism of the Italians. Daniel Bell, Suzanne Keller, and especially Talcott Parsons, who was closely associated with Paretian models of equilibrium and the Harvard "Pareto Circle," harped on Mills's unproven assumption of the congruity of elite interests.[19] Mills linked the upper classes and the power elite to the increasing functional specialization of elites, but these were incompatible, argued his critics.[20] In a reply, Mills conceded that his argument was not "unquestionably valid," which seemed to divorce Mills from the Italian methodology.[21] The methodological distortion will enable the second wave of pluralists to assume that Italians were the antecedents of an empirical, realistic elite tradition in political science.

Both Mills's *The Power Elite* and Dahl's *Preface to Democratic Theory* were published in 1956, which today makes Mills and Dahl seem like convenient

152   DEMOCRATIC ELITISM

counterparts of the "elite theory" debate between the pluralists who celebrated elite competition and their detractors who emphasized elite cohesion. But this framing obfuscates important elements of the genealogy of elite theory: Dahl may have been responding to Mills and other critics of the "conflict group" approach, but Mills was equally engaged with an earlier conception of pluralism that preceded Dahl, whose first work *Congress and Foreign Policy* (1950) had little to do with pluralism or elite theory.[22] It is only in 1953 that Dahl turns his interest to pluralism. As we will see below, Dahl's response to Mills and the latter's rejection of Italian elite theory moves pluralism in a new direction, a direction supposedly endowed with the empirical methodological authority of the Italian antecedents but divorced from their supposed conservative or authoritarian commitments.

Polyarchy and the Nouveau Elitism of Robert Dahl

Dahl's work is paradigmatic of a midcentury American political science movement I call "nouveau elitism." As the most successful expositor of this school of thought, Dahl's prolific contributions to American political science leave an indelible mark on our perception of the Italian School's thought and Schumpeter's thought. Although Dahl borrows heavily from both the Madisonian early interest-group pluralists and the Italians to develop "polyarchy" as a legitimate regime type, his pluralist system is more elitist than the normative model originally staked out by his predecessors. Dahl's pluralism bears closer resemblance to what we remember the Europeans to have advocated than what Pareto, Mosca, and Michels, and even Schumpeter actually argued. Dahl consistently attempts to distance himself from elite theory, but his writings appropriate the partial conclusions of Pareto, Mosca, Michels, and Schumpeter on representative governments, transforming them into a more idealistic, democracy-friendly model. Dahl's development of polyarchy reconfigures the European theories in a more optimistic light; what horrified the Italians, and even worried Schumpeter to some extent, gave Dahl infinite hope about the present and future of electoral democracy.

In *A Preface to Democratic Theory* (1956) Dahl introduced polyarchy as a new addition to the Aristotelian regime types, explaining why we should not consider representative institutions problematically oligarchic despite certain appearances to the contrary. This first iteration of polyarchy grafts elements of Michels's and Schumpeter's thought onto Dahl's own in the effort to reclassify modern representative governments as polyarchies. Dahl first draws upon Michels's speculation that the need for a ruling elite arises as a result of increased specialization and bureaucratization in the modern age. Secondly, he endorses Schumpeter's contention that in modern representative governments, "the rule of popular sovereignty" is most "closely approximated" in electoral moments.[23] In light of these two appropriations, and in response to the challenge Schumpeter posed in 1942, Dahl analyzes political systems according to different temporal moments within the electoral process: pre-voting, voting, post-voting, and inter-election periods.[24] Only on this basis, he argues, can one determine a particular regime's democratic character—by judging the extent to which it fulfills certain metrics of popular sovereignty at various junctures in the voting cycle.

Dahl thus defines polyarchy as a system that exhibits various degrees of popular sovereignty at different stages, but this criterion does not in itself distinguish it from oligarchy. In order to make such a distinction, Dahl combines the Schumpeterian trope of electoral competition with Mosca's insistence on the "multiplicities" of elites; in so doing, Dahl portrays elections as a more democratic institution than American political scientists currently consider it. Electoral competitions among elites, he claims, "vastly increase the size, number, and variety of minorities" who influence the political process. One can therefore distinguish polyarchy from other regimes by the criterion of "minorities rule" in the plural—"not minority rule" in the singular, which characterizes Aristotelian oligarchy. Though Dahl complains of the inordinate power that elites exert, he ultimately glorifies competitive elections among myriad elite groupings as the element that renders polyarchy an impressive, dynamic political system—quite certainly, he argues, the best of all possible and imaginable alternatives.[25]

The glorification of elite competition arises again in Dahl's next major work, *Who Governs?* In his case study of New Haven, Connecticut, Dahl advances his view that although American government is controlled by a ruling elite consisting of select professional politicians and socially prominent citizens, it should not be considered a cohesive, monolithic oligarchy. The argument here is similar to the one presented in his earlier work, but the emphasis on elite accountability derived from electoral competition draws on different elements of the Europeans' thought—specifically, Mosca's and Pareto's understanding of pluralities of minority groups who exercise control in a given society. Dahl contends that polyarchy cannot be considered oligarchy because, in the former, multiplicities of elite groups with access to different political resources compete for power. He traces a history of the ruling classes from the Patrician era of the American Republic when inequalities were "cumulative"—that is to say, when wealth, social standing, education, and political power were all in the hands of the same group.[26] America's peculiar history of industrialization

154   DEMOCRATIC ELITISM

and immigration resulted in a "gradual and peaceful revolution" away from these circumstances, he argues, where power passed through the hands of different elites until it created a multiplicity of groups with competing political resources—a system characterized by "dispersed inequalities."[27] Rather than relying exclusively on the Madisonian tradition of early pluralism, Dahl thus fuses a Paretian focus on the resources of elites with a historical example of how elites were replenished from the lower classes in a way that evokes what Mosca described as "the democratic impulse."

As a result of this peaceful revolution, Dahl argues, the United States enjoys a system of "executive" leadership with professionals acting as competitive "political entrepreneurs," as opposed to the "petty sovereignties" that dominated in the colonial era and in Europe.[28] Throughout this narrative, Dahl takes up Schumpeter's famous political economism to apply the economic language of competition to the political sphere in order to make a case for American exceptionalism. Yet, crucially, Dahl's history of a slow evolution in the makeup of elites contravenes Pareto's and Mosca's doubts that varied groups of elites accessing different pots of resources would be enough to eliminate a system's oligarchic or plutocratic dimensions. At this juncture Dahl can be likened to Pareto and Mosca in that all three study the transformation of elite composition throughout history and focus on a plurality of minority elite groups. However, whereas the Italians consider the consequences of minority rule to be necessarily antidemocratic, Dahl imbues his narrative with a tempered optimism regarding the compatibility of elite rule and quasi-democratic government.

Who Governs? reiterates the claim that polyarchy cannot be identified with oligarchy, despite the presence of a dominant elite, because diverse sets of leaders are rendered accountable to the populace through elections. While Dahl expresses this familiar defense of representative institutions, he also undermines this position, indicating that the accountability of leaders in the American context is determined by the extent to which the populace adheres to the "democratic creed," and the extent to which leaders attempt to exploit it. Dahl not only attributes the success of politicians like his beloved Mayor Richard Lee to such "political entrepreneurship," but in the last chapter he concedes that blind American adherence to the democratic creed makes polyarchy, in the form of competitive elections, stable.[29] In this sense, Dahl's answer to the question "Who governs?" seems to be "the democratic creed" and the politicians who utilize it; he thereby undermines his own efforts to accentuate the democratic-friendly dimension of polyarchy and to minimize its oligarchic character.

While this tension appears to parallel the Europeans' views—they all heavily stress the importance of a national myth of democracy—it is important to note that in his presentation of these myths Dahl dramatically deviates from his predecessors. On the one hand, Pareto, Mosca, Michels, and even Schumpeter provide historical accounts for why something like a democratic creed cannot be separated from the institution of elections in a way that exposes the oligarchic dimension of representation. Furthermore, they discuss the myth of democracy as part of a crucial process of demystification, which they believe poses a threat to the status quo of minority domination by depriving corrupt elites of the myths or symbolic structures that help preserve their legitimacy. Dahl, on the other hand, rather incongruously makes a similar point simply as a minor qualification within an otherwise overwhelmingly positive appraisal of the American development of electoral competition. Through this change in rhetorical expression and emphasis, Dahl divorces his predecessors' pessimistic suspicions from his own more sanguine presentation of electoral competition. Dahl's "democratic creed" is an American myth immune to European democratic demystification.

By omitting any explicit discussion of the Italian School while implicitly replacing their suspicious conclusions with a more optimistic assessment, Dahl appears to distance himself from their school of thought. Subsequently, in the 1960s, he attempts to inoculate his polyarchic model from aggressive critiques of nouveau elitism; and he vociferously denies that his theories have any association with elitism of any kind. In his article "A Critique of the Ruling Elite Model" (1958), Dahl attempts to debunk all elite theories, including those of the Italian and Schumpeterian variety, because they are unfalsifiable. For Dahl, the theory that a ruling elite exists can always be cast into a form that "makes it impossible to disprove." The idea that a ruling elite controls political decision-making cannot be "controverted by empirical evidence," thereby rendering it an "unscientific" and unusable theory. He asserts that any evidence for the existence of a ruling elite in the United States "or in any specific community" has not been properly examined, "because the examination has not employed satisfactory criteria to determine what constitutes a fair test of the basic hypothesis."[30]

In other words, Dahl rejects the project of identifying elite domination because it employs a patently unscientific methodology. This methodological criticism seems to undermine any parallel that critics might draw between Dahl and the Italian School and / or Schumpeter, and at the same time it raises the methodological bar so high that a "successful" discussion of elites is nearly impossible. On this score, readers may recall Mosca's protest against any scientific standard employed to judge social theories, on the grounds that scientific standards often inhibit honest discussion of elites and the identification of their power and privileges.[31] Dahl invokes social scientific standards to ward off efforts aimed at exposing minority domination, thereby attempting to insulate his own theories against charges of elitism.

In this vein, Dahl's article "Further Reflections on 'The Elitist Theory of Democracy'" responds to Jack Walker's accusation that Dahl is an "elite theorist of democracy"—that is, one who does not express confidence in the epistemic capacity of the masses to participate in politics.[32] Dahl sullies Walker's credibility by revealing the latter's poorly cited generalizations, bypassing any response to Walker's substantive criticisms with a call for a separation between normative and empirical inquiry in democratic thought so that "shallow" critiques like Walker's can be avoided.[33] This charge seems strange considering the fact that Dahl employs both approaches, and would continue to do so in the effort to further develop his idea of polyarchy. Nonetheless, the article demonstrates Dahl's effort to quash any perception of his thought as elitist, or even as "pessimistic," through his invocation of methodological standards and evasion of substantive engagement.

Despite his efforts, these rebuttals did not dispel Dahl's association with elitism or allow him to escape charges that his model does not recognize that some groups (economic elites and corporations) are too strong vis-à-vis other groups and vis-à-vis the state to make polyarchy a feasible quasi-democratic, non-oligarchic regime. Consequently, after his colleague and collaborator Charles Lindblom published a critique of pluralism, Dahl admits that polyarchy, and capitalism in polyarchical regimes, threatens popular sovereignty.[34] Dahl concedes as much in *A Preface to Economic Democracy*, which declares that if democratic accountability is morally defensible in the political realm, it must also be a normative aspiration in the economic sphere as well.[35] Scholars mark this period as the beginning of Dahl's turn to democratic socialism.[36] This bifurcation of his pre- and post-1980s views allowed Dahl to disassociate his model from the nouveau elitism that I contend he always espoused throughout his career.

Despite Dahl's concession that polyarchy may undermine popular sovereignty, I argue that this "socialist turn" did not substantively alter his democratic theory. I agree with Jeffrey Isaac that all of Dahl's works embody the "guiding thread" of the concerns expressed in his dissertation. Isaac contends that "Dahl's genuine intellectual interests and political inclinations were diverted by the academic and political mood of postwar liberal democracy. Once the appearance of liberal consensus began to crumble, so did Dahl's resistance to the more critical insights of socialist theory and practice."[37] This explanation beautifully captures how Dahl responded to the academic trends of his moment, and their influence on the articulation of his substantive positions. Dahl superficially co-opts criticisms impelling him to extend democratic principles to business enterprises while he continues to advance the same basic premises of the polyarchical regime that he first articulated in the 1950s. Even in his magnum opus, *Democracy and Its Critics* (1989), which combines a history of democratic thought with contemporary normative prescriptions, Dahl enumerates polyarchy's virtues and advances a modern, dynamic, pluralist (MDP) polyarchy as the desirable basis of a purported "third transformation" in democratic practice.[38]

Many view the critically acclaimed and incredibly influential *Democracy and Its Critics* as emblematic of Dahl's "democratic socialism" because he targets the Italians—whom he calls "theorists of minority domination"—as the main object of his critique. Although Mosca, Pareto, Michels, Marx, Lenin, and Gramsci all qualify as theorists of minority domination, Dahl mostly focuses on Mosca, Pareto, and Michels. The thrust of his criticism is that these theorists do not adequately weigh the extent to which elections make elites accountable to the demos. Curiously omitting Schumpeter from this discussion, Dahl claims that these theorists make the "elementary mistake" of not applying the theory of economic competition to the public sphere. "Even Pareto," he complains, "who as an economist insisted that competition would inevitably force firms to adapt their products to the preferences of consumers, failed as a sociologist to apply a similar notion to the party competition he acknowledged occurred in the electoral marketplace."[39]

This critique sounds very much like the Dahl of the 1950s and 1960s who extolled electoral competition and often applied economic categories to the political sphere. Yet by the end of the work, things change inexplicably. In the last chapter, devoted to his normative prescriptions for the advancement of democracy, he argues that we must abandon the standard "theoretical perspective" of treating human beings like consumers and we must resist applying economic principles to the political sphere. Dahl further argues that the future of democracy rests on an economic order that "serves not merely consumers but human beings in all the activities to which an economic order may contribute." He suggests that advancing his "theoretical vision of democracy" will be a tall order because on this score it "runs counter to more than a century of intellectual history in Europe and English-speaking countries."[40]

So, which one is it? Can the free-enterprise, capitalist paradigm be applied to the political sphere and democratic theory or not? Should a more socialist paradigm be adopted instead? Is the substantive problem with theories of minority domination that they "give little weight" to accountability achieved through the competition of political elites? Or should we completely reject this economic model of thinking for a more comprehensive political, social, personal discourse? Dahl never addresses this conflict that he establishes between his lifelong arguments and his latterly expressed normative aspirations. Be that as it may, Dahl's parting words give the false impression that his position has substantially evolved from his first writings.

Despite his long, prolific career, Dahl's oeuvre still constitutes a defining moment in the scholarly literature on democratic theory. His development of polyarchy appropriates and optimistically refashions the Italians' and Schumpeter's thought in a palatable way for positivist, postwar American political science throughout changing intellectual and disciplinary trends—but he does so at the cost of distorting their intellectual contributions. Pareto's, Mosca's, Michels's, and Schumpeter's pessimistic exposure of oligarchic elements of electoral competition are transformed by Dahl's hands into the optimistic system of polyarchy, a model supposedly more amenable to popular sovereignty than oligarchy—in fact, the best of all plausible alternatives and one that can even be interpreted as a regime type friendly to democratic socialism.

Dahl's intervention in the pluralist debates and his role in the American reception of elite theory cannot be overstated. His appropriation of the Europeans' partial conclusions and transformation of them into an optimistic ode to representative government laid the groundwork for later perversions of their thought. This redescription of Pareto, Mosca, Michels, and Schumpeter occurred in three phases of his career.

During the second half of the 1950s and 1960s, Dahl relies upon Pareto, Mosca, and Michels as methodological authority figures emblematic of a scientific position, and he does this so extensively that we can confirm that his thought descends from their work. Consequently, his submerging of their explicit preoccupation with economic plutocracy beneath a related but distinct concern over political oligarchy becomes imperceptible—so much so that scholars became inclined to blame the Italian theorists, and not American political science itself, for reorienting the debate *away* from plutocracy and toward oligarchy.[41]

During a second phase of his career, Dahl infused more hope into his presentation of representative institutions: he developed elite explanatory models to demonstrate that modern popular government is less "democratic" than Americans suppose; but also to excuse this reality by arguing that modern "democracies" still ought to be considered popular regimes because they are *more* free and democratic than their previous fascist and present communist antagonists. Dahl's hope for the prospects of fulfilling popular sovereignty despite the oligarchic quality of representative institutions distances his thought from the pessimistic orientation of both the Italian School and Schumpeter. It gave the impression that Dahl offered an alternative to Soviet communism that was conservative but distinctly more progressive than the preceding theories of elitism.

Finally, while the early Dahl distanced himself from all four Europeans through methodological critique, his work in the 1970s and 1980s professes to change course in a way that seems to fully sever any possible connection between his thought and that of his Italian, German, and Austrian predecessors. Nevertheless, as I demonstrated above, this purported normative reorientation toward "democratic socialism" did not substantively alter his commitments to the electoral and economic paradigms that he articulated in the 1950s and 1960s.

As previously mentioned, Dahl calls Pareto, Mosca, and Michels "theorists of minority domination." This is certainly a wonderful moniker for the Italian School. These theorists studied the ways that elites dominate political processes in order to expose these tendencies, and consequently to advance democratic theory and the asymptotic fulfillment of popular sovereignty. But for half a century Dahl relied only partially on their conclusions and ignored critical parts of their arguments in ways that made the Italians conveniently attractive enemies for postwar American political science. What is more, this encouraged audiences to perceive Dahl's polyarchy / pluralism model as a more democratic, albeit still "elitist," regime type. Herein lies the birth of democratic elitism.

Once Dahl was considered to be the paragon of a democratic kind of elitism, the Italian intellectuals came to be seen as proponents of oligarchy who celebrated the ways liberal political institutions suppress or contain mass / popular participation. This perversion of their thought was primarily facilitated by a willingness to ignore their melancholy dispositions and pessimistic philosophical inclinations. I have aimed to underscore the mood expressed in each historical moment discussed in the preceding chapters because rhetorical disposition should not simply be interpreted as a decorative literary technique— on the contrary, disposition substantively affects content. While we intuit this to be true, it is too often deemed acceptable to focus on explicit, expressed political prescriptions while dismissing rhetorical style or literary tone. Of course, Pareto, Mosca, Michels, and Dahl all ostensibly study minority domination. Yet if we do not appreciate how the Italian School's efforts to combat the tragic effects of minority domination on popular governance contrast with nouveau elitism's qualified endorsement of the oligarchy that modern representative institutions generate, then the difference between

160   DEMOCRATIC ELITISM

the two collapses. It consequently becomes tempting to assimilate all of these authors into one school of thought despite their conflicting conclusions, until we eventually forget that any intellectual and political differences exist at all.

Empirical Panic and the Birth of Democratic Elitism

Notwithstanding Dahl's distortion of the Italian School, the school of thought today known as democratic elitism would have never gained such footing in American political science had it not been for the panicked response of participatory democrats to nouveau elitism and the general popularity of Dahl (along with Seymour Lipset, Bernard Berelson, Giovanni Sartori, Harry Eckstein, David Truman, et al). While such a response was widespread, two major works accelerated the rise of democratic elitism as an orthodox model of democracy: Peter Bachrach's *The Theory of Democratic Elitism* and Carole Pateman's *Participation and Democratic Theory*.

Although rarely invoked today, Bachrach's *The Theory of Democratic Elitism* (1967) monumentally shifted the perception of elite theory and shaped the category known as democratic elitism.[42] It was continually cited in reference to the political contributions of the Italians, and Bachrach's subsidiary piece, "Two Faces of Power," coauthored with Morton Baratz, was one of the most cited articles in the political science discipline in the twentieth century.[43] In this widely read and taught pamphlet, Bachrach misinterprets the Italians' pessimism as expressing an elitist disdain for the political capacities of the masses and for democracy writ large, consequently misrepresenting their moral preoccupations and substantive contributions.[44] He then marries the Italians' views to Schumpeter's language of procedural, economic competition based on their supposed shared contempt for mass political agency and their methodological commitment to strict empiricism. Bachrach's polemic against the insufficiencies of democratic elitism, contained within his suspect genealogy, not only disappears the Italians' concerns about plutocracy, but also repackages their contributions so that later participatory democrats rendered their ideas similar to those propounded by the contemporary political science establishment of the 1950s and 1960s.

Bachrach contends that the current approach to democracy reverses the traditional relationship between masses and elites: instead of identifying elites as the main threat to the system (as classical democratic theory would have it), political scientists now borrow from the philosophy of elitism and assume that the perpetuation of democracy rests with the elites' ability to protect the system against the masses.

To explain how this inversion took place, Bachrach constructs a genealogy connecting the "fascist" and "aristocratic" "precursors"—Pareto, Mosca, and Schumpeter—to Bachrach's own contemporaries Dahl, Harrold Lasswell, Truman, V. O. Key, A. A. Berle, William Korhauser, Sartori, et al. These pillars of mainstream political science, he claims, used the Italian School to insidiously shift the discipline's attention toward the study of power and away from the true essence of democratic politics: mass participation. The genealogy is predicated on one basic assumption: that all varieties of elite theory and contemporary democratic theory share an unfavorable view of the masses; or more precisely, that all such theories consider the masses incompetent and practically worthless, at least as far as political participation is concerned.[45]

According to Bachrach, Pareto, Mosca, and Schumpeter (excluding Michels from the fascist lineage) are responsible for this inversion. In Tocquevillian fashion, Bachrach writes, Pareto's and Mosca's cynicism toward "the myth of democracy" prompted them to distinguish between liberalism and democracy, lauding the former and reviling the latter.[46] Bachrach presents Pareto's "ridicule" as emblematic of his hatred of democracy. Mosca's antipathy was also clear, Bachrach suggests, as Mosca thought electoral government can produce "the worst type of political organization and anonymous tyranny of those who win elections and speak in the name of the people."[47]

In the first sentence of the chapter, Bachrach admits that Pareto's and Mosca's primary aim was "to avert the catastrophe of a 'demagogic plutocracy.'"[48] Yet this element entirely drops out of his analysis thereafter. Instead of focusing on their concern for the way representative institutions foster plutocracy, he contends that the Italians were actually motivated to save liberalism from the perils of democratization by showing the illusory prospects of the latter. However, their concerns regarding demagogic plutocracy are crucial to an appropriate understanding of the distinction that Pareto and Mosca drew between liberalism and democracy. The Italians distinguished between these two political forms of organization because they feared that the illusory democratic expectations arising out of electoral, liberal institutions create the opportunity for a demagogic plutocrat to emerge. For the Italians, the conflation of democratic aspirations with exclusive reliance on representative institutions creates the conditions for a "shrewd" member of the plutocratic "elite" to create a demagogic tyranny in the first place.[49]

162   DEMOCRATIC ELITISM

In a footnote, Bachrach acknowledges that as "realists," the Italian theorists are exceptions to the general elitist paradigm he has proposed in that they believe "governing elites [rule] primarily in their own interest"—and *not* in the interest in the people.[50] But for some reason this does not impact his view that the Italians' chief object of disdain was mass participation. Although Pareto might have conceded that "in the parliamentary form of government . . . the governing elite 'must now and again bend the knee to the whims of the ignorant and domineering sovereigns or parliaments,'" Bachrach underscores Pareto's claim that "'they are soon back at their tenacious patient, never-ending work, which is of much the greater consequence.'"[51] For Bachrach, this means that while at times "the masses might have some influence on the ruling class," for the most part Pareto deprives ordinary citizens of any consequential agency.

But the thrust of Pareto's remark here has little to do with democracy or mass participation. Pareto claims that "the parliamentary form of government," government based on elections, may occasionally produce a situation in which the governing elite (a broader elite that may not necessarily hold political office) must obey the "ignorant and domineering sovereigns or parliaments" (that is, an ignorant and domineering *political* elite), but for the most part, the governing elite can tenaciously pursue its never-ending work of satisfying its own interest. "The ignorant and domineering parliaments" to which Pareto refers here are not the masses, but instead incompetent political elites who are unable to hold the broader ruling class accountable. Far too cynical to entertain the notion that the elite, through elections, can be held accountable to the people directly, Pareto declares that extra-parliamentary elites are rarely even accountable to the political elites that the people elect.

Bachrach similarly charges that Mosca's *Elementi* "is clearly an elitist and anti-democratic tract" because it denies any effective agency to ordinary citizens.[52] For Bachrach, the idea of a division between those who govern and those who are governed "is hardly shocking" but Mosca "adds an anti-democratic bite" to this commonplace view when he writes that "the first class, always the less numerous, performs all political functions, monopolizes power, and enjoys the advantages that power brings, whereas the second, the more numerous class, is directed and controlled by the first, in a manner that is now more or less legal, now more or less arbitrary and violent."[53]

According to Bachrach, the saving grace for both Mosca and Pareto can be found in their theories of elite pluralism and elite circulation, respectively. He sees Mosca's 1896 edition of *Elementi* as a purely elitist tract but contends that the six chapters Mosca added to his opus in the 1920s contain the democratic elements of his text. "In perceiving the insight underlying the apparent paradox that democratic methods prudently used can enhance the strength and stability of the ruling class," Bachrach writes, Mosca "finally [recognized] the utility of the elective and representative institutions." This development, for Bachrach, constitutes "the first formulation of democratic elitism" because Mosca does not as thoroughly emphasize minority domination over the majority in the second version of his treatise.[54]

To be sure, Bachrach writes, Mosca "remained essentially an elitist to the end," but whereas in the nineteenth century Mosca's interest lay in the "manipulation and exploitation of the masses by the elite," in the early twentieth century his "emphasis [radically] shifts . . . to the limitation and control of elites within the ruling class by the alignment of differing political forces in separate and opposing political institutions."[55] For Bachrach, elite pluralism obtained through elections defines Mosca's most "democratic" contribution to political science but paradoxically offers a democratic method to obtain a substantively elitist end: control of the masses.

Bachrach claims that Pareto's theory of elite circulation does not substantively contribute to the doctrine, but ultimately judges it inferior to Mosca's work. Bachrach interprets his insistence that the governing classes need to be constantly restored from lower socioeconomic classes, not as a warning to corrupt elites attempting to insulate themselves from such circulation through elections, but as a sign of Pareto's fatalism about the prospects of democratic accountability, given elite use of force.[56] Hence, in the conviction that "demagogic plutocracy" was a foreseen event, he writes, Pareto's mammoth study on social equilibrium closes on *a note of despair*.[57] For Bachrach, the pessimism pervading Pareto's analysis of how elections inhibit the proper circulation of elites translates into a fatalism and "despair" over the prospects of democratic accountability. Like many Anglo-American political scientists, Bachrach bristles at this kind of cynicism and equates this posture with resolutely antidemocratic proclivities.

Bachrach's aversion to pessimism becomes even more explicit in his comparison of the two Italian figures. "Unlike Pareto, whose scathing remarks on majority rule, equality, and the like continued unsubsided throughout his lifetime and who had little difficulty joining the fascist camp," Bachrach declares that Mosca attenuated his cynicism toward representative institutions later in life and therefore deserves more consideration as a democratic theorist.[58] Even though, substantively, Bachrach argues that the Italians posited virtually identical theories, he claims that Mosca should still be considered the first expositor of democratic elitism because he is more democratic (that is, liberal) than his peer: "Persistent Mosca won his fight, at least in the eyes of history, with his bitter rival, Pareto. For in adding six chapters to his major opus years after it was 'finished,' Mosca ended on a note of resolution, not despair."[59] Bachrach contends that Mosca was ultimately concerned with maintaining elite power, and nothing more. But unlike Pareto, with his ominous "despair," at least Mosca provided some type of "resolution"—something more positive, a concrete quasi-democratic "contribution" to political science. The quasi-democratic element of his thought consists only in the fact that he ultimately defended an institutionalization of elite pluralism through the mechanism of elections.[60] For Bachrach, the last iteration of Mosca's work is not as pessimistic as Pareto's exposition about the plutocratic propensities of liberal institutions, and therefore is more democratically valuable.

Nevertheless, Bachrach continues, Joseph Schumpeter is ultimately responsible for ushering Mosca into the canon of twentieth-century American political science. At the time of the publication of *Capitalism, Socialism and Democracy*, he says, an idea of democracy devoid of the commitment to the individual self-development and freedom that proliferates through mass engagement in politics was inconceivable. But armed with Mosca's defense of the elite pluralism that elections promote, Bachrach charges that Schumpeter stripped electoral politics of any attachment to democracy and defined it as a "political method" by promoting the competition through which Mosca's desired elite pluralism is attained.[61] In effect, readers became comfortable with "Mosca's theory of a stable and open political system ruled by elites," which "fits nicely in the democratic frame reconstructed by Joseph Schumpeter," because a theory of democracy predicated on the competition of elites allows political consumers some type of choice, and hence agency, when they vote to decide who rules them.[62]

In "following Schumpeter's lead," Bachrach declares that contemporary theorists generally agree that "democracy has no overriding purpose to promote" and that its singular function is to "choose leaders." In subsequent chapters of *The Theory of Democratic Elitism*, Bachrach thus connects establishment political scientists of both conservative and progressive persuasions—from Sidney Verba and V. O. Key to C. Wright Mills and A. A. Berle—to their "aristocratic" precursors Pareto, Mosca, and Schumpeter based on their distrust in mass participation in politics and their commitment to a procedural conception of democracy based on competitive elections.[63] Democratic realism, he insists throughout the text, developed out of the marriage of the two key presumptions of this elitist, aristocratic tradition.

Once Bachrach establishes Pareto, Mosca, and Schumpeter as enemies of democracy, interested only in the mechanics of elite power, his way of then identifying the shortcomings of such an approach implicitly acknowledges the empirical value of his new understanding of these theories. Although he initially derides the European precursors for exaggerating the influence of elites in modern society, in the second part of his book he admits that we must "fully recognize the elite-mass nature of modern industrial society and the implications of this fact for democratic theory." Ultimately, he concedes that elite explanatory models are "useful," but laments that they provide no "direction, perspective, or inspiration and fire to reach that which is presently unattainable."[64] Bachrach's anxiety that democratic theory will remain "content" with his rendering of the pessimistic, elite models dominates the text so pervasively that he inadvertently legitimizes their value and validity by portraying them as useful and accurate.

In sum, Bachrach creates a far more elitist position than Pareto and Mosca espoused, and then he inadvertently establishes the veracity of such a position (that is, that modern popular government must necessarily be driven by elite minorities) in his defensive critique of it. By connecting Italian elite circulation to Schumpeterian electoral competition based on shared contempt for popular agency, his anxiety amalgamates Pareto, Mosca, and Schumpeter with Bachrach's American contemporaries in a genealogy that formalizes a hitherto nonexistent school of democratic elitism.

To a certain extent, democracy and elitism had not been officially coupled so expansively until Bachrach did so with his genealogy, which was as faulty as it was influential. Earlier American elite theorists—including Lipset and Dahl in the 1950s and early 1960s—developed elite explanatory models to demonstrate that modern popular government is less "democratic" than Americans suppose and espouse; and to legitimate modern "democracies" as kinds of popular regimes because they are far *more* free and democratic than their communist and fascist alternatives.[65] Even in 1967 Dahl was unwilling to call his proposed regime type "democracy," and instead insists on the term "polyarchy" (and later "pluralism") as an attractive alternative to both democracy and oligarchy precisely because of modern representative government's patently undemocratic features.

Bachrach confirms this position for Dahl and other nouveau elitists by identifying such forms of political organization as being in some sense genuinely "democratic." His panic over the popularity of elite models prompts him to make a strategic error: he takes nouveau elitism one step further by creating a formal school of democratic elitism so that participatory movements would have a cohesive transhistorical establishment position to oppose. As a result, "radical" democratic theory, typified by Maure Goldschmidt, Lane Davis, Graeme Duncan and Steven Lukes, William Connolly, and even Sheldon

166 DEMOCRATIC ELITISM

Wolin, became obsessed with debating whether Bachrach's vision of the power-driven elite model provides an accurate depiction and a normative ideal, ignoring whether he constructed an accurate depiction of "the model" itself.[66]

Bachrach's contemporaries, specifically participatory democrats eager to discredit pluralism's popularity within American political science, deployed his genealogy, further solidifying democratic elitism's dominance of the discipline. Carole Pateman's influential *Participation and Democratic Theory* is the best example of such work. In this text Pateman explicitly credits Bachrach with the genealogy she uses to introduce her critique of democratic elitism. Yet Pateman's rendition offers an even more misleading characterization than did *A Theory of Democratic Elitism*. Bachrach at least acknowledges the anti-plutocratic motivations of the Italian School theorists, albeit in passing asides and footnotes, but Pateman omits such qualifications when she adopts Bachrach's lineage. She even declares that her summary of this approach, thanks to Bachrach, can be stated "without too great an oversimplification."[67]

Pateman explains "the empirical turn" in political science by essentially reproducing an abbreviated version of Bachrach's genealogy.[68] Given their descendance from fascist theorists disillusioned by failed participatory regimes, the state of the political science establishment can be explained, she claims, by a twofold problem that plagues contemporary elitist empiricists. First, all modern interpreters have accepted Schumpeter's purported call to evacuate democratic theory of normative content—that is to say, all democratic theorists problematically advance the view that a "modern theory of democracy must be descriptive in form and focus on the on-going political system."[69] Second, Schumpeter was able to convince democratic theorists to compare "political competition for votes to the operation of the (economic) market; voters like consumers choose between the policies (products) offered by competing political entrepreneurs, and the parties regulate the competition like trade associations in the economic sphere."[70] Through the glorification of economic competition, laments Pateman, Schumpeter economized political science, and everyone else has foolishly followed suit.

For Pateman, then, the Schumpeterian turn in political science not only was catastrophic for democratic theory on normative grounds, but also represented poor social scientific practice. Yet she makes the case for her participatory theory of democracy along the lines of the Schumpeterian model she describes, taking as its starting point the premise that cognitive capacity is strictly limited to the areas in which individuals have direct experience.[71] Pateman's strategy therefore takes the empirical evidence developed out of the contemporary school and argues for increased participation in the workplace. Increased worker participation in industry serves as a stand-in for the type of mass political participation that today, she implies, is hopelessly unrealistic.[72] In this sense, Pateman's participatory theory begins with the basic premises of Schumpeter's alternate theory.

Pateman demonstrates that proponents of participatory models can rely upon empirical evidence and develop explanatory theories just as effectively as the elite democratic theories currently do. But more to the point, she argues that the empirical evidence suggests that increased participation in the workplace would increase economic efficiency.[73] She uses the mining and car industries as examples and says that the facts actually indicate that a participatory system "is the most efficient way to run an enterprise."[74] Not only does she thus embrace an empirically oriented approach, but her exposition conflates economic and political categories and standards in the very ways that Schumpeter sarcastically beckoned future democratic theory to do—a "Schumpeterian" conflation of the economic and the political that, as we observed above, Pateman herself bemoans at the start of her book.

To further solidify the empirical orientation of her participatory model, Pateman ends the book with a case study of Yugoslavian worker movements. Her discussion of worker self-management clearly accepts Schumpeter's challenge to conduct political science *and* organize democracy along empirical and economic lines. Her conclusion suggests that these empirically demonstrable and economically affiliated paradigms can help us settle for increased participation in the workplace while leaving the representative political system largely intact.[75]

Participation and Democratic Theory achieved critical acclaim because it brilliantly employed the contemporary school's empirical findings to contrary ends. In this respect, it offered a more formal and successful critical response to the democratic realists in political science on their own terms than Bachrach's pamphlet had. Yet while the panicked pressure to respond to the nouveau elite theories of Dahl and Lasswell is understandable, the way Pateman spurred the conversation forward foreclosed potential avenues that American democratic theory discourse could have taken. Not only did her success change the American reception of the Italian School, but by accepting, and effectively employing, Schumpeter's dare to initiate an empirical turn and apply economic categories to political theory, Pateman does not correct Schumpeter's analysis. Instead, she puts it into practice.

Pateman's work was wildly influential in the literature on participatory and radical democracy, and inspired comment even from those who considered themselves far outside of the discussion. Most famously, after Pateman's acclaimed reception, Quentin Skinner intervenes in the debate as arbitrator between the pluralist and the participatory democrats on methodological grounds. From the standpoint of ordinary language analysis, says Skinner, the empirical elite theorists exhibit a "false, ideological move"—that is, the implicit assumption that the prevailing meaning and usage of the term "democracy" indicates that it is a regime type that "deserves to be commended." Yet as far as the methodological battle was concerned, Skinner defends Dahl against the assault of the participatory democrats. On the basis of objective neutrality, Skinner contends, Dahl's *Preface to Democratic Theory* emerges "more or less completely unscathed from the critical battery which has been directed against the work of the empirical theorists as a school," thereby granting the nouveau elitists seemingly more genuine scientific status than their detractors.[76] His more nuanced critique suggested that both the empirical theorists and their participatory critics were similarly afflicted by the delusion of a false premise; nonetheless, Skinner's status as a neutral umpire granted more credibility to the realist, albeit conservative, vision of democracy on empirical grounds.

Minimal Enthusiasm: "Pessimism Is Informed Optimism"

Given this gradual reduction of the Italians' and Schumpeter's thought to the category of democratic elitism, it may be tempting to think that the "minimal" theory, which narrowly affiliates democracy with free and fair elections, was generated directly through this descent. Nevertheless, notwithstanding participatory democrats prematurely labeling this theory the "orthodox" model, before the 1980s the equation of elections and democracy propagated by the democratic elitists still had not stuck; according to more neutral parties who, at the time, were describing the theoretical landscape, the equation of elections and democracy, though hotly debated, was still formally identified as the "revisionary" rather than the standard position.[77]

The "revisionary" theory, which identifies democracy with competitive leadership, could not have acquired the status of the reigning model had it been confined to the specific debate that raged between realist democrats and participatory democrats over the prospects of mass participatory politics in modern representative government. For this conception to become the dominant paradigm, it needed approval from all domains of political science: in particular, it needed sanction from socialist intellectuals. Adam Przeworski created this consensus. The equation of elections and democracy was cemented as the standard conception only after Przeworski's methodological intervention in both socialist and liberal debates.

In the 1980s Przeworski convinced socialist intellectuals to eliminate democracy from their vocabulary through a deft reconsideration of Marx's methodology vis-à-vis Schumpeter and Michels. In the 1990s Przeworski gained influence over mainstream political science through a similar methodological insistence, now associated with rational choice theory, and through a more thorough economization of democratic theory. In the late 1990s Przeworski's amalgamation of socialist and liberal thought coalesced into Schumpeterian minimalism, an approach that reduces democracy to competitive elections, not because popular sovereignty is most closely approximated at the electoral moment, but because of the hindrances to domination by elites that elections provide.

Przeworski's early work emerges within an entirely different conversation than the one that engrossed liberal political theorists (the debate over the philosophical origins of elite, realist theories of democracy). He starts his career in the 1980s as a founding member of the "Analytical Marxists" prompting his interlocutors to discard the connection between socialism and democracy that plagued Marxist philosophy and inhibited socialist transformation. His first book, *Capitalism and Social Democracy* (1985), poses this motivating question directly: Why has democracy, institutionalized through broad universal suffrage, not brought about the advent of socialism?[78]

Przeworski contends that "the error of the early socialists was to have thought that one could precipitate radical social transformation through the electoral process."[79] Socialists were deluded in thinking, not only that elections would help realize their goals of nationalizing the means of production, but also that democratic procedure would provide "a clear mandate for grand projects for a better future." Misinterpretations of Marxist theory thus led to the delusion that socialist transformation could be achieved through "the democratic method." But the structure of representational consensus, Przeworski argues, eliminates this possibility.[80]

Even if electoral procedure could produce a clear enough mandate in such heterogeneous societies, Przeworski denies that "anyone living under capitalism, including workers, would have good reasons to prefer socialism."[81] As he makes clear throughout the text, Przeworski believes that in this event workers would prioritize their own immediate material interest and support the continuity of capitalist system because they would be unwilling to disturb their short-term material well-being. Be that as it may, even if we close our eyes to the fact that "the democratic process"—that is, electoral procedure—is unlikely to yield socialist transformation because of the structure of consensus, we still should not expect it to bring about socialist outcomes.

What does Przeworski seek to advance in decoupling democratic procedure from socialist policies? To be clear, he says, his analysis does not disqualify him

170 DEMOCRATIC ELITISM

as a socialist. Somehow, his argument does not "lead to a rejection of social democracy," nor does it imply that "reforms are impossible" or that workers "would never opt for socialism." He is even unwilling to label his conclusions "pessimistic" about the future prospects of socialism. "Pessimism" is nothing but "informed optimism," and therefore, he writes, his grim projection about the potential for socialist transformation is not only "informed" but borders on the "optimistic."[82] As opposed to Pollyanna claims that democracy will give rise to socialism, his optimism aims to get an "informed" picture of what advances the socialist cause and what does not.

First, his socialist interlocutors must accept that socialism may be possible "only on the condition that the movement for socialism regains its integral scope" and leaves behind the view that democratic procedure will eventually procure socialist ends. Second, socialists need to eschew the idea that the socialist project should be predicated on "the continual improvement of material conditions of the working class." Socialism might become conceivable, he maintains, when it is reborn as "a social movement and not solely an economic one, when it learns from the women's movement, when it assimilates cultural issues."[83]

Although Przeworski remains silent about which issues ought to be assimilated, one thing is certain: as far as the revitalization of socialism is concerned, "the time is not near." At the present juncture, "there is every reason to expect that capitalism will continue to offer an opportunity to improve material conditions . . . while conditions for socialism continue to rot." He discourages his comrades from the unproductive optimism in "dreaming of utopia," because that distracts from the informed, optimistic "struggle to make capitalism more efficient and more humane." Right now, he claims, we must optimistically concentrate on "improving capitalism" through the electoral method of democracy, but this struggle for democracy must not be confused with "the quest for socialism."[84] Not only have socialism and democracy become analytically disconnected, but the recipient of the 1985 Socialist Review Book Award argues that any plans to develop what an alternative socialism might entail should be put on an indefinite hold.

Soon thereafter, Przeworski publishes *Paper Stones: A History of Electoral Socialism* in collaboration with John Sprague. At its most basic level, the text uses empirical data on social democratic parties to animate the electoral dilemma that socialist parties historically faced in choosing between class consciousness and winning electoral matches.[85] As he describes it in both *Capitalism and Social Democracy* and *Paper Stones*, when social democratic parties decided to participate in elections, they abandoned the possibility of socialist transformation: "by broadening their appeal to the 'masses'" in order to generate electoral support, "social democrats weaken the general salience of class as a determinant of political behavior of individuals."[86] Following Michels's analysis from 1915, in *Paper Stones* Przeworski details how in Belgium, France, Denmark, Germany, Norway, and Sweden, courting "small peasants," "petty bourgeois elements," and groups outside of the manual labor force meant that socialist parties could not continue the class-conscious program, because that message did not "appeal" to the "entire working population."[87] With empirical science at his command, Przeworski "analytically" demonstrates that the democratic procedure of elections will not procure socialist ends because "the working-class base of left-wing parties is being eroded"—or such parties are diluted by other groups in order to win the vote.[88]

Paper Stones thus provides an empirical account of the historical thesis Przeworski presents in *Capitalism and Social Democracy*, and simultaneously bridges the gap between his socialist interlocutors and liberal, mainstream American political science. The former are again asked to disassociate democratic procedures from socialism, because elections will only diminish the working-class basis of left-wing parties and destroy any possibility for socialist transformation. Instead, he repeats, socialists should focus on ameliorating the worst vicissitudes of capitalism, as opposed to doggedly standing by the conviction that democracy will eventually breed socialist policies. Liberal political scientists were of course quite pleased with the analysis that severed democracy from socialism, but more importantly they praised Przeworski's version of rational choice and "the rigorous modeling" and "data sets" he employed; they hailed the analytic, "methodological individualism" that Przeworski supposedly derives from Marxist theory.[89]

Paper Stones was one of the few books in the late 1980s that won endorsement from opposite ends of the political and methodological spectrums. On the one side, Felipe Pimentel insisted it was necessary reading for anyone "interested in the possibilities of radical transformation present within democratic capitalist society," and, on the other, Sidney Verba, proclaimed that the text ushered in an "important new standard for research in political history."[90] Przeworski's rational choice, or, depending on your political leanings, "methodological individualism," provided the terms on which all of political science could agree that, at the very least, democratic procedures do not produce socialist outcomes.

In 1991 Przeworski published *Democracy and the Market*. With the fall of the Soviet bloc, Przeworski was now free to wholly embrace the economic logic of market competition in his conception of democracy; he even ventures that we understand democracy in terms of a Paretian equilibrium model.[91] To be

172   DEMOCRATIC ELITISM

fair, his position does not change from his work in the 1980s, but rather than clinging to more precise language about "democratic procedure" or "democratic process," Przeworski now much more explicitly equates democracy *tout court* with elections through market logic.

Democracy and the Market begins with the self-proclaimed "informed optimistic" aim to "illuminate the obstacles typically confronted in building democracy and transforming economies." Free of Soviet oppression, Eastern European countries now find themselves "embracing capitalism," but "they are poor." A clear understanding of democracy will help these countries better combat "vacillations" between technocratic, market-oriented programs that ameliorate poverty and the participatory expectations that arise out of the new political conditions.[92]

Consequently, Przeworski proclaims, democracy should simply be understood as a system "in which parties lose elections"—and nothing more. He complains that even those definitions of democracy that make contestation the central feature, such as Dahl's, still ambivalently "treat participation on a par with contestation." While it may be "attractive" to discuss participation from a normative standpoint, "from the analytic point of view" he finds participation irrelevant: the mere "*possibility* of contestation by conflicting interests is sufficient to explain the dynamic of democracy," and no other feel-good hedging should be "analytically" entertained. At the end of the day, participation does not "universally" appear in democracies, Przeworski writes; it is neither a sufficient nor a necessary condition. Notice that we are no longer talking about democratic procedure or democratic method: all that is needed "to identify a political system as democratic," he maintains, is to ascertain whether elections provide the *opportunity* for certain [presumably elite] individuals to contest previous results through competition for those same positions.[93] Recall that for the Italians, the mere opportunity for contestation—as opposed it its continual application—is exactly how elite cohesion ossifies.

As Przeworski notes, even the most "elitist" or "realistic" theories of democracy are unwilling to eliminate the role of participation in electoral democracies, even though they effectively do so in their definitions. He insists on formally ending this charade, which feigns that participation has anything to do with the democratic character of a regime. More than any of his predecessors, Przeworski drastically confines democracy exclusively to the electoral function. Impressively, he does not even pretend that mass participation is involved through the enactment of electoral campaigns, and instead shifts the focus to the ability or mere possibility of elites to contest each other's positions (not the masses' ability to contest elites) and marshal just enough, but no more, votes to prevail.

HOPEFUL PANIC 173

In 1993 Przeworski leaves the founding group of Analytical Marxists.[94] In 1999 he publishes "A Minimalist Conception of Democracy: A Defense," a summary of the "minimalist" theory he latently developed over the preceding twenty years.[95] In this widely read piece, Przeworski is more transparent about the Schumpeterian sources of his thought: he seeks to defend a "minimalist," "Schumpeterian" conception in which democracy "is just a system in which rulers are selected by competitive elections." He again expresses annoyance with the "normatively attractive" definitions that predicate democracy on a random variable, such as participation, equality, representation, and so on. Readers must instead admit the suspicion that we all share: "All there is to democracy" is that "rulers are elected," and, presumably, can be unelected. The point of his exposition aims to determine, once and for all, whether this criterion is really "too little" to be valid.[96]

Do we really need all the other elements (participation, equality, accountability, and even representation) to make democracy stable and robust, and, Przeworski asks, even the most normatively attractive option? Surely "the quality of democracy" can always be asymptomatically improved, he admits, but in the end, "the *miracle* of democracy" lies in the fact that "conflicting political forces obey the results of voting."[97] The optimistic approach to democracy, he suggests, actually coincides with the realist, minimalist conception. Can you believe it, he marvels: in a democracy, "people who have guns obey those without them"?[98] In Przeworski's "analytic" hands, elections cease to provide the means through which we can satisfy the desired ends of participation, equality, or even representation; they are, in and of themselves, the ends that makes democracy a "miraculous" enterprise.

Electoralism is the feature that provides grounds for optimism. Although Przeworski spends most of the piece likening elections to a coin toss, ultimately he argues that they are more than random institutional devices that determine winners and losers. Elections are powerful because of the coercive power of voting. However, contrary to long-standing popular belief, this coercive power does not come from consent or the opportunity for participation that this consent implies; it does not, he insists, come from individuals agreeing "to accept decisions of as yet undetermined content as long as they can participate in the making of these decisions." Rather, he submits, the force of elections comes from the fact that they inform "everyone who would mutiny" if the results are not obeyed. In democracies, he explains, voting does not "reveal a unique collective will but it indicates limits to rule." Elections inform winners and losers of existing "passions, values, and interests," of the power and support certain factions garner, and how things would likely result if violent confrontation were

174 DEMOCRATIC ELITISM

to emerge between opposing forces. In other words, elections function as a barometer or signaling device to other elites: voting indicates to elites the limits of what they can push, of what they can and cannot get away with, and discourages violent "mutiny" *between them* as a result.[99]

Unlike democracies, dictatorships do not exhibit this feature, Przeworski argues, which is why they require "secret police." The information that elections generate for elites is what makes living in a democracy the better alternative. Put differently, the crucial element of democracies is that "voters can choose rulers through elections" and the information generated from this choice will constrain elites and inhibit violence. He admits that other conditions may need to be fulfilled for democracy to endure, but even if democracy "cannot be improved" beyond the mere presence of elections, this minimalist, Schumpeterian conception of democracy, he maintains, would still be the one "worth defending," both "empirically and normatively."[100]

This emphasis on elite limits brings us back full circle to the Italian position. The Italians acknowledged that elections can in some circumstances limit elite rule. Of course, at a basic level, forcing elites to compete with each other imposes some constraints on them, which is why, despite their critiques of liberalism, Pareto, Mosca, and Michels did not think that elections should be eliminated. Nevertheless, the Italians sought to underscore the fact that such institutions, without supplementation, encourage an incumbent ruling class toward corruption because elections do not necessarily allow true competition. Their critiques did not consist in the antidemocratic inclination that elections allow for too much mass participation. Rather, their view was that elections structurally engender the collusion of governing elites to stack the electoral deck in their own favor, and furthermore, that the plutocracy bred by elections insulates a corrupt ruling class from external pressure until it is too late and the legitimacy of elections is called into question by a demagogue with authoritarian aspirations.

Przeworski deploys Schumpeter's thought somewhat more faithfully. He disassociates democracy from socialism through a reconsideration of the history of socialist parties and through a reinterpretation of Marxist methodology via rational choice theory. Under the auspices of this new "methodological individualism," he unites liberals and socialists through a minimal, informed, but optimistic approach to democracy. This Schumpeterian definition champions descriptive facts of empirical science over normative prescriptions, uses the language of competition to conflate economic and political categories, and, most importantly, celebrates the possibility of contestation that electoral institutions engender as the integral element of democratic politics.

The Invisibility of Scientific Revolutions: A New Enemy

In the twenty-first century, Pareto, Mosca, and Michels are still remembered as proffering scientifically oriented, positivist conceptions of politics that would serve as the foundation of the behavioral revolution of American political science and the development of rational choice theory.[101] In this capacity, they simultaneously became the conservative source for empirical political science and the boogeyman of the current reigning theory of democracy as competitive elections.

Yet the Italians preemptively rejected these two characterizations. To take Pareto as the paradigmatic example, he scorned the application of economic thinking to the study of government, warning that such an approach would lead to "seriously significant misapprehensions."[102] And despite the fact that he would later be subsumed into the elitist paradigm, Pareto renounced pure forms of electoralism, proclaiming that "freedom is that regime where the citizens obey only the laws, rather than where they are governed by the whims of the few, *even if by them elected*."[103]

How did this erroneous reception of the Italian School come to pass? Why did American political scientists read the Italians so incorrectly on both methodological and political registers? Why were they inclined to ignore the Italian School's belabored critique of plutocratic rule and their anti-elitist orientation?

It is not my contention that American political scientists were simply obtuse readers, or that they were nefariously trying to pursue their own political agenda. To use Thomas Kuhn's oft-cited characterization, "what differentiated these various schools was not one or another failure of method—they were all 'scientific'—but what we shall come to call their incommensurable ways of seeing the world and of practicing science in it."[104] A deus ex machina that lay outside the postwar worldview was needed in order to forge ahead with a new scientific paradigm. There are three explanations that, taken together, enabled the development of such a contrivance device and render American political science's perversion of the Italian School more intelligible.

Most obviously, the Cold War and its effects on social science formation in the immediate postwar period played a significant role in the vilification of the Italian School. Writing between 1870 and 1923, especially Pareto and Mosca but even to some extent Michels were concerned that the plutocratic corruption of representative government would give rise to increased enthusiasm for illiberal alternatives. They predicted the emergence of a Hitler or a Mussolini, but certainly did not condone it.

176   DEMOCRATIC ELITISM

And yet after the "hot war," the Italian School authors were subsumed into a Cold War paradigm that divided the ideological landscape as a contest between liberalism and communist totalitarianism, rather than the fascism represented by Hitler's Germany or Mussolini's Italy. In an effort to provide an alternative to Soviet communism, American political science carved out a defense of liberal democracy that was free from any association with the supposed Italian apologists for fascism. The temptation to provide an alternative untainted by any Italian affiliation drove American and, as we have seen, even European political scientists to create more distance between their thought and the Italians—even if this distance was predicated on false assumptions about Pareto's, Mosca's, and Michels's political orientations.

Relatedly, but most importantly, in the postwar period plutocracy ceased to be a pressing political concern. The first wave of this sublimation occurred before the Second World War, when early twentieth-century democratic theorists in the United States were insensitive to the particularly plutocratic context of Risorgimento Italy, a post-unification environment that drastically exemplified the connections between plutocratic and electoral politics in a way that exponentially outstripped the turn of the century populist responses to the Gilded Age in the United States. Even Michels, a naturalized Italian, could not fully appreciate the extent to which identifying democracy as competitive elections obfuscated the plutocratic dangers of liberal representative governments.

The blindness to the connection between plutocratic and electoral politics was further fueled by the historically unprecedented socioeconomic conditions of the postwar period. An entire school of contemporary economic theory has recently demonstrated that between 1950 and 1980 economic inequality was at an all-time low in human history.[105] It thus became much easier for American political scientists like Lipset and Dahl to ignore the plutocratic context in which Pareto, Mosca, and Michels were writing, and to redescribe the problem in terms of oligarchy, where power is dispersed among financial, political, and intellectual elites. As a result, contemporary scholars have blamed the Italian theorists, and not the midcentury pluralist movement in American political science, for reorienting the debate away from plutocracy and toward oligarchy more generally understood.[106]

And finally, as I have suggested throughout this book, Americans succumbed to the temptation to vilify Pareto, Mosca, and Michels as "elitists" because they misunderstood their pessimistic worldview. Without sensitivity to their different approach to their political problems, it was easy for Lipset to ignore Michels's methodological claim that exposing plutocracy in liberal polities encourages the fulfillment of democracy. These differences in political context and philosophy permitted the Americans to champion an optimistic pluralism of competing elites over the fear of plutocratic capture that terrorized the Italians.

Alas, American political scientists in the postwar moment read Pareto, Mosca, and Michels not as pessimistic defenders of democracy but instead as conservative champions of authoritarian leadership. And although Michels was the only committed fascist of the trio, the Americans partially justified his work against the other Italian figures because Michels was more sanguine about the salutary effects of electoral competition. American political science thus took Schumpeter up on his challenge to redefine democracy as competitive elections by selectively incorporating Michels's celebration of elections and some of the Italians' partial claims and completely ignoring their worries about plutocracy. The uptake of Schumpeter's challenge to equate elections and democracy generated "elite," "realist" theories of democracy dating back to the Italian School, which granted them some empirical legitimacy but, through their association with Schumpeter, seemed to offer a less fascist orientation toward representative government—at least in terms of its democratic potential.

The construction of a founding myth beginning with the Italian School carried on by Schumpeter became a pervasive and dominant narrative in democratic theory and political science. The end result was that the definition of democracy as competitive elections became the primary one.

Democratic theorists became obsessed with debating whether elite theories of democracy provide a sufficient normative ideal, as opposed to questioning the theoretical grounding of the models themselves—that is, whether they were actually realistic. The Italians thought that elections required external anti-plutocratic measures to function, whereas the Americans happily thought that elections could perpetually stave off plutocratic capture. Political scientists of all stripes, then, began to use "elite," "minimal," or "realist" theories as the standard metric to attest to the presence of democracy in a polity. The perversion of the Italian School and the consequent debates surrounding democratic elitism shaped the discipline to think of democracy in terms of competitive elections. The irony is that the purported founders of democratic elitism knew that the definition of democracy as competitive elections was untenable, and they certainly did not mean for us to be stuck with it. There is some poetic justice in noting that today we confront the same plutocratic cum demagogic circumstances in which they found themselves.

Conclusion: A New Realism

Democracy as Good Government

Pessimism of the intellect, optimism of the will.

— ANTONIO GRAMSCI, *Discourse with the Anarchists*

The global political landscape indicates that the moment may be ripe for the untethering of democracy and election. Amid populist rejections of liberal representative governments across the world, the definition of democracy as free and fair election no longer seems to pass muster precisely because the plutocratic tendencies of electoralism have lost democratic credibility. In this sense, the reigning conception of realist democracy has come to be seen by many as entirely unrealistic.

Yet despite a decade of pointed attention to the contemporary political malaise, democratic theory still finds itself at an impasse. Two notable responses to the current turmoil within Western representative governments roughly correspond to the binary between the elites and the masses. Unsurprisingly, the two groups largely talk past each other.

One prevalent response among the elite, and especially among the intelligentsia, has been to worry about "democratic backsliding" or "democratic recession," a concept that most generally refers to the decline in popular support for electoral norms.[1] Often these commentators indulge in blaming this decline on the inherently dangerous features of mass politics. Some rail against ordinary people's cognitive incapacities to understand their own interests amid increased technocratic centralization and / or the erosion of bureaucratic institutions that serve the larger public.[2] Occasionally such critics describe the

CONCLUSION   179

rejection of the mainstream press or conspiracy movements as a type of semi-religious delusion characteristic of the masses who are ultimately unable to understand technocratic centralization or simply feel disgruntled by sweeping socioeconomic changes that jeopardize their economic interest or social sense of superiority.[3]

Even those who have been extremely sensitive to the rise of plutocracy and the accompanying rejection of liberal government have reflexively repeated the habit of looking for answers within electoral politics. If democracy is under attack, the reasoning goes, then the problem must lie in the decline of competitive elections. In this manner, intellectuals continue to insist that elections constitute the main organ of democratic politics in addition to some other supplemental criterion, whether that criterion lies in increased mass participation, deliberation, judicial proceduralism, or technocratic reorganization of bureaucratic apparatuses. According to this framework, the answer to the woes of liberal polities always lies in elections plus the incorporation of some additional element that implicitly assumes a subordinate role to electoral processes.

These responses strike the masses as tone-deaf, further fueling the rejection of liberal norms. The continued rise of support for demagogic leaders who promise to undermine representative practices once elected indicates that if democracy continues to be primarily predicated on the ideal of competitive election, even when supplemented by additional criteria, then that democratic chimera is not worth fighting for.[4] Support for populist leaders is defended not merely or even most importantly as support for a particular candidate but instead as an expression of rejection of the "establishment" or the "system"— that is to say, as the only way to indicate distrust in the apparent cohesion of the ruling electoral class. Now and in the past, the involuntary intellectual response is to discredit the cohesion of elites on empirical grounds, yet this mass sentiment is not as preposterous as the rigorous standards of scientific objectivity often suggest. In a system where electoral politics is the only meaningful instrument to express dissatisfaction with the democratic possibilities contained within elections, on some level, supporting demagogic leaders who denigrate the intractable insider-aspect of electoral procedures makes some psychological sense.[5]

Not only has mass disillusionment led to a rejection of the illusory picture of democracy as competitive election, but increasing majorities within representative governments are less inclined to appreciate the salutary effects of competitive electoral politics in their own right. This disillusionment has prompted mass publics to question the value of the rule of law, legitimate opposition, the peaceful transfer of political power, congressional and

180 DEMOCRATIC ELITISM

parliamentary deliberation among elite political actors, judicial neutrality, and other such cornerstones of popular representative government.[6]

In reviving the Italian School of Elitism, I do not mean to deny that elections are a crucial mechanism in modern mass popular government. Fixing elections to make them more free and fair is central to the functioning of the liberal state. But research on voter suppression, campaign finance reform, gerrymandering, the role of political appointments in the judiciary, and so on is important because it makes elections more *representative*; it does not make elections more democratic. Returning to the Italian School helps us understand why even if we could solve the problems of representation in modern mass government, it would not necessarily lead to more democratic outcomes: elections can never be democratic because, by their very structure, they generate plutocratic outcomes as a result of the financial incentives that encourage collusion between different sects of political, economic, and military elites. Even when we work to make the link between the electors and their elected more representative—that is, when we aim to achieve a status in which officials "mirror" their constituencies—the success of the governor depends on the ability to coordinate with other elites in order to serve the voting publics. After all, an elected official can deliver only if in a position to coordinate with other elites: to find the financial resources for legislation, to maneuver political compromise between warring factions, and to appease lobbied interest groups in order to satisfy the promises made to constituents.

For the Italians, the issue is not that we need to find checks to electoral corruption, as important as it is to do so. The problem runs deeper: in our attribution of democratic power to election. It holds us captive to an image of democracy as representative government that has made us lose track of what democracy is and what it should to be: counter-plutocratic, majoritarian institutions and procedures that fend off the most deleterious threats of the electoral process in order to level unequal political power.

The Italian School offers conceptual and diagnostic resources that recover a lost path to combat plutocracy and fulfill the democratic promise. First, they help us theoretically disconnect the seemingly "natural" connection between election and democracy. The Italians' bold claim is that competitive election is an instrument of representation, not an instrument of democracy.

Put differently, representation and democracy are two distinct concepts that work in a mutually constitutive way, in order to preserve the contemporary iteration of popular government we now call liberal democracy. This means that democracy requires constant vigilance against the ever-present threat of plutocracy internal to electoral systems through majoritarian institutions that

CONCLUSION   181

are external to elections. External mechanisms are crucial so that the inevitable influence of the wealthy does not result in plutocratic capture of the entire government, just as elections and constitutionally guaranteed rights are crucial in protecting minorities from the tyranny of the majority. Such external democratic institutions also help keep electoral contests competitive as an antidote to the elite cohesion that is somewhat paradoxically necessary to run any political campaign. As the Italians insisted, electoral processes can structurally encourage collusion, and therefore electoral procedures must enable the contestation of the ruling class that renders elections meaningfully competitive.

The warning against identifying democracy with election is not a merely semantic issue. The Italians diagnose two distinct but related threats to the legitimacy of popular government that can result from equating democracy and election.

First, equating elections and democracy conceals the plutocratic threats of representative systems. The Italians claimed that the connection between electoral institutions and plutocratic governance must be constantly exposed and combatted—not fallaciously described as democratic. Otherwise popular government devolves into a contest between competing sets of plutocrats that we unconvincingly call "democracy." This charade delegitimizes the value of electoral institutions in the eyes of the public. We currently face this precise conundrum in our own plutocratic moment: disillusioned citizens can, as the Italians warned, *credibly* contend that elections do not generate public officials who genuinely represent them—or even act in their interest.

The second risk in pairing election with democracy is the demagogic threat. Viewing elections as a democratic expression of popular sovereignty gives potential demagogues, many of whom are themselves plutocrats, the ability to claim that they truly represent the will of the people, speciously claiming a right to rule that becomes difficult to dispute.

When elections are understood as the democratic tool *par excellence*, elected leaders can claim democratic legitimacy to do as they please even though election alone does not confer that right. Election-winning demagogues proclaim, "The people have spoken!" as a mandate for unilateral rule. The democratic power we attribute to elections enables such leaders to characterize themselves as the voice of the people, allowing them to deal a death blow to popular government writ large.

Putting these two risks together reveals the Italians' realist critique of elections: the idea that more enfranchisement leads to more democracy is a dangerous fantasy. The reality is that mass enfranchisement does not necessarily encourage elite competition and it still allows for plutocracy to persist, leading to mass disillusionment with electoral government and loss of faith in the system. Therefore, they argued that identifying democracy with election is perilous because it conceals the threat of plutocracy and generates unrealistically democratic expectations that elections, on their own, will never deliver.

On one level, this account constitutes a pessimistic approach. The Italians simply refuse to be enthralled with the image of democracy that is at stake in the idea of competitive elections because it is dangerously unrealistic. No amount of electoral engineering can ever lead to a functioning democracy organized around the idea of elections, and it may even prompt the loss of faith in the benefits of representative government.

But in offering a deflationary account of what elections can possibly achieve, we may generate a more expansive vision of what democracy in modern mass government can entail. The standard refrain for the last century has been that we cannot expect more of democracy in modern mass polities other than increasingly competitive elections. This book has argued that, given the current crisis of popular government amid ever-increasing plutocratic capture, disconnecting democracy and competitive elections is the only realistic path forward. Such an approach constitutes a radically new kind of realism for American political science, but popular faith in both representation and democracy depends on it.

The Modern Machiavellians: Democratic Theorists of Elitism

If we analytically separate representation and democracy into distinct categories, what remains? Is there a feasible alternative to free and fair election that does not hinge on identifying a singular alternative procedural criterion as the heart of democracy? Is there a way for us to move past the stultifying definitions of democracy based on the binary offered between competitive elections and Athenian-inspired lottery?[7]

The Italian School provides resources for disentangling election and democracy. They also direct us toward a conceptual reconfiguration of what twenty-first-century democracy may entail. I have insisted that the Italian theorists, and Pareto and Mosca in particular, should be understood not as elite theorists of democracy, but instead as democratic theorists of elitism. In contrast to the Central European emphasis on the democratic potential contained within electoral competition, the Italians were concerned about plutocratic corruption engendered by electoral mechanisms. Their desire to

CONCLUSION   183

contain such collusion through the leveling of political inequality constitutes the democratic animus of their elite theory.

Some might still bristle at the characterization of Pareto and Mosca as democratic thinkers, on grounds of anachronism. After all, they despised "representative democracies" such as France and the United States and renounced the application of classical Athenian models to the modern world. In this sense, they rejected the two most salient definitions of democracy currently on offer. While contemporary political science accommodates a range of democratic theories outside of the binary of competitive elections versus Athenian assembly and lottery, for whatever reason, none of these conceptions has gained significant traction outside of the ivory tower.

The Italian School directs us toward a theory of democracy understood as *buon governo*, or good government, that might resonate with proponents of Western popular government who remain dissatisfied by strictly Marxist alternatives. Although they did not identify themselves as democrats, Pareto and Mosca each devoted his life's work to envisioning the criterion for what qualifies as good government. In line with his sober approach to the scholastic norms of his time, Mosca was more comfortable directly articulating the features of good government.[8] By contrast, Pareto, in his quintessentially contrarian fashion, claimed that he had given up on searching for the criteria of good government and merely sought to avoid a bad one.[9] Nevertheless, both authors developed their theories in conversation with this long-standing tradition of the political thought of the Italian medieval city-states. This tradition was codified as early as 1339 in Ambrogio Lorenzetti's *The Allegory of Good and Bad Government*, a series of frescoes that decorate the seed of Siena's commonwealth, La Sala dei Nove of the Palazzo Pubblico.[10] At least since then, Italian political philosophy has centered around this organizing concept.

Italian scholarship has defined *buon governo* in many ways familiar to Anglo-American and continental philosophy—good government as the rule of law; the government of good rulers; mixed government; the art of governing the good of the commonwealth, or *il bene comune*; and even the art of governing the well-being of private citizens.[11] Pareto and Mosca may have identified all such features as necessary elements of *buon governo*, but their thought attunes us to something particularly important about the connection between the good of the commonwealth and the necessarily democratic nature of good government.

Most broadly, these Italian thinkers help us appreciate democracy not primarily as a regime typology akin to oligarchy, monarchy, or forms of government that end with the root *arkhein* (to rule). *Arkhein* words denote the

184 DEMOCRATIC ELITISM

specific number of rulers that govern a particular polity. Instead, democracy and, incidentally, plutocracy and aristocracy are better understood as "principles" (Mosca's formulation), or as types of "power" (Pareto's) rather than as precise institutional arrangements. Pace Josiah Ober's recent articulation, democracy, plutocracy, and aristocracy—terms that etymologically all involve the ending *-kratia* (power)—focus our attention on who applies power in a ruling order in which it must be taken for granted that the few will be always "inherently strong and capable."[12] Put simply, the *-kratia* terms prompt us to ask who can legitimately be said to apply power in any institutional regime where there are only so many formally selected "governors." From the perspective of elite theory, all modern popular governments will identify a small cohort of formal leaders through their respective political procedures. Pareto and Mosca's motivating political question is therefore not simply "Who governs?" but instead, Who will exercise significant control over the leaders who govern officially? Will it be the *ploutos* (the wealthy) or the *demos* (the many, or the people)?

Considering the Renaissance ancestral heritage of *buon governo*, the distinction between democracy understood as a power or principle and democracy understood as a regime typology might lead one to suspect that the Italians should be classified, not as democratic thinkers, but instead as republican figures more comfortably placed within the Ciceronian articulation of the mixed regime.[13] Yet this paradigm is problematic on two registers. First and foremost, although Pareto and Mosca appropriate the neo-Roman categories of socioeconomic differentiation, the few and the many (the *grandi* and the *popolo*), the central claim of elite theory replaces civic harmony (*concordia*) as the end, the goal, of a political plurality with the presumption of perpetual antagonism between the two classes. In line with the revival of those who understand Machiavelli as an anti-Ciceronian thinker, Pareto and Mosca attempt to productively institutionalize the civil discord between the few and the many, or the elites and masses, in order to level the unequal political power that undergirds the regime's stability.[14]

We should therefore understand Pareto and Mosca as "Modern Machiavellians" in this spirit. Pareto confesses that despite his apparent focus on the few, his research agenda does not follow the Machiavelli of *The Prince*, but the Machiavelli of the *Discourses on Livy*, and specifically Machiavelli's idea "that the same desires and the same humors are always present in all peoples of all cities, as it has always been."[15] Similarly, although at the end of his career Mosca emphasized the importance of implementing "social balance" at the risk of eradicating representative practices, he always underscored that liberal procedures were never sufficient to generate the social balance between the elites

CONCLUSION 185

and the masses that is necessary for *buon governo*. Mosca identifies unfounded faith in the democratic potential of liberal procedure as one of the reasons for the breakdown of juridical defense, or the "rule of law," that precipitated the advent of fascism.[16]

Moreover, treating the Italian thinkers as proponents of a mixed regime obfuscates the extent to which Pareto and Mosca envisioned good government as necessarily democratic in many of the ways that we have come to understand the term—even if such elements often escape the current academic definitions on offer. Their shared conception of good government entails institutionalizing public orders of an inescapably democratic character. For these Italians, *buon governo* must exhibit three 'democratic' features: good government must be popular, anti-plutocratic, and pluralist. I now address each of these three features in turn.

Good government is popular: For Pareto and Mosca, a regime characterized strictly by electoral process can never alone qualify as *buon governo*. The only way to prevent oligarchic capture is to establish the government on popular foundations—through institutions that elevate democratic power such that its influence on the governing channels is considered *credible* by the vast majority of its people.

It has been suggested that elite theory ignores majorities. Pareto's account of history as an oscillation between the rule of two different typologies—the cunning foxes and authoritarian lions—seems to leave no space for majoritarian considerations. Recently the theory of elite circulation has been portrayed by reference to Pareto's metaphor of the river. "By the circulation of elites," Pareto offhandedly writes, "the governing elite is in a state of continuous and slow transformation. It flows like a river and what it is today is different from what it was yesterday. Every so often, there are sudden and violent disturbances. The river floods and breaks its banks. Then, afterwards . . . the river returns to its bed and flows once more freely on."[17] Contemporary readers rightly seize upon this metaphor to explain Pareto's view that when the power of a certain group of elites begins to decline, a government of the second typology emerges through assimilation or revolution.[18] Less rarely noted, however, is that the river must eventually "[return] to its beds" in order to "once more flow freely on." Just before he introduces the river metaphor, Pareto explains that a ruling class gains and loses its power based on its energy and its ability to respond to residues—the needs and sentimental desires—present in the population writ large.[19] The practice of elite circulation, whether through assimilation or revolution, bring elites back to their majoritarian source, which is what puts any elite into the governing class in the first place.[20]

186 DEMOCRATIC ELITISM

Mosca also insists that *buon governo* must be a popular government, or a government that is seen as convincingly responsive to majoritarian interests. From its first articulation in *Teorica* to one of his last works, *Storia delle dottrine politiche*, Mosca's theory of "the political formula" (*la formula politica*) contends that the ruling class's legitimacy always rests on the acceptance of the majority's beliefs and, most importantly, its "feelings."[21] As we saw in Chapter 2, his entire critique of universal suffrage hinged on the idea that the masses of the Mezzogiorno rejected claims that liberal parliamentarism was a popular or democratic mechanism, because they quite rightly did not see it as responsive to their interests, needs, and feelings; and this undermined their support for a unified Italian state.

Good government is anti-plutocratic: For Pareto and Mosca, the plutocratic threats that reside within liberal electoral governments must be continuously combated through public mechanisms. One way to make electoralism compatible with democracy is to include anti-plutocratic institutions in the procedural constitution. This element of their elite theory offers potential prescriptive recommendations for thinking about the future of democratic politics vis-à-vis plutocracy. First, they alert us to the importance of addressing *regional* economic inequality. A nation with dramatic geographic economic inequality, whether between Northern and Southern Italians or Coastal Elites and Middle Americans, will never fulfill democratic expectations or generate faith in the benefits of an electoral government.

Second, the Italians prompt us to think beyond the elite / mass binary to differentiate politically relevant elite minorities from other types. Surely speculators and rentiers still count as categories today. The Italians would urge contemporary political science to figure out ways to regulate speculating activity through preemptive measures against collusion between politicians and speculators, as opposed to post hoc redress. And finally, much like the recent literature on reimagining the referendum process, the Italian theorists recommend revisiting different types of referenda—as in the case of military action, for example—as a potential way to constrain plutocratic interests from permeating government.[22]

Good government is pluralist: Unlike Americans, the Italians do not see pluralism as consisting simply in the competition between different types of elites engendered through electoral contests or other informal avenues of competition. According to both Pareto's formulation of elite circulation and Mosca's articulation of the ruling class, elites will actually compete against each other only if majoritarian pressure is applied from below through institutional contestation.

CONCLUSION   187

As we saw in Chapter 1, Pareto, the most famous "elitist" theorist, claims that the surest way to generate *buon governo* is to infuse localized, participatory extra-electoral mechanisms into liberal governments—mechanisms of the Swiss variety, no less. Liberal governments on the verge of breakdown must be amended to avoid their degeneration into authoritarian regimes. Parallel to Machiavelli's appropriation of the Roman *tribunate*, Pareto suggests a public system of expelling or exiling corrupt elites—what he calls a system of egress— as one active mechanism to help maintain the productive circulation of elites that helps keep the system credible in the eyes of the majority. Without such systems in place, violent revolution is likely. Pareto often insists that he never offers any normative claims, yet he adjudicates that in many circumstances, such as the French Revolution, the use of force is a "chief merit" in advancing "the conditions determining social utility" for the society as a whole.[23]

Far more afraid of imminent violent revolution, Mosca routinely insists that elite pluralism requires properly allowing for contestation of the few by the many so that different types of elites can emerge, contest, and then successfully integrate into the ruling class on a slow but continuous basis. As Ettore Albertoni put it, Mosca's discussion of the middle class (*il ceto medio*) envisions how the "Italian middle- and lower-middle classes in the years that followed national unification" could be incorporated into the governing body in order to curtail elite (the Northern Piedmontese and Southern Baroni) neglect of lower socioeconomic classes—the masses.[24]

Consequently, Mosca has been described as a conservative proponent of the mixed regime because he insists that good government depends on the institution of countervailing "social forces" to aid in the constant renewal of the ruling class from the middle strata.[25] But the point of these countervailing social forces is to address the "contradiction between political and economic inequality," which means that there must be adequate channels of contestation for those lower socioeconomic classes that are barred access to cost-prohibitive electoral contests.[26] His elite pluralism thus requires internalizing economic class differentiation in way that is not sufficiently attended to by the mixed regime tradition.

Because they conceptualize democracy as a power or principle that serves as an instrument for *buon governo*, Pareto and Mosca judged that any regime that veers from the popular, anti-plutocratic, and pluralist foundation is a bad government. As such, they see democracy both as a crucial instrument of good government and also part and parcel to good government itself.

By thinking of democracy in terms of good government, the Italians enable us to dislocate our conception of democracy from the primacy of elections

188   DEMOCRATIC ELITISM

without reducing it to a singular alternative institution or inflating it to an expansive conception such as "contestation" or "agonism"—ideas that, however accurate, lack requisite specificity to appreciate the democratic form. Pareto's and Mosca's thought offers us the means to conceptualize democracy as a "people" power that must be erected through majoritarian practices—popular, anti-plutocratic, and pluralist mechanisms that are ultimately responsible for inhibiting elite collusion, thereby creating the groundwork for productive elite competition and the productive use of the representative mechanisms of good government. And is that not what we now *really* mean by the term, anyway?

Pessimism and the Elitism of Translation

The hardest thing to swallow about the democratic theorists of elitism is their pessimistic approach. For some, no matter how it is articulated, the division of society between mass and elite—the attitude that "the elite will always be with us"—constitutes a fatalistic abdication of the fight for a society of political equals before it even gets started.[27] If the "plebeian" among us must struggle to be recognized by mainstream democratic theory, how will an elite heuristic or the theory of democracy as good government ever stand a chance?

The Italian theorists were certainly cynical about the prospects of overcoming the propensity of elite domination, but they were not pessimistic about the potential for good government. To use Antonio Gramsci's interpretation of the Italian orientation, Pareto and Mosca maintained "pessimism of the intellect, optimism of the will."[28] Their ruthless theoretical (intellectual) pessimism was motivated by their optimistic political desire (will) to convince their peers that it was in their own interest to curtail their power by introducing democratic institutions for the maintenance and stability of good government. A crucial component of their theory thus insists that democratic thought must speak to an elite audience and convince them of the democratic basis of *buon governo*. The fact that elites were speaking to each other did not foreclose the democratic potential of their theories. Instead, they hoped this orientation might make elites more responsible for their political power and its abuses.

Along these lines, elite theory is not quietist or fatalistic. Despite their protestations to the contrary, the Italians' works exhibit an implicit challenge that there might be one way desiring members of the ruling class could indeed prove themselves genuine *aristoi*. Pareto and Mosca challenged their readership to show themselves to be elites not by identifying themselves as plebeian but instead by listening to and translating the message of the masses into a vocabulary that is accessible to their elite peers.

CONCLUSION 189

Even medieval expositors of the tradition of *buon governo* such as Francesco Petrarch and Giovanni Boccaccio assumed this approach. Much like Pareto and Mosca, the medieval laureates represent two different kinds of elites with opposing dispositions. Most scholarship treats Boccaccio as the elite representative of Florentine republicanism, favoring the participation of the masses and the use of the vernacular, and Petrarch as the stodgy elitist who insists on maintaining *alio stilo*, or high style.[29]

Their divergent approaches are famously illustrated in Petrarch's appropriation of the last story of Boccaccio's *Decameron*. In this tale, we are told of Griselda, the daughter of a plebeian, who marries Prince Gaultieri. In Boccaccio's recounting, the prince abuses Griselda until the end. After years of sadistic tests, including divorce and banishment, he introduces her to a twelve-year-old girl he claims is to be his new bride but who is really their daughter; Griselda wishes them well. At this, Gaultieri reveals their grown children to her and Griselda is restored to her place as wife and mother.

Petrarch translates the story into Latin from Boccaccio's vernacular Italian, shifting the perspective from Gaultieri to Griselda as the narrator. Commentators assume that the translation signfies an act of "defiance" by Petrarch against Boccaccio, a declaration that the priority of readership is the elites, or the international community of literati who can acess the Latin idiom.[30] But this reading misses something important about Petrarch's own explanation of his translation. Petrarch writes to Boccaccio that even though many people have urged him to claim this version of the story as his own, it is and will forever remain a translation of the *Decameron*'s last novella and insists that Boccaccio should remain the author and judge of Petrarch's intervention.[31]

Why would it please Boccaccio, as Petrarch claims, to have his novella out in Latin if he had made the decision to write in the vulgar? And why, despite the existence of the Latin translation and despite the renewed contexts of meanings that Petrarch acknowledges will result from this translation, should the authorial source of judgment remain with Boccaccio? Part of the reason lies in the fact that Petrarch suggests that Boccaccio will be happy to have the meaning of the story extended to a wider audience of cosmopolitan elites so that they too may learn something from the vulgar.

Petrarch makes this clear in two ways. First, he disavows French translations of the story as marital exemplum and Christian virtues of chastity and constancy. In his letter, Petrarch explains that the intended audience of the fable is not *matrons nostri temporis*, or matrons, but *legentes*, or elites. In translating it into Latin, he makes it available not only to ecclesiastics, but also to jurists, administrators, and "men of affairs."[32] Petrarch and Boccaccio are both included in the group along with "our friends," two of whom Petrarch later reports to have read the story. He discusses how they receive the tale as if their differing opinions reveal something eternal about the nature of the governing classes in all polities.

Petrarch's friends exemplify two possible elite responses typical of their class. The first response turns on incredulity; the Paduan elite is unmoved by the story because it is entirely unrealistic.[33] Petrarch criticizes this response, lamenting that the Paduan thinks that "whatever is difficult for them, [must be] impossible for everyone; and so they judge everything by their own measure as to put themselves in first place; whereas there have been many, and perhaps still are, for whom things that seem impossible *to the multitude are simple.*"[34]

Fortunately for the fate of Petrarch's own class, there is another response: The Veronese is moved to tears. Petrarch condones this response and says that he puts "a favorable construction on it." To his mind, here we see what it means to be part of the genuine *aristoi*—that is, this ability to listen, compassionately respond to vulgar needs and feelings, and then translate those needs in a way that other elites can understand and appropriately respond politically. In other words, the translation of the story into Latin suggests that mass suffering and minority domination need to be translated to the elite from the vulgar; moreover, there is something that men of affairs need to learn from Griselda's patient suffering.

After all, Petrarch describes Griselda as the epitome of political virtue often "hidden under so much poverty." "In her husband's absence," Petrarch writes, she "[arbitrated] and [settled] the country's disputes and the disagreements of the nobles with such grave pronouncements, such maturity and fairness of judgment, that everyone declared that this lady had been sent down from heaven for the public well-being."[35] Griselda is not merely epistemically capable of managing the state, but she also saves the public wheel when real elites are nowhere to be found.

If we are to extrapolate from the tradition of *buon governo*, there is more for both the elites and the masses to learn than the appropriate definition of democracy for the contemporary imaginary. Perhaps the lesson is that in listening to the vulgar, the elite literati and men of affairs might learn to be real elites and willingly curtail the domination that creates the conditions for tyrannical usurpation in the first place.

Notes

Acknowledgments

Index

Notes

Preface

All translations of text from non-English sources are my own unless otherwise indicated.

1. Nadia Urbinati, *Democracy Disfigured: Opinion, Truth, and the People* (Cambridge, MA: Harvard University Press, 2014); Jan-Werner Müller, *What Is Populism?* (Philadelphia: University of Pennsylvania Press, 2016).

2. Josiah Ober, *Demopolis: Democracy before Liberalism in Theory and Practice* (Cambridge: Cambridge University Press, 2017); Hélène Landemore, *Open Democracy: Reinventing Popular Rule for the Twenty-First Century* (Princeton, NJ: Princeton University Press, 2020).

3. John P. McCormick, *Machiavellian Democracy* (Cambridge: Cambridge University Press, 2011); Jeffrey E. Green, *The Shadow of Unfairness: A Plebeian Theory of Liberal Democracy* (Oxford: Oxford University Press, 2016); Camila Vergara, *Systemic Corruption: Constitutional Ideas for an Anti-oligarchic Republic* (Princeton, NJ: Princeton University Press, 2020).

4. Jason Brennan, *Against Democracy* (Princeton. NJ: Princeton University Press, 2016).

Introduction

Epigraph: Gilbert Ryle, *The Concept of Mind* (Abingdon: Routledge, 2009), 5.

1. The connection between Collodi and the Italian Risorgimento is well established in Collodi's own writings and in the secondary literature. Prior to writing *Le avventure di Pinocchio: Storia di un burattino* (The adventures of Pinocchio: The story of a puppet), Collodi was widely understood as a political satirist and author who promoted the Risorgimento through his own newspaper, *Il Lampione* (The lamppost), subtitled "Giornale per tutti" (Newspaper for everyone). He also wrote multiple books on the Risorgimento, including *Quattro uomini del Risorgimento* (Four men of the Risorgimento) and a three-volume book series, *Il viaggio per l'Italia di Giannettino* (Giannettino's trip to Italy), in which he recounts travels through Northern, Central, and Southern Italy, describing them as "fatto modestamente per dare ai ragazzi una mezza idea di quell'Italia, che è la loro nuova e gloriosa patria" (made modestly in order to give the kids a half idea of that Italy, which is their new and glorious *patria*). Carlo Collodi to Guido Biagi, November 4, 1882, Carteggio Biagi, Biblioteca nazionale centrale di Firenze. See also Benedetto Croce, "Pinocchio," in *La letteratura della nuova Italia*, vol. 5 (Bari: Laterza, 1957), 330–334. For contemporary research on the relationship between

194 NOTES TO PAGES 2–5

Collodi's entire body of work and the Risorgimento, see Vincenzo Cappelletti, Cosimo Ceccuti, and Daniela Marcheschi, *Carlo Lorenzini protagonista dell'unità d'Italia* (Pescia: Edizioni Fondazione Carlo Collodi, 2020). For an additional source on Collodi's *Pinocchio* in particular, see Susanna Ferlito, "Sonorous 'Mitezza': A Political Voice in Collodi's 'The Adventures of Pinocchio,'" *Italica* 94, no. 4 (Winter 2017): 709–725.

2. The Carbonari—the informal network of secret revolutionary societies that advanced Italian unification—began in Naples under the Napoleonic Wars. The Carbonari made it possible for Garibaldi to organize the Redshirts into the forces that won decisive battles against the armies of the Austrian Empire, the Kingdom of Two Sicilies, and The Papal States, ultimately culminating in the victorious Expedition of the Thousand in 1860.

3. Suzanne Stewart-Steinberg, *The Pinocchio Effect: On Making Italians, 1860–1920* (Chicago: University of Chicago Press, 2007).

4. Compare Giorgio Agamben's recent take in his *Pinocchio: The Adventures of a Puppet, Doubly Commented Upon and Triply Illustrated* (Chicago: University of Chicago Press, 2023). See also Giorgio Manganelli, *Pinocchio: Un libro parallelo* (Milan: Adelphi, 2002).

5. In the very first version of the fable, Pinocchio commits suicide. Collodi had killed off his character with no intent of resurrecting him, but the editor of *Giornale per i bambini* (Newspaper for children) pleaded with him to continue the series; so in 1882 and into 1883 Collodi published piecemeal "Le avventure di Pinocchio," which ultimately became chapters 16–36 of the book. Although the message became expressed less pessimistically, it remained consistent: the nation would survive only if the Mezzogiorno (Southern Italy) was resuscitated from the Northern plutocratic electoral stranglehold. Rebecca West, "Afterword," in Carlo Collodi, *Pinocchio* (New York: New York Review Books, 2009).

6. For some of the most famous models of democracy developed along the lines of elite theory, see Gabriel Almond and Sidney Verba, *The Civic Culture: Political Attitudes and Democracy in Five Nations* (Princeton, NJ: Princeton University Press, 1963); Bernard Berelson, Paul Lazarsfeld, and William McPhee, *Voting: A Study of Opinion Formation in a Presidential Campaign* (Chicago: University of Chicago Press, 1954); Norberto Bobbio, *The Future of Democracy* (Minneapolis: University of Minnesota Press, 1987); Anthony Downs, *An Economic Theory of Democracy* (New York: Harper and Row, 1957); William Domhoff, *Who Rules America? Power, Politics, and Social Change*, 5th ed. (New York: McGraw Hill, 2006); David Easton, *A Systems Analysis of Political Life* (New York: Wiley, 1965); Harold Lasswell, "The Elite Concept," in *Political Elites in a Democracy*, ed. Peter Bachrach (New Brunswick, NJ: Transaction, 1971); Robert Putnam, *The Comparative Study of Political Elites* (Englewood Cliffs, NJ: Prentice Hall, 1976); David Truman, *The Congressional Party: A Case Study* (New York: Wiley, 1959); Myron Weiner, "Empirical Democratic Theory and the Transition from Authoritarianism to Democracy," *PS: Political Science and Politics* 20, no. 4 (Autumn 1987): 861–866; Giovanni Sartori, *Democratic Theory* (New York: Praeger, 1965); Walter Lippmann, *Public Opinion* (New York: Harcourt, Brace, 1922).

7. For critiques of elite theories of democracy, whether through the lens of behavioralism, rational choice, social choice, or variants of classical sociological elite theory, consult Graeme Duncan and Steven Lukes, "The New Democracy," *Political Studies* 11, no. 2 (June 1963): 156–177; Benjamin Barber, *Strong Democracy: Participatory Politics for a New Age* (Berkeley: University of California Press, 1984); Lane Davis, "The Cost of Realism: Contemporary Restatements of Democracy," *Western Political Quarterly* 17, no. 1 (March 1964): 37–46; Kenneth Prewitt and Alan Stone, *The Ruling Elites: Elite Theory, Power, and American Democracy* (New York: Joanna Cotler Books, 1973);

Eva Etzioni-Halevy, *Classes and Elites in Democracy and Democratization* (New York: Garland, 1997); Maure Goldschmidt, "Democratic Theory and Contemporary Political Science," in *Apolitical Politics: A Critique of Behavioralism*, ed. Charles A. McCoy and John Playford (New York: Thomas Y. Cromwell, 1967); Quentin Skinner, "The Empirical Theorists of Democracy and Their Critics: A Plague on Both Their Houses," *Political Theory* 1, no. 3 (August 1973): 287–306; Thomas Bottomore, *Elites and Society*, 2nd ed. (New York: Routledge, 1993); John Dewey, *The Public and Its Problems* (New York: Henry Holt, 1927).

8. David Held, *Models of Democracy*, 3rd ed. (Stanford, CA: Stanford University Press, 2006); Edward Purcell, *The Crisis of Democratic Theory: Scientific Naturalism and the Problem of Value* (Lexington: University Press of Kentucky, 1973); John Higley and Michael Burton, *Elite Foundations of Liberal Democracy* (Lanham, MD: Rowman and Littlefield, 2006).

9. Jack Hayward, ed., *Elitism, Populism, and European Politics* (Oxford: Oxford University Press, 1996).

10. Bernard Manin, *The Principles of Representative Government* (Cambridge: Cambridge University Press, 1997).

11. For notable contemporary debates, see, for instance, Carole Pateman against Robert Dahl, John McCormick against the "Cambridge School," and Nadia Urbinati against Philip Pettit.

12. Robyn Marasco reconstructs an overlapping strain of twentieth-century German pessimism vis-à-vis "the dynamism of despair" to similar ends in *The Highway of Despair: Critical Theory after Hegel* (New York: Columbia University Press, 2015).

13. John Rawls, *A Theory of Justice*, rev. ed. (Cambridge, MA: Harvard University Press, 1999).

14. Jürgen Habermas, *The Theory of Communicative Action: Reason and the Rationalization of Society* (Cambridge: Polity Press, 1986); Sheldon Wolin, *Fugitive Democracy: And Other Essays* (Princeton, NJ: Princeton University Press, 2016).

15. Compare Hugo Drochon, "Robert Michels and the Iron Law of Oligarchy and Dynamic Democracy," *Constellations* 27, no. 2 (June 2020): 185–198; Chantal Mouffe, "Deliberative Democracy or Agonistic Pluralism?," *Social Research* 66, no. 3 (Fall 1999): 745–758.

16. Niccolò Machiavelli, *The Prince*, 2nd ed. (Chicago: University of Chicago Press, 1998); Francesco Petrarca, *In difesa dell'Italia (Contra eum qui maledixit Italie)*, ed. Giuliana Crevatin (Venice: Marsilio Editori, 1995).

17. Juan J. Linz, *Robert Michels, Political Sociology, and the Future of Democracy* (New Brunswick, NJ: Transaction, 2006), 63; Giovanni Sartori, *The Theory of Democracy Revisited* (Chatham, NJ: Chatham House, 1987), 149.

18. Thomas Piketty, *Capital in the Twenty-First Century*, trans. Arthur Goldhammer (Cambridge, MA: Belknap Press of Harvard University Press, 2014).

19. For one of the many accounts of the fragility of the Italian state and its character as an elite enterprise, see, most famously, Denis Mack Smith, "Italy," in *The New Cambridge Modern History*, vol. 10: *The Zenith of European Power, 1830–70*, ed. J. P. T. Bury (Cambridge: Cambridge University Press, 1960), 552. The unified Italian state was such a contested concept that even foreign investors did not believe in Italian sovereign debt until six years after unification. See Stéphanie Collet, "A Unified Italy? Sovereign Debt and Investor Skepticism" (unpublished paper, ESCP Europe, 2016), https://ssrn.com/abstract=2024636.

20. Although the United States experienced a populist response to the Gilded Age at the turn of the century, its previous existence as a nation and unique experience with the Civil War alleviated the existential threat posed to the nation itself, which was not the case with Italy.

196   NOTES TO PAGES 13–18

21. Rocco Rubini interprets the so-called Italian hermeneutic "difference" as a reception of Giambattista Vico's thought against the Cartesian strains of Continental philosophy (French, German, and their American elaborations). Rubini, *The Other Renaissance: Italian Humanism between Hegel and Heidegger* (Chicago: University of Chicago Press, 2014).

22. Even those who assimilate Pareto, Mosca, Michels, Weber, and Schumpeter into the tradition of democratic elitism are careful to methodologically distinguish the first three from Weber and Schumpeter on methodological grounds. Jan Pakulski describes the conventional wisdom well when he writes: "Weber never identified himself as part of the classical elite theoretical camp (as represented by Vilfredo Pareto, Gaetano Mosca and Robert Michels) perhaps mainly because of his anti-positivistic orientation and his skepticism concerning the nomothetic model of emergent political sociology." Jan Pakulski, "The Weberian Foundations of Modern Elite Theory and Democratic Elitism," *Historical Social Research*, 37, no. 1 (2012): 38–56.

23. While pessimism has been recognized as a German intellectual discourse, Joshua Dienstag demonstrates that pessimism is, at the very least, a broadly European tradition that dates back to the Enlightenment—if not the Renaissance. Dienstag illuminates the pessimistic orientation as a philosophical response to modernity and rescues the orientation from neglect in Western philosophy. I believe that Mosca, Pareto, Michels, and Schumpeter are a part of the tradition as Dienstag describes it. Joshua Foa Dienstag, *Pessimism: Philosophy, Ethic, Spirit* (Princeton, NJ: Princeton University Press, 2006). See also Frederick Beiser, *Weltschmerz: Pessimism in German Philosophy, 1860–1900* (Oxford: Oxford University Press, 2016).

24. Robert Nye, *The Anti-democratic Sources of Elite Theory: Pareto, Mosca, Michels* (London: Sage, 1977), 47.

1. An Angry Warning

Epigraph: Joseph Schumpeter, *Ten Great Economists* (San Diego, CA: Simon Publications, 2003), 110.

1. Talcott Parsons, *The Structure of Social Action: A Study in Social Theory with Special Reference to a Group of Recent European Writers* (Glencoe, IL: Free Press, 1949), 293.

2. Norberto Bobbio, *On Mosca and Pareto* (Geneva: Librairie Droz, 1972), 59; Raymond Aron, "Paretian Politics," in *Pareto & Mosca*, ed. James H. Meisel (Englewood Cliffs, NJ: Prentice-Hall, 1965), 115.

3. Tellingly, Pareto has often been called both the "Karl Marx of the Bourgeoisie" and the "Karl Marx of Fascism." See, respectively, Georges-Henri Bousquet, *Vilfredo Pareto, sa vie et son œuvre* (Paris: Payot, 1928), 23; Vincenzo Fani, quoted in Placido Bucolo, *The Other Pareto* (London: Scolar Press, 1980), 285–286.

4. Meisel, "Introduction: Pareto & Mosca," in *Pareto & Mosca*, 10. See also Lawrence Henderson, "The Science of Human Conduct: An Estimate of Pareto and One of His Greatest Works," *The Independent*, December 10, 1927; Parsons, *Structure of Social Action*, 299–300; Sidney Hook, "Pareto's Sociological System," *The Nation*, June 26, 1935, 747–748.

5. Karl Mannheim, *Ideology and Utopia: An Introduction to the Sociology of Knowledge* (New York: Harcourt, Brace, 1936), 119; Benedetto Croce, "The Validity of Pareto's Theories," *Saturday Review*, May 25, 1935, 13; R. V. Worthington, "Pareto: The Karl Marx of Fascism," *Economic Forum* 1, no. 1 (Summer / Fall 1933): 311–315; William McDougall, "Pareto as Psychologist," *Journal of Social Philosophy and Jurisprudence* 1, no. 1 (October 1935): 36n1; Ellsworth Faris, *The Nature of Human*

Nature: And Other Essays in Social Psychology (New York: McGraw-Hill, 1937), 190–201; Melvin Rader, *No Compromise: The Conflict between Two Worlds* (New York: Macmillan, 1939), 44–87, 93, 199–209.

6. Giorgio Volpe, *Italian Elitism and the Reshaping of Democracy in the United States* (New York: Routledge, 2021).

7. James W. Vander Zanden, "Pareto and Fascism Reconsidered," *American Journal of Economics and Sociology* 19, no. 4 (July 1960): 399. Fanciful theories were developed to explain Pareto's sudden change of heart. For Franz Borkenau, Pareto's counterrevolutionary positions were the result of an Oedipus complex. Franz Borkenau, *Pareto* (London: J. Wiley and Sons, 1936), 9–11. According to another view, Pareto's hatred of democracy can be explained by his being a "decayed nobleman," bitter about his failed parliamentary campaign. Werner Stark, *The Sociology of Knowledge: Toward a Deeper Understanding of the History of Ideas* (London: Routledge, 1958), 53. For H. Stuart Hughes, Pareto's about-face represents his response to his failed predictions about protectionism. H. Stuart Hughes, *Consciousness and Society: The Reorientation of European Social Thought, 1890–1930* (New York: Knopf, 1958), 261. All such theories have been debunked by Samuel Finer; yet Finer still maintains that Pareto's change was the response of a disappointed liberal whose disillusionment forced him to retreat from politics into academic life. Samuel Finer, "Pareto and Pluto-Democracy: The Retreat to Galapagos," *American Political Science Review* 62, no. 2 (June 1968): 440–450.

8. Richard Bellamy, *Modern Italian Social Theory: Ideology and Politics from Pareto to the Present* (Cambridge: Polity Press, 1987).

9. Renato Cirillo, "Was Vilfredo Pareto Really a 'Precursor' of Fascism?," *American Journal of Economics and Sociology* 42, no. 2 (April 1983): 235–245; Carl Friedrich, *The New Image of the Common Man* (Boston: Beacon Press, 1950), 265.

10. Charles Merriam, *The New Democracy and the New Despotism* (New York: McGraw-Hill, 1939), 29, 208–210; William J. Novak, Stephen W. Sawyer, and James T. Sparrow, "Democratic States of Unexception: Toward a New Genealogy of the American Political," in *The Many Hands of the State: Theorizing Political Authority and Social Control*, ed. Kimberly Morgan and Ann Shola Orloff (Cambridge: Cambridge University Press, 2017), 247.

11. Some have acknowledged that, like Georges Sorel, Pareto sought to dispel this political myth, but argue that without Sorel's proletarian bias, Pareto's exposure acquires an antidemocratic quality. Guy Perrin, "Thèmes pour une philosophie de l'histoire dans le 'Traité de sociologie générale,'" *Cahiers Vilfredo Pareto* 1, no. 1 (1963): 36–37.

12. Joseph Femia, *Pareto and Political Theory* (New York: Routledge, 2006), 5.

13. Joseph Schumpeter, *Ten Great Economists: From Marx to Keynes* (London: Routledge, 1997), 112–113.

14. William Selinger, *Parliamentarism: From Burke to Weber* (Cambridge: Cambridge University Press, 2019); Nadia Urbinati, "Condorcet's Democratic Theory of Representative Government," *European Journal of Political Theory* 3, no. 1 (January 2004): 53–75.

15. Vilfredo Pareto to Maffeo Pantaleoni, October 28, 1896, in Pareto, *Lettere a Maffeo Pantaleoni*, vol. 1, ed. Gabriele De Rosa (Rome: Banca Nazionale del Lavoro, 1960); Giovanni Busino, "Introduzione a Vilfredo Pareto," in *Vilfredo Pareto (1848–1923): L'uomo e lo scienziato*, ed. Gavino Manca (Milan: Libri Scheiwiller, 2002), 21.

16. Charles H. Powers, "Introduction: The Life and Times of Vilfredo Pareto," in *The Transformation of Democracy*, ed. Charles H. Powers, trans. Renata Girola (New Brunswick, NJ: Transaction Books, 1984), 5.

198 NOTES TO PAGES 21–23

17. Pareto published primarily in the *Giornale degli economisti* under the editorship of his friend Maffeo Pantaleoni, but he ceased contributing in 1898 after friction developed with the new editor, Antonio De Viti De Marco, due to, in De Viti De Marco's opinion, the excessively antiestablishment tone of Pareto's contributions. Vilfredo Pareto to Maffeo Pantaleoni, June 14 and August 1, 1897, in Vilfredo Pareto, *Lettere a Maffeo Pantaleoni*, vol. 2, ed. Gabriele De Rosa (Rome: Banca Nazionale del Lavoro, 1960).

18. Vilfredo Pareto to Luigi Minuti, January 24, 1894, in Vilfredo Pareto, *Oeuvres complètes*, vol. 30: *Lettres et correspondances: Compléments et additions*, ed. Giovanni Busino (Geneva: Librairie Droz, 1989), 222.

19. For a history of the concept, see Marco Valbruzzi, "Trasformismo," in *The Oxford Handbook of Italian Politics*, ed. Erik Jones and Gianfranco Pasquino (2015; online ed., Oxford Academic, February 11, 2016).

20. Busino, "Introduzione a Vilfredo Pareto," 23.

21. Richard Bellamy demonstrates the ways in which Pareto followed John Stuart Mill, but also notes that some of Pareto's conclusions have more in common with T. H. Green's "new liberalism" than with strict "classical liberalism." Bellamy, *Modern Italian Social Theory*, 15.

22. Vilfredo Pareto, "Considerazioni sui principi fondamentali dell'economia politica pura," *Giornale degli economisti* 4 (May 1892): 419–420.

23. Vilfredo Pareto, "Il movimento dei conti correnti presso le banche popolari ed altri istituti di credito," *L'Economista*, November 16, 1890, 726–727.

24. Vilfredo Pareto, "Operai disoccupati," *Il Secolo*, April 6–7, 1891, in Pareto, *Oeuvres complètes*, vol. 17: *Écrits politiques: Lo sviluppo del capitalismo, 1872–1895*, ed. Giovanni Busino (Geneva: Librairie Droz, 1974), 416–417; Pareto, "Lettre d'Italie," *Journal des économistes* (March 1891): 414; Pareto to Teodoro Moneta, May 15, 1892, in Pareto, *Oeuvres complètes*, vol. 31: *Nouvelles lettres (1870–1923)*, ed. Fiorenzo Mornati (Geneva: Librairie Droz, 2001), 41–42.

25. Vilfredo Pareto, "Lettre d'Italie," *Le monde économique*, August 6, 1892, 146, in Pareto, *Oeuvres complètes*, vol. 10: *Lettres d'Italie: Chroniques sociales et économiques*, ed. Giovanni Busino (Geneva: Librairie Droz, 1967), 86.

26. Vilfredo Pareto, "L'ora dei sacrifizi è suonata," *Il Secolo*, January 11, 1894, in Pareto, *Oeuvres complètes*, 17:705–706.

27. Vilfredo Pareto, "Lettre d'Italie," *Journal des économistes* (December 1891): 388–389; Pareto to Felice Cavallotti, October 28, 1890, in Pareto, *Oeuvres complètes*, 30:93.

28. Pareto to Cavallotti, October 28, 1890, in Pareto, *Oeuvres complètes*, 30:95.

29. Pareto, "Il movimento dei conti correnti."

30. Vilfredo Pareto, "L'equa protezione della fame," *Il Secolo*, February 2–3, 1892, in Pareto, *Oeuvres complètes*, 17:485–486.

31. "Mathematical economics supplied a proof that, in general, the direct effect of protection is a destruction of wealth. If one were to go on and add an axiom, which is implicitly taken for granted by many economists, that any destruction of wealth is an 'evil,' one could logically conclude that protection is an 'evil.' But before such a proposition can be granted the indirect economic effects . . . of protection have to be known. . . . [We] find that protection transfers a certain amount of wealth from a part, A, of the population to a part B, through the destruction of a certain amount of wealth, q, the amount representing the costs of the operation. If, as a result of this new distribution of wealth, the production of wealth . . . increases by a quantity greater than q, the operation is economically

NOTES TO PAGES 23–26 199

beneficial . . . [This] case is not to be barred a priori." Vilfredo Pareto, *The Mind and Society*, 4 vols., ed. Arthur Livingston, trans. Andrew Bongiorno, Arthur Livingston, and James Harvey Rogers (New York: Harcourt, Brace, 1935), vol. 4, §2208.

32. Vilfredo Pareto, "L'aumento della circolazione delle banche di emissione," *Il Secolo*, January 27, 1894, in Pareto, *Oeuvres complètes*, 17:714–716.

33. Vilfredo Pareto to Maffeo Pantaleoni, February 17, 1892, in Pareto, *Lettere a Maffeo Pantaleoni*, 1:184.

34. Vilfredo Pareto to Maffeo Pantaleoni, December 20, 1892, in Pareto, *Lettere a Maffeo Pantaleoni*, 1:329 (emphasis added). The point was reiterated in an address given by Pareto in Milan on December 16, 1892, published in *Corriere della Sera*, December 18–19, 1892; Pareto, *Cours d'économie politique: Professé à l'Université de Lausanne*, vol. 1 (Lausanne: F. Rouge, 1896), 370.

35. Vilfredo Pareto, "Les finances italiennes," *Journal des économistes* (April 1894): 24.

36. See Christopher Seton Watson, *Italy from Liberalism to Fascism, 1870–1925* (London: Methuen, 1967).

37. Vilfredo Pareto, "Le Crédit foncier," *Le monde économique*, May 2, 1891, in Pareto, *Oeuvres complètes*, 10:32–33.

38. Pareto, "Le Crédit foncier," in Pareto, *Oeuvres complètes*, 10:31–33; Pareto, "Lettre d'Italie," *Le monde économique*, April 25, 1891, in Pareto, *Oeuvres complètes*, 10:30.

39. Pareto, "Le Crédit foncier," in Pareto, *Oeuvres complètes*, 10:32–33.

40. Vilfredo Pareto, "Le verdict Tanlongo," *Gazette de Lausanne*, August 2, 1894, in Pareto, *Oeuvres complètes*, vol. 32: *Inédits et addenda*, ed. Fiorenzo Mornati (Geneva: Librairie Droz, 2005), 130.

41. Pareto, *Cours d'économie politique*, 1:352–353n1 (emphasis added).

42. Vilfredo Pareto, "L'intervention de l'état dans les banques d'émission en Italie," *Journal des économistes* (April 1893): 4.

43. Vilfredo Pareto, "Cronaca," *Giornale degli economisti* 5 (May 1893): 401.

44. Vilfredo Pareto to Teodoro Moneta, July 11, 1891, in Pareto, *Oeuvres complètes*, 31:26.

45. Vilfredo Pareto to Maffeo Pantaleoni, July 29, 1893, in Pareto, *Lettere a Maffeo Pantaleoni*, 1:388.

46. Vilfredo Pareto, "Carte in tavola," *L'Isola*, August 28–29, 1892, in Pareto, *Oeuvres complètes*, 17:543.

47. Vilfredo Pareto to Teodoro Moneta, October 18, 1891, in Pareto, *Oeuvres complètes*, 31:29.

48. Vilfredo Pareto, "The Parliamentary Régime in Italy," *Political Science Quarterly* (December 1893): 711–712. Later Pareto expressed his conviction that war is "the consequence of the rivalry between political classes, who wish to increase the number of their subjects, and, more particularly, of their taxpayers." Pareto, *Cours d'économie politique*, 1:135–136.

49. Vilfredo Pareto to Felice Cavallotti, August 14, 1892, in Pareto, *Oeuvres complètes*, 30:165.

50. Vilfredo Pareto to Francesco Papafava, August 14, 1892, and Pareto to Cavallotti, August 14, 1892, in Pareto, *Oeuvres complètes*, 30:165–166. Pareto defended the view proposed in Tiberio Squilletta's "La Nazione armata: Studio di un nuovo ordinamento dell'esercito," *Giornale degli economisti* 4 (September 1892): 183–221; (October 1892): 344–375; (November 1892): 428–478.

51. Vilfredo Pareto, address given at the Conferenza Pareto, *Il Secolo*, April 15–16, 1893.

52. Vilfredo Pareto, *Le spese militari e i mali dell'Italia* (Milan: Gattinoni, 1892), in Pareto, *Oeuvres complètes*, 17:562–567.

200 NOTES TO PAGES 26–29

53. Pareto, address, in *Il Secolo*, April 16–17, 1893.

54. Vilfredo Pareto, "Il discorso del presidente Cleveland," *Il Secolo*, April 8–9, 1893, in Pareto, *Oeuvres complètes*, 17:610.

55. Vilfredo Pareto to Emilia Peruzzi, December 18, 1892, in Pareto, *Oeuvres complètes* 27:2.

56. "Whom do I call the bourgeoisie? I call bourgeois all those who live comfortably and enjoy protective tariffs, get government jobs for their children and make money through the contractors, and, when the occasion arises, plunder the banks; and besides these, many rich and well-to-do persons, honest in their private lives but who think it necessary, so as to support their own class and not dry up the sources of money for their friends, to support knavery on the government's part." Vilfredo Pareto to Maffeo Pantaleoni, December 23, 1896, in Pareto, *Lettere a Maffeo Pantaleoni*, 1:500. For Pareto's critique of the pre-1860 nobility, see his writings from the "Florentine period" (1874–1893), which are full of even more savage references to the "gilded youth" and the families who "'sucked the blood' of the Italian poor." Pareto, *Dal carteggio con Carlo Placci*, ed. Tommaso Giacalone-Monaco (Padua: Cedam, 1957).

57. Vilfredo Pareto, "Dialoghi dei morti," *Giornale degli economisti* (March 1893): 167.

58. Vilfredo Pareto, "Cronaca," *Giornale degli economisti* 5 (August 1893): 181.

59. Vilfredo Pareto, "Cronaca" (August 1893), 181.

60. Vilfredo Pareto, "State Intervention in Italy," *The Speaker*, May 14, 1892, in Vilfredo Pareto, *Oeuvres complètes*, vol. 16: *Écrits épars*, ed. Giovanni Busino (Geneva: Librairie Droz, 1974), 50.

61. Vilfredo Pareto, "The Result of Italian Elections," *The Speaker*, November 26, 1892, in Pareto, *Oeuvres complètes*, 16:65.

62. Vilfredo Pareto, "The Coming Elections in Italy," *The Speaker*, October 29, 1892, in Pareto, *Oeuvres complètes*, 16:62.

63. Vilfredo Pareto, "L'Italie économique," *Revue des deux mondes*, October 15, 1891, in Vilfredo Pareto, *Oeuvres complètes*, vol. 2: *Le marché financier italien (1891–1899)*, ed. Giovanni Busino (Geneva: Librairie Droz, 1965), 2.

64. Pareto, "Parliamentary Régime in Italy," 710.

65. Tom Bottomore laments that Pareto did not appreciate the "heterogeneity of elites," even though Pareto often said that the unity of the ruling class was a Marxist fairy tale. Bottomore, *Elites and Society*, 2nd ed. (New York: Routledge, 1993), 4. Others see Pareto as denying agency to anyone but elites, thereby dividing society between elites and the masses. Peter Bachrach, *The Theory of Democratic Elitism: A Critique* (Washington, DC: University Press of America, 1980). Some argue that Pareto's interest in crowd psychology confirms that the division of elites and masses characterizes his thinking. Robert Nye, *The Anti-democratic Sources of Elite Theory: Pareto, Mosca, Michels* (London: Sage, 1977). Others maintain that Pareto's division of human activity between the logical and the nonlogical not only sorts society into two categories but also legitimized authoritarian politics. Bellamy, *Modern Italian Social Theory*. Still others, albeit aware that Pareto's categories were complicated, nevertheless understood this paradigm as the crucial one. Warren Samuels, *Pareto on Policy* (New Brunswick, NJ: Transaction, 2012).

66. Renzo Sereno, "The Anti-Aristotelianism of Gaetano Mosca and Its Fate," *Ethics* 48, no. 4 (July 1938): 514–515.

67. Julien Freund, *Pareto: La teoria dell'equilibrio* (Bari: Laterza, 1976), 1.

68. Vilfredo Pareto, *Cours d'économie politique: Professé à l'Université de Lausanne*, vol. 2 (Lausanne: F. Rouge, 1897).

NOTES TO PAGES 29–32   201

69. Joseph Femia, *Pareto and Political Theory* (New York: Routledge, 2006), 138.

70. Pareto, *The Mind and Society*, vol. 4, §2060.

71. In his previous academic works, Pareto calls this movement the "alternation of elites," but in the *Trattato* he collapses the terms "elite circulation" and "elite alternation."

72. Barbara Heyl, "The Harvard 'Pareto Circle,'" *Journal of the History of the Behavioral Sciences* 4, no. 4 (October 1968): 316–334. For more on this point, see James Meisel, "A Question of Affinities: Pareto and Marx II," *Cahiers Vilfredo Pareto* 3, no. 5 (1965): 164–174.

73. Even outside of political science, economists and sociologists tend to believe that Pareto's most "significant insight" was that "the history of all hitherto existing society is a history of social hierarchies." Joseph Persky, "Retrospectives: Pareto's Law," *Journal of Economic Perspectives* 6, no. 2 (Spring 1992): 191.

74. Pareto, *The Mind and Society*, vol. 4, §§2550–2553, 2586.

75. Pareto, *The Mind and Society*, vol. 2, §888.

76. Pareto, *The Mind and Society*, vol. 4, §2610.

77. Pareto, *The Mind and Society*, vol. 4, §§2227, 2259, 2274, 2585.

78. Pareto, *The Mind and Society*, vol. 2, §888.

79. Pareto, *The Mind and Society*, vol. 4, §2268. For a recent revival of Pareto's fox and lion metaphors in his explanation of social change, see Clayton Fordahl, "Lions and Foxes: Revisiting Pareto's Bestiary for the Age of Late Pluto-Democracy," *Distinktion: Journal of Social Theory* 21, no. 3 (April 2020): 316–333.

80. Pareto, *The Mind and Society*, vol. 4, §§2256, 2419–2421, 2493.

81. Samuel Finer, "Pareto and Pluto-Democracy," 446.

82. Giovanni Sartori, "Anti-elitism Revisited," *Government and Opposition* 13, no. 1 (Winter 1978): 58–80.

83. Pareto, *The Mind and Society*, vol. 4, §§2257, 2267, 2304–2307.

84. Pareto, *The Mind and Society*, vol. 4, §§2259, 2257n1.

85. "Polybius (*Historiae*, VI, 17, 1–4) notes, in particular, manipulations of public contracts by censors, especially the farming of taxes, and he remarks that virtually everybody was engaged in it. 'Some,' he says, 'get the contracts from the censors themselves, others are bondsmen, others mortgage their properties as bonds.' There, in its cradle, is the creature that will one day be named Plutocracy. An infant weakling, it remains subordinate. Once it gets and grows its muscle, it will claim dominion." Pareto, *The Mind and Society*, vol. 4, §2548.

86. Pareto, *The Mind and Society*, vol. 4, §2254.

87. Pareto, *The Mind and Society*, vol. 4, §2254.

88. Pareto, *The Mind and Society*, vol. 4, §2256.

89. Pareto, *The Mind and Society*, vol. 4, §2255.

90. Sometimes, Pareto says, politicians will cave to public sentiments, but only when they are forced to pay "ransom . . . for lucrative operations conducted by shrewd financiers, promoters, and other speculators." Pareto, *The Mind and Society*, vol. 4, §2253n1.

91. Pareto, *The Mind and Society*, vol. 4, §2240n1.

92. Pareto, *The Mind and Society*, vol. 4, §2240n1 (emphasis added).

93. Pareto, *The Mind and Society*, vol. 2, §§933–936, 967–970, 1220–1227; vol. 3, §§1511–1514, 1859.

94. Pareto, *The Mind and Society*, vol. 4, §2183.

95. Pareto, *The Mind and Society*, vol. 4, §2147.

202 NOTES TO PAGES 32–38

96. Vilfredo Pareto, "Universal Suffrage," from a lecture given to the Accademia dei Georgofili, June 29, 1872; in Bucolo, *The Other Pareto*, 19–23.

97. Vilfredo Pareto, "Proportional Representation," from a lecture given to the Accademia dei Georgofili, June 29, 1872. in Bucolo, *The Other Pareto*, 7–23.

98. Pareto, *The Mind and Society*, vol. 4, §2244.

99. Pareto, *The Mind and Society*, vol. 4, §2256n1.

100. Pareto, *The Mind and Society*, vol. 4, §§2582n2, 2583–2584.

101. Pareto, *The Mind and Society*, vol. 4, §2259.

102. Pareto, *The Mind and Society*, vol. 2, §888; Vilfredo Pareto, *Trasformazione della democrazia* (Rome: Editori Riunti, 1999), 41.

103. Pareto, *The Mind and Society*, vol. 4, §2540.

104. Many commentators held that this element of Pareto's thought epitomizes his conservatism because it denies human progress. See, for example, Morris Ginsberg, "The Sociology of Pareto," *Sociological Review* 28, no. 3 (July 1936): 221–245.

105. Pareto, *The Mind and Society*, vol. 3, §§2035–2036.

106. Pareto, *The Mind and Society*, vol. 4, §2485.

107. Pareto, *The Mind and Society*, vol. 4, §2485.

108. Pareto, *The Mind and Society*, vol. 4, §2485.

109. Pareto, *The Mind and Society*, vol. 4, §§2494, 2501.

110. Pareto, *The Mind and Society*, vol. 4, §2495.

111. Pareto, *The Mind and Society*, vol. 4, §2257.

112. Lewis Coser, *Masters of Sociological Thought: Ideas in Historical and Social Context* (New York: Harcourt Brace Jovanovich), 421.

113. This contention is a stable theme in Italian political thought. For Francesco Guicciardini's anticipation of this argument, see John Padgett, "Open Elite? Social Mobility, Marriage, and Family in Florence, 1282–1494," *Renaissance Quarterly* 63, no. 2 (Summer 2010): 357–411.

114. I exclude *Cours d'économie politique* from consideration because it contains little that is specifically Paretian. Even though the *Cours* demonstrates Pareto's long-standing interest in minority domination, on the whole the text constitutes Pareto's attempt to make good on his appointment as the Walras neoclassical chair at the University of Lausanne. Pareto refused to sanction a reprint or a second edition, and I accordingly take his lead regarding which texts best exemplify the particularity of his contribution.

115. Vilfredo Pareto, *Les systèmes socialistes* (Paris: V. Giard et E. Brière, 1902), 22.

116. Pareto, *Trasformazione della democrazia*, 39.

117. Pareto, *Trasformazione della democrazia*, 39, 40, 51, 83–84.

118. Pareto, *Trasformazione della democrazia*, 44.

119. Pareto, *Trasformazione della democrazia*, 47. Pareto intended to add another volume to the *Trattato* that would have examined contemporary events in light of his theories. He never finished that volume, and *Fatti e teorie* (1920) and *Trasformazione della democrazia* (1921) were written in its stead, initially appearing as a series of articles for the *Rivista di Milano* in 1920. Francesco Marchiano, "Introduzione," in *Trasformazione della democrazia*, ed. Francesco Marchiano (Rome: Castelvecchi, 2019), 5.

120. Pareto, *Trasformazione della democrazia*, 55, 56.

121. In *Fatti e Teorie*, written contemporaneously with *Trasformazione della democrazia*, Pareto claims that this division is analogous to Machiavelli's theory of the two humors presented in the

Discourses on Livy, and that the investigation of this division was the guiding thread of all his work. Vilfredo Pareto, *Fatti e teorie* (Firenze: Vallecchi, 1920), 321.

122. Pareto, *The Mind and Society*, vol. 4, §2180; Pareto, *Trasformazione della democrazia*, 63.

123. Pareto, *Trasformazione della democrazia*, 64, 55, 63.

124. Pareto, *The Mind and Society*, vol. 2, §868; Pareto, *Trasformazione della democrazia*, 41.

125. Pareto, *Trasformazione della democrazia*, 76, 64.

126. Pareto, *Trasformazione della democrazia*, 76. Jeffrey Winter demonstrates that even in Sweden the superrich set the taxes paid by the rich. Jeffrey Winters, *Oligarchy* (Cambridge: Cambridge University Press, 2011), 279. For a similar analysis along these lines, see Jeffrey Green, *The Shadow of Unfairness: A Plebeian Theory of Liberal Democracy* (Oxford: Oxford University Press, 2016).

127. Pareto, *Trasformazione della democrazia*, 81.

128. Pareto, *Trasformazione della democrazia*, 76, 85–86, 55, 112. For an analysis of Machiavelli's anticipation of this argument, see John P. McCormick, "Machiavelli's Greek Tyrant as Republican Reformer," in *The Radical Machiavelli: Politics, Philosophy and Language*, ed. Filippo Del Lucchese, Fabio Frosini, and Vittorio Morfino (Leiden: Brill, 2015), 337–348.

129. Pareto, *Trasformazione della democrazia*, 83–84.

130. "Consequently, modern parliamentary regimes follow the rhythms of all plutocracies: They prosper and decline, and their transformations, *also called transformations of democracy*, accompany the typical occurrences evident in all plutocracies." Pareto, *Trasformazione della democrazia*, 83–84 (emphasis added).

131. Pareto, *Trasformazione della democrazia*, 83–84, 76, 104.

132. Pareto, *Trasformazione della democrazia*, 83–84.

133. Pareto, *The Mind and Society*, vol. 4, §§2231, 2239.

134. Pareto, *Trasformazione della democrazia*, 83. For the famous elaboration of the same argument applied to the particularities of the Italian context, see Antonio Gramsci, "The Conflict between City and Countryside in Modern Italy," in *Italy from the Risorgimento to Fascism: An Inquiry into the Origins of the Totalitarian State*, ed. William Salomone (New York: Anchor Books, 1970), 397–412.

135. Pareto, *Trasformazione della democrazia*, 93–94, 95–96.

136. Pareto, *The Mind and Society*, vol. 4, §2227.

137. Pareto, *Trasformazione della democrazia*, 91. "From that standpoint," Pareto writes, "the interpretations of plain people are generally of greater importance than the interpretations of the scholar." Pareto, *The Mind and Society*, vol. 1, §260.

138. Pareto, *Trasformazione della democrazia*, 91–93.

139. Pareto, *Trasformazione della democrazia*, 91.

140. Pareto, *Trasformazione della democrazia*, 109.

141. Pareto, *Trasformazione della democrazia*, 109, 109–110, 110.

142. Pareto, *Trasformazione della democrazia*, 111, 112.

143. Pareto, *Trasformazione della democrazia*, 76, 113, 114.

144. Pareto, *Trasformazione della democrazia*, 104.

145. We may disagree about the implications of Pareto's critique of parliamentary government, but Giuseppe La Ferla is correct to note that although Pareto insisted that he had "a fixed idea not to believe in ethics," we agree that the work of this apparently cynical and cold man was inspired by "a high moral conscience." Giuseppe La Ferla, *Vilfredo Pareto, filosofo volteriano* (Firenze: La Nuova Italia, 1954), 166.

204 NOTES TO PAGES 43-46

146. Georges-Henri Bousquet, *Pareto (1848–1923): Le savant et l'homme* (Lausanne: Payot, 1960), 193–194n4.

147. Adrian Lyttelton, *Italian Fascisms from Pareto to Gentile* (London: Jonathan Cape, 1973), 22.

148. Schumpeter, *Ten Great Economists*, 114.

149. Vittorio Racca, "Working with Pareto," July 2, 1928, Livingston Papers, box 7, folder 13, Harry Ransom Center, University of Texas at Austin (my translation).

150. Racca, "Working with Pareto," 1 (my translation, emphasis added).

151. Hughes, *Consciousness and Society*, 415.

152. "That a scholar of his eminence had been obliged to seek employment abroad made him a sort of symbol of the injustice that the wicked tyranny at home was guilty of." Vittorio Racca, "Working with Pareto," *Revue européenne des sciences sociales* 16, no. 43 (1978): 163.

153. Spencer Di Scala and Emilio Gentile, eds. *Mussolini 1883–1915: Triumph and Transformation of a Revolutionary Socialist* (New York: Palgrave Macmillan, 2016), 5; 21.

154. Croce, "Validity of Pareto's Theories," 12–13. As Placido Bucolo describes, despite their "continual bickering" before Pareto's death, "Pareto and Croce always behaved correctly towards each other" and "with great esteem." Bucolo, *The Other Pareto*, 281. On Croce's "dictatorship" over Italian culture, also known as "idealism's hegemony," see Hughes, *Consciousness and Society*, 19, 62–65. For another perspective, see Norberto Bobbio, *Profilo ideologico del Novecento italiano* (Torino: Einaudi, 1986), 90–104.

155. For the most explicit accusation, see Gaetano Mosca, "Piccola polemica," *La riforma sociale* 17, no. 4 (1907): 329–331, in Gaetano Mosca, *Partiti e sindacati nella crisi del regime parlamentare* (Bari: Laterza, 1949), 115–120.

156. Alfonso de Pietri-Tonelli, "Mosca e Pareto," *Rivista internazionale di scienze sociali* 6, no. 4 (July 1935): 468–493; Luigi Einaudi, "Parlamenti e classe politica," *Corriere della Sera*, June 2, 1923, in Luigi Einaudi, *Cronache economiche e politiche di un trentennio (1893–1925)*, vol. 7 (Torino: Einaudi, 1963), 264–269.

157. "Le date sono certe: Mosca 1883 e 1896, Pareto 1900, 1902, 1906 e 1916 . . . Non occorre parlare di plagio . . . [ma] . . . la fama del Pareto va ingrandendo ed ora, dopo aver persuaso gli esclusivisti circoli accademici insulari d'Inghilterra, sta conquistando quelli nord-americani. La teoria delle élites va ormai correntemente sotto il nome di Pareto. Questa è l'ingiustizia." Luigi Einaudi, "Dove si discorre di Pareto, di Mosca ed anche di De Viti," *La Riforma Sociale* (November–December 1934): 707.

158. Bobbio, *Profilo ideologico del Novecento italiano*, 63–64.

159. In his first response to Einaudi, dated February 2, 1900, Pareto writes: "Caro Sig. Einaudi, ho solo avuto tempo di percorrere la prima parte del suo libro e quel poco che ho veduto mi è piaciuto assai perché ricco di dati sperimentali molto bene esposti. Ho letto con cura la seconda parte. Mi rincresce di non poter andare d'accordo con lei. Ella considera ancora con l'antico metodo i fenomeni economici come indipendenti. Dopo la teoria generale del fenomeno economico dovuta al Walras, credo che ciò non si possa più fare . . . Non si abbia per male se le ho scritto queste cose, anzi le abbia per una prova di amicizia" (Dear Mr. Einaudi, I had the time to read the first part of your book. I liked the little that I read as it is rich with well-argued experimental analysis. I also read the second part with great care. I regret that I cannot agree here, as you are still deploying the outdated method of treating economic subjects as independent variables. I believe it is no longer possible to do so after Walras's pathbreaking [marginal] revolution in general theoretical economic analysis. I hope you are not offended by my criticism, but instead consider it a proof of friendship). Carteggio

Einaudi-Pareto (1897–1923), fasc. *Vilfredo Pareto*, Archivio della Fondazione Luigi Einaudi, Fondo Luigi Einaudi.

160. Alberto Giordano, *Il pensiero politico di Luigi Einaudi* (Genova: Name, 2006), 37.

161. Giordano, *Il pensiero politico di Luigi Einaudi*, 37–41. In a letter dated January 3, 1935, Mosca praises his friend for "la onesta e coraggiosa difesa che hai fatto della mia priorità sul Pareto nella teoria della classe politica" (the honest and courageous defense of my precedence over Pareto in the theory of the political class). Carteggio Einaudi-Mosca, Archivio della Fondazione Luigi Einaudi, Fondo Luigi Einaudi.

162. Rodolfo de Mattei, "Embrioni e anticipazioni della teoria della classe politica," *Rivista internazionale di filosofia del diritto* (March–April 1932): 235. American audiences read of the controversy through Charles Merriam's student Renzo Sereno's "Note on Gaetano Mosca," *American Political Science Review* 46, no. 2 (June 1952): 603–605.

163. Vilfredo Pareto, "L'uomo delinquente di Cesare Lombroso," *Giornale degli economisti* (November 1896): 449–454; Pareto, *Lettere a Maffeo Pantaleoni*, 2:215.

164. In 1923, the year of Pareto's death, Croce wrote a glowing review of *Elementi*, which was reprinted as a forward to what for twenty-five years was the only available edition of *Elementi*.

165. Hughes, *Consciousness and Society*, 252.

166. James Meisel, *The Myth of the Ruling Class: Gaetano Mosca and the "Elite"* (Ann Arbor: University of Michigan Press, 1962), 180.

167. Many commentators maintain that thanks to his mother's French birth, his more abstract economic perspective, and his secluded life in Lausanne, Pareto was less enmeshed in the particularities of Italian parliamentarism than Mosca, who had experienced only the Italian context and served a long career as a public servant and a senator. The best case in point is H. Stuart Hughes, "Gaetano Mosca and the Political Lessons of History," in *Teachers of History: Essays in Honor of Laurence Bradford Packard*, ed. H. Stuart Hughes (Ithaca, NY: Cornell University Press, 1954), 146–167. I hope that this reconsideration of his thought raises questions about this assumption.

168. James Meisel offers the most comprehensive summary of the controversy in English, along with a comparison of their works and a particularly close investigation of Pareto's earlier work *Cours d'économie politique*. Meisel finds that although Pareto had not employed the term "elite" in his earlier work, he had been working on the same ideas with a distinct orientation. Meisel in fact emphasizes the difference in Pareto's applications of minority domination and the rejection of Aristotelian categories that always pervaded Pareto's thought. Meisel, *Myth of the Ruling Class*, 169–189. In recent Italian scholarship, Alberto Giordano, in *Il pensiero politico di Luigi Einaudi*, presents a fair view of the issue of precedence as it related to Luigi Einaudi.

169. Karl Popper, *The Open Society and Its Enemies* (Princeton, NJ: Princeton University Press, 2013), 38; Cirillo, "Was Vilfredo Pareto Really a 'Precursor'?"

170. Raymond Aron, "L'idéologie," *Recherches philosophiques* 6 (1936–1937): 65–84.

171. Raymond Aron, "Lectures de Pareto," *Contrepoint* 13 (1974): 175–191. As Campbell articulates, Aron acknowledged that throughout the course of his career he had written about "four different Paretos": the fascist, the authoritarian Machiavellian, the liberal Machiavellian, and the cynic. Stuart Campbell, "The Four Paretos of Raymond Aron," *Journal of the History of Ideas* 47, no. 2 (Spring 1986): 287–298. See also Aron's letter in Meisel, *Pareto & Mosca*, 42n166.

172. For an intellectual history of the Pareto circle, see Joel Isaac, *Working Knowledge: Making the Human Sciences from Parsons to Kuhn* (Cambridge, MA: Harvard University Press, 2012);

206   NOTES TO PAGES 47–52

Natasha Piano, "Squaring the Circle: Pareto at Harvard, 1930–1950," *Revue européenne des sciences sociales* 61–62, no. 2 (December 2023): 179–205.

173. Sidney Hook, "Pareto's Sociological System," 747–748.

174. Friedrich, *The New Image*, 242.

175. Merriam, *The New Democracy*, 209.

176. Merriam, *The New Democracy*, 209, 210, 208.

177. Hughes, *Consciousness and Society*, 270, 260, 253.

178. Hughes, *Consciousness and Society*, 393.

179. Meisel, *Myth of the Ruling Class*, 180.

180. Pareto, *The Mind and Society*, vol. 3, §2055.

2. Sober Cynicism

Epigraph: Giuseppe Tomasi di Lampedusa, *The Leopard*. Fair Access.

1. Vilfredo Pareto to Napoleone Colajanni, April 27, 1892, in Vilfredo Pareto, *Oeuvres complètes*, vol. 19, pt. 1: *Correspondance, 1890–1923*, ed. Giovanni Busino (Geneva: Librairie Droz, 1975), 185–186.

2. Fiorenzo Mornati has recently published a detailed discussion of Pareto's relationships and contacts within the Italian socialist party. Fiorenzo Mornati, *Vilfredo Pareto: An Intellectual Biography*, vol. 1: *From Science to Liberty (1848–1891)* (Basingstoke: Palgrave Macmillan, 2018), 163–166.

3. Vittorio Racca, "Working with Pareto," *Revue européenne des sciences sociales* 16, no. 43 (1978): 163.

4. Vilfredo Pareto, "The Parliamentary Régime in Italy," *Political Science Quarterly* (December 1893): 677–721.

5. Vilfredo Pareto to Maffeo Pantaleoni, July 3, 1920, in Pareto, *Lettere a Maffeo Pantaleoni*, vol. 3, ed. Gabriele De Rosa (Rome: Banca Nazionale del lavoro, 1960).

6. As Jan-Werner Müller has pointed out, arguably nowhere else did socialist and communist discourse "flourish for such a long time both as a party and as a form of political theorizing that had gained significant distance from Marx, but not necessarily broken with Leninism or, generally, an insurrectionary approach to politics." Jan-Werner Müller, "The Paradoxes of Post-War Italian Political Thought," *History of European Ideas* 39, no. 1 (2013): 80.

7. James H. Meisel, "Introduction: Pareto & Mosca," in *Pareto & Mosca* (Englewood Cliffs, NJ: Prentice-Hall, 1965), 10.

8. Even those who acknowledge Mosca's insistence upon a historical method underscore that his type of criticism "is evidently strictly inductive and hence comparable to the empirical method of the natural sciences." Franco Ferrarotti, "Sociology in Italy: Problems and Perspectives," in *Modern Sociological Theory in Continuity and Change*, ed. Howard Becker and Alvin Boskoff (New York: Dryden Press, 1957), 705–707.

9. Henry Stuart Hughes, "Gaetano Mosca and the Political Lessons of History," in *Teachers of History: Essays in Honor of Laurence Bradford Packard*, ed. Henry Stuart Hughes, Myron P. Gilmore, and Edwin C. Rozwenc (Ithaca, NY: Cornell University Press, 1954), 148–149.

10. For a point of departure on the vast historiography of the Risorgimento, see Alberto Mario Banti and Paul Ginsborg, eds., *Storia d'Italia: Annali 22, Il Risorgimento* (Torino: Einaudi, 2007); Mario Isnenghi and Eva Cecchinato, eds., *Fare l'Italia: Unità e disunità nel Risorgimento* (Torino: UTET, 2008). For a recent summary of these histories, see Maurizio Isabella, "Rethinking Italy's Nation-Building 150 Years Afterwards: The New Risorgimento Historiography," *Past & Present* 217, no. 1 (November 2012): 247–268.

NOTES TO PAGES 52–56   207

11. As Lucy Riall's analysis attests, "Garibaldi's success in Sicily represented a huge political opportunity for Italian democrats because it allowed them to seize back some initiative from Cavour and from Piedmont. However, Garibaldi's government failed to win the support of the landed elites, which benefitted the Piedmontese liberals." Lucy Riall, "Garibaldi's Dictatorship: The Reality of Government, May–November 1860," in *Sicily and the Unification of Italy: Liberal Policy and Local Power, 1859–1866* (Oxford: Oxford University Press, 1998).

12. Nadia Urbinati, "The South of Antonio Gramsci and the Concept of Hegemony," in *Italy's "Southern Question": Orientalism in One Country*, ed. Jane Schneider (New York: Routledge, 1998). For more on the connection between Mosca and Gramsci, see Maurice Finocchiaro, *Beyond Right and Left: Democratic Elitism in Mosca and Gramsci* (New Haven, CT: Yale University Press, 1999).

13. For a comprehensive study of this pessimistic orientation, see Eugenio Garin, *History of Italian Philosophy*, ed. Giorgio Pinton (New York: Rodopi, 2008).

14. Antonio Gramsci, "Notes on Italian History, History of the Subaltern Classes: Methodological Criteria," in *Selections from the Prison Notebooks of Antonio Gramsci*, ed. Quintin Hoare and Geoffrey Nowell Smith (New York: International, 1971), 59.

15. For a compelling account of the way Mosca's Sicilian experience colored his political thought, see Ettore Albertoni, *Mosca and the Theory of Elitism*, trans. Paul Goodrick (New York: Basil Blackwell, 1987), 110–120.

16. For a discussion of this theme as it applied to the Risorgimento, see Massimo Salvadori, *Il mito del buongoverno: La questione meridionale da Cavour a Gramsci*, 2nd ed. (Turin: Einaudi, 1963).

17. Michael Christensen, "The Social Facts of Democracy: Science Meets Politics with Mosca, Pareto, Michels, and Schumpeter," *Journal of Classical Sociology* 13, no. 4 (June 2013): 460–486; Jason Maloy, "A Genealogy of Rational Choice: Rationalism, Elitism, and Democracy," *Canadian Journal of Political Science* 41, no. 3 (September 2008): 749–771.

18. Gaetano Mosca, *Teorica dei governi e governo parlamentare*, in *Scritti politici*, ed. Giorgio Sola, vol. 1 (Torino: UTET, 1982), 198.

19. Mosca, *Teorica*, 198.

20. Mosca, *Teorica*, 199.

21. Mosca, *Teorica*, 200.

22. Gaetano Mosca, *A Short History of Political Philosophy*, trans. Sondra Koff (New York: Thomas Y. Crowell, 1972), 160–161, 178, 193–211; Bruno Brunello, *Il pensiero politico italiano dal Romagnosi al Croce* (Bologna: Zufli, 1949), 9.

23. Mosca, *Teorica*, 200.

24. Mosca, *Teorica*, 202–203.

25. Mosca, *Teorica*, 201. Mosca anticipates a methodology akin to what we now term comparative political theory. Andrew March, "What Is Comparative Political Theory?," *Review of Politics* 71, no. 4 (Fall 2009): 531–565.

26. Mosca, *Teorica*, 517.

27. The best treatment of Mosca's anti-Aristotelianism remains Renzo Sereno's "The Anti-Aristotelianism of Gaetano Mosca and Its Fate," *Ethics* 48, no. 4 (July 1938): 509–518.

28. Mosca, *Teorica*, 519.

29. Mosca, *Teorica*, 520–528.

30. Mosca, *Teorica*, 519.

31. Mosca, *Teorica*, 519–520.

32. Mosca, *Teorica*, 522–523.

208   NOTES TO PAGES 56–60

33. Mosca, *Teorica*, 523.

34. Mosca, *Teorica*, 523, 524, 523.

35. Mosca, *Teorica*, 524, 528n.

36. Mosca, *Teorica*, 527.

37. Mosca, *Teorica*, 528.

38. Mosca, *Teorica*, 528, 528n.

39. Mosca, *Teorica*, 528.

40. Mosca, *Teorica*, 528.

41. As Silvana Patriarca explains, in the first years of the liberal state "Garibaldi's democratic and republican views and his virulent polemics against the political class in power after 1861 made him a rather 'inconvenient' figure for the governing elites, but very popular in democratic and even socialist milieux." Patriarca, "Unmaking the Nation? Uses and Abuses of Garibaldi in Contemporary Italy," *Modern Italy* 15, no. 4 (2010): 467–483. Nevertheless, he was never absolved of the charge of political opportunism because of his continued contacts with the king after unification.

42. Mosca, *Teorica*, 528.

43. Mosca, *Teorica*, 532.

44. Mosca, *Teorica*, 532–533. For an explanation of Italian antagonism toward English analytic liberalism, see Mario Ricciardi, "Political Philosophy across the Atlantic: A Difficult Relationship?," *Journal of Modern Italian Studies* 10, no. 1 (2005): 59–77.

45. Mosca, *Teorica*, 533.

46. Mosca, *Teorica*, 525, 526, 534.

47. Francis Fukuyama has made a similar argument about the introduction of suffrage in modern Greece. See Fukuyama, *Political Order and Political Decay: From the Industrial Revolution to the Globalization of Democracy* (New York: Farrar, Straus and Giroux, 2014), 94–126.

48. This interpretive framework is elaborated in Gramsci's essay on the Southern Question in his *La costruzione del partito comunista, 1923–1926* (Torino: Einaudi, 1971), 146; and his notebook 19 on the Risorgimento, found in translation in Gramsci, "Notes on Italian History."

49. Gramsci, *La costruzione del partito comunista*, 79.

50. Gramsci, "Notes on Italian History," 44–120, esp. 57, 91.

51. Gaetano Mosca, *Che cosa è la mafia?*, in *Partiti e sindacati nella crisi del regime parlamentare* (Bari: Laterza, 1949), 214–256. In one of his many homages to Mosca's thought, Gramsci explains the attribution that Vittorio Emmanuele II "had the Action Party in his pocket." Everyone, especially in the Mezzogiorno, always knew that the Action Party (the party initially reorganized by Garibaldi which later was supposed to represent the "democratic" electoral representation of the "popular" Southern masses) was always formally led by the liberal capitalist bourgeois Moderate Party, both of which were informally led by "Cavour and the King." Gramsci, "The Problem of Political Leadership in the Formation and Development of the Nation and the Modern State in Italy," in "Notes on Italian History," 57. As Gramsci explains, "For the Action Party . . . to have succeeded at the very least in stamping the movement of the Risorgimento with a more markedly popular and democratic character . . . it would have had to counterpose to the 'empirical' activity of the Moderates . . . an organic programme of government which would reflect the essential demands of the popular masses, and in the first place of the peasantry." Gramsci, "Notes on Italian History," 61. In other words, the Action Party, for Gramsci, perfectly represents Piedmontese domination of the south through the Risorgimento's hollow promises of electoral politics. Gramsci, "Notes on Italian History," 89.

NOTES TO PAGES 60–66   209

52. Mosca elaborates this position in *Che cosa è la mafia?*

53. G. Lowell Field and John Higley, *Elitism* (London: Routledge and Kegan Paul, 1980).

54. Norman Lewis, *The Honoured Society: The Mafia Conspiracy Observed* (London: Collins, 1964), 35, in Richard Bellamy, *Modern Italian Social Theory: Ideology and Politics from Pareto to the Present* (Cambridge: Polity Press, 1987), 36.

55. Pareto illustrates a similar point in *The Mind and Society*, 4 vols., ed. Arthur Livingston, trans. Andrew Bongiorno, Arthur Livingston, and James Harvey Rogers (New York: Harcourt, Brace, 1935), vol. 4, §2180ft1.

56. Valentino Larcinese, "Enfranchisement and Representation: Italy 1909–1913," discussion paper presented at the London School of Economics, November 2011.

57. Larcinese, "Enfranchisement and Representation," 20, 31, 1; Gramsci, "Notes on Italian History," 89.

58. "The ordinary man from Northern Italy," Gramsci explains, "[thought that] if the Mezzogiorno made no progress after having been liberated from the fetters which the Bourbon regime placed in the way of a modern development, this meant that the causes of the poverty were . . . internal, innate in the population of the South." Gramsci, "Notes on Italian History," 70–71.

59. Alessio Cappone, "Il Terremoto dell'Irpinia: La tragedia che permise alla Camorra di diventare grande," *Antimafia*, November 22, 2021; Nello Trocchia, "Dal terremoto ai rifiuti: In Campania l'emergenza è una mangiatoia," *Domani*, November 24, 2021.

60. Gramsci, "Notes on Italian History," 89.

61. Gramsci, "Notes on Italian History," 90.

62. Gramsci, "Notes on Italian History," 90; Gramsci, *La costruzione del partito comunista*, 177.

63. Mosca, *Teorica*, 535, 537 (emphasis added).

64. Mosca, *Teorica*, 537. For a discussion on the relationship between wealth inequality and meritocracy, see Chapter 4.

65. Mosca, *Teorica*, 537.

66. Vilfredo Pareto, *The Mind and Society*, vol. 3, §2055.

67. Mosca, *Teorica*, 537. For an exposition of Mosca's anti-parliamentary orientation in context, see Mario delle Piane, "Introduzione: Il significato dell'antiparlamentarismo italiano del secolo scorso," in *Gaetano Mosca: Classe politica e liberalismo* (Napoli: Edizioni Scientifiche Italiane, 1952).

68. Mosca, *Teorica*, 537, 536.

69. Mosca, *Teorica*, 42.

70. Bellamy, *Modern Italian Social Theory*, 43.

71. Mosca, *Teorica*, 536, 201.

72. Mosca edited the English translation of *Elementi* alongside Arthur Livingston. That translation bears so many new additions to, and deletions from, the 1923 text that it constitutes a third edition in its own right. Gaetano Mosca, *The Ruling Class (Elementi di scienza politica)*, trans. Hannah Kahn, ed. Arthur Livingston (New York: McGraw-Hill, 1939).

73. At the time, Mosca engaged in a methodological critique of both abstract constitutionalism and Darwinian paradigms to employ a "historical political" approach. See Stefano Sicardi, "La scienza costituzionalistica italiana nella seconda metà del XIX secolo," *Diritto e società* 4 (1999): 648–654.

74. Mosca, *The Ruling Class*, 39.

75. Mosca, *The Ruling Class*, 114.

76. Mosca, *The Ruling Class*, 114.

210 NOTES TO PAGES 66-74

77. Mosca, *The Ruling Class*, 41, 47.

78. Mosca, *The Ruling Class*, 330.

79. James Meisel, *The Myth of the Ruling Class: Gaetano Mosca and the "Elite"* (Ann Arbor: University of Michigan Press, 1958), 10.

80. Mosca, *The Ruling Class*, 291.

81. Mosca, *The Ruling Class*, 332 (emphasis added).

82. Gaetano Mosca, *Elementi di scienza politica* (1896), in *Scritti politici*, ed. Giorgio Sola, vol. 2 (Torino: UTET, 1982), 894. Giulio Azzolini elegantly traces the normative implications of the shift in usage from *la classe politica* to *la classe dirigente* in "Gaetano Mosca e il problema 'dell'immanenza necessaria' delle classi dirigenti," *Annali dell'Istituto italiano per gli studi storici* (Milan) 29 (2016): 217–244.

83. "Relazione sul concorso al Premio Reale per le scienze sociali ed economiche, Scaduto il 31 dicembre 1895—Commissari: Boccardo, Bodio, Lampertico, Messedaglia e Ferraris," Gaetano Mosca (1881–1964), Archivi di famiglie e di persone, Archivi di personalità della politica e della pubblica amministrazione, busta 1, fasc. N 3, sottofasc. 4, Archivio Centrale dello Stato, Roma.

84. "Relazione sul concorso," 381.

85. "Relazione sul concorso," 381–382, 382, 381.

86. "Relazione sul concorso," 381.

87. For a parsimonious summary of Mosca's anti-fascism, see Joseph Femia, "Mosca Revisited," *European Journal of Political Research* 23, no. 2 (February 1993): 145–161.

88. Mosca, *The Ruling Class*, 326.

89. Arthur Livingston, "Introduction," in Mosca, *The Ruling Class*, xl.

90. Mosca, *The Ruling Class*, 415.

91. Mosca, *The Ruling Class*, 65.

92. Mosca, *The Ruling Class*, 438 (emphasis added).

93. Mosca, *The Ruling Class*, 336 (emphasis added), 53.

94. Antonio Gramsci, *Quaderni del carcere*, edizione critica dell'Istituto Gramsci, ed. Valentino Gerratana, 4 vols. (Torino: Einaudi, 1977). For more on Gramsci's development of Mosca's theory of the political class, see Francesca Chiarotto, "Mosca e Gramsci," in *Aspetti del realismo politico italiano: Gaetano Mosca e Guglielmo Ferrero*, ed. Lorella Cedroni (Rome: Aracne editrice S.r.l, 2013), 117–133.

95. Mosca, *The Ruling Class*, 395.

96. Mosca, *The Ruling Class*, 57, 58.

97. James Burnham, *The Machiavellians: Defenders of Freedom* (New York: John Day, 1943), 41.

98. Mosca, *The Ruling Class*, 415.

99. Mosca, *Teorica*, 521; Niccolo Machiavelli, *Discourses on Livy*, trans. Nathan Tarcov and Harvey Mansfield (Chicago: University of Chicago Press, 1998), I.39.

100. Mosca, *The Ruling Class*, 202.

101. Mosca, *The Ruling Class*, 202. Recent literature suggests that Mosca may have been uncharitable in offering this view. See Yves Winter, "A Government of Creditors: Machiavelli on Genoa, the Bank of San Giorgio, and the Financial Oligarchy," *Polity* 54, no. 4 (October 2022): 658–683; and Jérémie Barthas, "Machiavelli, the Republic, and the Financial Crisis," in *Machiavelli on Liberty and Conflict*, ed. David Johnston, Nadia Urbinati, and Camila Vergara (Chicago: University of Chicago Press, 2017), 257–279.

102. Hughes, "Gaetano Mosca," 148.

103. Mosca, *The Ruling Class*, 154.

104. Mosca, *The Ruling Class*, 491.

NOTES TO PAGES 76–83   211

105. Mosca, *Teorica*, 187–188.

106. Giuseppe Tomasi di Lampedusa, *Il Gattopardo* (Milan: Feltrinelli, 1958), 216.

107. Stephen P. Turner and Dirk Käsler eds., *Sociology Responds to Fascism* (New York: Routledge, 1992), 62–75.

108. Gramsci, "Notes on Italian History," 59–60.

109. Gaetano Mosca, *Partiti e sindacati nella crisi del regime parlamentare* (Bari: Laterza, 1949) 35.

110. Mosca, *Partiti e sindacati*, 35.

111. Meisel, *Myth of the Ruling Class*, 19.

112. Gaetano Mosca, Senato del Regno, tornata del 19 dicembre 1925, in *Discorsi parlamentari* (Milan: Il Mulino, 2003), 362.

113. Mosca, Senato del Regno, tornata del 19 dicembre 1925, 362.

114. Livingston Papers, Harry Ransom Center, University of Texas at Austin (hereafter cited as Livingston Papers), box 19, folder 3, Correspondence, February 1, 1921, and box 16, folder 2.

115. Livingston Papers, box 16, folder 2.

116. Livingston Papers, box 6, folder 5, Correspondence 1904–1944, Incoming Li–Lz 1912–1938, correspondence on March 17, 1930.

117. Charles Merriam, *The New Democracy and the New Despotism* (New York: McGraw-Hill, 1939), 29.

118. Joseph LaPalombara, "The Study of Gaetano Mosca in the United States," in *Studies on the Political Thought of Gaetano Mosca: The Theory of the Ruling Class and Its Development Abroad*, ed. Ettore Albertoni (Milan: Giuffre, 1982), 126.

119. Merriam, *The New Democracy*, 29, 208.

120. LaPalombara, "Study of Gaetano Mosca," 156.

121. Gabriel Almond, *Ventures in Political Science: Narratives and Reflections* (Boulder, CO: Lynne Rienner, 2002), 5; Harold Lasswell, *Politics: Who Gets What, When, How* (New York: McGraw-Hill, 1936).

122. For a more recent perspective on how these authors inappropriately used the Italian case, see Alfio Mastropaolo, "From the Other Shore: American Political Science and the 'Italian Case,'" *Modern Italy* 14, no. 3 (2009): 311–337.

123. Meisel, *Myth of the Ruling Class*, 175.

124. Louis Hartz, "Review of *The Myth of the Ruling Class: Gaetano Mosca and the "Elite*," *American Political Science Review* 53, no. 3 (1959): 804–806.

125. On Mosca's contribution to the founding of modern Italian political science, see Antonio Lombardo, "Sociologia e scienza politica in Gaetano Mosca," *Rivista italiana di scienza politica* 1, no. 2 (1971): 297–323.

3. The Edge of Fatalism

Epigraph: Friedrich Nietzsche, *Beyond Good and Evil*, trans. Walter Kaufman (New York: Vintage Books, 1989), §28.

1. David Beetham's paradigmatic study on Michels's transformation offers the most dedicated exposition, from this perspective, on Michels's transition to Fascism. David Beetham, "From Socialism to Fascism: The Relation between Theory and Practice in the Work of Robert Michels: II. The Fascist Ideologue," *Political Studies* 25, no. 2 (June 1977): 161–181. For other expressions of the view, see Arthur Mitzman, *Sociology and Estrangement: Three Sociologists of Imperial Germany* (New Brunswick, NJ: Transaction, 1973); Guenther Roth, *The Social Democrats*

212 NOTES TO PAGES 83–87

in Imperial Germany: A Study in Working-Class Isolation and National Integration (Totowa: Bedminster Press, 1963).

2. Alfred de Grazia, "Introduction," in *Roberto Michels's First Lectures in Political Sociology*, ed. Alfred de Grazia (Minneapolis: University of Minnesota Press, 1949), 4.

3. Lawrence Scaff, "Max Weber and Robert Michels," *American Journal of Sociology* 86, no. 6 (May 1981): 1280.

4. On the relationship between Pareto and Michels, see Pier Paolo Portinaro, "Robert Michels e Vilfredo Pareto," *Annali della Fondazione Luigi Einaudi* 11 (1977): 99–141; Corrado Malandrino, "Pareto e Michels: Riflessioni sul sentimento del patriottismo," in *Economia, sociologia e politica nell'opera di Vilfredo Pareto*, ed. Corrado Malandrino and Roberto Marchionatti (Florence: Leo S. Olschki, 2000), 363–382.

5. James Meisel, *The Myth of the Ruling Class: Gaetano Mosca and the "Elite"* (Ann Arbor: University of Michigan Press, 1958), vii; Philip Cook, "Robert Michels's Political Parties in Perspective," *Journal of Politics* 33, no. 3 (August 1971): 783.

6. Giorgio Volpe, "The Élites Vogue: La ricezione di Michels, Mosca e Pareto negli Stati Uniti," *Studi Storici* 56, no. 1 (January–March 2015): 116–117.

7. Joel Wolfe, "Robert Michels (1876–1936)," in *The Routledge Dictionary of Twentieth-Century Political Thinkers*, ed. Philip Green and Robert Benewick (London: Routledge, 1992), 175.

8. Robert Michels, *Political Parties: A Sociological Study of the Oligarchical Tendencies of Modern Democracy*, trans. Eden Paul and Cedar Paul (New York: Collier, 1962), 365.

9. Although the definitive Collier translation of Michels's text titles the work *Political Parties: A Sociological Study of the Oligarchical Tendencies of Modern Democracy*, I use my own translation of the German title (*Zur Soziologie des Parteiwesens in der modernen Demokratie. Untersuchungen über die oligarchischen Tendenzen des Gruppenlebens*) because it directly relates to the argument I proposed in this chapter. However, I rely on the Collier English translation because this edition will be the one used by postwar Anglo-American political science in their appropriation of Michels's work.

10. Peter LaVenia's reconsideration of Michels's thought also dispels the assumption that Michels had fascist proclivities in the period 1904–1915 and underscores Michels's discussion of "counter tendencies to oligarchy" during the period. However, LaVenia emphasizes these democratic propensities through the "structural dissimilarities" between *Sociology of the Party* and the Italian thinkers' works, as opposed to what I suggest here: that the continuities attest to Michels's counter-oligarchic tendencies, whereas the "dissimilarities" encouraged more authoritarian propensities. Peter LaVenia, "Rethinking Michels," *History of Political Thought* 40, no. 1 (2019): 112.

11. Scaff, "Max Weber and Robert Michels," 1279. Weber's letters to Michels can be found in Archivio Max Weber, Fondazione Luigi Einaudi: nos. 1–134 (hereafter cited as AMW), and in Archivio Roberto Michels, Fondazione Luigi Einaudi (hereafter cited as ARMFE). Most of Weber's commentary on Michels's work can be found in the AMW letters from March to August 1906 (AMW 2, 4, 6, 8–14).

12. For a close examination of the revolutionary and reformist impulses in Michels's thought, see Giorgio Volpe, "Riforma o rivoluzione sociale? Il problema della collocazione politica di R. Michels all'interno del movimento socialista," *Rivista di storia dell'Università di Torino* 1, no. 1 (2012): 43–85.

13. For the most comprehensive account of the way Michels's disillusionment determined his theoretical writings and political evolution, see Timm Genett, *Der Fremde im Kriege: Zur politischen*

NOTES TO PAGES 87–89 213

Theorie und Biographie von Robert Michels, 1876–1936 (Berlin: De Gruyter Akademie Forschung, 2008).

14. Roberto Michels to Gaetano Mosca, July 1, 1932, busta 2, sottofasc. N 1 / 5, Corrispondenza Personale in Entrata M-V, sottofasc. N 68: Robert Michels, document 1, Archivio centrale dello stato, Roma, 362; Roberto Michels, *Pagine autobiografiche*, ARMFE nos: 2–3, fasc. Michels Roberto, notizie biografiche, 1932, 15–16.

15. For some of the most famous discussions of Weber and Michels, see Wolfgang Mommsen, *Max Weber und die deutsche Politik, 1890–1920*, 2nd rev. ed. (Tübingen: Mohr, 1974), III–121, 144–145, 420–421; Roth, *The Social Democrats*, 249–257.

16. Robert Blank, "Die soziale Zusammensetzung der sozialdemokratischen Wahlerschaft Deutschlands," in *Il Pensiero politico: Rivista di storia delle idee politiche e sociali*, vol. 17 (Firenze: Leo S. Olschki, 1984), 221–224.

17. Weber, AMW 4.

18. Robert Michels, January 1, 1906, in Max Weber, *Max Weber Gesamtausgabe: Briefe, 1906–1908*, vol. 2, pt. 5, ed. M. Rainer Lepsius, Wolfgang Mommsen, Birgit Rudhard, and Manfred Schön (Tübingen: Mohr, 1990), 19.

19. Robert Michels, "Die deutsche Sozialdemokratie," *Archiv fur Sozialwissenschaft und Sozialpolitik* 23 (1906): 471–556, found in Italian translation as "La Socialdemocrazia tedesca" in *Potere ed Oligarchie: Antologia, 1900–1910*, ed. Ettore A. Albertoni, trans. Viviana Ravasi (Milan: Giuffre, 1989), 205–284. Weber read "Die deutsche Sozialdemokratie" during this period, promising Michels a "verbal response" to it, presumably conveyed on August 18, 1906, when Michels visited Weber in Heidelberg.

20. Michels, "Die deutsche Sozialdemokratie," 556.

21. This thesis depended heavily on James Bryce's *The American Commonwealth*, which Weber recommended to Michels on several occasions (AMW 4, 9, 60, 126). Although many commentators assume that "Weber had been strongly under the influence of M. Ostrogorski's monumental volumes on *Democracy and the Organization of Political Parties*" (Roth, *The Social Democrats*, 252), Lawrence Scaff argues that the letters to Michels suggest "that Bryce's influence was primary; Ostrogorski is in fact never mentioned." Scaff, "Max Weber and Robert Michels," 1279.

22. Scaff, "Max Weber and Robert Michels," 1279.

23. Robert Michels, "Die oligarchischen Tendenzen der Gesellschaft," *Archiv fiir Sozial wissenschaft und Sozialpolitik* 27 (1908): 73–135.

24. Michels, "Die oligarchischen Tendenzen," 73. Michels uses the same language in the German 1911 edition and the English 1915 edition of *Sociology of the Party*. See Robert Michels, *Zur Soziologie des Parteiwesens in der modernen Demokratie* (Leipzig: Klinkhardt, 1911), vi, 1–13, 375; Michels, *Political Parties*, 43–51, 353.

25. Michels, "Die oligarchischen Tendenzen," 73.

26. Robert Michels, "L'oligarchia organica costituzionale: Nuovi studi sulla classe politica," *La Riforma sociale: Rassegna di scienze sociali e politiche*, December 1907, 961–983, reprinted in Albertoni, *Potere ed Oligarchie*, 429–542. Ettore Albertoni describes this initial, openly hostile attitude toward Mosca and Pareto. Ettore Albertoni in Robert Michels, *Potere e Oligarchie: Organizzazione del partito ed ideologia socialista (1900–1910)* (Milan: Giuffre Editore, 1989), 33.

27. Michels, "L'oligarchia organica costituzionale," 983, 965.

28. Gaetano Mosca to Robert Michels, December 22, 1907, in ARMFE, sezz. 2–3, fasc. *Mosca Gaetano.*

214 NOTES TO PAGES 89–98

29. Gaetano Mosca to Robert Michels, August 4, 1908, in Weber, *Max Weber Gesamtausgabe*, 615.

30. For the same critique from two divergent perspectives, see Antonio Gramsci, *Quaderni del carcere*, vol. 1 (Torino: Einaudi, 1977), 236; Giovanni Sartori, *Democrazia e definizioni* (Bologna: Il Mulino, 1969), 99.

31. Robert Michels, *Sociologia del partito politico nella democrazia moderna: Studi sulle tendenze oligarchiche degli aggregati politici*, trans. Alfredo Polledro (Torino: Unione Tipografico, 1912), xvi.

32. Max Weber, "The Alleged 'Academic Freedom' of the German Universities," in *Max Weber on Universities*, ed. Edward Shils (Chicago: University of Chicago Press, 1974), 14–18.

33. Francesco Tuccari, "100 anni dopo: Le radici, le ragioni e l'inattualità della 'Sociologia del partito politico' di Robert Michels," *Annali della Fondazione Luigi Einaudi* 46 (2012): 55–84.

34. Gordon Hands, "Roberto Michels and the Study of Political Parties," *British Journal of Political Science* 1, no. 2 (April 1971): 170; Michels, *Political Parties*, 365.

35. Michels, *Political Parties*, 142, 129.

36. Michels, *Political Parties*, 150, 143.

37. Michels, *Political Parties*, 140.

38. Seymour Martin Lipset, "Introduction," in Michels, *Political Parties*, 16.

39. Michels, *Political Parties*, 140, 141.

40. Michels, *Political Parties*, 139, 142, 143.

41. Michels, *Political Parties*, 143.

42. Michels, *Political Parties*, 134, 147.

43. Michels, *Political Parties*, 132.

44. Michels, *Political Parties*, 147.

45. Michels, *Political Parties*, 147.

46. Michels, *Political Parties*, 221.

47. Michels, *Political Parties*, 221; Gerhard Lenski, "In Praise of Mosca and Michels," *Mid-American Review of Sociology* 5, no. 2 (Winter 1980): 7.

48. Michels, *Political Parties*, 264, 127 (emphasis added).

49. Michels, *Political Parties*, 148.

50. Michels, *Political Parties*, 148.

51. C. W. Cassinelli, "The Law of Oligarchy," *American Political Science Review* 47, no. 3 (September 1953): 777.

52. Jeffrey Winters criticizes Michels for purportedly obscuring the fact that since Aristotle's formulation, rule of the few has always meant rule of the rich. Jeffrey Winters, *Oligarchy* (Cambridge: Cambridge University Press, 2011), 16.

53. Beyond their personal affiliation, Mosca and Michels are often paired against Pareto on methodological grounds: Mosca and Michels seem to be more aligned as sociologists who study the "scientific question," whereas Pareto, as a trained economist, offered an economically oriented understanding of society. Lenski, "In Praise of Mosca and Michels," 2.

54. Giorgio Sola, *La teoria delle élites* (Bologna: Il Mulino, 2000), 93.

55. Michels, *Political Parties*, 62.

56. Michels, *Political Parties*, 61, 62, 61–62 (emphasis added), 166, 70.

57. Michels, *Political Parties*, 61.

58. Michels, *Political Parties*, 342, 202.

59. Gaetano Mosca, *The Ruling Class (Elementi di scienza politica)*, trans. Hannah Kahn, ed. Arthur Livingston (New York: McGraw-Hill, 1939), 145.

NOTES TO PAGES 98–105   215

60. Michels, *Political Parties*, 369.

61. Michels, *Political Parties*, 217. On the rehabilitation of Michels's theory of democracy understood as elite competition, see David Beetham, "Michels and His Critics," *European Journal of Sociology* 22, no. 1 (1981): 94; Hands, "Roberto Michels," 171; Juan J. Linz, *Robert Michels, Political Sociology, and the Future of Democracy* (New Brunswick, NJ: Transaction, 2006), l.

62. Michels, *Political Parties*, 339.

63. John D. May, "Democracy, Organization, Michels," *American Political Science Review* 59, no. 2 (June 1965): 418. For a discussion of Mosca's influence on Michels as a theorist of "democratization," see Ferdinand Kolegar, "Elite and the Ruling Class: Pareto and Mosca Re-examined," *Review of Politics* 29, no. 3 (July 1967): 364.

64. May, "Democracy, Organization, Michels," 421–422.

65. Michels, *Political Parties*, 342.

66. Michels, *Political Parties*, 216–217.

67. Lipset, "Introduction," 34; Michels, *Political Parties*, 73.

68. Michels, *Political Parties*, 70.

69. Cook, "Robert Michels's Political Parties," 776; Seymour Martin Lipset, *Political Man: The Social Bases of Politics* (New York: Doubleday, 1959).

70. Beetham, "From Socialism to Fascism"; and Scaff, "Max Weber and Robert Michels."

71. Robert Nye, *The Anti-democratic Sources of Elite Theory: Pareto, Mosca, Michels* (London: Sage, 1977).

72. Hugo Drochon, "Robert Michels and the Iron Law of Oligarchy and Dynamic Democracy," *Constellations* 27, no. 2 (June 2020): 185–198.

73. Michels, *Political Parties*, 142, 165, 310, 164.

74. According to Linz, for Michels corruption is the result of the leaders' "selfish purposes" despite their best intentions. Linz, *Robert Michels*, 40, 53.

75. Michels, *Political Parties*, 142, 310, 142, 165, 310, 164.

76. Michels, *Political Parties*, 164, 169.

77. Michels, *Political Parties*, 92–93, 364, 97.

78. Michels, *Political Parties*, 10, 205, 364, 205, referencing Le Bon's *Psychologie des foules*.

79. Michels, *Political Parties*, 364.

80. Michels, *Political Parties*, 365 (emphasis added).

81. Michels, *Political Parties*, 32.

82. Michels, *Political Parties*, 369–370.

83. Michels, *Political Parties*, 368.

84. Michels, *Political Parties*, 368, 369.

85. Hugo Drochon has recently explored the fact that *Sociology of the Party* ends on "a cheerier note, with Michels articulating how democracy will naturally give rise to two 'palliatives'—an increase in education and competition between different oligarchies—something that has often been overlooked in the secondary literature." Drochon, "Robert Michels," 186.

86. Michels, *Political Parties*, 370.

87. Michels, *Political Parties*, 368, 72, 370, 368 (emphasis added), 368.

88. James Burnham, *The Machiavellians: Defenders of Freedom* (New York: John Day, 1943).

89. Jeffrey Green, "Liberalism and the Problem of Plutocracy," *Constellations* 23, no. 1 (2016): 84.

90. Green, "Liberalism," 84.

216 NOTES TO PAGES 106–108

91. Michels, *Political Parties*, 71, 120. Michels would later be criticized for offering "no sharp distinction" between party "democracy" understood as "a party which aims at setting up, or supports, a democratic state government" versus "a party which has a democratic internal structure." As Gordon Hands demonstrates, Michels had both aims in mind and finds these definitions of democracy to be inextricably linked. Hands, "Roberto Michels."

92. LaVenia, "Rethinking Michels," 126.

93. De Grazia , *Roberto Michels's First Lectures*, 75.

94. Michels, *Political Parties*, 182.

95. For studies on Weber's and Michels's relationship that advance this view, see Francesco Tuccari, *Dilemmi della democrazia moderna: Max Weber e Robert Michels* (Bari: Laterza, 1993); Scaff, "Max Weber and Robert Michels"; Sandro Segre, "Notes and Queries: On Weber's Reception of Michels," *Max Weber Studies* 2, no. 1 (November 2001): 103–113.

96. Wolfgang Mommsen, "Robert Michels and Max Weber: Moral Conviction versus the Politics of Responsibility," in *Max Weber and His Contemporaries*, ed. Wolfgang J. Mommsen and Jurgen Osterhammel (London: Routledge, 1987), 132. Federico Trocini's archival reconstruction of the correspondence between Michels and Mussolini demonstrates that Michels began to participate in fascist politics and intellectual circles as early as 1920. Federico Trocini, "Robert Michels e il fascismo: Ragioni e circostanze di un rapporto problematico," in *Robert Michels: Un intellettuale di frontiera*, ed. Raffaele Federici (Milan: Meltemi, 2020).

97. Jeffrey E. Green, *The Eyes of the People: Democracy in an Age of Spectatorship* (Oxford: Oxford University Press, 2009); Wolfgang Mommsen, "Max Weber and Roberto Michels: An Asymmetrical Partnership," *European Journal of Sociology* 22, no. 1 (1981): 112–115.

98. H. Stuart Hughes, *Consciousness and Society* (New York: Knopf, 1958), 272.

99. Kolegar, "Elite and the Ruling Class," 364. David Beetham marvels that Michels was able to maintain relations with both Mosca and Pareto and argues that although the Italian context pushed Michels toward fascism, Michels's thought can be distinguished "by his scientific categories" located in the "historical . . . experience of pre–World War Europe." Beetham, "From Socialism to Fascism."

100. "Ma so una cosa, ed è che nessuno meglio di me sarà in grado di mantenere alta davanti alla scolaresca ed alla vita pubblica la fiamma del tuo pensiero scientifico" (But I know one thing, and that is that no one better than me will be able to keep the flame of your scientific thought alive before the altars of public and intellectual life). Norberto Michels to Gaetano Mosca, July 1, 1932, busta 2 / sottofasc. N 1 / 5, Corrispondenza Personale, Entrata M-V, sottofasc. N 68: Robert Michels, documento 2, Archivio centrale dello stato, Rome.

101. "Fin d'ora però posso assicurarti che l'influenza che tu credi che io possa esercitare (per conto tuo) per la soluzione dell'accennato affare è per lo meno molto esagerata" (However, I can already assure you that the influence you believe I can exercise [on your behalf] in resolving the aforementioned matter is at the very least very exaggerated). "Gaetano Mosca a Norberto Michels," busta 2 / sottofasc. N 1 / 5, Corrispondenza Personale, Entrata M-V, sottofasc. N 68: Robert Michels, documento 3, Archivio centrale dello stato, Rome.

102. Ettore Albertoni, *Mosca and the Theory of Elitism*, trans. Paul Goodrick (New York: Basil Blackwell, 1987), 114.

103. In 1925, in *Corriere della Sera*, Mosca wrote a positive review of Michels's original work, but this review preceded Michels's public conversion to Fascism. Gaetano Mosca, "La crisi della democrazia esaminata da Roberto Michels," in *Gaetano Mosca e il Corriere della Sera, 1897–1925*, ed. Alberto Martinelli (Milan: Rizzoli, 2013), 218–224. Although Michels had written to Mussolini as early as Jan-

uary 1923, and then met il Duce privately in 1924 and in March 1927, Michels did not publicly embrace to Fascism until 1927. Robert Michels, *Italien von heute* (Zurich: Orell Füssli, 1930), 269–270.

104. See Chapter 2 for a discussion of this episode.

105. Francesco Tuccari, "Discepolo o rivale? Robert Michels, Gaetano Mosca e la teoria delle élites," in *Classe dominante, classe politica ed élites negli scrittori politici dell'Ottocento e del Novecento*, vol. 1: *Dal 1850 alla prima guerra mondiale* (Firenze: Centro Editoriale Toscano, 2008); Albertoni, *Mosca and the Theory of Elitism*, 1–64.

106. Scaff, "Max Weber and Robert Michels," 1281.

107. Wilfried Rohrich, *Robert Michels: Vom Sozialistisch-syndikalistischen zum Faschistischen Credo* (Berlin: Duncker und Humblot, 1972), 52.

108. Timm Genett has contested interpretations of Michels as rebounding from an extreme left, socialist democratic position to an extreme right, fascist position, demonstrating that before his conversion to Fascism Michels also took up centrist and liberal conservative positions in keeping with the habits of a Swiss economics professor. Genett's descriptions contribute to the idea that Michels was willing to make his theoretical contributions fit a plethora of mutually exclusive political platforms, depending on the possibility of patronage. Genett, *Der Fremde*, 661–670, 722–738.

109. Roth, *The Social Democrats*, 250n3.

110. Robert Michels, *Sociologia del partito politico nella democrazia moderna: Studi sulle tendenze oligarchiche degli aggregati politici*, trans. Alfredo Polledro (Torino: Unione Tipografico, 1912), xvi.

111. "Sarà compito nostro esaminare . . . gli sforzi che furono fatti per sciogliere il problema della democrazia . . . In quanto l'analisi della democrazia verte sulle varie manifestazioni dello Stato e del partito pervenuto al potere l'esame fu già magistralmente compiuto da una serie di dotti, in cospicua parte italiani, tra i quali primeggia, oltre Vilfredo Pareto, il nostro Gaetano Mosca. Né avrei a tale opera alcunché di sostanziale da aggiungere o da variare. Però un altro terreno, forse non meno interessante per chi studi questi problemi, è rimasto, fino al giorno d'oggi, pressoché vergine: l'azione, cioè, della democrazia sulla vita interna dei partiti che si professano democratici" (It will be our task to examine . . . the efforts that were made to resolve the problem of democracy. . . . Since the analysis of democracy focuses on the various manifestations of the State and the party that has come to power, the examination has already been masterfully carried out by a series of scholars, a large part of whom are Italian, among whom, in addition to Vilfredo Pareto, our Gaetano Mosca stands out. Nor would I have anything substantial to add to or vary in this work. However, another area, perhaps no less interesting for those who study these problems, has remained, up to the present day, almost untouched: that is, the action of democracy on the internal life of parties that profess to be democratic). Michels, *Sociologia del partito politico*, xvi.

112. Robert Michels to Gustave Le Bon, 1913, Archivio Robert Michels della Fondazione Einaudi, fasc. *Le Bon Gustave*.

113. Tuccari, "100 anni dopo," 574.

114. Arthur Livingston, "Introduction," in Mosca, *The Ruling Class*, x.

115. Livingston, "Introduction," xxxvi.

116. Burnham, *The Machiavellians*, 121, 108–109, 120, 122, 125, 128–129.

117. "I must note that it is only with democracy in this traditional sense that I am here dealing." He notes that democracy can be defined in another way—in roughly the sense that Machiavelli gives to liberty. If that is done, Michels's analysis is largely irrelevant, and his conclusions inapplicable. Burnham, *The Machiavellians*, 127n*.

218 NOTES TO PAGES 112–117

118. Burnham, *The Machiavellians*, 151.

119. Burnham, *The Machiavellians*, 101, 102, 101.

120. Burnham, *The Machiavellians*, 102.

121. Burnham, *The Machiavellians*, 221.

4. Sardonic Irony

Epigraph: Robert Musil, *The Man without Qualities*, 2 vols., trans. from the German by Sophie Wilkins with Burton Pike (New York: Alfred A. Knopf, 1995), vol. 1, chapter 4, 11.

1. Both Bernard Manin and Nadia Urbinati demonstrate that the traditional expositors of representative democracy, from Rousseau to Mill, expected citizens to participate in ways that far exceeded the mere casting of votes. Schumpeter's alternate theory, as we shall see, reduces democratic participation exclusively to the moment of election. Bernard Manin, *The Principles of Representative Government* (Cambridge: Cambridge University Press, 1997); Nadia Urbinati, *Representative Democracy: Principles and Genealogy* (Chicago: University of Chicago Press, 2006).

2. Paul Samuelson, "Schumpeter as a Teacher and Economic Theorist," in *Schumpeter, Social Scientist*, ed. Seymour Harris (Cambridge, MA: Harvard University Press, 1951), 52.

3. Richard Swedberg has shown that Schumpeter's methodological aim was to connect "'theoretical economics,' 'economic sociology,' 'history,' and 'statistics' to each other in one broad concept he called *Sozialökonomik*." Swedberg, "Introduction," in Joseph Schumpeter, *The Economics and Sociology of Capitalism*, ed. Richard Swedberg (Princeton, NJ: Princeton University Press, 1991), vii.

4. John Medearis maintains that this evolution toward a methodologically pluralist approach happened later in Schumpeter's career. I instead interpret this view as Schumpeter's consistent response to the *Methodensreit* debate, which had diverse iterations dependent on the changing circumstances of his academic environment. John Medearis, *Joseph Schumpeter's Two Theories of Democracy* (Cambridge, MA: Harvard University Press, 2001), 16. For more on Schumpeter's eclectic methodological orientation cast in light of his position on *Methodenstreit*, see Richard Swedberg, *Schumpeter: A Biography* (Princeton, NJ: Princeton University Press, 1991).

5. Here I follow Jan-Werner Müller, who calls Schumpeter "Weber's sardonic adversary." Müller, *Contesting Democracy: Political Ideas in Twentieth Century Europe* (New Haven, CT: Yale University Press, 2011), 149.

6. For a few iconic examples of the standard genealogy, see Bert Hoselitz, "Introduction," in Joseph Schumpeter, *Imperialism and Social Classes: Two Essays by Joseph Schumpeter*, trans. Heinz Norden (Cleveland, OH: Meridian, 1955); Giovanni Sartori, *Democratic Theory* (New York: Praeger, 1965); Harold Lasswell, "The Elite Concept," in *Political Elites in a Democracy*, ed. Peter Bachrach (New Brunswick, NJ: Transaction, 1971); Norberto Bobbio, *The Future of Democracy* (Minneapolis: University of Minnesota Press, 1987); Medearis, *Joseph Schumpeter's Two Theories*; Gerry Mackie, *Democracy Defended* (Cambridge: Cambridge University Press, 2003); David Reisman, *Democracy and Exchange: Schumpeter, Galbraith, T. H. Marshall, Titmuss and Adam Smith* (Northampton, MA: Edward Elgar, 2005).

7. Ian Shapiro, *The State of Democratic Theory* (Princeton, NJ: Princeton University Press, 2003), 55.

8. Joseph Schumpeter, *Capitalism, Socialism and Democracy* (New York: Harper and Row, 1942), 269.

NOTES TO PAGES 117–123 219

9. John Gunnell, *Imagining the American Polity: Political Science and the Discourse of Democracy* (University Park: Penn State University Press, 2004); Philippe Schmitter and Terry Lynn Karl, "What Democracy Is ... and Is Not," *Journal of Democracy* 15, no. 3 (Summer 1991): 75–88; David Ricci, "Democracy Attenuated: Schumpeter, the Process Theory, and American Democratic Thought," *Journal of Politics* 32, no. 2 (May 1970): 239–267.

10. Schumpeter, *Capitalism, Socialism and Democracy*, 235.

11. As Richard Ashcraft notes, Schumpeter's "contextual linkage between socialism and democracy—long since severed by virtually all of the political scientists who have written about 'modern democracy'—must be characterized as one of the many historical ironies ... with which readers ... must come to terms." Richard Ashcraft, "Schumpeter and Democracy" (lecture, "Capitalism, Socialism and Democracy: A Fifty-Year Retrospective," UCLA, February 1, 1993).

12. Schumpeter, *Capitalism, Socialism and Democracy*, 236, 237.

13. Schumpeter, *Capitalism, Socialism and Democracy*, 237 (emphasis added).

14. Schumpeter, *Capitalism, Socialism and Democracy*, 238.

15. Schumpeter, *Capitalism, Socialism and Democracy*, 239.

16. Schumpeter, *Capitalism, Socialism and Democracy*, 55n7, 65, 124n5, 342.

17. Schumpeter, *Capitalism, Socialism and Democracy*, 239.

18. Schumpeter, *Capitalism, Socialism and Democracy*, 241.

19. Carole Pateman, *Participation and Democratic Theory* (Cambridge: Cambridge University Press, 1970), 20.

20. Schumpeter, *Capitalism, Socialism and Democracy*, 241.

21. Schumpeter, *Capitalism, Socialism and Democracy*, 243n9.

22. Peter Bachrach and Carole Pateman famously expressed this concern in the postwar period, yet this view has been carried on well into the twenty-first century. Some commentators have argued that it constitutes Schumpeter's reactionary response to the democratizing and socializing tendencies he identifies—or that the alternate theory should be read as his deeply conservative bid to prepare the future's elites for the management of a socialist society. John Medearis, "Schumpeter, the New Deal, and Democracy," *American Political Science Review* 91, no. 4 (December 1997): 830. For a different yet parallel view, see Peter J. Boettke, Solomon M. Stein, and Virgil Henry Storr, "Schumpeter, Socialism, and Irony," *Critical Review* 29, no. 4 (2017): 415–446.

23. Schumpeter, *Capitalism, Socialism and Democracy*, 243.

24. Schumpeter, *Capitalism, Socialism and Democracy*, 150, 161, 198.

25. Schumpeter, *Capitalism, Socialism and Democracy*, 404–405.

26. JanaLee Cherneski, "An Unacknowledged Adversary: Carl Schmitt, Joseph Schumpeter, and the Classical Doctrine of Democracy," *Critical Review* 29, no. 4 (20178): 447–472.

27. For a discussion of Wallas's influence on American political thought, see Tom Arnold-Forster, "Walter Lippmann and Public Opinion," *American Journalism* 40, no. 1 (2023): 51–79.

28. Schumpeter, *Capitalism, Socialism and Democracy*, 242, 283. For representatives of those who read Schumpeter as espousing an elitist *ressentiment* of mass capacities from opposing political positions, see Jerry Z. Muller, "Capitalism, Socialism and Irony: Understanding Schumpeter in Context," *Critical Review* 13, no. 3–4 (1999): 239–267; William Scheuerman, *Carl Schmitt: The End of Law* (Lanham, MD: Rowman and Littlefield, 1999), 206.

29. See Esben Sloth Anderson on the "elitist dichotomies" in Schumpeter's thinking. Anderson, *Schumpeter's Evolutionary Economics: A Theoretical, Historical and Statistical Analysis of the Engine of Capitalism* (New York: Anthem Press, 2009), 67.

220 NOTES TO PAGES 124–127

30. Schumpeter, *Capitalism, Socialism and Democracy*, 256.

31. To take a recent example, Kyong-Min Son shares the view that Schumpeter's use of Le Bon reflects the characteristic anxiety of postwar liberals about "ordinary people" and their capacity for governance. Kyong-Min Son, "A Discordant Universe of Pluralisms: Response to Wenman," *Political Theory* 43, no. 4 (August 2015): 537.

32. Vilfredo Pareto, *The Mind and Society*, ed. Arthur Livingston, trans. Andrew Bongiorno, Arthur Livingston, and James Harvey Rogers, 4 vols. (New York: Harcourt, Brace, 1935), vol. 2, §888.

33. Pareto, *The Mind and Society*, vol. 1, §§320, 361; vol. 2, §896.

34. Pareto, *The Mind and Society*, vol. 3, §1770; see vol. 2, §§885, 903, for Pareto's rejection of Spencer.

35. Pareto, *The Mind and Society*, vol. 2, §986.

36. Pareto, *The Mind and Society*, vol. 2, §§898–899.

37. For an incisive retelling of Pareto's account of human irrationality constituting "the interplay of creativity and inertia and enmeshed in complex reciprocal interactions with ideologies and social conditions," see Kam Shapiro, "Residues and Derivations: Vilfredo Pareto and Affective Politics," *Polity* 55, no. 4 (October 2023): 746.

38. See Marco di Giulio's recent intervention on this front, "Did Elitists Really Believe in Social Laws? Some Epistemological Challenges in the Work of Gaetano Mosca and Vilfredo Pareto," *Topoi* 41, no. 1 (October 2021): 57–67. Norberto Bobbio famously decried Pareto's taxonomies as inconsistent "ideologies chosen at random," in a work that "ruins weak stomachs and paralyzes strong." Norberto Bobbio, *On Mosca and Pareto* (Geneva: Librairie Droz, 1972), 56–58.

39. Pareto, *The Mind and Society*, vol. 1, §§35,162, as quoted in Robert Michels, *First Lectures in Political Sociology*, trans. Alfred de Grazia (Minneapolis: University of Minnesota Press, 1949), 23.

40. Alasdair Marshall, *Vilfredo Pareto's Sociology: A Framework for Political Psychology* (Burlington, VT: Ashgate, 2007), 38; Joseph Femia, *Pareto and Political Theory* (New York: Routledge, 2006), 56.

41. Vilfredo Pareto, "Il massimo di utilità dato dalla libera concorrenza," *Giornale degli economisti*, ser. 2, vol. 9 (year 5) (July 1894): 48–66, 4.

42. Schumpeter, *Capitalism, Socialism and Democracy*, 253.

43. Schumpeter, *Capitalism, Socialism and Democracy*, 257–258.

44. Schumpeter, *Capitalism, Socialism and Democracy*, 257.

45. Schumpeter suggests that Pareto perceived as much when he and his disciple Enrico Barone capitalized on Leon Walras's assumption that demand for every good equals supply. See Joseph Schumpeter, *Ten Great Economists: From Marx to Keynes* (London: Routledge, 1997), 79.

46. Schumpeter, *Capitalism, Socialism and Democracy*, 263.

47. Schumpeter, *Capitalism, Socialism and Democracy*, 258, 129–131. The existence of the people's will is *not* undermined by Schumpeter's claim that individuals do not construct their voting preferences independent of institutional structures. True, unlike *later* "economic" conceptions of democracy—which view voters as consumers who choose candidates in order to maximize preexisting values, interests, opinions, and preferences—Schumpeter challenges this view by arguing that voters are not an exogenous source of demand. Yet the endogenous character of voter preferences does not discredit the existence of a people's will (nor does it discredit the existence of a consumer desire); it only takes into consideration how this will (or desire) is constructed. On this point, see Jon Elster, "The Market and the Forum: Three Varieties of Political Theory," in *Foundations of Social Choice Theory*, ed. Jon Elster and Aanund Hylland (Cambridge: Cambridge University Press, 1986), 104.

NOTES TO PAGES 128–138   221

48. Walter Lippmann, *Public Opinion* (New York: Harcourt, Brace, 1922); Edward Bernays, *Propaganda* (New York: Ig, 2005). For representative examples of postwar realism, see Fred I. Greenstein, *The American Party System and the American People* (Englewood Cliffs, NJ: Prentice Hall, 1963), 10–14.

49. Peter Bachrach, *The Theory of Democratic Elitism: A Critique* (Washington, DC: University Press of America, 1980), ix.

50. Schumpeter, *Capitalism, Socialism and Democracy*, 161, 384, 153, 190.

51. Schumpeter, *Capitalism, Socialism and Democracy*, 153, 161, 190, 203, 247, 321, 322, 384.

52. Schumpeter, *Capitalism, Socialism and Democracy*, 171, 200, 269.

53. Schumpeter, *Capitalism, Socialism and Democracy*, 269.

54. Schumpeter, *Capitalism, Socialism and Democracy*, 270.

55. Schumpeter, *Capitalism, Socialism and Democracy*, 269.

56. Schumpeter, *Capitalism, Socialism and Democracy*, 270.

57. Schumpeter, *Capitalism, Socialism and Democracy*, 48, 56.

58. Schumpeter, *Capitalism, Socialism and Democracy*, 271.

59. Schumpeter, *Capitalism, Socialism and Democracy*, 273.

60. Gaetano Mosca, "Il principio aristocratico ed il democratico," in *Partiti e sindacati nella crisi del regime parlamentare* (Bari: Laterza, 1949), 11.

61. According to Mosca, Pareto's error is due to the fact that he had unreflectively plagiarized Giuseppe Rensi's endorsement of majoritarianism. Mosca, "Il principio aristocratico ed il democratico," 11.

62. Mosca, "Il principio aristocratico ed il democratico," 19–20; Mosca also confusingly calls *politeia* the only "true aristocracy" (23).

63. Mosca, "Il principio aristocratico ed il democratico," 5.

64. Mosca, "Il principio aristocratico ed il democratico," 21, 20, 23.

65. Mosca, "Il principio aristocratico ed il democratico," 13.

66. Gaetano Mosca, "Stato città e stato rappresentativo," in *Partiti e sindacati nella crisi del regime parlamentare* (Bari: Laterza, 1949), 50.

67. Mosca, "Il principio aristocratico ed il democratico," 14.

68. Mosca, "Stato città e stato rappresentativo," 52.

69. Mosca, "Stato città e stato rappresentativo," 53, 59–60.

70. Schumpeter, *Capitalism, Socialism and Democracy*, 284–285.

71. Schumpeter, *Capitalism, Socialism and Democracy*, 285.

72. Corey Robin, *The Reactionary Mind: Conservatism from Edmund Burke to Donald Trump* (Oxford: Oxford University Press, 2017), 150–160.

73. Josiah Ober, "Joseph Schumpeter's Caesarist Democracy," *Critical Review* 29, no. 4 (2017): 473–491.

74. Schumpeter, *Capitalism, Socialism and Democracy*, 289.

75. Schumpeter, *Capitalism, Socialism and Democracy*, 287.

76. Gaetano Mosca, *Elementi di scienza politica* (1923), in *Scritti politici*, ed. Giorgio Sola (Turin: UTET, 1982), 2:1043.

77. "Bisogna che esso plasmi la coscienza della maggioranza almeno della classe dirigente, e che diventi preponderante nel determinare il suo modo di pensare e quindi di sentire." Mosca, *Elementi* (1923), 1080.

78. Mosca, *Elementi* (1923), 116, 1037.

222 NOTES TO PAGES 138–148

79. Mosca, *Elementi* (1923), 1037.

80. Gaetano Mosca, "Cause e rimedi della crisi del regime parlamentare" (1928), in *Partiti e sindacati nella crisi del regime parlamentare* (Bari: Laterza, 1949) 87–115, 104.

81. Schumpeter's most generous readers argue that the "Schumpeterian" equation of elections and democracy is a necessary but insufficient condition for democratic politics, but they do not further develop this element of his theory or its relation to the alternate conception of democracy as a whole. See Tom Bottomore, *Elites and Society*, 2nd ed. (New York: Routledge, 1993), 93; Jeffrey Green, *The Eyes of The People: Democracy in an Age of Spectatorship* (Oxford: Oxford University Press, 2009); Ian Shapiro, *Politics against Domination* (Cambridge, MA: Harvard University Press, 2016); Adam Przeworski, "Minimalist Conception of Democracy: A Defense," in *Democracy's Value*, ed. Ian Shapiro and Casiano Hacker-Cordon (Cambridge: Cambridge University Press, 1999).

82. See Richard Bellamy, "Schumpeter and the Transformation of Capitalism, Liberalism, and Democracy," in *Rethinking Liberalism* (New York: Pinter, 2000); William Selinger, "Schumpeter on Democratic Survival," *Tocqueville Review / La revue Tocqueville* 36, no. 2 (2015): 127–157; Emilio Santoro, "Democratic Theory and Individual Autonomy: An Interpretation of Schumpeter's Doctrine of Democracy," *European Journal of Political Research* 23, no. 2 (February 1993): 121–143.

83. For a development of this argument, see Natasha Piano, "Schumpeter's Dare: On the Dangers of Democracy as Competitive Election," in *Democracy and Competition: Rethinking the Forms, Purposes, and Values of Competition in Democracy*, ed. Samuel Bagg and Alfred Moore (Oxford University Press, forthcoming).

84. Medearis, *Joseph Schumpeter's Two Theories*; Schumpeter, *Capitalism, Socialism and Democracy*, 266.

85. Schumpeter, *Capitalism, Socialism and Democracy*, 63, 162, 220, 297, 301.

86. Schumpeter, *Capitalism, Socialism and Democracy*, 199, 223, 324.

87. Schumpeter, *Capitalism, Socialism and Democracy*, 275, 305.

88. Schumpeter, *Capitalism, Socialism and Democracy*, 302.

89. Schumpeter, *Capitalism, Socialism and Democracy*, 123.

90. Marjorie Perloff, *Edge of Irony: Modernism in the Shadow of the Habsburg Empire* (Chicago: University of Chicago Press, 2016) 1.

91. Schumpeter, *Capitalism, Socialism and Democracy*, xvli.

92. Schumpeter, *Capitalism, Socialism and Democracy*, 6.

93. Nils Gilman, *Mandarins of the Future: Modernization Theory in Cold War America* (Baltimore: Johns Hopkins University Press, 2007), 48.

94. Joseph Schumpeter, *Essays: On Entrepreneurs, Innovations, Business Cycles and the Evolution of Capitalism*, ed. Richard Clemence (New Brunswick, NJ: Transaction, 1989), xviii.

95. Bobbio, *The Future of Democracy*; Lasswell, "The Elite Concept"; Sartori, *Democratic Theory*.

96. Manin, *Principles of Representative Government*, 161.

5. Hopeful Panic

Epigraph: Voltaire. Fair Access.

1. John Gunnell, "The Genealogy of American Pluralism: From Madison to Behavioralism," *International Political Science Review* 17, no. 3 (July 1996): 253–265.

2. Mary Earhart Dillon, "Pressure Groups," *American Political Science Review* 36, no. 3 (1942): 481.

3. Irving Howe, "Critics of American Socialism," *New International*, May–June 1952, 146.

4. C. Wright Mills, *The Power Elite* (New York: Oxford University Press, 1956), 4.

5. Mills, *The Power Elite*, 269–297; E. E. Schattschneider, *Party Government* (New York: Farrar and Rinehart, 1942), 53–61.

6. Mills, *The Power Elite*, 268, 325, 22–23.

7. Mills, *The Power Elite*, 245, 363.

8. Mills, *The Power Elite*, 9.

9. Mills, *The Power Elite*, 365; C. Wright Mills, *The Sociological Imagination*, 40th anniv. ed. (Oxford: Oxford University Press, 2000), 50–75.

10. Vilfredo Pareto, *The Mind and Society*, ed. Arthur Livingston, trans. Andrew Bongiorno, Arthur Livingston, and James Harvey Rogers, 4 vols. (New York: Harcourt, Brace, 1935), vol. 3, §2037.

11. Mills, *The Power Elite*, 172.

12. Mills, *The Power Elite*, 20, 96, 100.

13. Mills, *The Power Elite*, 28.

14. Mills, *The Power Elite*, 21, 243, 336.

15. Mills, *The Power Elite*, 326.

16. Jay Sigler, "The Political Philosophy of C. Wright Mills," *Science & Society* 30, no. 1 (Winter 1966): 41.

17. Mills, *The Power Elite*, 350.

18. C. Wright Mills, *The Causes of World War Three* (New York: Simon and Schuster, 1958), 156.

19. Natasha Piano, "Squaring the Circle: Pareto at Harvard, 1930–1950," *European Journal of Social Sciences* 61, no. 2 (2023): 179–205.

20. Suzanne Keller, *Beyond the Ruling Class: Strategic Elites in Modern Society* (New York: Random House, 1963), 108–109; Daniel Bell, "Is There a Ruling Class in America?," in *The End of Ideology* (New York: Free Press, 1960), 47–74; Talcott Parsons, "Review: The Distribution of Power in American Society," *World Politics* 10, no. 1 (October 1957): 123–143.

21. C. Wright Mills, "'The Power Elite': Comment on Criticism," *Dissent*, Winter 1957, 24.

22. See Robert A. Dahl and Margaret Levi, "A Conversation with Robert. A. Dahl," *Annual Review of Political Science* 12 (2009): 1–9.

23. Robert Dahl, *A Preface to Democratic Theory* (Chicago: University of Chicago Press, 1956), 73, 66.

24. Dahl, *Preface to Democratic Theory*, 84.

25. Dahl, *Preface to Democratic Theory*, 132, 81, 150.

26. Robert Dahl, *Who Governs? Democracy and Power in an American City* (New Haven, CT: Yale University Press, 1961), 11, 21, 85.

27. Dahl, *Who Governs?*, 11, 227.

28. Dahl, *Who Governs?*, 309.

29. Dahl, *Who Governs?*, 95, 317–318, 324, 309.

30. Robert Dahl, "A Critique of the Ruling Elite Model," *American Political Science Review* 52, no. 2 (June 1958): 463, 469.

31. Gaetano Mosca, *The Ruling Class (Elementi di scienza politica)*, trans. Hannah Kahn, ed. Arthur Livingston (New York: McGraw-Hill, 1939), 47.

32. Robert Dahl, "Further Reflections on 'The Elitist Theory of Democracy,'" *American Political Science Review* 60, no. 2 (June 1966): 296–305; Jack Walker, "A Critique of the Elitist Theory of Democracy," *American Political Science Review* 60, no. 2 (June 1966): 285–295.

33. Dahl, "Further Reflections," 298.

224 NOTES TO PAGES 156–165

34. Robert Dahl, "Polyarchy, Pluralism, and Scale," *Scandinavian Political Studies* 7, no. 4 (December 1984): 225–240.

35. Robert Dahl, *A Preface to Economic Democracy* (Berkeley: University of California Press, 1985).

36. Richard Krause, "Polyarchy & Participation: The Changing Democratic Theory of Robert Dahl," *Polity* 14, no. 3 (Spring 1982): 371–558; Robert Mayer, "Robert Dahl and the Right to Workplace Democracy," *Review of Politics* 63, no. 2 (Spring 2001): 221–247.

37. Jeffrey C. Isaac, "Dilemmas of Democratic Theory," in *Power, Inequality, and Democratic Politics: Essays in Honor of Robert A. Dahl*, ed. Ian Shapiro and Grant Reher (Boulder, CO: Westview Press, 1988), 132, 142.

38. Robert Dahl, *Democracy and Its Critics* (New Haven, CT: Yale University Press, 1989), 312.

39. Dahl, *Democracy and Its Critics*, 276, 275–276.

40. Dahl, *Democracy and Its Critics*, 325.

41. Jeffrey Winters, *Oligarchy* (Cambridge: Cambridge University Press, 2011), 3–8.

42. Peter Bachrach, *The Theory of Democratic Elitism: A Critique* (Washington, DC: University Press of America, 1980).

43. Peter Bachrach and Morton Baratz, "Two Faces of Power," *American Political Science Review* 56, no. 4 (December 1962): 947–952.

44. For a discussion of Bachrach's contribution to democratic theory see, Steven Lukes, "The Challenge of Peter Bachrach," *PS: Political Science and Politics* 43, no. 1 (January 2010): 91–93.

45. Bachrach, *Theory of Democratic Elitism*, 2, 8, 2.

46. Bachrach, *Theory of Democratic Elitism*, 10.

47. Bachrach, *Theory of Democratic Elitism*, 11. As quoted in Mosca, *The Ruling Class*, 157.

48. Bachrach, *Theory of Democratic Elitism*, 10.

49. Bachrach, *Theory of Democratic Elitism*, 11.

50. Bachrach, *Theory of Democratic Elitism*, 2n2.

51. Bachrach, *Theory of Democratic Elitism*, 11. As quoted in Pareto, *The Mind and Society*, vol. 4, §2253.

52. Bachrach, *Theory of Democratic Elitism*, 11.

53. Bachrach, *Theory of Democratic Elitism*, 11. As quoted in Mosca, *The Ruling Class*, 154.

54. Bachrach, *Theory of Democratic Elitism*, 10, 15, 16,10.

55. Bachrach, *Theory of Democratic Elitism*, 17, 15, 16.

56. Bachrach, *Theory of Democratic Elitism*, 13–14; Pareto, *The Mind and Society*, vol. 3, §§2054–2059.

57. Bachrach, *Theory of Democratic Elitism*, 14 (emphasis added). As quoted in Pareto, *The Mind and Society*, vol. 3, §2059.

58. Bachrach, *Theory of Democratic Elitism*, 11.

59. Bachrach, *Theory of Democratic Elitism*, 14.

60. Bachrach, *Theory of Democratic Elitism*, 15, 14.

61. Bachrach, *Theory of Democratic Elitism*, 18.

62. Bachrach, *Theory of Democratic Elitism*, 15–16, 18, 21.

63. Bachrach, *Theory of Democratic Elitism*, 21, 23.

64. Bachrach, *Theory of Democratic Elitism*, 6.

65. Mills, *The Power Elite*; Edward Banfield, *Political Influence* (New Brunswick, NJ: Transaction, 1961); Henry Bertram Mayo, *An Introduction to Democratic Theory* (Oxford: Oxford University Press, 1960; Harry Eckstein, *Division and Cohesion in Democracy: A Study of Norway*

(Princeton, NJ: Princeton University Press, 1966); Lester Milbrath and M. L. Goel, *Political Participation: How and Why Do People Get Involved in Politics?* (Chicago: Rand McNally, 1977).

66. Richard M. Merelman, "On the Neo-Elitist Critique of Community Power," *American Political Science Review* 62, no. 2 (June 1968): 451–460; Peter Medding, "'Elitist' Democracy: An Unsuccessful Critique of a Misunderstood Theory," *Journal of Politics* 31, no. 3 (August 1969): 641–654; Charles Allan McCoy and John Playford, eds., *Apolitical Politics: A Critique of Behavioralism* (New York: Thomas Y. Cromwell, 1967).

67. Carole Pateman, *Participation and Democratic Theory* (Cambridge: Cambridge University Press, 1970).

68. Pateman, *Participation and Democratic Theory*, 2–10.

69. Pateman, *Participation and Democratic Theory*, 7, 16–17.

70. Pateman, *Participation and Democratic Theory*, 4.

71. Pateman, *Participation and Democratic Theory*, 45–66.

72. Pateman, *Participation and Democratic Theory*, 45.

73. Pateman, *Participation and Democratic Theory*, 27, 83.

74. Pateman, *Participation and Democratic Theory*, 66.

75. Pateman, *Participation and Democratic Theory*, 110.

76. Quentin Skinner, "The Empirical Theorists of Democracy and Their Critics: A Plague on Both Their Houses," *Political Theory* 1, no. 3 (August 1973): 298, 289.

77. James Roland Pennock, *Democratic Political Theory* (Princeton, NJ: Princeton University Press, 1979), 286n23; Henry Kariel, ed., *Frontiers of Democratic Theory* (New York: Random House, 1970).

78. Adam Przeworski, *Capitalism and Social Democracy* (Cambridge: Cambridge University Press, 1985).

79. Przeworski, *Capitalism and Social Democracy*, 129.

80. Przeworski, *Capitalism and Social Democracy*, 223, 238.

81. Przeworski, *Capitalism and Social Democracy*, 223, 238.

82. Przeworski, *Capitalism and Social Democracy*, 239.

83. Przeworski, *Capitalism and Social Democracy*, 248.

84. Przeworski, *Capitalism and Social Democracy*, 248.

85. Adam Przeworski and John Sprague, *Paper Stones: A History of Electoral Socialism* (Chicago: University of Chicago Press), 1–3.

86. Przeworski, *Capitalism and Social Democracy*, 27.

87. Robert Michels, *Political Parties: A Sociological Study of the Oligarchical Tendencies of Modern Democracy*, trans. Eden Paul and Cedar Paul (New York: Collier, 1962), 228; Przeworski, *Capitalism and Social Democracy*, 100; Przeworski and Sprague, *Paper Stones*, 8.

88. Przeworski and Sprague, *Paper Stones*.

89. Przeworski and Sprague, *Paper Stones*.

90. Przeworski and Sprague, *Paper Stones*.

91. Adam Przeworski, *Democracy and the Market: Political and Economic Reforms in Eastern Europe and Latin America* (Cambridge: Cambridge University Press, 1991), 26–34.

92. Przeworski, *Democracy and the Market*, xii, 191.

93. Przeworski, *Democracy and the Market*, 10, 11n2, 11, 10 (emphasis added).

94. G. A. Cohen, *Karl Marx's Theory of History: A Defence* (Princeton, NJ: Princeton University Press, 2000).

226 NOTES TO PAGES 173–183

95. Adam Przeworski, "Minimalist Conception of Democracy: A Defense," in *Democracy's Value*, ed. Ian Shapiro and Casiano Hacker-Cordón (Cambridge: Cambridge University Press, 1999).

96. Przeworski, "Minimalist Conception of Democracy," 12, 14.

97. Przeworski, "Minimalist Conception of Democracy," 15–16 (emphasis added).

98. Przeworski, "Minimalist Conception of Democracy," 16.

99. Przeworski, "Minimalist Conception of Democracy," 13, 15.

100. Przeworski, "Minimalist Conception of Democracy," 15, 16.

101. Jason Maloy, "A Genealogy of Rational Choice: Rationalism, Elitism, and Democracy," *Canadian Journal of Political Science* 41, no. 3 (September 2008): 749–771.

102. Vilfredo Pareto, "Considerazioni sui principi fondamentali dell'economia politica pura," *Giornale degli economisti* 5 (May 1892): 419–420.

103. Vilfredo Pareto, "Dialoghi dei morti," *Giornale degli economisti* (March 1893): 171 (emphasis added).

104. Thomas Kuhn, *The Structure of Scientific Revolutions* (Chicago: University of Chicago Press, 1962), 4.

105. Thomas Piketty, *Capital in the Twenty-First Century*, trans. Arthur Goldhammer (Cambridge, MA: Harvard University Press, 2014).

106. Bernard Manin, *The Principles of Representative Government* (Cambridge: Cambridge University Press, 1997); Jeffrey Green, *The Eyes of the People: Democracy in an Age of Spectatorship* (Oxford: Oxford University Press, 2009); Winters, *Oligarchy*.

Conclusion

Epigraph: Joseph Schumpeter, *Capitalism, Socialism and Democracy* (New York: Harper Perennial, 1949), 6.

1. David Waldner and Ellen Lust, "Unwelcome Change: Combing to Terms with Democratic Backsliding," *Annual Review of Political Science* 21 (2018): 93–112.

2. David Graeber, *The Utopia of Rules: On Technology, Stupidity, and the Increasing Joys of Bureaucracy* (Brooklyn: Melville House, 2015).

3. Steven Livitsky and Daniel Ziblatt, *How Democracies Die* (New York: Crown, 2018); Arlie Hochschild, *Strangers in Their Own land: Anger and Mourning on the American Right* (New York: New Press, 2016).

4. Yascha Mounk, *The People vs. Democracy: Why Our Freedom Is in Danger and How to Save It* (Cambridge. MA: Harvard University Press, 2018).

5. Arlie Hochchild, *Stolen Pride: Loss, Shame, and the Rise of the Right* (New York: New Press, 2024).

6. See Alexander Kirshner's compelling distinction between democracy and legitimate opposition in *Legitimate Opposition* (New Haven, CT: Yale University Press, 2022).

7. Nadia Urbinati, "The Sovereignty of Chance: Can Lottery Save Democracy," *Common Knowledge* (forthcoming).

8. Norberto Bobbio, "Il buon governo," June 26, 1981, *Atti della Accademia nazionale dei Lincei* 8, no. 5 (1983): 242; as cited in Paolo Silvestri, "Il buon governo: Di Einaudi e Mosca, tra governo o della legge e governo degli uomini," in *Annali della Fondazione Luigi Einaudi*, vol. 40 (Florence: Leo S. Olschki Editore, 2006), 159.

9. Vilfredo Pareto, "Il crepuscolo della libertà," *Rivista d'Italia* (February 1905), 436.

10. Nicolai Rubinstein, "Political Ideas in Sienese Art: The Frescoes by Ambrogio Lorenzetti and Taddeo di Bartolo in the Palazzo Pubblico," *Journal of the Warburg and Courtauld Institutes* 21, no. 3 / 4 (July–December 1958): 179–207.

11. Silvestri, "Il buon governo."

12. Josiah Ober, *Demopolis: Democracy before Liberalism in Theory and Practice* (Cambridge: Cambridge University Press, 2017), 27n15.

13. Bobbio, "Il buon governo," 242, as cited in Silvestri, "Il buon governo," 159.

14. Yves Winter, *Machiavelli and the Orders of Violence* (Cambridge: Cambridge University Press, 2018).

15. "Sia pure sotto i veli dell'empirismo, un concetto analogo in quanto scrive il Machiavelli . . . 'e si conosce facilmente per chi considera le cose presenti e le antiche, come in tutte le città e in tutti i popoli sono quelli medesimi desideri e quelli medesimi umori, e come vi furono sempre'" (Even if under the guise of empiricism, we find a similar concept in Machiavelli . . . "and it is easily recognized by those who consider present and ancient things, as in all cities and in all peoples there are the same desires and the same humors, and as there have always been"). Vilfredo Pareto, *Fatti e teorie* (Florence: Vallechi Editore, 1920), 321.

16. Ettore Albertoni, "The Evolution of Mosca's Thought," in *Studies on the Political Thought of Gaetano Mosca: The Theory of the Ruling Class and Its Development Abroad* (Milan: Giuffre, 1982), 25.

17. Vilfredo Pareto, *The Mind and Society*, 4 vols., ed. Arthur Livingston, trans. Andrew Bongiorno, Arthur Livingston, and James Harvey Rogers (New York: Harcourt, Brace, 1935).

18. Evan Osnos, "The Rules of the Ruling Class," *New Yorker*, January 22, 2024.

19. Pareto, *The Mind and Society*, §2054.

20. Pareto, *The Mind and Society*, §2044.

21. "In tutti i paesi . . . la classe politica giustifica il suo potere appogiandolo ad una credenza o ad un sentimento in quell'epoca ed in quel popolo generalmente accettati" (In all countries . . . the political class justifies its power by supporting it with a belief or a sentiment generally accepted in that era and among that people). Gaetano Mosca, *Storia delle dottrine politiche* (Bari: Laterza, 1965), 296.

22. John Matsusaka, "When Do Legislators Represent Their Constituents? Evidence from Roll-Call and Referendum Votes," USC CLASS Research Paper No. CLASS15-18, July 21, 2022; Francis Cheneval and Alice el-Wakil, "The Institutional Design of Referendums: Bottom-Up and Binding," *Swiss Political Science Review* 24, no. 3 (September 2018): 294–304.

23. Pareto, *The Mind and Society*, §2191n3.

24. Albertoni, "Evolution of Mosca's Thought," 25.

25. Bobbio, "Il buon governo," 242, as cited in Silvestri, "Il buon governo," 159.

26. Gaetano Mosca to Guglielmo Ferrero, February 26, 1934, *Gaetano Mosca–Guglielmo Ferrero: Carteggio (1896–1934)*, in *Opere di Gaetano Mosca*, ed. Carlo Mongardini, vol. 6, pt. 1 (Milan: Giuffre, 1980), 455–456.

27. Camila Vergara, *Systemic Corruption: Constitutional Ideas for an Anti-oligarchic Republic* (Princeton, NJ: Princeton University Press, 2020); Jeffrey Green, *The Shadow of Unfairness: A Plebeian Theory of Liberal Democracy* (Oxford: Oxford University Press, 2016).

28. In a 1920 editorial for *L'Ordine Nuovo*, Gramsci attributes this saying to Romain Rolland, thereafter developing this idea and adopting it as his motto throughout his writings until his death. Antonio Gramsci, "L'Ordine Nuovo" (April 1920), in *Discorso agli anarchici*, n43, 3–10.

228   NOTES TO PAGES 189–190

29. See, for example, David Wallace, *Chaucerian Polity: Absolutist Lineages and Association Forms in England and Italy* (Palo Alto, CA: Stanford University Press, 1999); Massimo Verdicchio, "Griselda between Boccaccio and Petrarch," *Italica* 97, no. 1 (Spring 2020): 5–31.

30. Rocco Rubini, *Posterity* (Chicago: University of Chicago Press, 2021), 65.

31. Francesco Petrarch, *Letters on Familiar Matters*, trans. Aldo Bernardo, vol. 2 (New York: Italica Press, 2005), 656.

32. Ann Middleton, "The Clerk and His Tale: Some Literary Contexts," *Studies in the Age of Chaucer* 2 (1980): 121–150, 128.

33. Petrarch, *Letters on Familiar Matters*, 670.

34. Petrarch, *Letters on Familiar Matters*, 670 (emphasis added).

35. Petrarch, *Letters on Familiar Matters*, 661.

Acknowledgments

After a decade working on this project, I have accrued many debts. John McCormick, Linda Zerilli, Jennifer Pitts, and Joel Isaac have all been tremendous readers and mentors, but their influence on me cannot be constrained to the confines of professional guidance.

I owe everything to John McCormick. John embodies the purest commitment to the study of politics without any semblance of pretense. His raw humanism continues to inspire me, and I cannot imagine having done any of this without him.

Upon my arrival in Hyde Park, Linda's precise expression of her political intuitions forced me to accept that I, too, am a political theorist and that I could not ignore the call to this vocation, however much I feigned dispassionate ambivalence. Jennifer somehow combines grace and disarming sophistication to deploy the most incisive criticism and provoke powerful self-reflection. Since the beginning, I have sought her academic advice, but she also serves as a reminder of how I strive to comport myself in all concerns. Joel's work moved me long before his arrival in Chicago. At key moments, his writing encouraged me to pursue a direction which, at the time, seemed like a fool's errand within the political science discipline.

The University of Chicago is a thrilling intellectual community that fed my soul for ten years. During my graduate and postdoctoral studies, I looked forward to every class, meeting, and workshop in a way divorced from how one normally views professional obligations. I must thank the following people for creating this world, for including me in it, and for providing crucial support at various stages: Chiara Cordelli, Robert Gooding-Williams, Daragh Grant, Sarah Johnson, Demetra Kasimis, Matthew Landauer, Jonathan Levy, Sankar Muthu, Emma Saunders-Hastings, and James Wilson, as well as Julie Cooper,

230 ACKNOWLEDGMENTS

Adom Getachew, Gary Herrigal, Patchen Markell, James Sparrow, Nathan Tarcov, and Lisa Wedeen. Luigi Zingales combines virtuosity and empathy in every one of his endeavors, and I am fortunate to have benefited from his intellectual generosity. I am especially grateful to have crossed paths with Rocco Rubini, whose writing encourages me to continue the application of Italian humanism to new corners of Anglo-American scholarship.

Several people read the manuscript in its entirety. James Farr, Katrina Forrester, Alison McQueen, Josiah Ober, and Ian Shapiro worked laboriously through each part of the text, and their ideas propelled me forward at a critical juncture in the process. I was privileged to receive penetrating comments from Alberto Giordano, Duncan Kelly, Steven Klein, Robyn Marasco, and Matt Simonton on select chapters that exponentially improved the overall product. Surya Gowda served as the most impressive research assistant, and from the beginning she has always been more of a teacher than a student. Two anonymous reviewers for Harvard University Press offered astute responses and wise suggestions that served as my guide for the final revision.

Although the manuscript was nearly completed by the time I arrived at UCLA, my colleagues Anthony Pagden, Davide Panagia, Tejas Parasher, and Giulia Sissa have contributed paradigm-shifting insights that have found their way into this book. My deepest gratitude goes to Joshua Dienstag, who saw a spark of something valuable in my work from its earliest stages. He is a pessimist's guardian angel.

This book owes its existence to a team of incredible editors. Joseph Pomp invested time and energy to ensure that the manuscript remained true to its original vision. I could not have asked for better editorial guidance. I thank Brian Ostrander for seeing the manuscript through the production process and Wendy Nelson for bringing a sharp eye to copyediting. Lucia Senesi also copyedited the manuscript and has been a key interlocutor in the final stages of the process but means so much more to me and my family.

My undergraduate supervisor Ellen Kennedy taught me how to pair rigor with eccentricity, and the creativity that can result from such a combination. I hope that she sees herself these pages, for I surely do. In some sense, this project began when Jeffrey Green formally introduced me to democratic elitism. I thank them both for stirring political theory within me.

For their friendship during the highs and, more importantly, the lows of this last decade, I would like to thank Milena Ang, Gordon Arlen, Giulio Azzolini, Simcha Barkai, Mattias Breuer, Jonny Bunning, Danielle Charette, Anastatia Curley, Oliver Cussen, Yonah Freemark, Jake Garrett, David Gudhurz, Will Levine, Daniel Luban, Emma Stone Mackinnon, Amanda Moure, Daniel

Nichanian, Ethan Porter, Lucille Richard, Katherine Robiadek, Tania Islas Weinstein, Adam Woodhouse, and Samuel Zeitlin. No words can express my gratitude to Mark Jurdjevic, Heather Hyde Minor, Gabriele Pedullà, and Yves Winter, who provided invaluable advice and good humor on my worst days. Much of this work profited from the late nights spent with Rossana Aliota, Andrea Cola, Giampaolo Demma, Paola Fabretti, Francesca Ippoliti, Filippo Marongiu, Stefano Meo, and Fabiana Tribusson. Allyson Levine, Stacy Levyn, Regina Marchese, Heather Serden, Sarena Snider, and Danielle Yadegar know the story of this book without having read any part of it.

Finally, I must thank my parents, Laura Quartulli, Steven Piano, and Mckey and Jim Berkman. They endured with me the heartache that comes along with any labor of love, and for that I will never be able to exaggerate my gratitude.

This book has benefited from the financial and institutional support of the George J. Stigler Center for the Study of the Economy and the State, the Notre Dame Archive Project, the Harry Ransom Center, The William Rainey Harper Trust, and the University of Chicago Division of Social Sciences. I was lucky to have presented parts of the work at the Università di Genova and the Seminar in Political Thought and Intellectual History at Cambridge University. I owe special thanks to the archivists at the Harry Ransom Center Archives, L'Archivio Centrale dello Stato, il Fondo Vilfredo Pareto della Banca Popolare di Sondrio, and the Walras-Pareto Centre Archive at the University of Lausanne. I'm especially grateful to Francois Allisson and Haro Maas for the warm hospitality during my stay in Lausanne.

Long before graduate school, my nonna Rosa tutored me in the art of translation; more specifically, in the ability to export components of Italian philosophy to contexts which do not seem to crave its lessons. For the longest time, my brother Alessio and I questioned the utility of this endeavor, but ten years ago my husband, Philip, imbued the pursuit with new meaning. I thank him for suffering through countless pages and my tempestuous demeanor to provide me with patience and emotional support I never dreamed possible. Our relationship exemplifies the differences between Italian and American styles, and how their combination can result in the most edifying and electrifying result. *Ubi tu Gaius, ego Gaia.*

Los Angeles, October 2024

Much of the text from "Revisiting Democratic Elitism: The Italian School of Elitism, American Political Science, and the Problem of Plutocracy," published in 2019 in the *Journal of Politics* 81, no. 2, is integrated into this book.

Index

Action Party, 208n51

Agnini, Gregorio, 23

Albertoni, Ettore, 108, 187, 213n26

Allegory of Good and Bad Government, The (Lorenzetti), 183

Almond, Gabriel, 80; *The Civic Culture,* 81

Alsace-Lorraine: Franco-German dispute over, 25–26

alternate theory of democracy. *See* theory of competitive leadership

Amba Alagi, Battle of, 26

American plutocracy, 72

American Political Science Review, 95

Analytical Marxists, 169, 173

Anglo-American political science: behavioral turn, 13, 145; defense of liberal democracy, 176, 177; Italian School of Elitism and, 13, 15, 80, 145, 147, 161–162, 175–177; key figures of, 146, 147–148; popularity of pluralism within, 166

"applied democracy," 100, 105

aristocracy, 133, 184

Aristotle, 55, 69, 132, 134, 214n52

Aron, Raymond, x, 47, 205n171

Ashcraft, Richard, 219n11

Athenian democracy, 8, 30, 34

Austro-Modernism, 141

autocracy: democracy and, 120; of European nations, 74; majoritarian politics and, 119–

120; oligarchic conditions and, 133; socialism and, 120–121

autocratic state, 30

Azzolini, Giulio, 210n82

Bachrach, Peter: critique of democratic elitism, 17, 160–166; on Dahl, 165; on demagogic plutocracy, 161, 163; on democracy, 164; on elections, 11; influence of, 146; on Mosca's *Elementi,* 162–163; pessimism of, 163; on pluralism, 147, 163; on relationships between elites and masses, 160–161, 162; on Schumpeter, 219n22; *The Theory of Democratic Elitism,* 160, 164, 166; "Two Faces of Power," 160

Balbo, Cesare, 55

Banca Nazionale, 24

Banca Romana's financial scandals, 24

Banfield, Edward, 80; *The Moral Basis of a Backward Society,* 81

Baratz, Morton, 160

Barone, Enrico, 220n45

Beetham, David, 100, 216n99

behavioralism, 6, 14, 127

Bell, Daniel, 151

Bellamy, Richard, 64, 198n21

Bentley, Arthur, 147

Berelson, Bernard, 160

Berle, A. A., 161, 164

Bernays, Edward, 127

234 INDEX

"Bloody '98" (popular insurrection of 1898), 44
Bobbio, Norberto, 143, 220n38
Boccaccio, Giovanni: *Decameron*, 189; Petrarch's translation of, 189–190
Bonald, Louis de, 8
Borkenau, Franz, 197n7
Bottomore, Tom, 200n65
bourgeoisie, 200n56
Bruni, Leonardo, 16
Bryan, William Jennings, 31
Bryce, James, 86, 213n21
Bucolo, Placido, 204n154
Burnham, James, x, 12, 72, 111, 112, 113; *The Managerial Revolution*, 111
Byzantine state, 30, 31, 34, 39, 43

Cambridge School, 147
Campbell, Stuart, 47, 205n171
Canetti, Elias, 141
Capital (Marx), 117
Capital in the Twenty-First Century (Piketty), 12
Capitalism, Socialism and Democracy (Schumpeter), 164; on classical justification of democracy, 123; contribution to elite theory, 115; on elites, 116; influence of, 11, 115–116, 117, 146; on liberal capitalism, 141–142; on liberalism, 121–122; on mass psychology, 124; new definition of democracy, 135–137; on people's will, 123–124; political psychology of, 123; on socialism, 117–119, 120–121, 122; on totalitarian autocracy, 121, 122–123
Capitalism and Social Democracy (Przeworski), 169, 170, 171
Carbonari movements, 52, 194n2, 207n11
Cassinelli, C. W., 95
Catholic Church, 51, 93
"centrifugal" dispersion of power, 34, 38
"centripetal" accumulation of power, 34, 38
charismatic authority, 106, 107, 108, 109
Cherneski, Jana Lee, 122
Cicero, 5, 184
Cirillo, Renato, 47
Civic Culture, The (Almond and Verba), 81

classe dirigente (ruling class), 29, 30, 38, 67, 68, 69, 72
classe politica (political class), 30, 38, 68
class struggle, 51, 67, 97
clientelist state, 30
Collodi, Carlo: books of, 193n1 (intro.); *Pinocchio*, 1–3, 194n5
competitive elections: vs. Athenian assembly and lottery, 183; criticism of, 27; decline of, 179; demagogues and, ix; democracy as, 11, 17, 116–117, 130, 131–132, 137, 142, 146–147, 164, 169, 175–177, 182; polyarchy and, 154
competitive leadership. *See* theory of competitive leadership
Comte, Auguste, 55, 66
Condorcet, Jean-Antoine-Nicolas de Caritat, marquis de, 20
Congress and Foreign Policy (Dahl), 152
Connolly, William, 165
Consciousness and Society (Hughes), 48
Corriere della Sera, 60
Crispi, Francesco, 22
"Critique of the Ruling Elite Model, A" (Dahl), 155
Croce, Benedetto, 45, 76, 204n154, 205n164
crowd psychology, 102
Cuoco, Vincenzo, 53, 55, 76

Dahl, Robert: "A Critique of the Ruling Elite Model," 155; Bachrach's critique of, 165; *Congress and Foreign Policy*, 152; on consequences of minority rule, 154; criticism of, 156, 168; *Democracy and Its Critics*, 157; on democratic creed, 154, 155; on elections, 9, 11, 81, 153; elite theory of, 15, 17, 151–153, 155, 156, 165, 167; evolution of political thought of, 156–157; "Further Reflections on 'The Elitist Theory of Democracy,'" 156; on future of democracy, 157; idea of polyarchy, 97, 152–153, 154, 156, 158, 159, 165; influence of, 146, 160; Italian School and, x, 12–13, 147, 152–153, 154, 155, 157–160; on oligarchy, 176; pluralism of, 152; on popular sovereignty, 159; *A Preface to Democratic Theory*, 151,

152–153, 156, 168; reorientation toward "democratic socialism," 159; on representative institutions, 153, 158–159; *Who Governs?*, 13, 14, 153, 154

Darwin, Charles, 55

Davis, Lane, 165

Decameron (Boccaccio), 189–190

demagogic leaders, ix, 39, 179

demagogic plutocracy, 33, 35, 37–39, 41, 74–75, 88, 133, 161, 163

de Mattei, Rodolfo, 46

democracy: association between elections and, 10, 33, 43, 57, 64, 73, 74–75, 85, 99, 105–107, 168–169, 172, 181–182, 222n81; Athenian-style, 8, 30, 34; autocratic threat to, 120, 122; as *buon governo*, xi, 8–9, 17, 183–188; communism and, 5; as competitive elections, 5–6, 11, 17, 116–117, 130, 137, 142, 146–147, 164, 169, 175–177, 182; critique of classical justification of, 123; definitions of, x, 36–37, 140, 172, 178; elitism and, 165; enfranchisement and, 181–182; failure of, 88–89; as free and fair elections, x, 4, 6, 9, 81, 113, 117, 147, 168, 178, 180; function of, 164; ideal (pure), 88, 132; law and, 134; liberalism and, 129, 130, 131, 161; market and, 172; "minimalist" conception of, 168, 173, 174, 177; oppression of minorities in, 119–120; organization and, 99; palliatives of, 215n85; parliamentary politics and, 73; participatory theory of, 8, 32, 117, 129, 166–167, 172; as a "people" power, 188; pessimistic accounts of, 14–15, 31–32, 179, 182; plutocratic threat to, 180, 181; as *politeia*, 132; as popular sovereignty, 37, 112; as principle, 184; procedural conception of, 137, 139, 164; "realist" theory of, 177; as religious creed, 32; vs. representation, x, 10, 32, 180–181; "revisionary" theory of, 168; as self-government, 113; socialism and, 118–119, 122, 169, 170–171, 219n11, 219n22; studies of, ix–x, 81; universal suffrage and, 169

Democracy, Italian Style (LaPalombara), 81

Democracy and Its Critics (Dahl), 157

Democracy and the Market (Przeworski), 171–172

democratic elitism, 5, 6, 16–17, 160, 163, 166

democratic impulse, 71, 97–98

democratic representation, 33, 62

"democratic" states, 31–32

de Pietri-Tonelli, Alfonso, 45

De Sanctis, Francesco, 76; *Un viaggio elettorale* (An electoral journey), 53

de Viti de Marco, Antonio, 46, 198n17

dictatorship of the proletariat, 29, 118

dictatorships, 174

Dienstag, Joshua, 196n23

Discourses on Livy (Machiavelli), 184

Donoso Cortés, Juan, 8

Downs, Anthony, 127

Dreyfus affair, 91

Drochon, Hugo, 215n85

Duncan, Graeme, 165

Eckstein, Harry, 80, 160

economic inequality, 55–56, 176

Einaudi, Luigi, 45–46, 110, 204n159

Einaudi, Mario, 110

elections: accountability of leadership and, 33; association between democracy and, 10, 33, 43, 57, 64, 73, 74–75, 85, 99, 105–107, 168–169, 172, 181–182, 222n81; corruption and, 180; critical importance of, 180; elites and, 60, 174; as expression of people's will, 128; freedom and, 64; function of, 174; Herfindel-Hirshman index of, 61; as instruments of inequality, 57–58; Italians' realist critique of, 181; mass participation and, 174; oligarchy and, 106; plutocracy and, 14, 58; as popular sovereignty, 59; prevention of failure of, 139; socialist view of, 169; voters and, 62, 127, 173, 220n47. *See also* competitive elections

Elementi di scienza politica (*The Ruling Class*) (Mosca): Accademia dei Lincei's prize competition, 68, 69; advocacy for reform of the ruling class, 68; call for historical approach, 66; critique of, 52, 68–69, 162–163; Croce's review of, 76–77, 205n164; editions, 55, 65, 68, 69, 70, 71, 73, 80, 111, 162; English translation of, 70, 209n72; on Marxism, 66–67; on

236 INDEX

Elementi di scienza politica (The Ruling Class)
(Mosca) (*continued*)
minority domination, 71; on parliamentary
democracy, 73; on positivism, 65, 66; on representative government, 73–74; on "scientific"
approaches to social science, 65–66
elite circulation: theory of, 28, 33, 34, 162, 163,
185, 201n71
elite domination: accountability and, 101; effect
on popular governance, 159; elections and, 7;
inevitability of, 13, 71, 97, 132, 138–139; "juridical defense" against, 69; Marxism on the end
of, 118; modern democracy and, 142; pessimistic orientation toward, 76; possibility of
socialist eradication of, 67; problem of, 28,
55–56; representative government and, 84;
Risorgimento's transfer of power and, 76;
ruling-class theory on, 71, 75; social equilibrium and, 29; struggle against, 97; studies of,
76, 144, 155–156, 157, 159, 188
elite pluralism: theory of, 162–163, 164, 187
elites: cohesion of, 7, 200n65; competition
among, 10–11, 98–99, 150, 153, 186; democratic contestation of, 34–35; historical development and, 150; incompetence of, 100; in
modern society, 165; monopoly on violence,
149; multiplicities of, 70, 99, 153; "openness"
and "closedness" of, 34; popular government
and, 165; power of, 71, 85; problem of elimination of, 55–56; relationships between
masses and, 48, 129, 160–161, 162, 178, 186,
188, 190; responsiveness to majority needs,
139; specialization and bureaucratization of,
151, 152–153; studies of, 13–14; types of, 30, 34
elite theories of democracy, 4, 6–7, 12, 15, 16, 117
English political institutions, 59
Expedition of the Thousand, 52, 58

fascism: democracy and, 5; influence of, 69;
origin of, 63; theoretical platform of, 43, 47,
76; united front against, 76–77
Fatti e teorie (Pareto), 202n119, 202n121
Femia, Joseph, 29, 125
Finer, Samuel, 30, 197n7
First World War, 25–26, 79

Frankfurt School of critical theory, 8
freedom of speech, 131
French Socialist Party, 92, 93
Freud, Sigmund, 124
Friedrich, Carl, x, 48
"Further Reflections on 'The Elitist Theory of
Democracy'" (Dahl), 156

Galbraith, John, 148
Garibaldi, Giuseppe, 58, 75–76, 194n2, 207n11,
208n41, 208n51
general will, 88
Genett, Timm, 217n108
Gentile, Giovanni, 51
German political pessimism, 105, 107
Gilman, Nils, 142
Gioberti, Vincenzo, 55
Giolitti, Giovanni, 22, 41, 42, 46, 60
Giordano, Alberto, 46
Gobetti, Piero, 77, 79
Goldschmidt, Maure, 165
good government (*buon governo*): anti-
plutocratic nature of, 8–9, 186; conception
of, xi, 8, 17, 183, 185; pessimism about, 188; as
popular government, 186–187
Gosnell, Harold, 80
governments: types of, 30
Gramsci, Antonio: application of Mosca's
ruling-class theory, 52–53, 62; concept of
hegemony, 60, 62, 77; on democracy, 52, 53,
62, 76, 79, 208n51; on Italian Fascism, 63, 77;
on situation in Southern Italy, 209n58; as
theorists of minority domination, 157
Green, Jeffrey, 105
Green, T. H., 198n21
Guicciardini, Francesco, 5, 16

Habermas, Jürgen, 9
Harrington, James, 5
Hartz, Louis, 81–82
Hegel, Georg Wilhelm Friedrich, 67
hegemony: concept of, 60, 62, 77
Henderson, Lawrence, 47
Herfindel-Hirshman index of electoral compe-
tition, 61

Herring, Pendleton, 147
Howe, Irving, 148
Hughes, H. Stuart, 47, 73, 81, 107, 197n7; *Consciousness and Society*, 48
Humanité, L' (newspaper), 91
human rationality, 123–126, 220n37
human sentiments, 124, 125
Hunter, Floyd, 148

iron law of oligarchy, 10, 83, 84, 86, 90, 95, 102–103, 112, 116
Isaac, Jeffrey, 156
Istituto di Credito Fondiario, 24
Italian Fascism, 63
Italian political pessimism, 53, 74, 105, 107
Italian political thought, 53, 146
Italian School of Elitism: American political science and, 175–177; Cold War paradigm, 176; contributions to theory of democracy, x–xi; critique of, 12, 147, 152–153, 154, 155, 157–160, 161; on democracy, 9, 183; on democratic elitism, 12; influence of, 11–13, 15, 144–145, 147, 175–176; leading figures of, x, 5, 6, 45–46, 53, 99, 111, 114, 144; on liberal government, 8; misappropriations of, 14, 145–146, 147; pessimism of, 15, 108; *Pinocchio* as metaphor of, 3–4; on plutocracy, 6, 7, 10, 13; re-emergence of, 16; theoretical legacy of, 180, 182
Italy: banking system, 24; corruption, 44; Giolitti's government, 41–42; intellectual and political landscape, 46; liberalism in, 21–22; monetary policy, 23–24, 25; nation-building, 3; parliamentary plutocracy, 5, 10, 13, 14, 24–25, 28, 41, 42; privatization in, 22; protectionism, 23; regional economic disparity, 8, 23–24, 26, 51–52, 58, 75, 186; socialist policies, 50; studies of democracy, 81; totalitarian transformation, 78–79; unification of, 10, 52, 58, 195n19, 208n41
Italy: A Difficult Democracy (Spotts and Wiser), 81

Kafka, Franz, 141
Keller, Suzanne, 151

Key, V. O., 80, 161, 164
Kingdom of the Two Sicilies, 52, 75
Korhauser, William, 161
Kraus, Karl, 141
Kuhn, Thomas, 175

Labriola, Antonio, 51, 109
La Ferla, Giuseppe, 203n145
Lampedusa, Tomasi di: *The Leopard*, 75–76
LaPalombara, Joseph: *Democracy, Italian Style*, 81
Larcinese, Valentino, 61
Laski, Harold, 80, 147
Lasswell, Harrold, 80, 143, 161, 167
Lathan, Earl, 168
LaVenia, Peter, 106, 212n10
Le Bon, Gustave, 100, 102, 110, 124, 220n31
Lee, Richard, 154
Lenin, Vladimir, 157
Leninism, 206n6
Leopard, The (Lampedusa), 75–76
Levellers, 60
liberal institutions, 8, 10
liberalism: anti-majoritarian features of, 121; democracy and, 161; popular rejection of, 178–179; vs. totalitarianism, 121
Liberal Party, 77
liberty: Greek and Roman conception of, 134
Lindblom, Charles, 156
Lippmann, Walter, 80, 127, 147
Lipset, Seymour Martin: on democracy, 12–13, 165; on elections, 81; influence of Italian School on, x; introduction to *Political Parties* (*Sociology of the Party*), 103, 104; "nouveau elitism" of, 15; on officials' control of means of communication, 91; on oligarchy, 176; popularity of, 160; on popular representation, 100
Livingston, Arthur, 69, 80, 209n72; *The Machiavellians*, 111; *The Ruling Class*, 111
Lombroso, Cesare, 46
Lorenzetti, Ambrogio: *The Allegory of Good and Bad Government*, 183
Loria, Achille, 46, 110

238 INDEX

lower classes, 35, 41, 57, 65, 68, 98, 104
Lukes, Steven, 165

Machiavelli, Niccolò: appropriation of the Roman *tribunate*, 187; *Discourses on Livy*, 184; influence of, 16, 30, 107, 109, 111, 112–113, 141; *The Prince*, 10, 184; realist approach to politics, 72–73, 106, 132, 184; theory of the two humors, 202n121
Machiavellians: Defenders of Freedom, The (Burnham), 111
Maine, Henry Sumner, 37
Maistre, Joseph de, 8
majoritarian politics, 119–120, 121, 130, 139
Making Democracy Work (Putnam), 81
Managerial Revolution, The (Burnham), 111
Manifesto of Anti-Fascist Intellectuals, 69
Manin, Bernard, 218n1; *The Principles of Representative Government*, 5
market competition, 131
Marshall, Alasdair, 125
Marx, Karl, 125, 157; *Capital*, 117
Marxism: on connection between socialism and democracy, 169; critique of, 67, 125, 127; on elimination of economic inequalities, 55; on the end of elite domination, 118; on management of society, 66–67; optimistic hubris of, 66; popularity of, 51; positivism and, 66; on social classes, 29
masses: capacity for governance, 123; crowd psychology of, 102, 124; disdain for liberal capitalism, 129; oligarchy and, 96; oppression of, 101; organization of, 96–97; passivity of, 101–102, 103; political participation of, 162, 179; relationships between elites and, 48, 129, 160–161, 162, 178, 186, 188, 190; resistance of, 96
mathematical economics, 198n31
May, John, 99
Mazzini, Giuseppe, 21, 55
Medearis, John, 115
Meisel, James, 67, 81–82, 108, 205n168
meritocracy, 133
Merriam, Charles, x, 12, 19, 48, 80, 81, 147

Mezzogiorno (Southern Italy): backwardness of, 209n58; capitalist exploitation of, 53, 60; electoral practices, 60–61, 62, 79, 208n51; extension of suffrage in, 61; feudal corruption in, 57; hegemony of the North over, 62, 75; obedience to mafia, 58–59, 60; plutocratic exploitation of, 52; suspicion of democracy, 76
Michels, Manon, 110
Michels, Robert: background, 83–84; career, 84, 90, 109–110; on charismatic authority, 106, 107, 108; on class struggle, 97; on competition between elite groups, 97–98; *Corso di sociologia politica (First Lectures on Political Sociology)*, 84; criticism of, 144, 176, 214n52; death of, 110; on democracy, x, 9, 85, 88–89, 97, 99–100, 103–106, 216n91, 217n111; "Die oligarchischen Tendenzen der Gesellschaft" (The oligarchic tendencies of society), 88; on elections, 4, 84, 85, 105–106, 174; Fascist sympathies, 83–84, 90, 100, 103, 110, 212n10, 217n108; influence of, 110–111, 145, 147, 152; interest in crowd psychology, 100–101; "L'oligarchia organica costituzionale" (Organic constitutional oligarchy), 89; on masses, 96, 100–102, 103; methodological approach of, 196n22, 214n53; Mosca and, 84, 85, 89–90, 98, 108, 109, 110, 213n26, 216n99; Mussolini and, 83, 85, 216n96, 216–217n103; as "neo-Machiavellian," 111; on oligarchy, 10, 83, 84, 85, 86, 89, 90, 95–97, 102–103, 106; Pareto and, 84, 85, 89–90, 109, 110, 213n26, 216n99; pessimism of, 14, 97, 105, 107, 108–109, 143; on plutocracy, 91–93, 96, 175; on political parties, 90–95, 99; *Political Parties*, 103, 104, 107, 212n9; political thought of, 10–11, 84, 85, 86; on popular sovereignty, 88–89; relations with Mosca, 108, 109, 110, 216n99; on remuneration to elected officials, 92–93; on representative government, 97, 99–100; on ruling elites, 7, 8, 84–85, 101, 103, 106, 107–108; on socialism, 87, 104; *On the Sociology of the Party System in Modern Democracy*, 84, 85, 86, 88, 90, 100–104, 105–107, 109–110, 111, 116, 213n24, 215n85; study of the German Social

Democratic Party, 86–88, 92, 119; as theorist of democratic elitism, 5, 12, 157, 159; Weber and, 86, 87, 88, 109, 110

middle class (*il ceto medio*), 134, 187

Mill, John Stuart, 20, 198n21, 218n1

Mills, C. Wright: critique of Italian School, x, 147, 149–150, 151; on democracy, 11, 150–151; elite theory of, 148–149, 150–152; on history of the American republic, 148; influence of, 146, 148; on intelligentsia, 151; *The Power Elite*, 148, 151–152

"Minimalist Conception of Democracy, A" (Przeworski), 173

minority domination. *See* elite domination

Moderate Party, 208n51

modern, dynamic, pluralist (MDP) polyarchy, 157

"Modern Machiavellians," 105, 111, 113, 184

Mommsen, Wolfgang, 107

Moral Basis of a Backward Society, The (Banfield), 81

Mosca, Gaetano: academic career, 132; Anglo-American literature on, 72, 176; anti-fascism of, 69, 76–77; anti-positivism of, 54; on association between democracy and election, 9, 73, 111, 116; calls for a "new science," 54–55; on combat of corruption, 134; on conception of freedom, 64; on constitutionalism, 209n73; critique of, 64, 65, 81–82, 99, 149–150, 161–165; on Darwinian paradigms, 209n73; on demagogic dangers, 4; on democracy, x, 134–135; on democratic impulse, 71, 97–98; on democratic potential of liberal procedure, 184–185; differences between Pareto and, 135, 184–185; on economic inequality, 8, 51, 55, 56; Einaudi and, 110; on elections, 57–62, 65, 174; *Elementi di scienza politica* (*The Ruling Class*), 52, 54, 55, 65–71, 73–74, 76–77, 80, 111, 138, 162–163, 205n164, 209n72; elite theory of, 5, 7, 8, 10, 14, 45–46, 47, 64, 132, 163, 182–183, 187, 188; on English political institutions, 59; friends and allies, 45, 46; on good government, 183, 185; on government neutrality, 56; identification as a "liberal," 77–78; "Il principio aristocratico ed il democratico," 132; influence of, 80–82, 85, 100, 111, 112, 145, 147, 152; interpretation of the democratic principle, 133; interwar receptions of, 144; on law, 134; on liberal institutions, 73; on liberalism, 65, 74, 77, 134; Liberal Party and, 77; on mafia dominance, 60; Marxist debates, 51, 54, 55–56, 66–67; on meritocracy, 133; methodological approach of, 196n22, 214n53; on middle class (*il ceto medio*), 187; on minority domination, 76, 138–139, 157, 159; on mixed regime, 187; as modern Machiavellian, 72–73, 112, 184; on monitoring of the minorities in power, 64; on moral progress, 67; on Mussolini, 77, 108; on oligarchy, 70, 95–96; on organized minorities, 71, 73; on parliamentarism, 63–64, 69, 78, 112; pessimism of, 14, 105, 106, 108, 143, 188; *Piccola polemica* (*A short polemic*), 89; on plutocracy, 53, 70, 71–72, 96, 175; political views of, 78, 82; popularization of, 80; on popular sovereignty, 88–89; on preemptive redistributive measures, 58; on problem of elimination of elites, 55–56; on progress, 53–54, 65; public career of, 205n167; on regime decay, 133; relations with Michels, 84, 108, 109, 110; on representative government, 73–74, 98, 134; ruling-class theory, 29, 62–63, 68, 70–71, 75, 79, 138, 186; *A Short History of Political Philosophy*, 55; on socialism, 51, 56, 65, 74, 87, 206n8; on Southern Question, 52; "Stato città e stato rappresentativo," 133; *Teorica dei governi e governo parlamentare* (*Theory of Governments and Parliamentary Government*), 52, 54–64, 68, 74, 78, 186; theory of "political history" of, 64; theory of "the political formula," 186; on totalitarian transformation of Italy, 78–79; translations of works of, 111; on universal suffrage, 57, 61, 79; on uprising of the working class, 59

Musil, Robert, 141

Mussolini, Benito: Mosca's influence on, 73, 84, 85, 216n96, 216n103; Pareto's influence on, 45, 76; popular support of, 78; rise to power, 69, 73

National Dante Society, 80

"negative" liberty, 131

240 INDEX

Nietzsche, Friedrich, 14, 124, 125
nouveau elitism, 15, 152, 155, 160, 165, 167–168
Nye, Robert, 100

Ober, Josiah, 184
oligarchy: masses and, 96; vs. polyarchy, 153, 154, 156; power of, 70, 95–96. *See also* iron law of oligarchy
On the Sociology of the Party System in Modern Democracy (Michels): dedication, 110; on democracy, 88, 107, 215n85; on distinction between democracy and electoral institutions, 105–106; editions and translations of, 86, 106, 107, 109–110, 213n24; on electoral politics, 90, 116; Italian influences, 110; Lipset's introduction to, 103, 104; Machiavellian tradition, 111; on Marxist doctrine, 84, 89; on plutocracy, 91; on political leaders, 101; on political parties, 90; on ruling class, 106–107
organization: as weapon of the weak, 96–97
Ortega y Gasset, José, 14
Ostrogorski, M., 86, 213n21

Pakulski, Jan, 196n22
Pantaleoni, Maffeo, 198n17
Paper Stones: A History of Electoral Socialism (Przeworski), 170, 171
Papini, Giovanni, 46
Pareto, Genoese Marchese Raffaele, 21
Pareto, Vilfredo: academic career, 21, 28, 44, 202n114, 204n152; Anglo-American scholarship on, 43–44, 176; anti-protectionist crusade, 23; association with fascism, 43, 45, 47; attacks on Giolitti administration, 41, 42; background of, 18, 205n167; on bourgeoisie, 200n56; on charismatic authority, 107; conception of social equilibrium, 29; conservatism of, 202n104; contribution to political science, 45–48, 82, 99, 198n21, 201n73; on corruption, 19; critique of, 48, 149, 161–162, 163, 205n171, 220n38, 220n45; Croce and, 204n154; death of, 29, 45; on demagogic plutocracy, 4, 39, 133; on democracy, x, 9, 19, 26–27, 28, 31–32, 36–37, 111, 116, 197n7,

203n145; differences between Mosca and, 135; on distinction between speculators and rentiers, 40; on division between urban and rural workers, 40; on division of human activity, 200n65; economic studies of, 22–23, 24, 26, 29; on elections, 20, 27, 33, 36, 111, 116, 174; on Ethiopian model for Italy, 26; exile to Paris, 21; *Fatti e teorie*, 202n119, 202n121; fox and lion metaphors, 30, 38, 185; on good government, 183, 185, 187; on human rationality, 123–126, 220n37; influence of, 80, 81, 85, 111, 124, 144–145, 147, 152, 154; interest in crowd psychology, 200n65; on irrational sentiments, 125; Italian unification and, 19, 20, 21, 48; *Les systèmes socialistes*, 36, 50, 132; letter to Einaudi, 204n159; on liberalism, 22, 74; on "logico-experimental" reasoning, 124, 125; on majoritarianism, 132, 134; *Manuale d'economia politica*, 36; Marxist debates, 47, 51, 125; on mass participation, 19; on mathematical economics, 198n31; methodological approach of, 196n22, 214n53; on minority domination, 28–29, 157, 159, 202n114, 205n168; as Modern Machiavellian, 184; on monetary policy, 23–24, 25; Paris course, 35–36; on parliamentarism, 20–21; passion for the public policies, 20; pessimism of, 14, 19, 20, 36, 105, 106, 108, 143, 188; on plutocracy, 19, 25, 35, 40–41, 48–49, 175; on popular sovereignty, 88–89, 126; posthumous reputation, 42–49; on principle of nonrepresentation of minorities, 32; on prospects of democratic accountability, 163; publications of, 198n17, 202n114; relations with Michels, 84, 109, 110; on representative governments, 37–39, 42–43; on ruling class, 14, 26, 27, 38, 40, 75; on sale of the railways, 22; on socialism, 50–51, 74, 87; on Sorel, 197n11; study of elites, 5, 7, 8, 12, 35, 45–48, 182–183, 188; theories of equilibrium, 28; theory of elite circulation, 28, 162, 163, 201n71; translations of, 111; *Trasformazione della democrazia* (*The Transformation of Democracy*), 20, 36, 40–41, 202n119; *Trattato di sociologia generale* (*The Mind and Society*), 29–30, 34, 35, 37, 40, 125, 202n119; on Triple Alliance, 25–26; typology

of political regimes, 33–34; on universal suffrage, 20, 28, 32–33, 48; on war, 199n48
"Pareto Circle," 47, 151
parliamentarism: corruption and, 27; democracy and, 33, 40, 73; plutocracy and, 57–58, 69, 71, 203n130
Parsons, Talcott, 18, 47, 151
Participation and Democratic Theory (Pateman), 160, 166, 167
participatory governance, 8
Pateman, Carole: on Bachrach, 166; critique of Italian School, 147, 166–167; on elections and democracy, 11; influence of, 146, 167–168; *Participation and Democratic Theory*, 160, 166, 167; on political science, 166; on Schumpeter, 120, 135, 219n22
Patriarca, Silvana, 208n41
Peasant Communism in Southern Italy (Tarrow), 81
people's will, 117, 123–124, 126–127, 128, 139, 220n47
Perloff, Marjorie, 141
pessimism: philosophical tradition of, 8, 9–10, 14–15, 196n23
Petrarch, Francesco, 10, 16, 189–190
Piccola polemica (A short polemic) (Mosca), 89
Piedmontese House of Savoy, 52
Pietri-Tonelli, Alfonso de, 45
Piketty, Thomas: *Capital in the Twenty-First Century*, 12
Pimentel, Felipe, 171
Pinocchio (Collodi): first version of, 194n5; as representation of Italy, 1, 2–3
plebiscitary democracy, 107
pluralism, 147, 148, 154, 186
plutocracy: autocracy and, 117; critique of, 41–42, 48–49, 71–72; definition of, 96, 201n85; demagogic autocracy and, 122; electoral politics and, 14, 42, 71, 106, 176, 181; inevitability of, 71; liberal institutions and, 6; parliamentary systems and, 40–41, 57–58; political parties and, 7, 91–95; as principle, 184; representative governments and, 33, 39, 161; rise of, 179
political parties: electoral systems and, 94; finances of, 90–91, 94; nepotism, 94; oligarchic

transformation of, 111–112; plutocratic features of, 7, 90, 91–95; as "state in miniature," 90
Political Parties (Michels), 103, 104, 107, 212n9
polity: forms of, 30
polyarchy: conception of, 30, 97, 152–153, 159; electoral competition and, 153; forms of, 33, 34; vs. oligarchy, 153, 154, 156; popular sovereignty and, 156
Polybius, 201n85
Popper, Karl, 47
popular government, 37
popular sovereignty: critique of doctrine of, 7, 19, 38, 104, 123–124, 126–129, 135; elections and, 59; as "ideal democracy," 88–89, 112, 158–159; polyarchy and, 156; as popular judgment, 141
populism, ix–x, 179
positivism, 6, 54, 65, 66
Power Elite, The (Mills), 148, 151
Preface to Democratic Theory, A (Dahl), 151, 152–153, 156, 168
Prince, The (Machiavelli), 10, 184
"Principio aristocratico ed il democratico, Il" (Mosca), 132
Principles of Representative Government, The (Manin), 5
progress: conception of, 53–54, 65
proportional representation, 79
Przeworski, Adam: amalgamation of socialist and liberal thought, 168–169; "A Minimalist Conception of Democracy," 173; Analytical Marxists and, 173; *Capitalism and Social Democracy*, 169, 170, 171; career of, 169; *Democracy and the Market*, 171–172; on dictatorships, 174; on elections and democracy, x, 9, 11, 172, 173; influence of, 146; on market and democracy, 171–172; *Paper Stones: A History of Electoral Socialism*, 170, 171; on pessimism, 170; on Schumpeter's "minimalist" theory, 135, 147; on socialism and democracy, 169–170, 174; use of rational choice theory, 171; on violence, 130
public contracts, 201n85
Publius, 5
Putnam, Robert: *Making Democracy Work*, 81

242 INDEX

Racca, Vittorio, 44, 50

"radical" democratic theory, 165

Reisman, David, 148

Renaissance trope, 16, 17

Rensi, Giuseppe, 221n61

representative government: citizens and, 115, 131; criticism of, 38–39; vs. democracy, 32; "negative" liberty practiced in, 131; plutocratic challenges of, 7, 39, 73–74, 161, 181; transfer of power in, 98

Republican Rome: form of government in, 30, 34

Riall, Lucy, 207n11

Riesman, David, 150

Risorgimento, 10, 13, 28, 55, 75, 193n1 (intro.)

Rohrich, Wilfred, 109

Romagnosi, Gian Domenico, 55

Roth, Joseph, 141

Rousseau, Jean-Jacques, 88, 218n1

Rubini, Rocco, 196n21

Rudini, Antonio Starabba di, 22, 24

rule of the few, 214n52

ruling-class theory, 29, 62–63, 68, 70–71, 75, 79, 186

ruling elites: competence of, 137–139; corruption of, 72–73; cycle of oppression, 67–68; democratic creed of, 154–155; democratic renewal of, 133; denial of unity of, 31; masses and, 129; plutocratic elite and, 69; types of, 30; use of the term, 68

Saint-Simon, Claude-Henri de, 66

Salvemini, Gaetano, 77

Sartori, Giovanni, 30, 143, 160, 161

Scaff, Lawrence, 87, 213n21

Schattschneider, E. E., 148

Schumpeter, Joseph: academic career, 114–115; *Capitalism, Socialism and Democracy*, 11, 115–116, 117–119, 120–121, 122–124, 135–137, 141–142, 146, 164; on classical democratic doctrine, 117, 128–129; criticism of, 164–165, 166–167; on democracy, 116, 118, 129–130, 131, 135, 139–140, 173, 177, 222n81; on electoral politics, 131, 137–138, 139, 164; on elite domination, 129, 139, 142; on German Social Democratic Party, 119; on individual voting preferences, 127, 220n47; influence of, 11, 128, 135, 143, 147, 152, 154, 166–167; on lack of individual rationality, 126; on liberalism, 121–122, 139–140, 141; on majoritarian politics, 119–120, 121, 130, 139; on Marxist doctrine, 118, 127; methodological approach to politics, 117, 128, 135, 141–142, 196n22, 218nn3–4; on Pareto, 20, 44, 126, 220n45; on people's will, 123–124, 126–127; pessimism of, 15, 109, 114, 115–116, 141, 142, 143; on popular sovereignty, 127–128, 129, 140; on socialism, 117, 118–119, 120–121, 122, 219n11, 219n22; on Soviet Union, 118, 119, 120; as theorist of democratic elitism, 5, 11, 12, 143; theory of competitive leadership of, 11, 116–118, 135–138, 139–143, 218n1; on totalitarian autocracy, 121, 122–123

Sereno, Renzo, 80

Shapiro, Ian, 117

Short History of Political Philosophy, A (Mosca), 55

Sicilian mafia (*Cosa nostra*), 58–59, 60

Sicily: Garibaldi's success in, 207n11; governments in, 75

Sieyès, Emmanuel, 5; *What Is the Third Estate?*, 60

Simon, Herbert, 80

Skinner, Quentin, 146, 147, 168

Smith, Adam: *The Wealth of Nations*, 117

Social Democratic Party (SPD): aristocratic composition of, 92; bureaucratic apparatus, 95; masses and, 93, 95; Michels' membership in, 83–84, 86; organizational structure of, 94, 119; plutocratic means of oppression, 94–95; social scientific study of, 86–88, 119

social equilibrium, 29, 35, 148

socialism: autocracy and, 120–121; democracy and, 118–119, 122, 169, 170–171, 219n11, 219n22; elite domination and, 56; optimism about the future of, 104

social science: Cold War paradigm, 12–13, 120, 176

Sola, Giorgio, 96

Son, Kyong-Min, 220n31

Sorel, Georges, 111, 197n11

Soviet Union: Nazi coalition with, 120, 122; political regime in, 118–119, 120, 122

Sparta, 30, 35

Spotts, Frederic: *Italy: A Difficult Democracy*, 81

"Stato città e stato rappresentativo" (Mosca), 133

Strauss, Leo, 13

Swedberg, Richard, 218n3

systèmes socialistes, Les (Pareto), 50, 132

Tarrow, Sidney: *Peasant Communism in Southern Italy*, 81

Teorica dei governi e governo parlamentare (Theory of Governments and Parliamentary Government) (Mosca): on action against the plutocratic domination, 64; on comparative study of governments, 55; criticism of electoral systems, 57–58, 59–62, 78; on economic redistribution, 63; on Italian parliamentarism, 63; on negative liberty, 56–57; on problem of elimination of elites, 55–56; publication of, 52; on representative government, 74; on ruling class, 68, 186; on social question, 55; on "systematic" historical investigation of human affairs, 54–55

theory of balance, 148

theory of competitive leadership: critique of, 139–140, 143; definition of democracy, 11, 116–117, 135; formulation of, 11; on freedom, 131; influence of, 129, 142; on power of government, 141

Theory of Democratic Elitism, The (Bachrach), 160, 164, 166

totalitarianism, 12, 115, 121–122

Trasformazione della democrazia (The Transformation of Democracy) (Pareto), 20, 36, 40–41, 202n119

Trattato di sociologia generale (The Mind and Society) (Pareto), 29–30, 34, 35, 37, 40, 125, 202n119

Triple Alliance, 25–26

trope: notion of, 16

Truman, David, 80, 148, 160, 161

Tuccari, Francesco, 108

Turati, Filippo, 51

"Two Faces of Power" (Bachrach and Barat), 160

United States: democracy in, 32; populism, 195n20; power elites in, 150–151, 153–154; system of "executive" leadership, 154

universal suffrage: criticism of, 48, 57, 61, 186; democracy and, 20, 32–33, 169; Italian parliamentarism and, 28, 79; regional economic disparity and, 3, 10

Un viaggio elettorale (An electoral journey) (De Sanctis), 53

Urbinati, Nadia, 218n1

Vailati, Giovani, 46

Venice's ruling classes, 35

Verba, Sidney, 164, 171; *The Civic Culture*, 81

Vico, Giambattista, 54, 55, 196n21

Vittorio Emmanuele II, King of Italy, 58, 208n51

Voltaire, 151

Walker, Jack, 156

Wallas, Graham, 123, 202n114, 204n159, 220n45

Wealth of Nations, The (Smith), 117

Weber, Max: anti-positivism of, 196n22; critique of, 147; definition of elite, 149; "Die deutsche Sozialdemokratie" (German social democracy), 87; influence of, 86, 87, 88; Michels and, 109, 110; Ostrogorski's influence on, 213n21; pessimism of, 14; on plebiscitarian democracy, 107; on Social Democratic Party, 87–88

Weimar Republic, 5

What Is the Third Estate? (Sieyes), 60

Who Governs? (Dahl), 13, 14, 153, 154

Wilson, Woodrow, 31

Winters, Jeffrey, 203n126, 214n52

Wiser, Theodore: *Italy: A Difficult Democracy*, 81

Wittgenstein, Ludwig, 141

Wolin, Sheldon, 9, 128, 165–166

Zaller, John, 127